The Bibliographic Record and Information Technology

SECOND EDITION

The Bibliographic Record and Information Technology

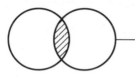

SECOND EDITION

Ronald Hagler

1991

American Library Association
Chicago

Canadian Library Association
Ottawa

Cover design by Charles Bozett
Text design by Dianne Rooney
Composed in TEX by Digital Graphics, Inc. in Times-Roman
Printed on 50-pound Glatfelter, a pH-neutral stock, and bound in Holliston Roxite linen
cloth by Braun-Brumfield, Inc.

The paper used in this publication meets the minimum requirements of American National
Standard for Information Sciences—Permanence of Paper for Printed Library Materials,
ANSI Z39.48–1984. ⊗

Canadian Cataloguing in Publication Data

Hagler, Ronald.
    The bibliographic record and information technology
2nd ed.
Includes index.
ISBN 0-888802-261-1 (CLA) - ISBN 0-8389-0554-4 (ALA)
    1. Machine-readable bibliographic data.
2. Bibliography—Methodology—Data processing.
3. Cataloguing—Data processing. I. Canadian Library
Association. II. American Library Association.
III. Title
Z699.H26   1991   026.3'16   C91-090205-4

Library of Congress Cataloging-in-Publication Data

Hagler, Ronald.
    The bibliographic record and information technology / by Ronald
  Hagler. — 2nd ed.
        p. cm.
    Includes bibliographical references and index.
    ISBN 0-8389-0554-4 (alk. paper)
    1. Machine-readable bibliographic data. 2. Bibliography—
Methodology—Data processing. 3. Bibliographical services—
Automation. 4. Cataloging—Data processing. 5. Information
technology. 6. Libraries—Automation. I. Title.
Z699.35.M28H34   1991
025.3'16—16dc20   90-45317
                                                    CIP

Printed in the United States of America.

95 94 93 92 91   5 4 3 2 1

CONTENTS

PREFACE

Eight years ago, a colleague and I completed *The Bibliographic Record and Information Technology* (Chicago: American Library Association, 1982). It described practices then prevalent in the manual and automated uses of bibliographic information in libraries in the historical context necessary to understand them. The book also represented an attempt to look ahead and we felt that a four- or five-year lifespan was as much as could be asked of the book our students came to know as BRIT. We were right. This revision began in 1985 but early drafts were constantly overtaken by the rapid pace of events in bibliographic control. Programs for processing full MARC records on a microcomputer, the CD/ROM revolution, the spread and the variety of the so-called online public-access catalogue, the changing functions of networks, the increasing computer-literacy of persons entering graduate library schools—all demanded a quite different model to replace the 1982 BRIT. My 1982 co-author proceeded to other professional activities and I began trying to keep pace with the changes needed in successive drafts.

Perhaps nothing demonstrates the rapid changes in this field as dramatically as the fate of the 1982 BRIT at the hands of the Library of Congress subject cataloguers. Three subject access points were assigned to it for Cataloging-in-Publication on its appearance (see the original record 82-14706, located at a-008-847 in the *National Union Catalog* of January, 1983). Just over two years later, a revision saw one of the original three subject access points retained and five others added—among them, the one most clearly stating what I think the book is about, namely **BIBLIOGRAPHIC RECORDS** (see NUC record a-680-844 of February, 1985). Three-and-a-half years after that, one of the original 1982 subject access points was restored, one was retained from the 1985 set, and three additional ones were added (see NUC record c-206-484 of September, 1988). At this time, my preferred one, mentioned above, was not only removed from the access points assigned to the first edition of this book, it was entirely expunged from the authorized list of Library of Congress subject access points. Now, the verso of the title leaf of this edition shows the five subject access points assigned in 1988 augmented by a sixth! In the meantime, the British Library contented itself with an access point I also fancy this book is about, **BIBLIOGRAPHIC CONTROL**, another topic yet unrecognized in the North American context.

The publisher insisted on retaining the 1982 title because the scope, purpose, and approach remain essentially the same. Chapters 2, 6, 9, the appendix, and parts of chapters 4 and 8 are revisions of the corresponding parts of the 1982 edition; the rest is newly conceived. The 1982 book related primarily to one comprehensive required course in a particular library school's curriculum. Although that course has disappeared in the inevitable curriculum revision, this new book has close connections to at least five current courses at the same school. The integrative approach implied in this breadth was generally welcomed by reviewers of the 1982 book and is here confirmed and strengthened. The bibliographic record is reviewed in its widest possible context, favouring neither the library catalogue, the abstracting and indexing publication, nor the commercial monographic bibliography as its most efficient and effective means of dissemination and use in libraries. While the focus is thus the library, neither the archival repository, the gallery, nor the museum is forgotten: all have documents to catalogue and index. The basic premise of both this book and its 1982 predecessor is that the bibliographic record in the three types of tool and the four types of agency is becoming ever more nearly the same thing in practice as well as in theory.

Even as library administrators prided themselves on transferring many cataloguing processes to distant computers owned by consortia, etc., CD/ROM and the microcomputer were poised to bring the same processes home again. Those who remember the purchase of Library of Congress proofslips to copy into the local catalogue smile as they watch the pendulum swing so rapidly. The essence of derived cataloguing, however, has not changed since Jewett first proposed it in the 1850s. If this edition lasts longer than the 1982 one did, it will be because the past thirty years of teaching courses on bibliographic control have taught me not to be cautious about looking for central unifying principles in the mass of detail and the confusion of change. Through all the change, the essentials really do remain the same.

While the concepts analyzed in this book have immediate practical application, this is not a *how-to* book but a *why?* book addressed to those to whom that question must come naturally: people educated as—or being educated to be—librarians. This is the profession which created the bibliographic record, automated it, and still knows best how to use it. There must, however, be a limit to this book's scope. Although planning for future management of bibliographic files is based on the application of principles analyzed in this book, how to implement that planning in detail is the concern of other works on such specialized topics as systems analysis, the selection of appropriate hardware and software, the application of particular cataloguing rules, effective search strategies in particular cases, and financial and personnel administration.

The reader is assumed to have some acquaintance with bibliographic data and organization, at least from having created footnotes and lists of readings for term papers and from having used library catalogues, periodical indices, and other published bibliographies. This book expands on those experiences primarily in the context of the professional work of the librarian (whether the job title be cataloguer, reference librarian, freelance information broker, or administrator). The reader is also assumed to have minimal acquaintance with what a computer can do, namely (1) receive and store digitized data, (2) compare any two sequences of data (character strings) for similarity or dissimilarity, and (3) transfer data, whether internally for processing purposes or externally to and from storage or display devices. Intelligent use of a desktop microcomputer as a word processor provides sufficient background knowledge.

As was the case in the 1982 edition, there is no bibliography at the end of this book and only the following types of material are cited as footnotes: (1) source documents, such as standards, (2) a few seminal writings which have changed the course of bibliographic control, and (3) items quoted directly. The concepts treated herein are the common currency of people professionally concerned with the many aspects of bibliographic control; I claim only to arrange these concepts systematically. In any case, books and articles on the practical details of bibliographic control still become obsolete remarkably quickly. The annual literature reviews in *Library Resources & Technical Services* and in *Annual Review of Information Science and Technology* may be considered as the ongoing bibliography for this book.

Any writer who tries to analyze this field comprehensively and in an integrated fashion is fighting constantly against the noncomprehensive and nonintegrated terminology of its everyday practitioners. The treatment of terminology in chapter 1 explains why I overthrew my initial qualms about occasionally introducing perhaps unexpected terminology (consistently and clearly, I hope) in order to ensure that the relationship of like concepts is clarified. In addition, recent changes in terminology regarding the two most central issues in this book—from *entry* to *record* and from *heading* to *access point*—are carried out consistently herein because the newer terms foster greater clarity of thinking about the subject.

My students continue to be my most valued teachers, but two colleagues, Peter Simmons and Mary Sue Stephenson, taught me what I know about automation. The latter read the penultimate draft of this book thoroughly and thoughtfully and greatly improved the organization and expression of the parts dealing with automated database management and file structures. Any remaining ambiguities are my own fault.

Vancouver, Canada
December, 1990

I Principles of Bibliographic Control

For a thousand years, the writings deliberately preserved and organized for posterity consisted of substantial bound monographs, at first manuscript, more recently printed. Libraries listed and indexed these in their catalogues so that they could later be retrieved and consulted. When the journal article appeared in the seventeenth century, it was awkward to include in the existing system, based by then primarily on recording the output of commercial book printers. A separate type of indexing service therefore grew up to list the writings in this genre. The arrival of the nonprint media of the twentieth century saw the rise of additional separate retrieval systems and often different administrative agencies to serve the users of information in these media. Most recently, information in its newest form, the machine-readable database, provides its own internal potential for automated self-indexing and has generated its own institutions and priesthood of Information Scientists.

That different information storage and retrieval techniques have become associated with different formats, subjects, and information-service agencies is no surprise since each has its own history. That this is neither theoretically ideal nor even efficient is and should continue to be a concern of librarians, the scope of whose professional activity is both information in its broadest sense and user requests at their most specific. Certain characteristics of information itself and of the reasons and ways users search for it are the same regardless of the processing technology, physical medium, or human organization involved in its dissemination. Nobody, not even the super-librarian, can attempt to cope with all of information per se. Librarians can only attempt to keep track of the documents, in all their variety, which contain information. Part I of this book analyzes the most basic *principles* underlying methods of doing so from the points of view of history, technology, and economics. Part II describes specific current library *practices* in the context of these principles, that is, how a standardized bibliographic description is created and indexed for searching in a computer-based system.

1

1
DOCUMENTS AND BIBLIOGRAPHIC CONTROL

This book's title indicates that its focus is something called a bibliographic record. A search under that term in the subject catalogue of a North American library might lead one to suspect that this is an obscure topic. It is neither that nor some new invention; it is the old library catalogue entry and its near relatives, the products of the ancient art of bringing relevant documents to the attention of those who are looking for the information they contain. There have been many books about the content, production, and use of the information to be found in catalogues and bibliographies. Those directed primarily to the producers of this information are likely to appear in a subject listing under **CATALOGING** because their focus is the function more than its product or its users. In contrast, this book is addressed not solely to prospective or practising cataloguers but to *all* who compile and use bibliographic information, particularly in machine-readable form, both within and outside the traditional library institution. Cataloguers, reference librarians, online searchers, interlibrary-loan librarians, and bibliographic systems consultants all use bibliographic data in the broader and more unified context we now call bibliographic control. This book treats the single bibliographic record, a standardized description of a single document, in that context.

Documents and Information

People receive information in many ways. We observe natural phenomena and converse with others nearby or at a distance. We read personal letters and reflect on some of what the mass media bombard our eyes and ears with. We look at antiquities and at contemporary works of art. We read books, articles, government publications, and technical and administrative reports. We note the influence of actions, whether of our own, of others, or of nature. Our minds process and interconnect vast quantities of information, deliberately fixing in memory bits of it whose later use can be foreseen; much more is semiconsciously stored for later (and often unexpected) recollection when it suddenly becomes relevant.

Absorbing, remembering, and recalling meet basic information needs for survival, but as society becomes more varied and complex, the information-retrieval technique of personal memory is more and more inadequate. We must also locate information externally. How to do so is not an inborn skill. Even the well educated often have no clearer idea of how to go about it than to "find someone who knows" or "go to the library" in recognition that much of the information they seek has already been processed and interconnected by someone else. More important, it has been fixed—in words, pictures, symbols, or otherwise—in a physical container of information generically called a document. The physical forms are many: a videocassette, a manuscript diary, a baked clay tablet, a painting, a pitted aluminum disk, a statue, a holograph, a photograph, and a sheet of paper containing writing or printing are all documents.

Nondocumentary methods of disseminating information (for example, attending a lecture, broadcasting, and using a telephone) are also important, but physical documents are the only *permanent* memory of the human race. A radio broadcast is preserved by being captured on a vinyl or tape sound recording: an aural document. Ideas shared at a conference are made permanent in printed proceedings, in the manuscript notes of participants, or in videorecordings: all are documents. Documents embody the knowledge people need to progress from the technical achievements of the past; to understand human nature, relationships, and culture; or just to give the emotions a needed lift—the latter at times the most useful purpose of all.

Because of their importance, people have always lavished care and creative skill on documents as physical objects. To see a beautiful book is itself an uplifting aesthetic experience. Except for this view of the document as art, however, the lay user rarely makes a conscious distinction between the document-as-physical-object and its intellectual content. The latter is the user's usual goal; the former only an annoyance: hard to locate, too expensive, inconvenient to use—and to top it all, the library wants it back before the user is finished with it. The instant photocopy, telefacsimile transmission (FAX), and the storage of the entire verbal and graphic content of documents in centralized machine-readable databases are all blurring the distinction between the document-as-object, its bibliographic citation, and its content. To preserve rare original documents intact, libraries provide copies for day-to-day use. To disseminate information more efficiently, they send copies on interlibrary loan and do not ask for their return. To store information more cheaply, they acquire it in electronic form, then create and destroy in-house copies on disk, tape, terminal screen, or paper almost indiscriminately.[1] Nevertheless, the library must identify, acquire, and maintain stock of physical documents in order to service the information within them. The bibliographic citation and the library's catalogue record therefore still distinguish between the two. Both traditionally describe the document more immediately and thoroughly than the work, or information, contained within it. Implications of this sometimes confusing, sometimes inefficient work/document distinction arise throughout this book. The difficulties it causes in bibliographic control cannot be totally resolved.

Society's Document-Collecting Institutions

Much of both formal and informal education is devoted to learning how to locate those documents which can provide the information or inspiration a person needs at any given time. We are constantly told that this is the Information Age. Although this book is primarily concerned with the librarian's role in this process, libraries are not the oldest of society's institutions to amass and service documents. As public institutions and private organizations developed, their employees would select and preserve the documentary record of their functions and achievements: the policy decisions, the correspondence, the books, the tapestries and paintings, the objects of warfare and commerce. Institutions whose *primary* function is to amass and organize documents arose from such activities and from the collecting instincts of private individuals. Eventually, the scope and cost of institutional collecting and/or organizing activities meant that many became dependent on public funding. In return, the resulting collections and services were put at the disposal of the public at large. The shift from secret and private to public information-servicing agencies is a necessary part of the transition to democratic forms of societal organization, a fact seen dramatically in the tax-supported public library movement of the nineteenth century.

A hundred years ago, the types of public agency engaging in this work were not as clearly differentiated as they are now. As recently as 1973, when its library function was separated from it by the establishment of the British Library, the British Museum as a single organization administered collections of library materials, archival records, museum objects, and works of fine art. Gradually, however, the archival repository, the art gallery, the library, and the museum of natural, historical, and/or anthropological objects began to define themselves as distinct types of institutions based largely on the nature of the documents each deals with. In the simplest terms, the document published in many copies is in the library, the original document created in the course of a person's or

---

1. It took two hundred fifty years after Gutenberg to establish the concept of copyright as a step toward resolving the ethical and commercial concerns associated with the ownership of information disseminated in the form of copies of printed documents. These concerns, reactivated by the uses of electronic technology in libraries, are beyond the scope of this book.

organization's activity is in the archival repository, the document whose prime purpose is aesthetic is in the gallery, and anything else is in the museum. The exact lines of demarcation will never be totally clear; for example, it is hard to know whether native American crafts are to be found in an art gallery or in a museum, or whether historical photographs of a community will be housed in its local public or college library or in the municipal archive. Furthermore, many librarians administer art galleries as part of their institutions and in most archives, galleries, and museums there is a library department containing books and journals.

The ever-growing quantity of documents of all types prevents any single institution, whether private or public, from attempting comprehensiveness unless its field of collecting is well defined and extremely limited. Institutions must therefore be able to share information about the documents they own, and at times share the documents themselves. This can be done efficiently only through the acceptance of compatible systems for describing and listing documents of all kinds. Archivists, gallery curators, librarians, and museologists are increasingly concerned with developing consistent practices. There is fortunately much common ground in what they do to list the contents of their collections. Whether the resulting list is called a catalogue, a finding aid, or an inventory, the goal is to list the institution's holdings so that a searcher can locate document descriptions (and hence the documents they represent) based on the same meaningful characteristics—names, dates, places, titles, forms, physical appearance, and subjects. Since no document can be fully understood in isolation from others, a good listing also attempts to note how certain documents are related to one another.

At more detailed and technical levels of practice, however, professionals working with each major type of document tend to develop specialized methods of description and indexing independently for that type. This is partly because archivists, curators, librarians, and museologists are sometimes more concerned with emphasizing the unique aspects of their work or goals than the aspects common to all. Many of the differences became entrenched through the separate education and training of these professionals and through the separation of the administration of their institutions over the past century. Today, the application of common computer techniques is rapidly making archival finding aids, library catalogues, and the listings of museum and gallery collections more and more similar to each other. Computer technology provides some common basis for the education of personnel from all four types of institution in integrated methods of listing and indexing their collections. Since it is a new technology for all four groups, it also makes them more willing to learn from one another.

There remain, nevertheless, good reasons for variation in details of applying the basic principles. A major reason is that, while libraries now deal primarily in the information within documents available in many copies, the other three types of institution deal primarily with original and unique objects and must therefore be at least as concerned with the objects as with the information they embody. Physical characteristics and the typical patterns of their use also differentiate what is contained in the four types of institution. Rules for identifying and indexing documents will always reflect such differences. The library handles information in its greatest diversity, if not necessarily at its deepest levels of meaning. The books and articles written by people who work with the documents held in archives, galleries, and museums enter library collections. Even the aesthetic experience of museum and gallery objects is transferred, if imperfectly, to the pages of art and archaeology books as illustrations. The original object held in an archive, gallery, or museum must therefore also be identified in the library catalogue or bibliography when it is the subject of a later book or article. These are good enough reasons why librarians have taken the lead in developing standards for listing and indexing documents of all types. It should be no surprise that they also began the automation of these processes. Libraries were also the first to take interagency standardization seriously, since it is easiest for them to share and loan their materials.

The Bibliographic Control of Library Materials

Bibliographic control is the goal of operations involved in identifying documents themselves, as distinguished from operations directed toward identifying the needs of users of the documents. The term thus relates to what are generally described in the library's administrative organization as the technical services, as distinguished from the public services. Bibliographic control bridges the two: it enables people to identify the existence of documents useful for their purposes by using indexed lists of documents. How to locate the actual documents and how and why to use the information *within* them are not treated in detail in this book but are left to works dealing more specifically with such operations as collection development, physical housing, interlibrary loan and other forms of document delivery, and reference services. Bibliographic control is at the centre of the information professions, both supporting and being supported by those other functions.

Although in reality bibliographic control cannot mean assembling and indexing in any one institution a copy of every relevant document in existence, in the abstract its functions may be itemized as:

1) identifying the existence of all possible documents produced in every physical medium
2) identifying the works contained within these documents or as parts of them (including articles in journals, papers published in conference proceedings, the contents of anthologies, etc.)

3) producing lists of these documents and works prepared according to standard rules for citation
4) providing all useful access points (indices) to these lists, including at least some access by name, title, and subject and
5) providing some means of locating a copy of each document in a library or other accessible collection.

Bibliographic control does not necessarily imply the application of computer technology to the above tasks, but in practice the computer is rapidly becoming the appropriate technology for the purpose. Institutions now unable to afford it must aspire to and plan for its eventual use. Computers enhance control through better and more comprehensive integrated document listings. They can also centralize access to the actual content of documents as the full text of documents is increasingly committed to machine-readable form for storage in combined databases.

Libraries pursue the goal of bibliographic control primarily by organizing information about the documents they collect. The process is still usually called cataloguing, a word increasingly limiting and antiquated as a description of what now happens in the new and broader context. However much it has changed in recent years, library cataloguing still clearly shows its origins in over three centuries of development before the computer when library collections consisted almost exclusively of printed books. Modern practice should make no essential difference between identifying a printed book, a manuscript deed, a portfolio of lithographs, a pop-up book for children, or a machine-readable file of current census data on a floppy disk. It is intended that the reader visualize examples in all such media even if the printed book and/or its language-based (rather than visual) content is generally used as the example in this book, for familiarity's sake, to illustrate a point.

Library catalogues have been compiled at least since the time of the Alexandrian Library, but for centuries thereafter, each book was still a unique manuscript, and a single identifying element (an author's name, a style of binding, etc.) often sufficed to identify it in a particular collection. In the fifteenth century, when many copies of the same arrangement of type (that is, an edition) began to come from printing presses and many editions of the same work were produced in different formats at different places, it became necessary to refine methods of *description* so that any given book could be identified as being part of a particular edition. When the number of different books/editions became large enough that it was no longer feasible to browse a list of them to find the desired one, standards were also needed for *access* (more loosely called indexing), that is, for providing a predictable place in a list—now called a heading or access point—where a searcher could find a single description among many. Systematic sets of rules for both description and access, called cataloguing codes, appeared by the late seventeenth century. By the mid-twentieth century, applying these rules had become a complex and costly operation and was inefficiently repeated for the same document not only in different libraries but throughout a single library's various in-house processes: selection, ordering, receipt, cataloguing, physical marking and protection, the search for the document by users including the reference staff, and finally circulation and interlibrary loan. Until the computer made it possible to integrate these processes, they tended to remain administratively, functionally, and psychologically separate, often with undesirable consequences for bibliographic services in the library. In particular, when cataloguing is thought of only as nitpicking done in a cataloguing department by people who never meet a user, its rules and practices tend to be forgotten by those who most need to know them: the reference librarians who must use the same principles to interpret bibliographic data from many sources (not only the library's catalogue) to users. To break down the psychology of separate functions is essential and is a principal goal of this book. The computer revolution is making it possible.

The Vocabulary of Bibliographic Control

Integration

Preparing clay, papyrus, paper, or vellum; manufacturing writing instrument, ink, press, and binding equipment; copy-editing drafts; making and transporting the finished product: each of these processes requires equipment and skills very different from one another. Many different crafts, each with its own context and terminology, converge to produce a single document. Today, raw data enters a computer's central processing unit through linked peripherals and emerges through other linked peripherals as a finished document on a display terminal or printer anywhere in the world without ever leaving the control of a unified set of instructions, such as the word-processing package, statistical package, or database management system. Previously, there was no one thing to which people could apply so generic a term as *information technology*, *data processing*, or even *bibliographic control*. The introduction of the computer brought a need for such terms. It is this degree of technological integration, not merely speed or accuracy, which accounts for the impact of the computer revolution, particularly for the amount of administrative disorientation it causes in every field to which it is introduced. It makes the cataloguer a word processor and an accountant, using the same programs and terminology as those used in a business office. It makes everyone a manager and a systems analyst.

In this context, the pre-computer processes of producing and using bibliographies and catalogues were many and had no single name as a whole. By the late 1960s, automation was making librarians see the whole as a single function for which they invented the term *bibliographic control*, even though the older term *cataloguing* is still often used with almost the same scope. In the same way, the computer revolution changed the nature of many parts of bibliographic control and made new names for them desirable. In addition to integration, there are four reasons for the pervasive changes of the past twenty years in the terminology of bibliographic control in libraries:

1) printed materials are no longer the only, or even necessarily the principal, documents processed; a new set of generic terms is replacing those whose primary meanings relate to books and to print
2) libraries now share many record-keeping practices with businesses and other types of institution; people involved in all of these must understand each other, and terms based on older, library-based methods are no longer necessarily the most appropriate
3) the jargon of computer technology has been combined with, and is sometimes replacing, that used for related manual processes and products and
4) the field is growing more international, requiring a review even of English-language terms which had been used differently on the two sides of the Atlantic.

These changes are analogous to, and just as far-reaching as, the decade-long task of devising and putting into effect an acceptable nonsexist terminology. As in that case, the new terminology often seems strained.

Adapting to a largely new terminology is perhaps most difficult for librarians in mid-career whose formal education gave them a now obsolescent sense of the scope and tools of their work. Experience updates practice but nobody comes along to update a librarian's vocabulary systematically. The student learns the concepts of the new era at library school but is confused when encountering both old and new terms in the literature. Each term of a technical vocabulary exists to convey a distinction, often subtle, sometimes meaningless to the outsider, but nonetheless essential. Computer-based jargon is usually easy enough to identify and is now generally accepted as a precise special-purpose vocabulary. Understanding the traditional vocabulary of bibliography is often more difficult. It includes many terms used nontechnically and often imprecisely outside the field, for example, *bibliography* and *index*. This unfortunately encourages librarians to forget or fail to distinguish their several precise and technical uses. Terms most basic to the concepts of any field tend to acquire a variety of meanings over time, hence to lose precision; yet they cannot be wished out of existence in favour of unambiguous replacements. It takes practical experience to know how to understand such a term in a given changing context. Examples in bibliography include the terms *edition, serial, title,* and *work*. One need not be a librarian to command a working definition of any of these or to recognize a given title, work, etc. as such, but additional distinctions may be needed to resolve a conflict or to define a specific procedure. For example, whether an item is a serial publication or a monograph is a critical distinction in many practical aspects of a library's operation. Yet even within the same library, the reference librarian seeking to identify an article in a particular serial, the clerk in the serials check-in unit, the serials cataloguer, the librarian who selects serials for purchase, the administrator who divides the collections budget between mono-graphic and serial purchases, and the bookbinder each probably has a slightly different working definition of what a serial publication is. As another example, figure 1 on page 28 illustrates the potential for disagreement about what words on a title page actually constitute the title of the item. To interpret the chang-ing vocabulary of automated bibliographic control intelligently requires broad experience of a variety of bibliographic situations.

The terminology of any field is a living thing: new trainees speak a different jargon from those about to retire, even when the ideas to be conveyed are similar. "Check the card catalogue" is still heard even in libraries where cards have disappeared as a catalogue form. "Look in the database" implies to most people a search of any kind of machine-readable file, but to a public-services librarian a database is still likely to mean some file *other than* the library's own catalogue. "Consult the catalogue" may seem totally neutral, but when the catalogue was merely a list of the books held in one department or branch, the phrase had a quite different meaning than it has now that the machine-readable catalogue may comprise several in-house and external databases. To help forestall problems of understanding in later chapters, the remainder of this one attempts to clarify some of the present terminological morass. In so doing, it also presents the context of the principal concepts treated in the following chapters. Where there remains a choice of terms for the same concept, process, etc., this book will use the one that general library practice appears to have adopted. In the index to this book, various terms for essentially the same concept are linked by cross-references to make it easier to relate what is found in other and earlier writings to the same concepts treated herein.

The Collections

As already noted, the document is the physical object produced on a printing press, tape recorder, computer disk drive, etc. An adjective is often attached to the word *document* to give it a superficially specialized but usually not very meaningful connotation (for example, technical document, government docu-ment). What the author, composer, or illustrator created—the intellectual content of a document—is more properly called a *work*. Bibliographic control involves both the physical document and the intellectual content (the work) it embodies, a fact which complicates both listing and searching. However, the document usually takes precedence because the primary function of most librarians is not to interpret a work to users but to *find* that work in the form of one or more physical documents. Libraries collect primarily editions or publications: documents produced in many copies and made available through a distribution system. Whichever word is used in the following chapters, the context makes clear what is at issue: a document (item, publication, edition) or a work (its intellectual content). Nevertheless, the uniqueness of a particular single copy of a publication can be of critical importance to a library or user. Someone may ask for

1) the one existing copy of Thomas Paine's *Common Sense* which has George Washington's autograph on its flyleaf
2) any copy of the first British edition of *Common Sense* or
3) Paine's words in any form, whether manuscript, print, recorded on a cassette, or projected on a screen from a computer file or a filmstrip.

In the last of these three situations, the user wants the work; in the second, a particular edition; in the first, a particular document, or copy. To say that the user in any of these cases wants a particular book is totally ambiguous.

From the mid-fifteenth century through the nineteenth, publishing almost always involved printing. The generic terms used for all published material naturally acquired print connotations, for example, *book, imprint, collation.* A library now also collects films, games, recordings, etc. and therefore quantifies its collection not as the number of books but of items. *Collation* has also given way to the more neutral term *physical description.* Where a specific nonprint medium is referred to, some specialized terms, such as *discography* and *filmography*, are becoming accepted. I have even seen a list of the films featuring Sylvester Stallone entitled a *Rambography.* However, no such generic term as *mediography* has yet surfaced, and the print-bound word *bibliography* and its cognates are unlikely to be replaced by anything more generic. Neither logic nor modernity can be expected always to prevail.

The Processes

When it defines a process, the word *bibliography* is used in two very different contexts: (1) the discovery of what documents are pertinent to some purpose and (2) the detailed study of the physical nature of a document. The former is more precisely called enumerative bibliography or systematic bibliography. The latter, called either analytical bibliography or critical bibliography, serves to authenticate both the document and its intellectual content. The specialized investigations of analytical bibliography are undertaken more often by chemists, historians, textual critics, etc. than by librarians. Such studies help determine whether the Hitler diaries are genuine and whether Melville called it a *soiled* or a *coiled* fish of the sea. Important though it may be, analytical bibliography as such is not a topic of this book. Bibliography as the process of describing documents stems from both the above processes and is the origin of the bibliographic record.[2]

2. Roy Stokes, *The Function of Bibliography*, 2nd ed. (Aldershot, Hants.: Gower, 1982), expands on the various uses of what is encompassed by the term bibliography.

When *bibliographic control* was making its appearance in the late 1960s, it had some competition as a generic term. The French word *documentation*, having approximately the same connotations, was easily adopted as an English word and is still sometimes used outside of North America. It is more abstract and lacks the narrowly bookish air of any term containing the root *biblio-*. As an English word, *documentation* connotes the practical application of up-to-date theories of information retrieval, usually though not necessarily in the computer context. Within North America, the term *information science* is gaining favour for some of the same purposes. It implies theoretical more than practical concerns; an interest in all types of information, not merely bibliographic information; and certainly the use of computers, mathematical modelling, the statistical orientation of bibliometrics, etc. Whether information science should be considered a subset of traditional librarianship or vice-versa, or whether they are quite separate fields, is a matter of more than passing concern in education for the information professions today.

The People

The connotations of the term *librarian* seem old-fashioned, clerical, and limiting to those in the profession who seek a new image and status enhancement in the growing field of commercial information services. The terms *documentalist* and *information scientist* arose with the names of newer processes mentioned previously. The former, like its cognate, documentation, had a short life in North America. The latter is being adopted both by some academic theoreticians and by many freelance practitioners. *Information broker*, *information manager*, and *information specialist* are other titles assumed particularly by private-sector suppliers of information (bibliographic or other) derived from computerized databases. The term *information professional* is suitably generic and abstract, and is appearing more and more frequently.

The functions of bibliographic control are called the technical services in library administration. They are embedded in the job descriptions of the acquisitions librarian, the circulation librarian, the cataloguer, the classifier, and the subject cataloguer or subject analyst. The term *bibliographer* is more ambiguous, now has antique connotations, and is less and less used in libraries. Some libraries still apply it to a person who selects materials rather than to one who catalogues them; the curator/cataloguer of a rare-book collection is often called a bibliographer. Outside the library context, a bibliographer seems to be anyone who makes lists of books, articles, etc.

Two quite different functions are undertaken by the person usually identified in a library's organization chart as a cataloguer:

1) describing a document's physical identity and establishing the names of persons, and entities involved in its creation and

2) stating its intellectual content both in words denoting its subject(s) and in the logical context of a classification scheme.

These functions are different primarily because the first involves the use of objective evidences while the second demands subjective judgement concerning a document's potential value to its users. A few very large libraries still divide these two functions between the descriptive cataloguer and the subject cataloguer, respectively.[3] The word *cataloguer* has institutional implications relating to libraries or large bookstores, so a person engaged in the same kind of work in any other type of organization or as a freelancer is more likely to be called an indexer, a bibliographer, or perhaps an information specialist. As professional cataloguers in libraries spend more of their time on supervision, policy making, and systems implementation, the more routine cataloguing functions have been passing to a group of paraprofessionals who have formal training in bibliographic practices but do not necessarily have a university education. In Canada, they are called library technicians.

The patron or library user can become quite adept in locating what is needed in catalogues and bibliographies without professional help. As computer technology replaces manual file searching, the patron may be temporarily less self-reliant, but part of the purpose of computerization is to give the user greater control and confidence in pursuing the search alone. Acknowledging this changing relationship between the patron and the information professional, the former is now often referred to as an *end-user* in order to emphasize the function of the librarian as an intermediary in the search for information. Thus the term *end-user searching* generally means the use of a machine-readable database without the intervention of a library employee.

The Organizations

Important as it may be, the library is not the only type of organization in which tasks related to the bibliographic control of published materials are accomplished. Nor are these tasks done only by persons trained as librarians, although such people do work in many of the other organizations described. Among the major producers of bibliographic lists today, whether in print or in machine-readable form, are the many commercial businesses and nonprofit organizations known collectively as the abstracting and indexing services, now commonly known as A&I services. They produce the A&I publications: listings, principally but not exclusively of journal articles, in almost every field of knowledge. The *Readers' Guide to Periodical Literature* and the *Magazine Index* are perhaps the best known of these although less typical of the genre than are such topically limited ones as *Environment Ab-*

3. The term *classifier* refers to a definable operation but has no practical significance in libraries in North America, where it is rare for a person's work to consist only of applying a classification scheme.

stracts. Indexers in the A&I services are typically hired from the ranks of subject specialists but many are also graduates of library schools. In addition to libraries and the A&I services, commercial and nonprofit publishers regularly produce bibliographies covering every possible topic to fill the reference shelves of any library. These may be compiled by members of a publisher's staff but more often are done on contract or even as a labour of love by someone whose direct monetary reward for the considerable work involved is usually meagre.

The Lists

The terms *bibliography*, *catalogue*, and *index* are used more or less interchangeably by the layperson to refer to a list of documents. The first of these is unfortunately often used as a catchall term: any few citations appearing at the end of a term paper are called a bibliography. If indeed the few items cited constitute the only possible sources of information on the topic, the usage is correct. If the items are only a selection, however, their listing might better be called a *List of Selected Readings* or *Sources Consulted*, thus reserving the term *bibliography* for a more exhaustive survey of the documents pertinent to a defined field. A list including critical comment on the items and/or summaries of their content is called an annotated bibliography; if it appears as consecutive prose it is called a narrative bibliography or a bibliographic essay.

The term *catalogue* is used properly when the list describes only items permanently or temporarily gathered in a single collection, for example, a bookseller's catalogue, an exhibition catalogue. A combined listing of the holdings of several libraries is called a union list or union catalogue. Why the former of these two terms should be preferred when the listing includes only serials, but the latter when it is comprehensive or restricted to monographs, is inexplicable until one knows the historical accident of the titling of two early lists which became models of their types. The *National Union Catalog* includes principally monographs whereas the *Union List of Serials* includes only serial publications.

Even as applied to an individual library's list(s) of its own holdings, the implications of the word *catalogue* have expanded. Twenty-five years ago, a library's card catalogue showed only what it owned and had fully processed for use. Various other files listed items on order, items received but not yet processed, items in circulation or at the bindery, etc. Today, a single database, the library's so-called online public-access catalogue or OPAC, may contain all these files of bibliographic information and more, searchable in a single process. Many libraries are giving their OPACs individualized names (for example, Orion or Gladys) not merely as a fad or a ploy to attract support for a technical novelty but also as an invitation to the user to consider it as something significantly different from the manual catalogue it replaces.

A distinction is deliberately made here between the word *database* and the word *file*. The latter is a very old word casually used, both as a noun and as a verb, synonymously with the word *list*. A list, or file, is a sequence of itemized descriptions of anything, organized for searching (that is, indexed) according to any defined principle(s). A person dealing with one of these in machine-readable form never speaks of a list, but rather of a file. In a computer-based system, it is possible and often desirable to integrate different files (lists) of data under the control of a single software package for searching or output. Such a combination of machine-readable files is called a database; the software package is called a database management system (see pages 86–87).

A century and a half ago when William Frederick Poole published *An Alphabetical Index to Subjects Treated in the Reviews and Other Periodicals to Which No Indexes Have Been Published*, the words *alphabetical* and *subject* had to be included in the title because in 1847 the word *index* conveyed only the act of pointing out or showing, without context. In the title of his continuation of Poole's work a half century later, H. W. Wilson used only the word *guide* (*Readers' Guide to Periodical Literature*); he felt he could take the other two words for granted. *Index* remains a loosely used catchall term. Whether as a noun or a verb, it suffers from so much overexposure that it should not be used without making the intended context explicit. Still widely used of a bibliographic file, *index* is also used of any alphabetic list of names, concepts, etc. without attached bibliographic data, as in an index at the back of a book or a telephone index (directory). Users often call a library's catalogue an index, or index file.

Poole's and Wilson's many successors in the A&I field launched what might seem a whimsical search for different words to imply a listing of documents. Some of them are underlined in the titles of the following A&I publications:

>   Accounting Articles*
>   Current Geographical Publications
>   Current Index to Journals in Education*
>   Excerpta Criminologica*
>   International Bibliography of Historical Sciences
>   Library Literature
>   Public Affairs Information Service Bulletin*
>   Resources in Education*
>   Sociology Abstracts*

An asterisk indicates that the list includes abstracts, that is, summaries of articles in addition to their citations. Such a list is still sometimes called an abstracting tool or abstract service, but the term *A&I publication* (or, less elegantly, *tool*) now tends to prevail for any subject-organized listing of journal articles and similar material whether abstracts are included or not. The above examples show that one cannot identify the presence of abstracts from the title alone.

The Individual Records in a File

A bibliographic file is an organized sequence of document descriptions. The abbreviation *bibfile* has come into use among cataloguers when they need to distinguish this from an authority file, which is a file containing only access points (see page 81). The single document description is the focus of this book. When it appears in a group of footnotes or a reading list, such a description is usually called a reference or a citation because it refers to (cites) a book, article, etc. When found in a library catalogue, it is likely still to be called a catalogue entry.[4] An information scientist may call it a document surrogate. In a machine-readable file, a single description is called a record in the jargon of computer programmers, who divide all databases into files and all files into records (see page 86). A single such description may be written or printed on an individual 3-by-5-inch (or any other size) card or slip. Along with others, it may be written or printed on a sheet of paper; photographed onto a piece of plastic fiche; pitted onto a compact disc; or magnetically charged onto a silicon chip, piece of magnetic tape, or disk (floppy or hard). This book deals with descriptions of all types of documents stored in all these ways. For much of the earlier part of this century, the listing of a book in a library's catalogue was considered only a distant relative of the listing of a journal article in an A&I publication because the two were created in administratively separate environments (the cataloguing department of a library versus an A&I service) and in different physical media (the individual card versus the printed page). The common treatment of all kinds of document descriptions in machine-readable form has brought the term *bibliographic record* into favour as a means of avoiding the limiting and separate contexts of all the earlier terms.

The Searchable Elements of a Record (Access Points)

We speak of searching in an index under a heading for a name, a concept, or a citation. Specialized terms like *name heading*, *author heading*, and *subject heading* are used when the search is for a word. When the search is for a number or symbol, however, the word *heading* seems inappropriate, so we speak of searching for a stock code or a classification number (rather than for a classification heading). Both words and codes/numbers have been used for centuries to locate a citation in a predictable place in some meaningful and useful arrangement for

4. The noun *entry* and its corresponding verb, to *enter*, are the deepest sandtraps in the vocabulary of bibliographic control because they have come to mean too many things, many of them technical and some now obsolete. The word is therefore avoided in this book. It may be better to use *entry* only as a synonym for a bibliographic record in a file and not to use the verb at all.

easy retrieval. The term *subject heading* is no longer generic; it now applies precisely to only one of several kinds of verbal subject identification system. Terms arising since 1950 to apply to other such systems are *descriptor*, *index string*, and *uniterm*. The latter fell rapidly from use; the others are distinguished in chapter 7.

The computer divorced the physical arrangement of records from the way they are searched as described in chapters 3 and 4. Furthermore, the word *heading* (something at the top of a card or preceding a group of records to show its filing sequence) is too restrictive to describe what can be typed on a keyboard, touched on the menu displayed on a touch-terminal screen, pointed to with the arrow controlled by a mouse, or wanded with a light pen. The computer programmer uses the term *search key*, which neatly describes any searchable element in a file. A computer can automatically generate search keys from the data when it creates indices according to a program: these are therefore called *derived* search keys in order to distinguish them from search keys individually assigned by a human indexer. A user is said to input a search key at a terminal when keying in what is to be searched or browsed to see if the file contains anything relevant to it.

In the manual context, the term *access point* was introduced to the librarian's vocabulary by the new descriptive cataloguing code of 1978, *Anglo-American Cataloguing Rules*, second edition (AACR2). That code does not deal with subject retrieval; nevertheless, this book uses *access point* to designate a subject term as well as any other characteristic which can be searched in a file. Because a whole access point can be fairly long, it may be desirable to refer in particular to its first part because that determines where it is locatable in a sequential (usually alphabetic) arrangement. If so, this part is sometimes referred to as the leading element. Here, the term *access element* is used; for example, the surname is the access element in the typical personal name.

The Technology

The term *information technology* is as easy and as difficult to annotate as are its two separate words. More evocative than the term *data processing*, which preceded it, *information technology* refers to the hardware of the digital computer along with all peripherals and software used to store, repackage, and display information of any kind, bibliographic or other. The few specific hardware and software terms used in the following chapters are defined in the context of bibliographic control wherever they appear. Because these terms are generally new, they carry little of the troublesome historical baggage of those defined earlier.

Standardization

The best guide to any information, including bibliographic information, is not a list but a knowledgeable person with whom the searcher can interact. Unfortunately, it is the nature of most library collections to be too large for any one staff member to recall the presence and value of each item. In any case, such a paragon needs time off. So we make lists. Many people are amazed to discover what a large part of a library's so-called reference collection consists of compilations of bibliographic citations rather than of other kinds of information (biographical, statistical, directory, etc.): up to half the reference collection of a typical academic library, and certainly more than half its cost. Add to this the footnotes and lists of selected readings appended to most non-creative writing and the total stock of bibliographic records in a library is overwhelming. It is no surprise that it takes the firm hand of standardization and great care with detail to ensure that the bibliographic structure leading the user through the library collection is sound. It could so easily collapse into complete chaos. Users must consult a number of catalogues, union catalogues, A&I publications, and other bibliographic lists representing the work of many people and the policies of many institutions. The transition from one to another can be transparent to the user and bibliographic data can be shared among institutions only if techniques of bibliographic control adhere to widely accepted standards.

First Principles

Two first principles, adequate identification and consistency, apply to the setting of these standards. The principles ensure that

1) no two documents can be confused with each other
2) the description of a document can be accessed in a list by any datum (for example, name, subject, series) relevant to that list's use and
3) the many details comprising each description are presented in a uniform manner so that they can be interpreted without unnecessary ambiguity.

Both principles are relative, not absolute. It is unreasonable to expect every list to describe an item in equal fullness of detail. What is bibliographically significant about a particular document depends on the purpose of the list in which it is included and/or of the institution housing it. How much and what information is needed for adequate identification is explored at the end of chapter 2. As for consistency, one would think that, five hundred years after Gutenberg, we would have universal conventions for the arrangement and presentation of the data pertaining to at least printed books. Alas, that is not the case: variants continue to appear and become entrenched for one or another reason. Conventions adopted by the library community and by the A&I services, however, are becoming more and more standardized. These are the fairly consistent practices described in part II.

Models and Rules

Within the framework of the two first principles, detailed rules and guidelines are needed for the day-to-day work of compiling bibliographies, catalogues, and A&I publications. Sir Thomas Bodley's first librarian at Oxford saw this need in the seventeenth century. Then, as now, a university library encountered some very difficult bibliographic problems and set an expert staff to decide how best to deal with them. Unfortunately, libraries in the past tended to create their own rules of practice quite independently of one another and to instruct staff by word-of-mouth and in-service training rather than through conference workshops and written policy decisions. The catalogues of libraries like the Bodleian, the Department of Printed Books of the British Museum, the Library of Congress, and the New York Public Library are more than landmarks in library history because, as models often imitated by the less creative, they still influence cataloguing practice elsewhere. However, they embody a variety of differing and sometimes conflicting practices.

Adhering to common rules means that different institutions can

1) contribute records to a useful union catalogue, facilitating the location and sharing of documents via interlibrary loan and
2) use each other's records interchangeably or acquire records produced from a central source.

Since these have been goals of the profession for the past century, particularly in the Anglo-American world, standards for their implementation have been actively pursued. With personnel and financial resources probably unmatched anywhere else, the Library of Congress became the pre-eminent rule-maker and model to imitate within its country, the continent, and to an astonishing degree the whole world. Because the standards and practices developed for the internal needs of a unique institution cannot be totally appropriate for other types and sizes of collection, a love-hate relationship with the Library of Congress is inevitable among other institutions. Nevertheless, to understand how bibliographic control functions anywhere today one must understand the history of its practices.

The unilateral dictates of the Library of Congress are less pervasive than they were a few decades ago. No longer anxious to bear total responsibility for everyone's good or bad practices, the Library has increasingly joined in co-operative arrangements. Initially, it only sought agreement with national library associations in the United States and the United Kingdom on rules for descriptive cataloguing. Since the Second World War, the Library has taken part in many international ventures in standards development, often through participation in projects of the International Federation of Library Associations and Institutions (IFLA) and with national bibliographic agencies of other countries. Within the United States, it now cooperates with numerous committees of the American Library Association (ALA) and other professional groups in discussing the development and practical application of standards for description, subject access, and automation. The Library's contributions to bibliographic control dominate every chapter of this book. That this institution looms so large should not, of course, detract from the recognition due other institutions and also the individuals both on the Library's staff and elsewhere whose ideas and incentive spurred the developments described herein. The single most pervasive result of all these developments in the English-speaking world is the codification of practice known as the Anglo-American Cataloguing Rules (AACR), the direct or indirect topic of all of part II of this book and the appendix, except for the chapter on subject access points.

Conservatism versus Change

Bibliography is an extremely conservative art, both as a whole and in individual applications. It deals with documents, the only permanent means of conserving the thought and values of society. Of all types of bibliographic list, a library catalogue must be approached with the greatest respect for the past because it is an accumulation of records created over decades, even centuries. Resistance to significant change in the catalogue's structure is desirable in the interest of internal consistency but, having been resisted, any change is the greater by the time it finally takes place. Change may arise from economic circumstances which from time to time allow elaboration or demand retrenchment of bibliographic services. Relationships between public-sector institutions and commercial agencies alter the nature and balance of services provided by each. New technology for producing and searching bibliographic lists has been a major spur to recent changes. A less obvious but equally persuasive cause for change lies in the documents themselves. Serial publications were once few and simple in their titling, patterns of issuing, etc. Published conference proceedings were once restricted to regular meetings of associations. Corporate names once followed a few standard patterns, for example, Department of [function]. Items in other than printed formats rarely appeared in library catalogues. Finally, change begets change. As users become accustomed to higher levels of search control and more access points in computerized systems, they bring increased expectations and demands to all bibliographic services. The integration made possible by computer-based systems also gives users little sympathy for historically based differences among bibliographic files originating from different sources.

When such external facts change, so must cataloguing rules and practices. Following a period of relative stability through the first half of the twentieth century, all these factors have pressed with particular vigour during the past generation. Many libraries have simply given up on old catalogues and systems and have started again from scratch. Others bravely attempt some degree of amalgamation of old and new practices. The most significant changes caused by automation are yet to come. They will involve the fuller practical implementation of methods of searching introduced in chapter 4 and the amalgamation of library catalogues with files of bibliographic records created and once separately maintained by other agencies. Whenever changes to bibliographic standards, procedures, and products are required, a period of uncertainty and even of policy conflict among institutions is inevitable. The present is such a period. When a more stable and conservative period will return is another uncertainty, but the very nature of the art demands it.

The Administration of Bibliographic Control

All aspects of bibliographic control are now organized more efficiently than in the days when each book was separately catalogued and cards for it individually typed in each of the thousands of libraries holding a copy of it. In a high proportion of libraries, bibliographic records are now copied electronically from centralized databases whose creation is a shared effort. Yet every library's collection and users differ from every other. No bibliography or catalogue is ever entirely correct or complete; supplements and revisions are being forever compiled, often by people other than those who did the original work. The increasing presence of commercial interests in bibliographic control means a rise in the number of competing services and products which deliberately duplicate each other's coverage at least in part and offer overlapping or even conflicting features. For example, when different searching services make exactly the same database available, they do so using different database management systems and user interfaces. Just to use computers brings problems of incompatibility because competing hardware and software companies have little interest in industry-wide standardization. A degree of efficiency which might please a private company's auditor remains an elusive goal.

Every administrator of a library, an A&I service, or a house that publishes monographic bibliographies must try to get the best value from a very considerable expenditure. At the 1985 annual conference of the American Library Association, a Library of Congress administrator was heard to say that the cost to that library of cataloguing a single new document from scratch and getting the record into machine-readable form exceeded one hundred U.S. dollars. This cost estimate, not subsequently committed to print, cannot be blamed on the inefficiency of a large government bureaucracy; it is the price of the complexity of the job and the care taken. So much bibliographic work is either subsidized, voluntary, or hidden in other accounting columns that the true total cost of preparing much published bibliographic work is not reflected in its retail price.

To make bibliographic lists worth their real cost, they must be of more use than the average member of the lay public can fathom. End-users are encouraged to use bibliographic lists and are instructed in appropriate techniques by information provided in prefaces, signs at the catalogue, workshops on database searching, etc. Yet as the lists and the information they contain become ever more complex, so grows the dependence of the inexperienced end-user on a professional interpreter of their scope, structure, and indexing vocabulary.

Three distinct groups of information professionals are involved in a library's making and use of bibliographic tools. Using terms common in library organization charts, these are:

1) technical services librarians, who create the various in-house catalogues
2) public services librarians, or reference librarians, who interpret to inquirers both the in-house lists and those acquired from external sources—and who also create specialized lists ad hoc and
3) administrators, who must balance the two groups in staffing and budgeting.

Outside the individual library are the faculty of the library schools who must train candidates for the three functions in the context not only of present but also of future uses of bibliographic information. There is an unfortunate history of mutual recrimination among all four groups. Those in the technical services often do not meet the public directly; their work patterns are different; there tends to be little personnel crossover between the technical and public services. Reference librarians claim that cataloguers hide information under obscure access points or classify items for shelving where no user would think to look. Cataloguers complain that reference librarians do not learn the standards and systems well enough to make the best use of them and that they fail to appreciate either the need for, or the benefit of, periodic changes to those standards and systems. Administrators, who may come from either stream, are routinely accused of favouring whichever segment of the operation they know best. They must attempt to apply performance measures but may seem to do so too rigidly. They complain that library school faculty slight the practical training needed for immediate effectiveness in applying current techniques. Tensions exist here as in every profession between the practitioners and the teachers. Happily, there is a growing tendency, particularly within consortia and associations, to raise the consciousness of each group toward the purposes of the others and to resolve differences through more systematic contacts.

Has the money poured into technical-service automation over the past twenty years detracted from the materials budget and from public-service staffing? Difficult as it is to quantify the value to end-users of either the collection or of reference and advisory services, it must be noted that a large part of the total cost of bibliographic control is the cost of the end-user's own time spent in searching bibliographic tools. In the private sector, the time of that user is considered accountable in the institutional budget. If a searching tool (for example, the library's catalogue) is well constructed and an appropriate technology for its use perfected, the end-user finds information efficiently and with less need for help from the public-service staff. If, on the other hand, the bibliographic tools or technology are inadequate, the user wastes time and, in addition, must demand more help from library staff. In other words, all else being equal, money spent on creating good tools for bibliographic control not only saves the patrons their time and money, it also saves the institution's public-service budget.

Automation brought major problems for the administrator of the 1960s in determining how to introduce a wholly new technology into bibliographic services. That today's major problems are no longer technological is small consolation when major budget- and personnel-based problems remain. These include the need to shift the traditional balance of a budget between

1) technical and public services costs
2) capital and operating costs
3) machine and human labour costs and
4) permanent staff and owned equipment costs, and the purchase of equivalent services commercially or from freelance professionals.

Such shifts are never administratively easy; in the face of union contracts they can be devastating. Difficulties in this area have toppled many library administrations. How to retrain staff to work in an automated environment is also an administrative minefield.

Bibliographic Judgement

The study of bibliographic control is laden with detail, much of which may seem confusing and irrelevant until one acquires through careful observation and experience the context in which to judge why a particular fact is significant and for what purposes. Designing, making, or using any bibliographic list, particularly a computer-based one, requires constant attention to detail so that nothing passes by without due consideration even if it appears inconsequential at first. To be effective one must develop the detective instinct of a Sherlock Holmes. People are not born with this instinct. It comes more easily to some than to others but anyone who consciously rejects this type of mental discipline will find neither self-fulfillment nor much success in the information professions. However, no single detail is of consequence alone. Its *context* is what makes it significant. The reader should consciously attempt to relate what is presented in this book to

1) its application to past personal experiences in looking up information in bibliographic tools of all types
2) practices observed in various types and sizes of libraries, archives, galleries, and museums and
3) information gained in studying about all other aspects of librarianship.

It bothers many students beginning a graduate programme in librarianship that so little in the study of bibliographic theory or practice is tangible or quantifiable. Everything is presented as relative. This is particularly disturbing to those who had been misguided into believing that bibliographic citation and library cataloguing consist of the application of concrete and rigid rules to situations which fit those rules unambiguously. I have always found the hardest student question to answer to be the perennial "But what is the *right* way?" The only honest answer is almost always "It depends on . . . . " One of the things it depends on, for better or for worse, is often an administrator's subjective assessment of the issues involved and judgement of the priorities to be applied. Any option is the "right" one if its premises are conceded.

Fewer premises are conceded today than ever before. The recent changes most difficult to deal with have been caused neither by new cataloguing codes nor by the computer but by the fact that a library rarely acts alone anymore in the purchase or creation of bibliographic records. The politics of compromise and consensus-seeking among cooperating libraries, the politics of lobbying government to support expensive cooperative ventures, and the politics of arriving at commercial decisions in an environment of competitive, profit-motivated bibliographic enterprises have become integral parts of bibliographic control. This book cannot usurp the prerogative of practitioners and administrators in deciding what is "right" in a given situation. All it can do is illustrate what circumstances and reasoning have led to certain practical applications. This book is concerned to show what *has* been done and what *can* be done, not to presume what *should* be done. Early in this century, Charles Ammi Cutter feared that the influence of the Library of Congress for standardization might mark the end of what he called the "golden age of cataloging." We are now in a new golden age where Cutter's view of cataloguing (by implication today, all of bibliographic control) as "an art, not a science" is still valid.[5] This view has one overriding implication for the student: one does not learn to deal with bibliographic records so much by studying their construction or reading a book like this one, as by *experiencing* their use.

---

5. Charles A. Cutter, *Rules for a Dictionary Catalog*, 4th ed., rewritten, U.S. Bureau of Education, Special Report on Public Libraries, Part II (Washington: Government Printing Office, 1904), p. 6. Reprint: London: Library Association, 1935.

2

BIBLIOGRAPHIC DATA
AND RELATIONSHIPS

The elements of bibliographic data which together identify a document are the building blocks of bibliographic control. They include the familiar data found in any citation, for example, author's name, title, publisher, date, and more esoteric information less frequently encountered. The purpose of this chapter is to itemize the most significant bibliographic data elements and to analyze their uses. In general, data elements serve:

1) to identify a particular document uniquely in order to distinguish it from others (for example, a date of publication or a count of the number of pages in a printed book)

2) to show how two or more documents are associated with one another (for example, in that they have a common author or that one is a continuation or reprint of the other) and

3) to provide the basis for access points which enable a searcher to locate the record of a document in a file; these may relate to

   a) objective facts about the document itself (for example, its title or the fact that it constitutes the proceedings of a conference) or

   b) the topic(s) and concept(s) treated in its intellectual content; simplistically, the subject(s) of the document.

No creator of bibliographic records can claim to be doing an adequate job if the first of these purposes is not fulfilled. Many ignore one or both of the other two either because their need is not perceived or because they are far more difficult and expensive to accomplish than the first. Libraries generally treat all three as of equal importance in compiling the bibliographic tools for which they are responsible. The third use of bibliographic data noted above, namely to generate access points, is a direct concern of only the final section of this chapter. It is the primary focus of chapter 3 and all of part II.

Value judgements have no place in bibliographic control. The price of an item at the time of its publication is an element of bibliographic data since it can help identify a particular issue or format of the publication; a judgement that the item is or is not worth the price is bibliographically irrelevant. A title's primary value to most end-users is as a description of the content of the document, to assist in making a value judgement about whether to purchase or consult the item. To the bibliographer, however, the title's prime purpose is not to describe the document's content but to name (and thus identify) the document itself in the same objective way as a personal name identifies the person in a passport.

The Language of Bibliographic Statements

Bibliographic data are communicated by means of a language. Since they are expressed in the words of a language such as English or French, it may seem that no other language is involved, but bibliographic language is also present with its own syntax. The "sentences" of bibliographese have a rigid structure and their expression is concise and often elliptical. As with any other language, the beginner can quickly comprehend much, but instruction and experience are needed before all the details and subtleties are either noticed or understood. Like any other language, the language of bibliography is nothing but a set of commonly accepted conventions. A cataloguer expresses bibliographic situations in that language; a reference librarian interprets bibliographic expressions to users who do not fully understand their implications. Both activities require judgement based on

1) broad experience of various bibliographic situations
2) familiarity with bibliographic language and
3) knowledge of the purpose of the listing in question.

As with any other language, the words and syntax of this language can be misunderstood and misinterpreted. Its words are the focus of this chapter; its syntax is the focus of chapter 8.

Someone without experience of the layout of title pages and/or with little knowledge of the English language might look at the pages reproduced in figure 1 and transcribe the titles as, respectively, *The Story of Whaling Harpooned* and *The Conversions of a Bishop*. Anyone who knows title-page layout and/or English-language style has no doubt that the first title page reads as *Harpooned; the Story of Whaling*. What is the correct reading of the other? If the title is *The Conversions of a Bishop*, what does one make of the preceding words, Dom Helder Camara? An author's name often precedes the title on a title page but, on the other hand, Camara might be the *Bishop* of the title, that is, the book's subject, and therefore more properly part of the title. The title page is ambiguous but so is the nature of the book's content, an extended interview with Camara.

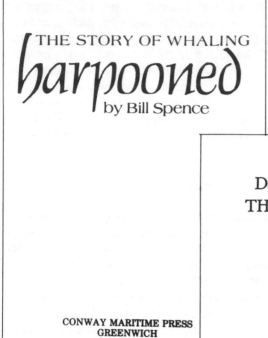

Broucker, José de
  Dom Helder Camara, the conversions of a bishop : an interview
  with José de Broucker / translated [from the French] by Hilary
  Davies. — London [etc.] : Collins, 1979. — [1],222p ; 22cm.
  Translation of: 'Dom Helder Camara'. Paris : Éditions du Seuil, 1977.
  ISBN 0-00-216460-4 : £4.95
  1.Ti 2.Camara, Helder 3.Conversions of a bishop

                                                    (B79-17299)

                                                            COLLINS

Câmara, Hélder, 1909-
    The conversions of a bishop : an interview with José de
  Broucker / Dom Helder Camara ; translated [from the French]
  by Hilary Davies. — London ; Cleveland : Collins, 1979.
    [1], 222 p. ; 22 cm.   GB79-17299
    Translation of Les conversions d'un évêque.
    ISBN 0-529-05624-0 (U.S.) : $9.95
      1. Câmara, Hélder, 1909-   . 2. Catholic Church—Bishops—Biography.
  3. Bishops—Brazil—Biography.   I. Broucker, José de.   II. Title.
  BX4705.C2625A3313 1979   78-74858
                      282'.092'4
                      79   MARC

FIGURE 1. Two different bibliographic records were prepared from one of these title pages: the
upper one is from the *British National Bibliography*, the lower from the *National Union Catalog*.

The whim of the bibliographer has no place in determining bibliographic data. They are transcribed from, or objectively based on, tangible evidences in the document itself. Yet both catalogue records reproduced in figure 1 were composed from the same title page using the same cataloguing rules. How is it possible for experienced cataloguers in national bibliographic agencies to differ in their interpretation of the same evidence? The cataloguing code used by both cataloguers defines a title as "the name of a work," which is neither more nor less a definition than the poet's "A title is a title is a title."[1] Although the publisher fixed the wording and layout of the title page, it is the librarian, a person with experience of how titles are used for bibliographic purposes, who must decide how the objective evidence best fits into the item's bibliographic record. Thus subjective judgement and ad hoc judgement (not whim) do have a place in determining bibliographic data when the objective evidence is ambiguous—but not to the extent of ignoring or distorting that evidence.

Since creating and using bibliographic records depend on interpreting the meaning and functions of their many component data elements, each element is discussed in the remainder of this chapter in the context of how it helps fulfil the purposes of bibliographic control. The formal definitions found in current cataloguing rules and glossaries can rarely be adequately understood without experience of how the data elements serve the purpose of retrieval and identification in catalogues and bibliographies. The following sections are intended to amplify what a person familiar with basic footnoting practice and library-catalogue searching should already know. The order in which the elements are treated below may seem familiar, but it is not the order generally prescribed for citations: chapter 8 deals with that. Here, the elements are grouped according to their functions.

Title(s)

In the myths and fables, one has control over what one can name. This is certainly true also of bibliographic identification. In the manuscript period, a title literally named an individual document or copy, since each was unique. Today there are many identical copies of a printed document and, although it may be convenient to say that a title names a *work*, it is best for purposes of bibliographic listing to say that it names a *publication*. The distinctions made on page 11 among the terms *document* (or *item*), *work*, and *publication* may be reinforced by noting that all copies of the same publication necessarily have the

1. AACR2 defines a title proper as "the chief name of an item." This is not much more help but it does recognize a distinction between a publication (item) and a work. The bibliographic records in figure 1 show that the two cataloguers chose different titles at least partly because of another difference of opinion between them, namely who should be considered the principal author of the work.

same title (they come from the same printing plates), but that different editions of a work often have different titles, as in *The Holy Scriptures* versus *The Old and New Testaments*, or *Die Dreigroschenoper* versus *The Threepenny Opera*. Just as different persons may have the same name, so may different publications and works have the same title: copyright cannot be claimed for a title. There are dozens of *Principles of Economics* and more than a few books entitled *The Second World War*. Although it cannot do so absolutely, a title still distinguishes one publication from all others more often than can any other single element of bibliographic data. This is why a title has been the one essential ingredient in every bibliographic citation since the advent of printing.

Most people expect a title to indicate the subject of the intellectual content of the item, as in *Famous Japanese Gardens*, but it may consist of, or include, words designating an author, publisher, date, form, or other information, as in the case of the following titles:

> *The Complete Shakespeare*
> *Macmillan Bible Atlas*
> *The 1981 Proceedings of the Conference on Aging*
> *Selected Poems*
> *The Barbara Kraus Calorie Guide*

An authoritative statement of a book's title is expected on its title page (see page 57), but a different one may appear on its cover, spine, running heads, etc. Among nonprint items consisting of more than one physical piece, this is all too common; for example, the box containing a particular kit displays the title *Regional Geography of Canada, an Economic and Urban Study*, while the guide accompanying the filmstrip inside bears the title *Geography of Canada, a Regional Survey*. One title must be chosen for any one publication as its principal title, something the cataloguer now calls a title proper. Ideally, every cataloguer would choose the same one, usually on the basis of typographic prominence or where it appears. In reality, alas, this is not always the case, as figure 1 shows. Since a given user may remember any of several wordings as an item's title, it is useful to note them all in its bibliographic record; however, this is rarely done in simpler records, such as footnote citations.

Where a title *ends* may be a matter of concern, for example, when creating a title index. How many users are unable to find *Time* magazine in a library's catalogue because its title is filed after the title *The Time of Your Life* as *Time, the Weekly Newsmagazine*? A title is a grammatical unit; if it can be separated into subunits, the first such subunit is the title proper. The remainder, including anything once called a subtitle, is now called other title information. In the following title, only the first four words are the title proper, and there are two units of other title information: *Nuclear Plant Emergency Plans, an Administrative Response to the Alarm Bell, a Selected Bibliography*.

When two or more works are published together, as is the case in a collection or anthology, the publication is usually given a collective title, for example, *Ten Classic Tales of Mystery*, *The Father Brown Stories*, or *The Wasteland and Other Poems*. None of these titles, even the last, merely identifies a single work. Each identifies a publication in which several works have been brought together. Figure 2 shows an example of both a collective title *and* the titles of the individual works in the collection appearing on a title page. Figure 3 shows two examples from different media in which no collective title appears to have been intended by their publishers.   This is relatively common in the case of the long-playing or compact disc containing music but relatively rare in the case of the printed book. Here, the titles and authors of the individual works must together serve as the title of the whole publication.   In both cases in figure 3, however, the names of the authors are presented separately from the titles of the works

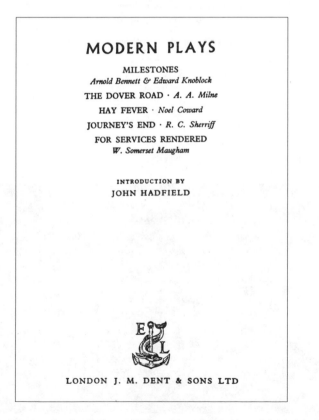

FIGURE 2. A title page bearing both a collective title and the titles of the independent works contained in the book. See figure 32 (page 259) for two types of bibliographic record for this book: one for the book as a whole and another for one of its component works (that is, for a single play within it).

FIGURE 3. The title page of a book and the label on a long-playing disc, each containing more than one independent work but no collective title. There are additional works by these same composers on the other side of the disc.

contained in the collection, as well as each in conjunction with the title of his or her separate work. It is a reflection of different bibliographic instincts brought by librarians of the past to the different media that, while no cataloguer is ever likely to have thought of *Clara Reeve—Horace Walpole* as a collective title for the printed book, there is precedent for making *Riegger/Prokofiev/Copland* serve as a collective title for the disc.

As a final example, the title page of another anthology is shown in figure 4. A title is usually presented as the first, or topmost, element on a title page, but placing an author's name before it is a well-known variant, perhaps more among British publishers than among American ones. James Russell Lowell is clearly named as the author whose selections (of what?) comprise the majority of the book. To say that the book's title is *Representative Selections . . .* is therefore reasonable. The single word *Lowell* is stamped on the front cover and the spine reads "Lowell *Clark and Foerster". The majority of undergraduates

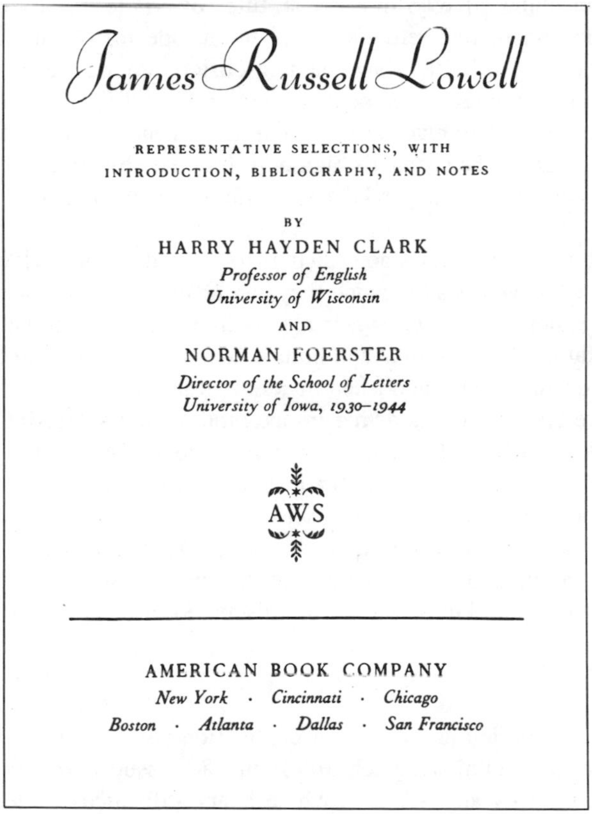

$$\mathcal{J}ames \; \mathcal{R}ussell \; \mathcal{L}owell$$

REPRESENTATIVE SELECTIONS, WITH
INTRODUCTION, BIBLIOGRAPHY, AND NOTES

BY
HARRY HAYDEN CLARK
Professor of English
University of Wisconsin

AND

NORMAN FOERSTER
Director of the School of Letters
University of Iowa, 1930–1944

AWS

AMERICAN BOOK COMPANY
New York · Cincinnati · Chicago
Boston · Atlanta · Dallas · San Francisco

FIGURE 4. A title page whose typographic layout invites the use of the author's name as the title proper.

who need to make a footnote reference to this book would show Clark as its principal author and *James Russell Lowell* as the title, without recognizing the resulting implication that this is a biography of Lowell. Every cataloguer would show Lowell as the author; most would transcribe the book's title as *James Russell Lowell : Representative Selections* more because of the layout of the title page than because of the sequence of its words. These points are belaboured here because of the critical importance of a title as the primary identifier of a publication. Recognition of a title is a matter of linguistic interpretation in the light of knowledge of both publication practices and searchers' retrieval habits.

Over the centuries, fashions in titling have gone through cycles. In one period, titles tend to be lengthy and/or explicit; in another, they are brief and/or allusive. Other title information, including any subtitle, has been used in various ways, the current fashion in trade books being to make it explain what is alluded to obliquely in the title proper. The contemporary English-language trade book rarely has more than four or five words in its titling which convey any substantive meaning directly. In contrast, titles of articles in academic journals tend to avoid connotative references and to include many substantive words, a practice encouraged by the long-standing custom among the A&I services of using title words to index the contents of such articles. In popular journals, there is a growing tendency to place as a caption at the head of an article a quotation from its text to catch the scanner's attention, followed by the title. People citing the article may unfortunately take this combination to be a title followed by a subtitle.

Although many brief news notes, letters to the editor, and reviews in journals and newspapers have titles by which they can be cited, many others do not. The lack of an explicit title of its own is also common among unique unpublished items, for example, manuscripts and homemade slide sets, videorecordings, and cassettes. It occurs among published materials, for example, when items issued separately are later brought together in one binding and a description is needed for the made-up whole. If an untitled item is to be listed in a catalogue or footnote, a title must be made up for it. Such a title must not be mistaken for one transcribed from the document itself; hence the convention of enclosing a supplied or made-up title within square brackets.[2] Titles can also be links relating publications to one another. In the section on these relationships beginning on page 45, several more kinds of titles are discussed in this context.

Serials

A serial (magazine, journal, etc.) is a publication issued in parts and intended to be continued indefinitely. Each article in each issue normally has its own title and occasionally an issue as a whole bears a distinctive title, but there is

---

2. Brackets [ ] are *not* parentheses ( ). The two marks of punctuation have different conventional functions in bibliographic description and must not be confused with one another.

also a title for the whole serial which presents special problems, most of them stemming from two facts:

1) Since it is printed on each separate issue produced over a long period under various editors and designers, the title can, and in many cases does, change from time to time in major and minor ways, resulting in successive titles for what its subscribers consider to be the same journal.

2) Much more often than in the case of monographs, totally different serials bear the same (or almost the same) title, vitiating the important function of a title as a means of distinguishing one publication from another.

The latter is an insidious problem. If several monographs are entitled simply *The Second World War* (among them, those of Sir Winston Churchill, Tim Healey, and Charles Messenger), each is likely to be cited by both its author *and* its title, so they are easily and naturally distinguished from one another. Among serials, there are thousands entitled *Annual Report*. Once again, no person citing any one of them would fail to indicate which body's annual report is meant, but it is usually more of a problem to identify clearly a body than a person in a file, a fact demonstrated on pages 155–61. However, many serials are not closely associated with a known body, for example, the dozens of serials entitled *Dialogue*. While a few of these may be clearly associated with societies or institutions, most are known to their casual users only by that title. These titles must therefore be qualified by some other data element in order to distinguish them as access points.

Title display on the cover of a serial is often deliberately ambiguous. Two experienced cataloguers may well disagree on what constitute the titles proper of the serials illustrated in figure 5. A flipped coin may be as good an arbiter as any. Bilingual and multilingual serials exist in significant numbers and pose problems such as that illustrated in the top two parts of figure 6, a problem shared by the much smaller proportion of monographs whose titling and content are in more than one language. The presence of a title in more than one language on the same title page, cover, etc., as illustrated here is not quite the same problem as that of a single physical item with more than one title page in different languages.[3] Figure 6 also shows the need to inform a user about the various successive titles a serial publication has appeared under throughout its life.

Especially in scientific fields where serials are cited much more frequently than are monographs, there is a natural tendency to want to use an abbreviation rather than a serial's full title. This has led to attempts to standardize a unique

3. These include items in which the entire content appears in two (or more) languages in separate sections, for example, the so-called or tête-bêche, or inverted, publications. In such cases, the practice of many libraries is to pretend that anything in the item not in its own working language does not exist, while in a bibliography the item may be treated almost as if each different-language part is a separate publication.

THE BRITISH LIBRARY   BIBLIOGRAPHIC SERVICES

Newsletter

NO. 49 JUNE 1989
ISSN 0268-9707

■■■*SELECT*■■■■   NATIONAL BIBLIOGRAPHIC SERVICE

Newsletter

NO. 1 JUNE/JULY 1990
ISSN 0960-1570

FIGURE 5. The publication statement on the June 1989 issue reads "The British Library Bibliographic Services Newsletter is published by The British Library . . . . " The publication statement on the June/July 1990 issue reads "Select is published by the British Library . . . . " The change of numbering and of the ISSN are also indications of an intended title change. Despite the prominence of the word *Newsletter* on both issues, it appears not to be the intended title proper of either issue!

brief titling for each serial. Today, the covers of many journal issues bear a suggested citation title in the form of a mnemonic abbreviation, for example, *Int.j.cir.theor.appl.* for the *International Journal of Circuit Theory and Applications*. In the 1950s, an attempt at cooperative standardization led to a central agency assigning to each serial that would accept and promote it a unique designation called a coden. At first a coden consisted of four characters taken from the title, but this proved insufficient to distinguish large numbers of journals. A coden now consists of six characters, of which the last two are often not derived from the title, for example, ICTACV for the preceding journal. The application of the coden system has not spread much outside the scientific community. It has been overtaken, but not entirely replaced, since 1970 by the establishment of ISDS, the International Serials Data System, and its master file of so-called key-titles. Each key-title is unique to one serial title and is exactly matched by the assignment of an International Standard Serial Number (ISSN), as described on page 56.[4] As a rather confusing result, several kinds of titling are to

4. For the ISSN/key-title system, see UNISIST, International Serials Data System, *Guidelines for ISDS* (Paris: Unesco, 1973). The coden system is now administered by Chemical Abstracts Service of Columbus, Ohio.

FIGURE 6. Successive titles of the official journal of the Canadian Library Association; the journal's numbering has continued in an unbroken sequence from the first title shown above to the present. The top two versions of the titling are in two languages; in the top three versions, there is a further question of whether the title includes the name of the association.

be found on many a serial issue: (1) a bibliographic title or title proper, (2) a coden, (3) an ISSN and a key-title, and (4) a suggested citation title! Whether this simplifies the bibliographic control of serial publications or complicates it depends on one's point of view.

Responsibility for Intellectual Content

In a simpler era, the typical printed book prominently claimed one personal author. Any additional disclosure of persons and/or corporate bodies involved in the intellectual content was discreetly buried in a preface or a statement of acknowledgements. Authorship is increasingly difficult to define as more and more works are the products of combinations of persons interacting in varied ways, whether as individuals or as members of corporate bodies (committees, institutions, government agencies, etc.). The statement in a book claiming that it is "by the editors of Sunset Books and Sunset Magazine" reveals the existence of specific personal authors but not their individual names. There is no implication in this statement that any corporate entity takes collective responsibility for the book's intellectual content. A corporate body as such, however, is unquestionably the author of such things as its own annual report, even if some person(s) had to write the actual words. On reading wording such as the following, one is left in more doubt about the nature and extent of corporate control exercised over the content of the publication; examination of prefatory matter or the text of the item may lead to firmer conclusions.

> *A College in the City: an Alternative.* "a report from Educational Facilities Laboratories . . . . The primary author . . . was Evans Clinchy."

> *The City Fights Back, a Nation-Wide Survey* . . . , "narrated and edited by Hal Burton from material developed by the Central Business District Council of the Urban Land Institute."

The words *editor* and *compiler* appear frequently. A person so designated may perform any one or more of the following functions:

1) cause a work to come into existence by conceiving its scope, general focus, and arrangement, then convincing others to do the actual writing
2) reconstruct a deceased author's intended text by examining existing editions, manuscripts, and other evidence
3) add a commentary, glosses, footnotes, bibliography, etc. (together called critical apparatus) to an existing work by someone else
4) abridge, revise, paraphrase, bowdlerize, or otherwise modify an existing work by someone else
5) select for inclusion in a new publication material which was created for other purposes by one or many persons or bodies (this activity is often called compiling, as in the case of an anthology, but it may also be called editing, as in the case of conference proceedings)[5]
6) collaborate with an author in putting the latter's ideas into acceptable verbal or visual form for publication (this activity may be called ghostwriting when it is done by a freelance writer rather than by a staff or contract member of a publishing firm) or
7) go over a writer's work to ensure consistency and/or correctness of style, punctuation, orthography, etc. but without authority to make substantial changes (this activity is called copy editing).

Cataloguing rules of the past made significant practical distinctions among many of these functions, but the functions are becoming less sharply distinguished in practice. In the first five cases, the editor or compiler is usually prominently named in the publication and the telltale word (editor, compiled,

---

5. As a variation of this case, a person is often said to compile a bibliography even though every citation in it is originally written solely by that person.

etc.) may even be omitted. In the last two cases, although a ghostwriter is often named as a co-author, it is more usual for the contribution not to be mentioned in the document (except perhaps among prefatory acknowledgements) and to be ignored in citations.

A performance is reproduced in the sound recording, motion picture, video-recording, etc. The performers warrant recognition in the bibliographic records for such documents. Some art forms emphasize, others blur, the distinction between creator (author, composer, etc.) and performer. The latter may undertake functions similar to most of the types of editing. A sufficiently idiosyncratic performance of a piece of music may even be accepted as a new work, no longer ascribed directly to the original composer(s).

The expression on a title page, disc label, etc. of any of the above facts concerning the intellectual origin of the work is called a statement of responsibility. Such a statement may be clear and explicit or vague and ambiguous; some interpretation is always needed to determine which of the named persons or bodies have acted so centrally to the creation of the intellectual content of the item as to warrant mention in the bibliographic record. Even the medium may be a consideration: while the layout designer of a prose text is almost certain to be ignored, the designer of an art book or a computer-graphics software package probably warrants inclusion as a descriptive data element and perhaps also as an access point. These days, everyone involved in the slightest way in a publication seems to demand recognition in the article's caption or on the book's title leaf—at least its verso. Recent scandals in academe reveal that a contribution to authorship may be explicitly ascribed on a document to someone who has never seen the text in question. As more designers, layout artists, jacket illustrators, copy editors, research assistants, advisors, consultants, etc. pry their way into the sanctum, a title leaf looks more and more like motion picture credits. Obviously, many feel that it should. The most basic function of authorship is always noted in the bibliographic record, but which others should also be recorded depends on the purposes of the various types of list.

As for access points, an index of so-called authors may include names of persons acting as writers, editors, compilers, illustrators, performers, creators of related works, photographers, writers of forewords and introductions, etc., and corporate bodies acting as publishers, sponsors, conference sites, and granting agencies.[6] Finally, the name of the author of an academic book or article is commonly followed by the name of the person's university, company, laboratory, etc. Such corporate affiliation has not traditionally been recorded in the library catalogue because it does not necessarily remain current. To reveal what publications derive from work done in a particular laboratory, etc. is a legitimate purpose of other bibliographic tools; they may not only state but also index the corporate affiliations of authors.

6. It is not necessary for every name appearing in a bibliographic record also to be indexed (that is, formulated as an access point for that record). The difference between description and the provision of access points is discussed at the end of this chapter and in the next.

Just as there may be multiple functions of authorship to account for, so any one function may be represented by more than one name, for example, five persons jointly writing a textbook. In an attempt to keep the amount of bibliographic data and the number of access points manageable, library cataloguing rules have traditionally required mention of only up to three different contributors per function: the appearance of four or more results in only the first one being recorded. Although totally arbitrary, this rule-of-three is familiar in several areas of cataloguing. It is less common in the A&I publications, in which each of fifteen authors of an article on psychology expects a listing. It also breaks down in the face of the demands of nonprint, and particularly performance, media. What is the use of naming only the first (or even the first three) soloists in an opera recording?

Publication/Distribution/Manufacturing Data

Information concerning the printer and the place and date of printing constitute the imprint, a word which betrays its origin as a statement of the facts of printing the item. The imprint was naturally placed on the final page (as a colophon, a tail) when the printer (or, earlier, the manuscript writer) completed production. The publisher separated from the printer by the eighteenth century. It is now the former from whom one acquires the item (while it is in print) and who therefore wishes to display a corporate name for product identification. The information therefore drifted from the colophon to the foot of the title page for greater prominence. Today, the manufacturer's name may appear in the colophon, on the title-leaf verso, or not at all. In any case, it is ignored in all but the more detailed bibliographic descriptions, except when the publisher is not named and cannot readily be deduced. It may be difficult to distinguish publishing from modern manufacturing functions. Firms exist to make and sell single-copy photographic reproductions of out-of-print items, whether in hard copy or in microform, as they are ordered. In some citation practices, such a firm is recorded as the publisher; in others, it is considered merely the manufacturer of an additional copy of an existing item and therefore is ignored in the citation.

Publication information, like most other bibliographic data, is of value in identifying both the content (the work) and the document. Despite the existence of many multinational houses, publishing is still largely a reflection of the culture of a place. Identifying that place therefore alerts a reference librarian or selector to a possible national or regional emphasis. The publisher's name may also guarantee quality standards (or warn of a lack thereof) and indicate a point of view or emphasis on a subject specialty. For these purposes, publication information is permanently useful even if the item can no longer be obtained from the originating publisher. There are many small firms not listed in standard publishers' directories, so even a street address can be useful in a citation. Many publishers, particularly of nonprint materials, now contract out the functions of distribution (warehousing, wholesaling, invoicing, shipping, and stock control) to a separate agency with whom the buyer is expected to deal. Therefore, a distributor named in the item should also be recorded in any citation intended to be of help in acquiring the item. Outside a publisher's own country, however, distribution arrangements are notoriously unstable. Canadian librarians therefore rarely include the name of a Canadian distributor in the catalogue record for an imported publication even when it is prominently displayed in the publication.

At one time, it was expected that a book published in both the United Kingdom and the United States would be set in type in the two countries separately, with consequent changes in spelling and sometimes in vocabulary, style, terms of measurement, etc. Today, international manufacturing arrangements are increasingly common. Either the same type image is used by printers in each country or the item is produced in only one place for sale worldwide by different publishers. The names of the different publishers may appear on the same title page whether shown with equal prominence or not. When this is so, it is reasonable for, say, a Briton to cite the item in a footnote naming only its British publisher while an American cites an identical copy naming only the American one. This may seem harmless, or even useful in indicating where to acquire the item in one's own country, but it can mislead the searcher into thinking there are two editions which differ in some significant respect. It avoids confusion, therefore, if a citation always indicates at least the first-named publisher. Instead of sharing the same title page with another publisher elsewhere, a publisher may have a different title page printed naming only itself although the item is in every other respect identical to that sold by the other publisher. Conventionally in library cataloguing, the existence of differing title pages suffices to require separate records for otherwise identical publications, probably because libraries in most countries are unlikely to receive the same content under more than one imprint.[7] By the same conventions, a difference in the binding or dust wrapper alone does not create a different bibliographic item and therefore a separate record.

The analogous situation of the reprint edition brings special problems for both cataloguer and reference librarian. This is not a reprint made by the item's original publisher to keep it available. It is a reissue of a publication by a publisher other than the original one because the latter no longer exists or no longer wishes to keep the work in print. The work may be in the public domain (meaning that anyone may legally copy it), or the copyright may be acquired by the reprint publisher. Reprint publishing is hundreds of years old but is especially active to replenish damaged libraries (for example, after the two World Wars) and to stock new ones (for example, in the explosion of post-secondary education in the 1960s). The reprint is now photographically produced and is therefore

---

7. In Canada, such multiple receipt happens often enough that the cataloguer may consider it a justifiable economy to consider the work rather than the publication, that is, to treat the one received later as merely a copy of the first.

identical to the original unless new material is added. The reprint publisher's name may appear on a new or additional title page, may be added to the original one, or may only appear on a stick-on label on an inner cover! The problem again arises of whether the work or the publication should take precedence in bibliographic identification. Both library cataloguing practice and style manuals for footnotes have vacillated over the years on this issue, treating the reprint sometimes as a variant or copy of the original, sometimes as a new publication. If a library has both the reprint and its original, the former method is an economy and may be less confusing for users, but this is not often the case since a library is most likely to buy a reprint precisely because it does not own the original publication. Further implications of the preceding bibliographic relationships among editions are discussed on pages 47–50.

Date

Four different kinds of date are pertinent to works and publications, all normally expressed in a citation only as a year.

1) The publication date is the year in which the *first* group of copies made from a given set of printing plates, magnetic signals, photographic negatives, etc. is issued for distribution by the publisher named in the publication data.

2) The manufacturing date pertains to the object in hand. It is the year in which the type image is actually inked and transferred to those very sheets of paper, the sound recording matrix actually stamped into that piece of vinyl, the magnetic impulses actually copied onto that reel of tape, etc.

3) The copyright date designates the year when legal claim is laid to some aspect of the intellectual content as literary property or to the typographic or other format as design.

4) The original date is the date when the work is first published any-where, not merely in the publication or manufactured item in hand, for example, 1850 in the case of Hawthorne's *The Scarlet Letter*.

The first type of date relates to the publication, the second to the object in hand (the copy), and the last two to the work. By far the majority of all works are published and manufactured only once, almost immediately after being completed. For these, the same year serves as all four types of date. However, the small minority of cases in which some or all these dates differ includes anything that could be called a classic: a work issued and re-edited over and over. Sometimes too few dates are mentioned in the item itself; sometimes, too many. An anthology comprising different works created and/or originally published at different times often presents many dates to interpret, some for the anthology and others for each separate work within it.

The following is a representative presentation of date information on the verso of a book's title leaf:

First published, 1931
Second edition, 1932
Third revised edition, 1954
Fourth impression, 1958
Fifth impression, 1963
Fourth revised edition, 1967
Fifth revised edition, 1981
New impression, 1986
Copyright ©1967, 1981

A work first available in print in 1931 was likely completed in manuscript some time in that or the preceding year. In 1954, 1967, and 1981, enough changes were made to the content that the publications of those years are called revised editions. The word *impression* implies no change in content but only the publisher's attempt to keep the work available by manufacturing more copies when stock has run low. One might suspect that the 1932 issuance is also merely a new impression even though the word *edition* is used; however, in those days it was not uncommon to print very few copies at first so the market could be tested and typographic errors and other minor details changed for an early and almost-but-not-quite-identical reprint.

There is nothing wrong with including more than one of these dates in the bibliographic record as long as it is clear which one relates to which function. Cataloguing rules give priority to a date of publication as defined earlier, rather than to that of the work's creation or the individual copy's manufacture. Thus the date 1981 must be recorded even if no other is; that is the year in which the version of the text in hand—its fifth revised edition—was first published. Many publications now show their publication history as in the preceding example, so a reader wanting to know when the book was originally written need only look in any edition of it. The user wanting to know the date of first publication of an older literary, musical, or similar creative work is expected to find that information in a reference work such as an encyclopaedia or a biographical dictionary. When cataloguing a rare book, it is common to try to distinguish each copy by noting when it was printed. For newer items, omitting the manufacturing date (unless it must serve as a substitute for an unknown publication and/or copyright date) means that no new catalogue record need be made for a different impression of a printed book: a convenience since the library can continue to use the existing record when it has replaced a worn-out or lost copy with a newer impression. This may be inconsistent with the practice noted earlier of making separate records when only the publisher's name differs, but a different publisher's name is a more likely clue to a possible change in content than is a different manufacturing date.

The nature and uses of a copyright date are complex matters governed by ever-changing national laws and international agreements. There is separate legal protection for the intellectual content of a document and, where relevant, for its performance on a sound recording or videorecording. A new claim, and therefore another year in the copyright statement, may indicate anything from total revision of the content to the addition of only a few sentences of prefatory matter or the updating of some statistics in a computer file. A totally unchanged new impression by the same publisher is not entitled to an updated copyright claim. However, in the United States before 1978, two copyright dates twenty-eight years apart indicate no more than a renewal of the original copyright claim without any change in the content.

The presence of several different copyright dates in an anthology may only indicate the separate claims to copyright by the various authors of works contained in it. The absence of a copyright claim in a work before the mid-1950s is of no significance because before their adherence to the Universal Copyright Convention, most of the world's developed countries (but not the United States) recognized the legal claim of copyright without requiring formal notification in the publication. In the United States, however, a copyright date has appeared as a legal requirement of protection for over a century. Since it dates the intellectual content of a publication more certainly than its publication date does, North American cataloguing practice has been to give both years in the record if they differ significantly and to use the year of copyright as a preferred substitute if no publication date is known. Thus a 1989 reprint edition showing a 1910 copyright date gets both years recorded.

Terms of Availability

Data relating to price, conditions of sale or distribution, etc. now tend to be of short-lived validity. They are valuable additions to records intended to aid in the selection and acquisition of newly published items. National and trade bibliographies therefore include such data but most retrospective ones do not. The constantly changing price of a serial publication is likely to be found only in its own issues and advertisements.

Physical Characteristics

The count and description of the material pieces composing a document is the very basis of bibliography as the study of the document-as-physical-object, the second function of bibliography noted on page 12. Such description helps distinguish documents from one another and provides information for the practical needs of conserving collections and restoring damaged items. The amount of such detail recorded varies greatly. Early and valuable items and those whose authenticity has been questioned are subjected to detailed inspection using the analytical methods of physics, chemistry, spectroscopy, etc. The results of such inspection might form part of a particularly detailed bibliographic record. At the other extreme, an average footnote or citation contains little or no data of this kind.

An object's medium (paper, acetate, etc.), the number of its component parts (pages, frames, reels, pieces, etc.), and the method by which they are assembled (binding, container, etc.) are its basic physical characteristics. Newer media are more technically complex (or at least less familiar) than paper-and-ink media. The type of magnetic coating on a strip of plastic, the acidity of the frame in which a slide is mounted, the density of the image electronically produced from a videorecording, or the transfer process of the emulsion on a piece of photographic film can all be significant. A type image is readable whether bound in hard or soft covers and whether printed on white or brown paper, but the intellectual content of some items is inaccessible without a specific mechanical or electronic aid. These requirements must be noted in detail, if at all; for example, the turntable speed and cartridge or stylus type needed to play a disc recording, or the amount of random-access memory needed to process a computer file. Machine-readable documents offer the greatest challenge because the same content may be permanently or temporarily in any of several different physical forms, for example, as core, hard-disk, or floppy-disk storage or with coding for any of several operating systems. An acceptable resolution of most of the outstanding problems in the physical description of computer files was reached only in time for publication in the latest (1988) revision of AACR.

In many media other than computer files, identical intellectual content is routinely issued in a number of different physical formats and the question again arises whether the work or the physical document should be the primary focus of the description. For example, should separate records be made for the vinyl, tape, and compact-disc recordings of the same performance—or for the unpublished microform copy of a complete book, made for preservation purposes, and the original from which it was photographed? Alternative cataloguing practices are still being explored.[8]

An Item's Relationships with Other Items

Information concerning one document's relationships with others can be almost endless. This is the most difficult type of bibliographic data to deal with, if only

---

8. This problem, called the multiple-versions problem, is of great concern to members of the North American consortia because of their interest in sharing records. It has been discussed extensively throughout the 1980s. The most recent summary of these discussions is *Multiple Versions Forum Report: Report from a Meeting held December 6–8, 1989, Airlie, Virginia* (Washington: Network Development and MARC Standards Office, Library of Congress, 1990).

because such information is not always easily found within the related documents themselves. For example, when a publication first appears, it is usually impossible to know how it might relate to future publications. The bibliographer must be prepared to investigate outside the item in hand to ascertain all possible connections. Significant types of relationship include the following:

1) Only physical characteristics may differ; for example,
    a) the same content is issued on paper, on microfilm, or as machine-readable data on CD/ROM
    b) a book is issued with a hard cover, paper cover, or library binding.
2) Other aspects of the bibliographic identity may differ while the intellectual content remains essentially the same; for example,
    a) the same content is published under different titles
    b) the same content is republished later as a reprint edition by a different publisher
    c) items which originated independently are later issued together as a new unit; for example, a previously published phonograph record accompanies a book on music in a pocket attached to the inner rear cover; ten original Civil War pamphlets are now bound into one book for a collector.
3) Finally, the intellectual content of the related documents may differ; for example,
    a) different editions of the same work exist involving revision of text, addition of prefatory or supplementary material, illustrations, colour versus black-and-white reproduction, etc.
    b) publications exist containing some content in common but also some which varies from one to the other (for example, many anthologies; reprint editions containing new material)
    c) different publications are issued in the same series
    d) different publications exist, one being a sequel to another (as in fiction), a supplement to another (as in a Christmas supplement to a magazine), or a continuation of another (as when a serial changes its title).

These conditions are not all mutually exclusive: many permutations occur. Publishers are devilishly inventive.

The study of bibliographic relationships is usually a necessary step in the process of textual criticism. Because library cataloguers attempt to inform users about the intellectual content of publications, not merely about their physical manifestation, they undertake this function—to a limited degree. Only a rare-book cataloguer does original investigation; others copy what relevant information can be easily uncovered in existing sources, often sources within the item being catalogued. As in any detective work, the skill lies not so much in locating the required information as in knowing what to look for. The more complex relationships are topics for lengthy investigation, usually by subject specialists rather than by bibliographers *per se*; for example, one consults a study in comparative literature, not a bibliography, to discover the links among the various mediaeval Tristan legends. Yet to trace the successive texts of *Moby Dick* is basically bibliographic work whether its results be detailed in a thick volume of prose or sketched in a few words on a thin catalogue card for each variant located. It always takes skill to state relationships succinctly, unambiguously, and intelligibly.

The most common, easy-to-express, and important bibliographic relationships, those stated in most citations and catalogue records, are normally revealed within the document itself. They are the relationships among

1) editions of the same work
2) sequels, continuations, etc.
3) items both physically and bibliographically separate from one another but issued and intended to be used together
4) important separately identifiable works contained within one publication and
5) items in the same series.

Each rule for bibliographic description prescribes its own way of showing some or all of these relationships. The result is a record which describes not one bibliographic entity or level alone but as many entities or levels as are involved in the relationship described, a technique discussed more fully on pages 256–60. One of these must be chosen as the primary entity to be fully described and indexed under all access points pertinent to it. Any other occupies a secondary position in the record and is described much more briefly, allowing less latitude for access points. Thus the typical series statement and the typical contents note on a catalogue record consist of little more than a title and perhaps an author's name. Comments on each of the five most common types of bibliographic relationship follow.

Edition

This term probably has more numerous, significantly different, and confusing uses than any other technical term in bibliography. An edition is most basically defined as the total number of copies of a publication produced from the same master copy by the same publisher. There is an implication of change in intellectual content between different editions (for example, in a third edition, an illustrated edition, or an edition in another language), but the change can range from almost total to a few barely noticeable corrections, as suggested on page 43 in the discussion of dates. The cataloguer neither can nor should attempt to count the quantity or judge the significance of changes between editions; that is the job of the textual critic. One wishes every author or publisher would state how the intellectual content differs in any new edition. To do so as concisely as is illustrated in figure 7 is commendable. The reader usually has to read pages of prefatory material to get less information.

First Published 2 November 1922
Second Edition October 1937
Third Edition with an Appendix October 1946
Fourth Edition with further Appendix April 1950
Fifth Edition July 1951
Sixth Edition, revised, 1956
Reprinted 1960

This book, originally published in 1922, consisted of the text of Dr. Einstein's Stafford Little Lectures, delivered in May 1921 at Princeton University. For the third edition, Dr. Einstein added an appendix discussing certain advances in the theory of relativity since 1921. To the fourth edition, Dr. Einstein added Appendix II on his Generalized Theory of Gravitation. In the fifth edition the proof in Appendix II was revised.

In the present (sixth) edition Appendix II has been rewritten. This edition and the Princeton University Press fifth edition, revised (1955), are identical.

The text of the first edition was translated by Edwin Plimpton Adams, the first appendix by Ernst G. Straus and the second appendix by Sonja Bargmann.

FIGURE 7. From the verso of the title leaf of Albert Einstein, *The Meaning of Relativity*, 6th ed., rev. (London: Methuen, 1956).

The same content as published by a particular firm in a particular physical format or at a particular time is also called an edition. The Bantam Edition of *Bleak House*, or the 1923 Edition, or the Limited Edition may all be identical, word for word, their differences being only in paper, typography, binding, price, and perhaps the publisher's name. It is not very helpful to know that "not one word of the original has been omitted" if the version of the work being republished in the book in hand is not explicitly identified. When editions are numbered or otherwise designated in a sequence, the titling and authorship usually do not change. The third edition of *Basic Programming* by Kemeny and Kurtz can be assumed to follow a first (but probably unnumbered) and a second edition of the same title by the same authors. This very book shows that this is not always the case, as do three more complex examples:

1) The ninth edition of *Guide to Reference Books* is by Eugene P. Sheehy; the eighth edition of the same title was by Constance Winchell; earlier

editions numbered in the same sequence, compiled by Isadore Gilbert Mudge and by Alice Bertha Kroeger, bore slightly different titles.

2) There is an *Introduction to Respiratory Physiology* by Harold A. Braun, Frederick W. Cheney, Jr., and C. Paul Loehnen, 2nd ed. (Boston: Little, Brown, 1980), but there was never an earlier edition bearing that title or issued by that publisher. The book's predecessor is *Physiologic Bases for Respiratory Care* by Cheryl E. Beall, Harold A. Braun, and Frederick W. Cheney (Missoula, Mont.: Mountain Press Publishing Co., 1974).

3) Editions of *Reference Books for Elementary and Junior High Libraries* by Carolyn Sue Peterson appeared in 1970 and 1975. The latter calls itself a second edition. The subsequent 1982 revision of the same material was published as *Reference Books for Children*, bears the name of an additional author (Ann D. Fenton), and has no edition number.

A reprint edition was casually described on page 41 as a later impression of the same content by a different publisher. It is often more than that. New material, such as a critical introduction or updated bibliography, is frequently added. Not all reprint publishers care to state prominently that they are selling an old work; it is possible to make a reprint appear to be a newly published or revised text without actually telling a lie. Only by comparing the bibliographic evidence of the item in hand with that in copies of other editions, or by comparing their descriptions in reliable bibliographic sources, can one be certain how a reprint varies from its original. Figure 8 shows a fairly complex reprint relationship honestly presented by its publisher. In preparing the bibliographic record for a reprint, it is essential to distinguish data relevant only to the original publication from those relevant only to the reprint and to present these unambiguously in conjunction with data (usually only the title and author's name) common to both.

Whoever interprets bibliographic records must be aware of the publication relationships discussed on pages 41–44—for example, that an item cited with an American imprint might in fact be a British publication (perhaps even one with a different title in that country) or that an item with a 1983 publication date may contain no information later than 1929 because it is a reprint edition. The acquisitions librarian must try to avoid wasting money buying another version not significantly different from something already available in the collection. The reference librarian presented with a footnote, which cannot be expected to express any of the relevant relationships, must be aware that if the library does not own the exact publication cited, it may have a reprint whose edition and publication details are not identical yet whose content answers the user's needs. It is the cataloguer's responsibility to understand and unambiguously express all the facts of a work's publication history which might affect the accessibility to searchers of its various editions.

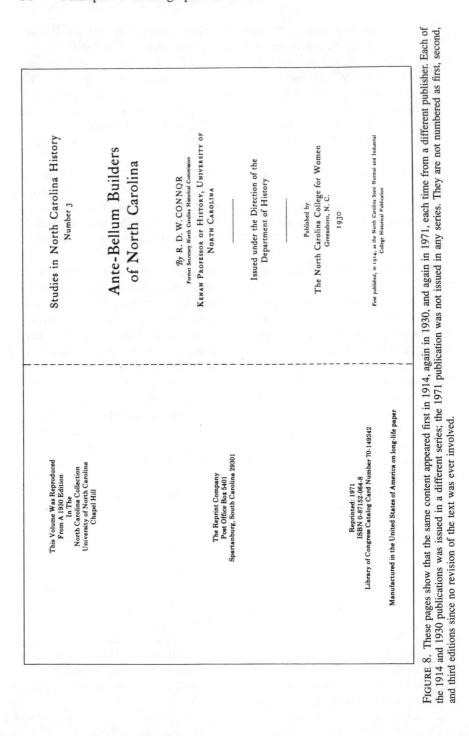

FIGURE 8. These pages show that the same content appeared first in 1914, again in 1930, and again in 1971, each time from a different publisher. Each of the 1914 and 1930 publications was issued in a different series; the 1971 publication was not issued in any series. They are not numbered as first, second, and third editions since no revision of the text was ever involved.

Continuations and Sequels

When there is more than one title in the sequence of a serial, as illustrated in figure 6 on page 37, the record must identify that one title was preceded or continued by, and/or was merged into, separated from, etc., another title. That *The Empire Strikes Back* is a sequel to *Star Wars* is also significant. The relationship works both ways, but of course at the time of release of *Star Wars* it was not known what the title of its sequel would be, even though the probability of a sequel was evident. Announced sequels, reprints, and even new publications sometimes never see the light of day. Such ectoplasmic titles and edition numbers, called bibliographic ghosts, float around the world of bibliographic citation haunting acquisitions librarians who will never be able to lay hands on the actual item. A bibliographic statement should be made only after it is verified as a fact.

Accompanying Items

A book and a sound recording are often brought together to be sold as a unit. So are a teacher's manual and a language text. Statistical tables on a microfiche are inserted in a pocket affixed to the inner cover of a study of economics. A pocket containing a map is tipped onto the flyleaf of a travel book. In some such cases, the two are conceived as integral parts of the whole and each bears the same title. In others, the parts have different titles, were brought together artificially after their creation, and/or are usable independently. In any case, they have different physical characteristics to be recorded, and the fact that they have been brought together as a unit requires that their relationship to one another be noted. The most trouble-free way is to make a separate bibliographic record for each, mentioning on it the existence of the other; but the closer the use-dependency of the one on the other, the less desirable is this technique. Interdependence makes a single record desirable but requires the cataloguer to decide with which of the separate parts to begin the description. This is not always an easy judgement to make. If a filmstrip and a cassette sound recording are produced for use together in a synchronized projector, should the combination be described as a sound recording accompanied by a filmstrip or as a filmstrip accompanied by a sound recording? A neutral solution is to treat the combination as a single unit, a kit, but this may not solve the problem of which title to begin with if the parts of the kit have different titles. Since every bibliographic identification is a linear sequence of data, it is inevitable that the description of one medium will take precedence over that of the other.

Contents: The Parts of a Single Publication

Most longer writing is divided into chapters or parts, musical compositions into movements, plays into acts, etc. Such divisions of a work have no bibliographic significance if they are never separately published or likely to be separately sought. But the parts of some works do have their own identity and are sometimes separately published and studied, for example, a song from a Broadway musical or The Lord's Prayer from the Bible. Thus a title, author, date, physical quantity, etc. can relate to a part of a publication as well as to a complete publication. The parts of any publication known as a collection are, in some more or less significant sense, separate works. *Collection* is a generic term; such terms as *anthology, conference proceedings, Festschrift, kit,* or *record album* describe some specialized types of collection. A journal or magazine is, by its very nature, almost always a collection of separate works called articles. The collection as a whole is also a work in its own right, as is clear when an anthology becomes as famous as Palgrave's *The Golden Treasury* or the *Anthologia Graeca* and is itself translated, issued in different editions, and made the subject of study and criticism. Some titling problems related to collections are illustrated in figures 2–4 on pages 31–33. If a printed-book collection has a collective title, it is most usual to find the identification of the individual works in the collection not on the title page but only in the table of contents. This practice gave rise to the contents note in the bibliographic record as a means of recording the existence of the separate works contained in a single publication. The question of whether to provide these works with their own access points is a separate issue. The use of the contents note and that of the formats known as the analytic record and the multilevel description (two other methods of identifying parts of larger bibliographic units) are discussed on pages 256–60.

Series

A publisher creates a series by giving the same title to each publication in a group, although each also has its own separate (and different) title. The publisher also usually imposes common editorial standards and a uniform physical design on the group. A noted person is often named series editor as a witness of quality as well as (sometimes) its guarantor. The publisher then advertises the series as a unit, hoping that the buyer who has liked one publication in it will notice and buy others, perhaps all. A library's acquisitions procedures are simplified by establishing a standing order for a series rather than ordering each publication separately. Therefore, in times of adequate collections budgets, administrators encourage subscribing to the series even if some items in it would not individually be selected for purchase. Everyone benefits as long as the quality and relevance of the individual publications in the series remains high. The number of monographs issued in series was very small only a half century ago. Now, at least in the more specialized academic and technical fields, it is unusual *not* to see a series title in a monograph.

The degree of topical connection among items in a series is not bibliographically relevant. In a series like *Pelican Books* or *The World's Classics* it is minimal. A series title is useful

1)   to identify the item wanted in a request like "Give me the *Everyman's Library* edition of Chaucer" and/or
2)   to find an item for the person who knows its series title (often from a less-than-adequate citation) but not its individual title.

In the first case, mention of the series title in the bibliographic record suffices; in the second, the series title must also be an access point. As an example of the second situation, a citation may provide only the information *University of London Institute of Education. Studies in Education* when referring to the monograph whose title page is shown in figure 9, although its title as a monograph is *The Arts and Current Tendencies in Education.*

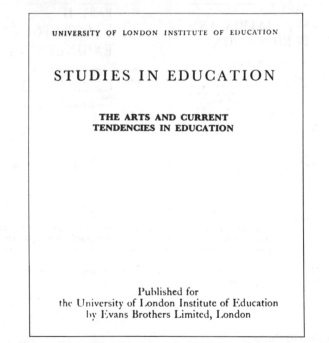

UNIVERSITY OF LONDON INSTITUTE OF EDUCATION

STUDIES IN EDUCATION

**THE ARTS AND CURRENT
TENDENCIES IN EDUCATION**

Published for
the University of London Institute of Education
by Evans Brothers Limited, London

FIGURE 9. A title page illustrating ambiguity as to which is the title of the monograph and which is the title of the series.

If items are intended to be added to a series indefinitely, the series is also a serial (see page 34). Many series are serials, but many others are not. If the number of possible items in the series is finite, the complete series is called a set. A.B. Paterson's literary writings appear under the title *Complete Works*, in two volumes. The volume containing the works written to 1900 is entitled

Singer of the Bush; the volume containing the later works is entitled *Song of the Pen*. Since Paterson is dead, there will not be a third volume.[9] In relation to the collective title *Complete Works*, the other two titles are items contained within the whole (see the previous subsection on contents). In relation to the title of either of the separate volumes, the title *Complete Works* is a series title. A single part or volume of a series need not be a single physical volume. Figure 10 is an example of two works with different titles which together comprise volume 3 of the thirteen-volume set *Technique of Organic Chemistry*.

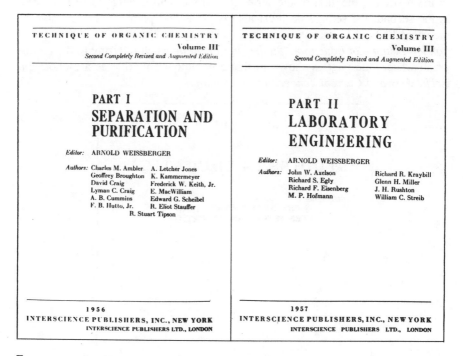

FIGURE 10. The title pages of two separate books which together form one bibliographic unit (volume 3) within a yet larger work.

Other Relationships

The following brief statements quoted from particular publications show something of the possible range of relationships other than those already described:

> The dictionary section was taken from *Polygraph Wörterbuch der graphischen Industrie in 6 Sprachen*.

9. A supplementary volume could appear containing corrections and newly discovered writings. That would complicate the record for the item, but would not change the nature of the series/set.

"Text adapted from *Of Them He Chose Twelve*, by Clarence
   Macartney."
Supplement to *Zulu ethnography*, 1976.

Bibliographic relationships can be multidimensional. For example, the second
edition of a work may be published in a different series from that in which the
first edition appeared; a reissue of a rock music recording may contain one new
song replacing a single band of the recording as originally issued; a microform
collection often comprises material from a number of publications.

Coding Intended to Identify an Item Uniquely

A judicious selection of the above bibliographic data elements assembled without ambiguity should suffice to identify any publication or work and provide
the means of its retrieval from a file via appropriate access points. However, the computer era has focused increased attention on the value of numeric identifiers for more accurate and efficient retrieval. Telephone numbers, social insurance numbers, bank account and credit card numbers, etc.
have long identified persons and their activities. It still takes only about a
dozen digits to provide each telephone line in the world with a unique number. Numbers have also been used bibliographically for a very long time;
for example, a serial number in the *Gesamtkatalog der Wiegendrucke* identifies a particular fifteenth-century printed edition, a Superintendent of Documents number uniquely identifies a United States government publication,
a Köchel number uniquely identifies a composition by Mozart, and an LC
Control Number identifies a single catalogue record created by the Library
of Congress. To these and many other bibliographically oriented numbers,
British publishers added the Standard Book Number (SBN) in the mid-1960s.
It was so quickly accepted worldwide as the International Standard Book
Number (ISBN) that librarians added the International Standard Serial Number (ISSN) in the 1970s. These two are now the most universal bibliographic
numbering systems.

   Publishers devised the ISBN for their computerized inventory control and
financial accounting systems. The number is therefore intended to identify any
form of a publication its publisher might invoice separately. Thus a quality paperback, a hardback, and a limited leatherbound edition of the same publication
each receives a different ISBN even if they are produced from the same printing plates and would be represented by the same catalogue record in a library.
Similarly, a multivolume set is assigned an ISBN for the set as a whole as well
as a different one for each of its separate volumes. The same book with two
publishers' imprints (for example, one American and one British) has a separate
ISBN relating to each publisher. Thus there cannot be an absolute one-to-one

relationship either between an ISBN and a work or between an ISBN and a library catalogue record.

The ten characters of an ISBN are conventionally shown in four segments divided by hyphens:

> 0-949946-29-X
> 3-7825-0052-0
> 92-67-10017-3

The fourth segment is a check digit—a single numeral or the letter X (see pages 128–29). Each of the other three segments can vary in length and consists of numerals only. The first two uniquely identify the publisher; the third identifies the publication. The first segment alone originally identified a language area rather loosely: for example, a publishing house in France, Quebec, or French-speaking Switzerland uses the prefix 2 and the English-language publishers of the industrialized world use 0 (zero) or 1 (one). Now, as a country joins the system, it is assigned a number; for example, Ghana is 996. The second segment identifies an individual publishing house within that country or language area. General control over the systematic application of ISBNs is in the hands of an independent publisher-sponsored agency, the International Standard Book Numbering Agency in Frankfurt. A national agency in each country, usually the national library, coordinates local application principally by assigning publisher numbers.

An ISSN consists of eight characters: seven numerals followed by a check digit. As in the ISBN, the check digit may be a numeral or an X. An ISSN is conventionally shown as two four-digit segments separated by a hyphen. Unlike an ISBN, it has no meaningful parts; two ISSNs in sequence therefore do not necessarily represent serials in any way related. An ISSN uniquely identifies all issues of a serial publication while they have the same key-title (see page 36). When a serial publication changes title, the issues under the new title have a new ISSN and a corresponding new key-title. UNISIST's International Serials Data System coordinates the assignment of ISSNs and key-titles by national agencies, again usually a national library. International Standard Numbering (ISN) schemes have been proposed for various nonprint formats but none has yet come to fruition, perhaps because the ISBN system seems to be serving the publishers of kits, computer programs, slide sets, etc. to identify their products as well. A numbering scheme peculiar to published music is close to realization.

Information Peculiar to One Copy or Process

Whether there are dozens, hundreds, or thousands of copies of a given edition and format of a publication, they are all identical with respect to the data elements identified so far in this chapter. It may be desirable to record further information peculiar to a single copy; for example, if it has fore-edge painting, a handmade binding, an author's autograph, or some association with a significant person, event, etc. If the library's copy is not complete as published, such facts as missing leaves or damage may also be significant.

When listed in a catalogue or bibliography, a document is an abstraction. In a library, it is a material object to be ordered, paid for, moved from branch to branch, circulated to borrowers, rebound, etc. Information needed to identify a single copy in order to record and manage these in-house processes may include such diverse facts as price, copy number, and branch location. These are not strictly bibliographic data but they must be attached to the bibliographic identification of the document. At one time, a library kept many different records for the same item, one for each purpose. In an integrated machine-readable database, temporary and constantly changing information on the circulation status (out to which borrower? due when? missing?) and on the processing status (received when? where located in the backlog? at the bindery?) can now be part of the permanent bibliographic record. Depending on the library's policy, some, all, or none of the temporary processing data can be made available to the public through the same access techniques as the permanent bibliographic data.

Finally, some accounting system is needed for the bibliographic record itself, as distinguished from the document it describes; for example, one must be able to locate each of the several access points established for the record in case any must be changed or deleted. In a manual card system, the access points are listed at the bottom of the card as what are called tracings. In a computer-based system, a record-identifier number unites every piece of data associated with that record.

Sources of Data

A title is useful as the principal identifier of a document because it is usually located where every reader expects to find it: at or near the top of a title page, at the beginning of a magazine article, as the largest printing on the container of a kit or the label of a sound recording, etc. In the case of books, a standard selection of the data elements discussed in this chapter has been presented on title pages, usually in the same sequence, for hundreds of years. That is why these elements and that sequence still dominate the standard library formats analyzed in chapter 8, and probably always will. As the title pages of books have in recent years tended to turn from staid recitations of bibliographic data into advertising and design statements, some data elements drifted to other locations, the most common being the verso of the title leaf. The group of leaves of a printed book up to and including the title leaf are called the preliminaries. These, and the now rarely used colophon, constitute the expected locations of most bibliographic data.[10] The title page, still the usual location of most of the useful data in their most formal presentation, is called the chief source of information. If no title page exists, needed information may have to be sought elsewhere within the item (for example, in running heads or on the cover) or from outside sources. Data included in the record but not taken from an expected source are enclosed in brackets (see page 34).

Defining the expected sources of bibliographic data for printed items of modern design, and particularly for nonprint media, is a problem only recently tackled. The cartouche of a map and the title frame of a filmstrip may be close analogies of the title page, but from which source should the title proper of a machine-readable document be transcribed: the image on the terminal screen or the wording of accompanying printed documentation? It took at least two hundred years for printed title pages to settle into a predictable pattern; one cannot expect newer media to be standardized instantly. Equally reasonable sources sometimes perversely contradict each other: for example, when the two labels of a disc sound recording give only the titles of dozens of individual songs while the slipjacket reads *Favorite Songs by Schubert* and an inserted folder providing the lyrics is headed *Excerpts from Die Schöne Müllerin and Die Winterreise*. An example of different title wording on parts of a kit is given on page 30. Since one title proper must be chosen for each item, rules must help define one chief source of information for each medium so that the same basis for selecting its bibliographic data is used by every cataloguer.

The positioning of data elements, particularly the names of corporate bodies, on a title page is significant. It is reasonable to interpret a corporate name at the foot of the page as the publisher. A corporate name at the middle or top sends a more ambiguous signal about what the body has done, especially if a personal name also appears there. While the whim of a layout artist may be the only explanation for the positioning of data, established publishers, including large corporations and government printing offices, tend to know bibliographic practice and to adhere to traditions in title-page layout. Familiarity with these traditions helps in interpreting the results. The most difficult type of title page to interpret is the ad hoc one made up, for example, by a departmental secretary for a typescript of a conference proceedings.

Not every document displays every desired data element openly. People making footnotes are likely to ignore anything not immediately evident. The library cataloguer accepts more responsibility to look elsewhere for information on the anonymous work, the undated film, or the serial whose ISSN does not appear on the issue in hand. It takes time and skill to locate needed information, particularly if secondary reference sources contradict one another. Some documents display fictitious information, as in the imprint of a clandestine publisher or a

---

10. To print bibliographic information in a colophon is increasingly rare in the English-speaking world, but still common in some other countries. There are national characteristics even in bibliography!

writer's pseudonym. Again, reference sources may reveal the truth—but they may not; the need to consult them is known only to the cataloguer's instinct. It is a cliché that a problem does not exist until it is recognized. Unrecognized pseudonyms, fictitious imprints, etc. do not vanish: these failures of the bibliographic instinct inevitably surface to haunt the cataloguer and confound the reference librarian. Perfection is the goal; imperfection, the reality. How much time to spend on verification and outside investigation of details is usually left to the individual cataloguer's professional judgement in a smaller institution; in a larger one, some tangible policy must be suggested by the administration.

As stated on page 29, a title is not some abbreviation, paraphrase, or translation of what appears on the item's title page (or, in its absence, some other internal source), but a transcription of *exactly* what is found there. Library cataloguing rules respect the integrity of information taken from the item in the transcription of statements of responsibility, edition naming, etc. Where abbreviation or truncation is sanctioned, that is also governed by stated rules. Other types of citation rules discourage changing the wording of a title but are more cavalier about the treatment of other elements; for example, a simple style manual may suggest using the formula "ed. J. Smith" instead of copying "John Smith, compiler." from the item's title page.

Data for Unique Unpublished Items

An unpublished item (for example, a manuscript or a locally made video recording of an amateur show) rarely has a formalized source of bibliographic data. Data elements need to be imposed on, more than extracted from, the document and are often only analogous to those for published items. For example, data relating to the manufacture of the item and the production of its content replace publication information; the cataloguer's concise description of the content replaces a lacking title. Archivists are now in the process of establishing data-element directories and rules for citation and description for the unpublished materials which are their particular domain.

How Much Is Enough?

Before the invention of printing, more than one copy of the same work was rarely available in one place and even if they were, each, being unique, had its own errors and other idiosyncracies. The concept of an exact quotation which could be documented by item and page number was unknown.[11] So was the

---

11. The very few instances such as Scriptural texts significant for salvation and memorized by "chapter and verse" are the exceptions which prove this rule. Even so, these did not involve citation by edition and page but reference to a relative location within conventional divisions of the text.

concept of an exact title: works were alluded to rather than named. Aristotle's *Metaphysics* is nothing more than the work which followed his *Physics*; Homer's *Odyssey* is the story of the character Odysseus. As often, a work was referred to only by identifying its author; for example, "The Stygirite [that is, Aristotle] states that . . . . " Even today, the author's name alone may provide sufficient identification if the person wrote only one famous work, for example, Mary Baker Eddy.

Today's total quantity of documents and the large number of separate publications containing the same work impose much stricter requirements of bibliographic identification. Yet these are too likely to be shortcut even by writers and publishers. Such unacceptable footnotes and citations as the following, copied from actual publications, serve only to give unnecessary work to an interlibrary-loan librarian:

> *Aristotle*. Columbia University Press 26
> *Quaternary Research*. University of Washington, 1970.

Nevertheless, some documents are so famous that an even briefer description can elicit instant recognition. Most educated English speakers recognize *The First Folio* or *Shakespeare. Folio. 1623* more immediately than they would recognize a description of the same book compiled according to current library cataloguing rules:

> Mr. William Shakespeares comedies, histories, & tragedies : published according to the true originall copies. — London : Printed by Isaac Jaggard, and Ed. Blount, 1623. — [18], 303, 100, [2], 69–232, [30], 993 [i.e. 299] p. : ill. (woodcuts) ; 33 cm. (fol.)

Yet the latter is still far from adequate for a student of textual criticism. The importance of the First Folio in the establishment of the Shakespearean text and the vicissitudes of its printing occasioned an extraordinarily thorough bibliographic study of it by Charlton Hinman. His two-volume bibliographic description of the known copies of the First Folio is over a thousand pages long: rather too much information to fit on a 7.5-by-12.5-cm. card or indeed on any library catalogue record! Not one publication in a hundred thousand warrants such detailed description. Unfortunately, it is impossible to predict when the appearance of a new publication with the same title, of a new edition or translation of the same work, of another work by the same author, or the need to identify a forgery will render a previously satisfactory citation too brief to serve the principle of adequate identification.

Over the centuries, a different number and combination of data elements have been found useful and have therefore come to be expected in bibliographic records serving somewhat different purposes. A library catalogue record contains more data than a footnote; a listing in an author bibliography contains yet more. A library's bibliographic records are used in more contexts and for more varied purposes than most other types of record. It has always been considered wiser to start with a fuller record than might seem necessary rather than with one that proves too brief and later needs upgrading. The student who consults the library's catalogue only to find a call number for browsing can ignore the unnecessary detail; the bookseller verifying a first printing of a Ben Jonson play is grateful for it. Some tolerance is useful in cataloguing codes to permit one library to abridge records more than another would and to permit a cataloguer to use judgement in considering the bibliographic nature and importance of the individual item. Figure 11 shows descriptions of the same item in six different bibliographies and catalogues. All are very brief, yet they differ in (1) the number of data elements given and (2) their arrangement and presentation.

With regard to completeness, library practice has changed over time. As an example, early in this century it was considered desirable for a physical description to specify the existence of each leaf within a printed book, for example,

1 p.l., iii–xi, [1], 13–401, [7] p. [where p.l. means preliminary leaf]

AACR requires the cataloguer to record only the highest number appearing on any major sequence of pages and "401 p." suffices to replace all the above detail. At the other extreme, rare-book description may still require collation by (1) format and size, followed by (2) details of each separate signature, and finally (3) pagination, as shown in the following example where these three groups are separated by periods. The signature-descriptions of the second group include their signing, folding, and order.[12]

Demy 8° (227 × 142 mm. uncut). $[A]^2 B^8 (-B^8 + B^{8'}) C-D^8 E^8 (\pm E2)$ $F^8 (-F6 + F6') G^8 H^8 (-H2,3 + H2:3) I-Z^8 2A^2$. Pp. [i] title, [iii]–iv preface, 1–356 text.

Data Elements for Description and for Access

The data elements discussed in this chapter describe a document, distinguish it from others, and help the user decide if it might serve a given need. Some of these elements are also used for the related but different purpose taken up in the next two chapters, namely *finding*, or *accessing*, the record in a file. For the user, accessing a record must precede any judgement as to whether and how it might prove useful, but the producer of records must approach it the other way because access arises from the data elements described in this chapter. The title-page wording "edited, with an introduction, by Fred Hoyle" is a statement of responsibility. The searcher knows that access is normally provided for personal names and so looks under the personal name within this data element, using the

12. The example is from Philip Gaskell, *A New Introduction to Bibliography* [1st ed.] repr. with corr. (Oxford: Clarendon Press, 1979), 374.

—— Report of the Tripartite Economic Survey of the Eastern
Caribbean. January–April 1966. [Leader, J. R. Sargent.]
pp. xxi. 278. *London*, 1967. 8°.   B.S. 251/66.

Report of the Tripartite Economic Survey of the Eastern
Caribbean, Jan.–Apr. 1966. London, H. M. S. O., 1967.
xxi. 279 p. diagr., tables. 25 cm. £2/10/–

              (B•••)

At head of title: Ministry of Overseas Development.

**Report of the tripartite economic survey of the
Eastern Caribbean [appointed by the governments
of the United Kingdom, Canada and the United
States of America, carried out] January-April
1960. London. H.M.S.O., 50/-. [dFeb] 1967.
xxi, 279p. tables, diagrs. 24½cm. Pbk.**

Report of the Tripartite Economic Survey of
the Eastern Caribbean, Jan.-Apr. 1966. London,
H.M. Stationery Off., 1967.
  xxi, 278 p. 25 cm.
  At head of title: Ministry of Overseas
Development.
   "To the Governments of the United Kingdom
of Great Britain and Northern Ireland, of Canada
and of the United States of America".—p. iii.
  50/- pa.

---

*Report of the Tripartite Economic Survey of the Eastern Caribbean, January-
 April 1966*, Ministry of Overseas Development, H.M.S.O., London,
 1967.

Tripartite Economic Survey of the Eastern Caribbean, January-April 1966.

FIGURE 11. From top to bottom, these records are from the catalogue of the British Museum
Department of Printed Books; the *National Union Catalog*; the *British National Bibliography*;
Canadiana; Sir Harold Mitchell, *Caribbean Patterns* (Edinburgh: Chambers, 1967); and Aaron
Segal, *The Politics of Caribbean Economic Integration*, Special Study no. 6 (Rio Piedras, P.R.:
Institute of Caribbean Studies, University of Puerto Rico, 1968).

convention of locating not the given name but the surname, *Hoyle, Fred*, to find the item. An ISBN alone is a great access point, much better than an author and/or title because there is no question of guessing what form it will take in an alphanumeric listing. It serves such practical library purposes as looking for an existing catalogue record to match with a book in hand, but it will be a long time before a reader's advisor suggests that 0-226-81620-6 is a good book to read. A serial is more likely to be referred to by its citation title (see page 36), which is at least mnemonic—"Where is volume 28 of BAPS?"—but certainly not by its ISSN. Among the more meaningful identifications, people still most often rely on a title alone ("Read *Future Shock*"), but common sense indicates that it is not sufficient to tell a friend to look up *Principles of Chemistry* or *Statistical Report for 1981*. Although frequently adequate for both description and access, reference by title along with author's name must be supplemented by additional information, such as an edition number, physical medium, date, or publisher's name if the user is interested, for example, only in the second edition of the *Anglo-American Cataloguing Rules* (not the first), or a recording in cassette form only of Beethoven's *Fifth Symphony* (not one on compact disc), or the Northwestern/Newberry edition of Melville's *Typee* (not the Bantam paperback). Any retrieval system must incorporate the possibility of using such data elements as part of the means of accessing a record.

If the variety of purposes prevents the establishment of any one rule for either description or access, so does the infinite variety of the presentation of data within individual documents. It can seem to a beginner that (1) almost every item presents a slightly different challenge in the selection and arrangement of its bibliographic data and (2) almost every different bibliography presents a slightly different arrangement of data, access points, etc. This is either the joy or the despair of bibliography, depending on one's point of view. Libraries are dedicated to the exchange of bibliographic data and documents and therefore need standardized bibliographic practices more than other agencies do. Over the past hundred years, librarians have worked hard to develop rules accepted nationally and even internationally for (1) describing documents using standard data elements and (2) applying name and subject access points to retrieve the resulting records from large files. Librarians' early application of computers to bibliographic work has expedited agreement on standardization. The principles of access and its efficient operation in manual and automated files occupy the next two chapters.

3

ACCESS POINTS

The purpose of every activity in bibliographic control is to provide the most direct possible access to the content of a particular document which can satisfy a stated informational need. The naive beginner asks where the documents are in order to browse shelves, vertical files, or boxes of them. While this can be enjoyable, how does one find out on which shelf to start? What if relevant documents are loaned out temporarily, in storage, or at the bindery? Consulting a complete and organized file of document descriptions—bibliographic records—to discover what is relevant and where to find it is usually preferable even if it adds a step to the search. The person who wants to browse can browse the records too. Everyone does this from time to time with small files, such as bibliographic lists at ends of chapters. Browsing is not to be rejected as an access technique: serendipity produces valuable results and is occasionally the only way to find an elusive fact or document. However, it is usually a less efficient and more time-consuming method than using some systematic means of direct access.

Sheer quantity is the greatest barrier to direct access. Whether the user is looking for the actual document on a shelf or in a filing cabinet or for the bibliographic record representing it in a catalogue or A&I publication, the item or its record is buried among thousands or millions of others. It is natural for some end-users to feel that both a library as a whole and its catalogue in particular are impenetrable jungles and that librarians keep things complicated to preserve their jobs as intermediaries in information retrieval. Yet every user wants the largest possible assemblage of potentially relevant material to be available for any search because the larger the library or file, the more likely something of value can be found there.

The compiler of any bibliography, catalogue, or A&I publication has always been expected to build into the file a consistent and predictable system for accessing the descriptions of single documents and groups of documents. The wise searcher learns how to use that system to find what is needed. The bibliographic files used, and usually created, by librarians are among the best organized of any kind of information-access tools in existence. That many of them are large and complex, however, means that their most effective and efficient user is usually also a professional librarian. This and the next chapter describe in the abstract the types and methods of access to records in files. Chapters 6 and 7 discuss the principles and rules adopted by librarians to choose the actual name forms and subject access points to use in those files.

Access implies a mechanism for isolating a single record or a related group of them from among many others. This is accomplished by (1) arranging and/or (2) indexing the records. Both processes involve

1) selecting one or more useful access points for each document from among its data elements
2) structuring and arranging these access points in a predictable way so that an informed user can find the one(s) useful in any particular search
3) linking each access point with the records to which it applies and often (but not always)
4) linking related access points with each other.

The two latter functions are particularly technology-dependent; the type of file makes a great deal of difference to how they operate and they are therefore discussed also in the next chapter. The first and last functions are particularly cost-sensitive: access costs money; more access points and links cost more money.

Each access point (in current cataloguer's jargon), index term (in typical user's jargon), or search key (in computer programmer's jargon) states a single occurrence of a bibliographic data element pertinent to a document and considered useful for retrieving it.[1] An access point locates a bibliographic record and ultimately the document itself; for example, the title is one of several possible access points for a document. To find a record for a document, the user looks in a predictable (for example, alphabetic) file sequence for a type of data element (for example, a government publishing agency) which in the user's experience was likely to have been chosen as an access point. Thus,

1. An older synonym for access point / index term / search key, still widely used, is the word *heading*, as in *name heading* or *subject heading*. The word *entry* is also used with this meaning, as in "The entry is Smith, John," but this ambiguous usage should be avoided. If the word is to be used at all, it is better to call the whole bibliographic record an entry, not just one of its access points (see also footnote 4 on page 17). The word *index* is another problem, as noted on page 16. Although it is less likely to be misinterpreted than the words *entry* and *heading*, *index* is avoided in this book as a noun. As a verb, it is usually replaced with the more awkward but perhaps clearer expression "to provide access," whether this is by means of extracting data elements from an existing document description as implied here or by imposing appropriate access points on it as described beginning on page 74.

knowing that the publication required was issued by the Environmental Protection Agency, the user expects to find it by looking under that body's name.[2] Any name, date, title, single word of a title, inventory number, etc. found in a document is a potentially useful characteristic for its retrieval because anyone who has seen the document itself or a footnote or other citation is likely to have copied one or another of these data elements from it for future reference. One might therefore derive the following access points from a particular document: (1) **Eastwood, Terry**; (2) **Bureau of Canadian Archivists**; (3) **1986**; (4) *Toward Descriptive Standards*; (5) *Standards*; (6) **0-88925-680-2**; and (7) **C86-091272-8**.[3]

Arranging Access Points

Humans search an alphanumeric arrangement with minimal effort and maximum confidence. The roman letters used in English and the ten arabic numerals together number only thirty-six and everyone knows their basic order.[4] Fortunately, most types of information sought from bibliographic files can be alphanumerically expressed, for example, personal, corporate, and place names; titles; dates; subjects expressed in words; and classification symbols, such as a Dewey or Library of Congress class number. However, there can be many ways of arranging the same *type* of access point, some not expressable in an alphanumeric sequence. Arranging personal names alphabetically by surname is convenient for locating material by or about individuals. If their relationship to historical events is of greater consequence to the purpose of the list, it may be better to arrange them chronologically by each person's birthdate— one has the choice of forward or reverse order. This is an equally simple alphanumeric sequence to express and to understand. If family relationships are to be shown, however, the only arrangement to serve the purpose efficiently is a genealogical-table arrangement, which cannot be reduced to an alphanumeric sequence.

2. The actual *forms* prescribed by library practice (for example, whether one should look for this body under *E* for Environmental or under *U* for United States) and the actual filing rules which determine their sequence are discussed in part II.

3. Items 6 and 7 are the document's ISBN and its *Canadiana* record-identifier number, respectively. Throughout this book, an access point is shown to be such by the use of boldface shown here. **Upper/Lower Case** is used for a personal/corporate/place name; **FULL CAPITALS** for a topical (subject) access point; *italics* for a title or any word(s) taken from a title; and **000** (digits) as relevant for a numeric code. Particularly in part I, use of boldface type does not imply that the access point in question is authorized by any one particular cataloguing code or access-point system; the context explains which principles are at issue.

4. This is not to say that alphanumeric arrangement offers no problems but, as shown in chapter 9, these problems relate to the meanings and uses of the access points being arranged, not to the order of their component symbols.

In a geographic arrangement of access points, Alert Bay must be placed very close to Zeballos (they are only a few miles apart); in an alphanumeric file, it is much closer to Alabama. The subjects **CATAPULT** and **CATASTROPHE** may be causally related on occasion but the relationship is not a deep and meaningful one. One way to locate documents about catapults, howitzers, and other military ordnance together is to arrange either the documents themselves or their bibliographic records according to access points derived from a classification scheme, for example, in the Dewey Decimal Classification, the group **623** or in the Library of Congress Classification, the group **UF**. The alphanumeric arrangement of those classification symbols as access points locates material about military weapons together and separates it from material about natural catastrophes.

Still, the *use* of military ordnance is also closely related to such things as economics and politics, which are not part of the linear juxtapositions reflected in the classification groups just noted. To locate documents on the basis not only of unilinear sequences (alphanumeric or other) but also of multidimensional relationships has always been a goal of information retrieval. Postcoordination was the computer's first notable advance toward this goal; further development of artificial intelligence and of database management systems based on relational models (for example, hypertext) offer possibilities for interdisciplinary searching inconceivable in the sequential files of book or card catalogues. Developments in these fields, discussed in the next chapter, will have far-reaching consequences for access to documents. However, before proceeding to methods of access in computer-based files, the uses of different types of data element as access points must be examined. This is done first in the context of manual file production and searching; that is, as if no computer were involved. The applicability of the same principles to computer-based files is discussed later.

Access to Single Data Elements in Manual Files

Single Access

The most uncomplicated manner of providing access to records in a manual list is very familiar: the one access point considered most important for each document forms the basis for arranging a single copy of each record. For efficient transaction-processing purposes, a single-access file is almost essential. Thus a file of all the circulating books in a library arranged by their bar-code numbers is at the heart of a circulation system. For information-retrieval purposes, however, a single-access file is much less useful. Although very many of them are in existence with more constantly being created, they are now generally small ones for manual consultation, for example, a bibliography at the back of a book. Multiple access using duplicate records or cross-references is not cost-effective in a list small enough to be browsed. The fact that some very large single-access lists were once a most important type of bibliographic resource makes their characteristics worth brief exploration.[5]

Which Access Point to Choose for a Single-Access List?   If only one access point per document is permitted, what it should be depends on the type of document listed and/or the purpose of the list. The chief purpose of citations appended to an article or book is to document what others have written about the topic in question. The text of the article or book already provides the subject context, making a subject-based arrangement of the citations redundant. An author-based arrangement more naturally fulfils the purpose of a list of citations. This explains why most style manuals for academic citation prefer the author's name as the first element of a citation. It also explains why these names are presented in normal filing order, surname first, only when the references are grouped in one place, as at the end of the paper or article. This is the basis of the long-standing Western bibliographic tradition of treating the name of the personal creator (or the principal one) of a document's intellectual content—the author, composer, artist, etc.—as the usual access point by which to arrange a single-access list.[6]

For purely economic reasons, some of the largest and most important of all bibliographic files were once essentially single-access ones, for example, the published book-catalogues of the British Museum's Department of Printed Books, of the Bibliothèque Nationale, and of the Library of Congress, as well as most manual union catalogues and many booktrade lists. Regardless of limitations to their use, it was either too expensive for the originating institution to provide multiple access or too expensive for others to purchase and update the much larger printed lists which multiple access would require. To find anything in a single-access list, one needs to know not only what type(s) of access point to permit (an author's name cannot serve in the case of anonymous work), but also the method of applying the principle for each publication listed; for example, what is defined as an author; whose name to use if there are many authors; whether real names or pseudonyms should be used. Rules for determining a publication's so-called main entry heading—the one, or principal, access point under which its record is to be found in a single-access list—became very complex over the years. In English-speaking countries, these rules invariably specify a primary author, or a substitute based on the title, as the principal access point (main entry heading). But a large list accessible only in this manner is useless if one simply does not know who wrote the desired item(s) or if the

5. In practice, some lists known as essentially single-access ones permit multiple access under a *type* of access point; for example, if the type is authors' names and an item has more than one author, it is accessible under the name of each author. The large library catalogues described here are essentially but not purely single-access files because of this feature and because most have admitted some cross-references as additional access points.

6. This fixation on the importance of the person-as-creator is far from universal: in the bibliographic practice of the Far East, for example, authorship is not so primary a consideration.

request mentions only, say, a subject. The primary uses of a single-access list have therefore been specialized ones rather than general information retrieval; namely

1) to verify the existence and location of items discovered through other sources, such as subject reference tools and footnotes, and
2) to provide the local cataloguer with authoritative bibliographic records for items in hand.

Multiple Access

It is not hard to justify providing in a list more than one access point for the same document. Being usually both more memorable than an author's name and associated with the document's subject content, words in the title (not necessarily or only the first one) undoubtedly serve the largest number of useful retrieval purposes. Other types of access point also satisfy known and pressing retrieval needs. The authors of many early works are unknown, so anonymous classics and folk literature are best cited by a conventional title adopted by tradition and called a uniform title by cataloguers, for example, *Song of Roland*; *Arabian Nights*. Some works are largely unknown except by the names of their publishers (for example, a Chilton automobile repair manual, a Sunset garden book, a Time-Life cookbook). Publisher access is also useful in book-trade listings: it is the primary access provided in lists like *Publishers' Trade List Annual*. In a rapidly changing technological field, the date of a document may be its most immediately significant characteristic, making a chronological arrangement of citations more useful than any other. Thus different elements serve best for different documents and for different retrieval purposes. One can find single-access lists arranged by almost every conceivable characteristic, but to be most helpful, one must provide access points of various types for the same document. The publishers of almost all the large single-access lists of the past responded to the need for multiple access as economics permitted over the years. The complex history of the publication of the *National Union Catalog* and of the several parts of the earlier but related *Library of Congress Catalog* is a useful case study illustrating the problems of single-access lists and the gradual process of adding access points under more names, then subjects, and finally titles and series. Few if any single-access manual lists too large to be easily browsed are now being produced, so the issue of choosing a single principal access point (main entry heading) for a document is no longer relevant for this purpose. Its other, and still valid, purpose is discussed on pages 169–71 and 270.

Types of access point appear in greatest variety in monographic bibliographies because these respond to the particular demands of the subject or type of material listed. For example, a bibliography of published reports of sightings of unexplained phenomena includes access points, in separate sequences, of (1) locations of sightings in a geographic (not alphabetic) arrangement by state/city, etc., (2) subjects, using terms governed by a glossary within the bibliography, (3) names of observers, and (4) ethnic groups. Dates chronologically arranged are frequent access points in historical bibliographies. In the general library catalogue or A&I publication covering all subject areas, there must be a more standardized—even arbitrary—approach to access-point types because the special characteristics of one subject area or user-group cannot be allowed to take precedence over others. The cliché of the manual listing is that one can find an item under its author(s), title(s) (each title accessible only under its first word), or subject(s); that is, under who is responsible for its intellectual content, under its identifying name, and under term(s) denoting what it is about as a whole. Each of the three is a very different type of approach; together, they cover what most end-users are interested in most of the time.

Multiple access is technically achieved by

1) displaying a complete copy of the record of an item under each of several different access points or
2) displaying a complete record only once (usually under the access point judged most useful for most of the foreseen uses of the file) and referring to it from one or more indices, each consisting only of other access points or
3) displaying each record only once as in (2), but interspersing the sequence of records with additional access points in the form of cross-references or abbreviated descriptions (this technique is a compromise between the other two).

The first of these techniques, called the unit-record system, is common in lists produced as, or derived from, card-based files. The second is employed in most printed monographic bibliographies.

There exist bibliographies using the second technique in which the records themselves are arranged only in the order in which the documents were received or listed. Since this order is useful for very few kinds of search, consulting the file is normally a two-step process: first to an index, then to the file of document descriptions. Originally a pure economy measure for the producer, this type of file arrangement is increasingly used for large continuing bibliographies produced in microform, for example, the *National Union Catalog* (NUC) since 1983, whose monthly fiches containing the new full records need never be replaced by cumulations. Only the fiches containing the name, subject, title, etc. access points, which refer to the complete records via their sequential serial numbers, are cumulated and reissued regularly. The saving lies in the fact that only a small part of the whole listing—the indices—needs to be cumulated and reissued in order to update everything. This file format is known as a register (more properly a register with indices), the word *register* being used in the old meaning of a sequence to which additions are appended as events occur. In the NUC and in many other register files, just enough bibliographic information is added to the access-point indices that the user often does not need to refer to the complete record at all.

It is most usual for each different type of access point (authors, titles, dates, subject terms, etc.) to occupy its own separate index or section of the complete listing. Yet for most of the twentieth century, some of the most widely known lists adopted the so-called dictionary arrangement: a single alphanumeric sequence considered more user-friendly because all types of access point are interfiled. These lists included most North American library catalogues and popular (as distinguished from academic) A&I publications. Libraries began abandoning the dictionary arrangement in the 1960s to revert to one or another type of multiple-sequence, or divided, catalogue in which topical-subject access points are separated from other access points. There is less consensus on such matters as whether authors and titles should also be separated from one another, whether names used as subjects (for example, of biographies or literary criticisms) should be interfiled with names used as authors, editors, etc., or whether corporate names should be interfiled with personal names. Good arguments can be found for each of many different solutions to these questions and library catalogues are not as similar to one another in these respects as formerly. Searching any machine-readable file for different types of data element is normally accomplished by approaching each of several access-point indices separately (see page 266). The machine-readable format adopted (see chapter 8) is therefore now the primary determinant of how access points are divided into different types for searching.

Limits to Multiple Access in Manual Files

To provide access to every possible data element useful to any searcher would cause a manual file in card or book form to become more intimidating and less useful because of its very size. Furthermore, each access point provided is a small but measurable budgetary drain not merely at the time of creation and production but also for storage and continued maintenance throughout the lifetime of the list. In selecting access points, demands considered frivolous have always been ignored. The student told to read any three books from a particular reading list wants the three shortest ones but probably cannot find any listing arranged by the number of pages in the items. Other demands, if not frivolous, are better answered by a different type of reference tool and those who compile bibliographic lists feel they do not need to duplicate the work. The user who wants a novel by a New Zealand author is expected to find some appropriate names and/or titles in, for example, a monographic bibliography of Commonwealth writing or a literary encyclopaedia, before going to the library's catalogue. To search the catalogue under **NEW ZEALAND FICTION** (or any other single access point) would be unproductive. No bibliographic list is an island. Each depends on others for its most productive use.

In addition to reasonable limits on the *types* of access points provided, arbitrary limits on their *number*, also based on practical limitations on the size of manual lists, have long been taken for granted. Of many authors, only the first might be made accessible (or the first three: see page 40). Of all the words in titles, many of which have some value for subject access, only the first (other than an initial article) was made accessible in most manual lists until the 1950s because it was deemed impracticable to do so for every word of a title, except in small catalogues covering very specialized subject matter.[7] In fact, it was long common not to provide any title access at all if

1) the first word is unmemorable (for example, *Introduction*, *Proceedings*) or

2) the title is identical to a subject heading assigned to the same item, because the two would file in the same place in a dictionary catalogue.

The impact of such limitations on divided files, in which titles and subjects appear in different alphabets, tended to be ignored.

That more than one subject-based access point per document should be permitted has always been taken for granted, but in the manual file their number is kept under firm control by various practices, principally:

1) indexing only the one or few topic(s) constituting the focus of the document *as a whole*, not the many topics treated in its separate chapters and sections and

2) combining, or pre-coordinating, several concepts into a single access point, for example, using the single access point **PHOTOGRAPHY OF ANIMALS** instead of two separate ones: **PHOTOGRAPHY** and **ANIMALS** (for further discussion of pre-coordination, see pages 95–97).

Still, the desire for more access points led to experimentation as soon as practical limitations could be overcome or minimized. Keyword-in-context (KWIC) and keyword-out-of-context (KWOC) title lists inaugurated the automation of bibliographic files forty years ago, before computerized applications, using electromechanical equipment for quick sorting and printing. In a KWIC or KWOC list, as illustrated in figure 12, each word in a document's title becomes an access point except those on a stop-list of words to be bypassed as access points,

---

7. To provide access to *some* additional word(s) of a title for quasi subject access was occasionally done but required ad hoc judgements which could be hard to justify because they had to be based on exception, not rule or principle. Seymour Lubetzky argues cogently against the practice in the context of the dictionary catalogue of the time in his "Titles: Fifth Column of the Catalog," *Library Quarterly* 11 (October 1941): 412–30.

for example, articles. Like other early attempts to improve access to library catalogues, this one was rendered obsolete by the computer-based developments discussed in the next chapter.

```
  600 Users Meet the COM  Catalog
Two Years with a Closed  Catalog
        Closing the Card  Catalog      the New York Experience
Card Catalog to On-Line  Catalog      the Transitional Process
                   Card  Catalog      the On-Line Catalog: the T
    Living amid Closed  Catalogs
   The Effect of Closed  Catalogs     on Public Access
                         Catalogue    Use Survey
   Alternative Forms of  Catalogues   in Large Research Libraries
```

```
Catalog     600 Users Meet the COM Catalog
Catalog     Card Catalog to On-Line Catalog: the Transitional Process
Catalog     Closing the Card Catalog: the New York Experience
Catalog     Two Years with a Closed Catalog
Catalogs    The Effect of Closed Catalogs on Public Access
Catalogs    Living amid Closed Catalogs
Catalogue   Catalogue Use Survey
Catalogues  Alternative Forms of Catalogues in Large Research Libraries
```

FIGURE 12. Above, a portion of a KWIC index; below, a KWOC index covering the same items. In the former, the titles are arranged by the keyword plus any following words. In the latter, subarrangement under a keyword is by the first nonarticle word of the title (sometimes by the author's surname).

Casual library users are more likely to prefer access by subject classification than by subject words. As mentioned at the beginning of this chapter, they like to browse. North American libraries have encouraged browsing on open shelves, but not everything is there: items may be misshelved, in circulation, or in storage. More important, shelf browsing is only possible under one classification-based access point per item, not under such multiple subject terms as may be provided in a catalogue. Only recently have many general libraries made it possible for users to browse a classified arrangement of records, that is, a sequence of subjects arranged according to the classification symbols under which the documents are shelved (see pages 187–88).

Before the advent of the computer, libraries and the A&I services adopted approximately the same limitations on access. In fact, the latter went farther, many providing no title access but only author/subject access. The effective searcher became adept at ways of getting around all these limitations. What is most amazing in retrospect is how librarians made a virtue of necessity. The limitations described above were viewed as positive aids to searching because they restricted the potential for confusion by requiring the searcher to have a clear searching strategy—an idea of what is needed and how to reach it—*before* approaching the file or an organized shelving arrangement. There is danger of losing sight of the desirability of doing this. Access is ideally neither hit-or-miss nor ferretting through the haystack. The old cliché *garbage in, garbage out* is if anything more relevant to access in the computer mode with its potential for speed and quantity than in the manual mode where files must be more compact. Manual and computer-based modes of searching, and the file structures which support them, are compared in the next chapter.

Uncontrolled versus Controlled Access Points

Seven different access points were suggested for the book on archival description used as an example on page 66. In cataloguers' jargon, these seven are said to be uncontrolled because the cataloguer does not govern their form, except in such minimal ways as transposing a surname to precede the given name(s) for filing. Another way of stating the same thing is to call them natural-language terms because they are copied without change from the wording of the document's various data elements, a wording established by the document's author or producer, not by its later cataloguer.

One function of an access point is to identify and/or locate a single document. Natural-language access points are very helpful for this purpose precisely because they are the same words as those commonly copied from the document into citations. There are bibliographic tools whose only access points are natural-language ones. Compiling such access points is relatively quick and cheap and very amenable to automation. An experienced clerk can quickly identify those words and terms to be copied from the document or from an existing record and input into a particular data-element index, for example, authors, titles, and dates which are clearly identified as such on title pages or captions (heads). Title words are made to suffice for subject identification (see pages 179–84). A computer program separates the elements into their types, puts the words of each type into alphabetic order, and either prints the result or makes it available for searching at a computer terminal. In fields whose subject vocabulary is relatively predictable, automated extraction of the data elements already in a machine-readable bibliographic database and their assembly into a useful index further reduces the human labour involved.

However, natural-language access points do not serve all the expectations of searchers. Despite the lack of the following words in its title, the above document might well be sought in an index under a term such as **ARCHIVAL MATERIALS**, and perhaps also under **CATALOGUING**, even though that term is less widely used by archivists than by librarians. Then it turns out that Terry Eastwood is also known and cited as Terence M. Eastwood and that the Bureau of Canadian Archivists also has a name in French: Bureau canadien des archivistes. Even that does not complete the matter. Thorough access to the *work* in question would have to include access to the title and ISBN of its separately issued

French-language version, and a bilingual catalogue would also require one or more access points designating the subject in French, whether or not taken from the French-language title. In other words, while some natural-language access points (for example, a title as such or an ISBN) are clearly desirable in almost any index, access points *not* directly copied from the document in hand can be equally desirable.

Most users expect more of bibliographic access points than to find single documents known through citations, etc. They want to locate documents which share a common characteristic (identified on page 46) or which deal with the same subject: documents related to each other and therefore usefully consulted together. The goal of bringing related items together in a file is difficult to achieve. Natural-language access points do not serve well; what is required is some control over the access-point vocabulary. To reach this goal, the first objective must be to establish which documents do share the characteristic under consideration, for example, the same author. This is not always self-evident. To say a particular anonymous or pseudonymous work has the same author as another work, it is necessary to discover who wrote it! Having identified the related documents, the next step is to survey all the ways the characteristic in question is expressed, both in the documents and in outside sources. Only then can one decide what access point(s) best express that characteristic in a standard way.

To pursue the previous example, taking these steps means discovering that

1) the descriptive standards mentioned in the document's title refer to the listing of archival material in finding aids but that archivists have not yet established a standardized terminology for the process and
2) the Terry Eastwood of this document and the Terence M. Eastwood in his institution's directory are the same person.

If Mr. Eastwood identified himself openly in everything he wrote, always using exactly the same form of name, the second problem would not arise. This is in fact the case in a high proportion of instances involving personal names: only a minority cause the kinds of problems suggested here and discussed in detail in chapter 6, but to discover which are the problematic ones is itself a major challenge. If names *sometimes* cause problems of this kind, one may assume that identifying subject concepts *always* does, as suggested earlier and discussed further in chapter 7.

To summarize using different examples, if a list is to reveal everything written by and/or about the author of *Huckleberry Finn*, one must first discover every different name form ever used in any context to identify this person. *Mark Twain*, *Samuel L. Clemens*, and *Samuel Langhorne Clemens* prove to be only three of many. Furthermore, one must discover whether there exist any documents by him in which he is hidden under the cloak of anonymity so that these, too, may be displayed along with the others in response to a request for his works. One must then ensure that every document in the file by or about this person can be located regardless of whether the searcher first looks under **Clemens**, under **Twain**, or under any of the other surnames or pseudonyms that author used (ignoring access under a given name may be taken for granted). To give a parallel example of a subject search, if the file is to reveal everything dealing with rail-based urban transportation vehicles, the first problem is to determine exactly what is the scope of this concept. The second is to ensure that all the documents listed in the file which deal with the concept are indexed under the same subject term(s), regardless of what words appear in their titles. The final problem is to ensure that the searcher can find all these documents, whether the first approach to the file is under **STREETCAR**, under **TRAM**, under **LIGHT RAIL VEHICLE**, or under any other synonym, classification symbol, or code representing the same topic.

Authority Work

The processes outlined in the above examples are called authority work. They involve

1) determining that a relationship exists and
2) establishing and linking all the possible access points which could reasonably express it.

Authority work usually (always, in the case of subjects) requires professional judgement. It is time-consuming because *every* name and *every* topic encountered must be examined closely, whether in the end it proves to be problematic or not. Despite the obvious expense of careful authority work, it has been a feature of library cataloguing for at least two hundred years in the case of names, and since about the beginning of the twentieth century in the much more difficult case of subjects. Among other bibliographic services, it is not an all-or-nothing matter; for example, some A&I services do authority work for subjects but not for names, while others ignore it (except in the case of particular names or subjects where its application is clearly desirable to avoid a known potential for confusion). As usual, monographic bibliographies cannot be categorized in this respect; they vary too much in their individual approaches to this problem.

The Controlled Vocabulary: Terms Plus Their Links

Authority work imposes a cataloguer's decisions on how best to organize and display the identities (of persons, bodies, etc.) and the meanings (of concepts) implicit in the uncontrolled words and terms of natural language. Carefully done authority work results in what is known as authority control but is perhaps better described as access-point control or vocabulary control. If a file of bibliographic records is subject to this control, its searcher can feel confident that its access points lead to relevant information in a thorough and organized way. To use a file most effectively, therefore, one must be aware of whether controlled access points or only natural-language ones appear in it, yet it is not always possible to tell the difference between the two merely by looking at them.

A controlled vocabulary is the total of all the identified access points and all the linkages established among them resulting from all the authority work done on the names and/or subjects within a defined scope, a scope often limited to what appears in a particular bibliographic file. Three different types of relationship are defined in the linkages:

1) the equivalence relationship, in which two or more terms are synonymous (as judged by the indexer and within the context of a given controlled vocabulary)
2) the hierarchical relationship, in which one of two terms names a definable part of what is encompassed by the other and
3) the associative relationship, in which terms are related in some manner different from either (1) or (2) but still closely enough that they should be linked.[8]

All three types of relationship linkage are essential parts of any controlled vocabulary of subject concepts. In a controlled vocabulary of names, the equivalence relationship is very common because variant forms of any kind of name can exist. A corporate body may have parent or subordinate units warranting links to show a hierarchical relationship between them or an earlier-later name sequence warranting an associative-relationship link.

The most familiar method of showing a linkage in a manual (card, fiche, book) listing is to use what is called a cross-reference. Traditionally, a *see* reference expresses the equivalence relationship while the other two types are not distinguished from each other, both being expressed in a *see also* reference. How vocabulary control in automated files presents links to the user is sketched in the following discussion.

The Equivalence Relationship.   The notion that only one of several name forms for a person, corporate body, etc. (or of several synonyms for a concept) can be a *correct* access point has long been fostered by the use in library catalogues of *see* references, such as

8. This terminology is used in sections 8.2–8.4 of standard ISO2788 of the International Organization for Standardization, "Documentation—Guidelines for the Establishment and Development of Monolingual Thesauri" in *Documentation and Information*, 3rd ed., ISO Standards Handbook 1 (Geneva: ISO Central Secretariat, 1988). This is the equivalent of standard BS:5723 of the British Standards Institution. Standard Z39.19 of the National Information Standards Organization covers the same concepts but has not been revised as recently. Standard ISO5963 (BS:6529), "Documentation—Methods for Examining Documents, Determining Their Subjects, and Selecting Index Terms," is also relevant.

Clemens, Samuel Langhorne
for works by and about this person, look under **Twain, Mark.**

In other words, the searcher who looks first for the "wrong" name is more or less brusquely told that the document(s) wanted can only be found under the "right" name, but choosing the right one requires the application of the technical rules and practices discussed in chapters 6 and 7. This is a poor approach in theory as well as in practice. An important purpose of authority control is indeed to determine which of several possible names or terms best serves the searcher in identifying a particular person, subject, etc. However, its *primary* purpose is only to ensure that records representing the entity sought can be located regardless of which (reasonable) term is sought first. Thus **Twain**, chosen as the "right" surname in the preceding cross-reference, is not merely the natural-language surname by which that writer is most often identified in his own works. What makes it part of a controlled vocabulary is that, through the process of authority work, it is linked to all other possible access points for this person, including in this example the surname Clemens. As for the "wrong" surname (Clemens), the link in the controlled vocabulary makes it just as much an access point as is the "right" one: either of the two leads to documents by and about the person in question. The technical reason for opting for a *preferred* access point (not a "correct" one) when two or more are deemed to be equivalent is that the preferred one can be the base for any required linkage. Such a base is needed in both automated and most manual files, although for different purposes.

The user is best served if *each* access point (**Twain** *and* **Clemens** *and* [any other name]) is directly attached to the description of *each* item by or about him, without regard to which is the better access point (option 1 on page 70). In Twain's case, this requires at least a tenfold increase in the number of separate complete bibliographic records because of his many pseudonyms. What card, fiche, or book file can be so prolific? A *see* reference, such as the one illustrated atop this page, is used precisely to avoid this (option 3 on page 70). Compilers of most monographic bibliographies use a different technique which bypasses the need to establish the priority of one synonym over another. They separate at least some access points entirely from the item-descriptions, placing the access points in a separate index (or more than one) (option 2 on page 70). Thus in a name index devoid of both item-descriptions and cross-references, **Clemens** and **Twain** can each separately lead to the same description of *Huckleberry Finn*, which is in its own file or sequence consisting only of item-descriptions (see figure 13). Could this leave a searcher in any doubt that Mr. Clemens and Mr. Twain are the same person? Is it a proper function of the bibliographic tool to make this explicit when either name can lead directly to the document(s) wanted?

In addition to not making the searcher pause to consider the linkages as such, this is a more democratic system: it makes *every* searcher take two

. . . . .

2506   The Letters of Edward Gibbon. London: Special Editions Club,
        1974.

2507   Huckleberry Finn, by Mark Twain (S.L. Clemens). London: Special
        Editions Club, 1974.

2508   On the Origin of Species, by Charles Darwin. London: Special
        Editions Club, 1975.

. . . . .

— — — — — — — — — — — — —

. . . . .
Clemens, Richard: 278
Clemens, Samuel Langhorne: 532, 675, 1893, 2507, 3855, 4580
Clement, H. Albert: 2638, 5993
. . . . .
Tuohy, Adrian C.: 1083, 1084
Twain, Mark: 532, 675, 1893, 2507, 3855, 4580
Twistleton, Frederick: 559
. . . . .

FIGURE 13. Links to the same description from different, but equivalent, access points. In this hypothetical example, the full records (top) are arranged by publisher and date; each is identified by a sequential serial number. In the name index (bottom) all name forms for the same person, including *Clemens* and *Twain*, lead to the same records.

steps to find the description of *Huckleberry Finn*: first to locate any form of the author's name in an index, then to go from that index to the citation. Is this more efficient than requiring the two-step search only of those who first look under a "wrong" form of name? Surely they will remember the "right" one the next time. Yet this is how all computer-based searching is done. First, the index commonly called the authority file (see page 81) is searched. Then each retrieved index term is matched via a record-identifier number to the single copy of each related complete bibliographic record stored in the bibliographic file. Because the computer goes automatically from one file to the other and makes the matches, the need for two steps per search is no drawback; it takes so little time that the human searcher is not aware of the process.

The Hierarchical and Associative Relationships.   Like a person, a subject may be called by different names, for example, **TRAM** or **STREETCAR**. Synonymous subject terms are equivalents to be treated in exactly the same way as pseudonyms and other variant name forms. However, the hierarchical and associative relationships are equally important, if not more so, in subject searching. Trams/streetcars, for example, are one type of public transit vehicle. If the file has material on both public-transit vehicles (in general) and streetcars (in particular), it is usually advisable to index these concepts separately. They are not synonymous. But the searcher who locates **PUBLIC TRANSIT VEHICLES** should be informed that material on a more specific part of the same concept is also available under another access point: material whose focus is a part of anything cannot help but deal as well with aspects of the whole, and vice-versa. A hierarchical link is warranted. Similarly, streetcars are not the same things as buses, nor is one a part of the other, but a searcher looking for either of these topics might appreciate being reminded of the existence of the other in the list by an associative link. In manual listings of the past, the *see also* cross-reference usually served to identify both hierarchical and associative linkages, for example,

> **BUSES**
> *for related material, search also under* **STREETCARS**

and

> **STREETCARS**
> *for related material, search also under* **PUBLIC TRANSIT
> VEHICLES**.

As discussed in more detail beginning on page 204, it is now more common to separate hierarchical from associative links and, in the case of the former, to show the direction (broader or narrower) of the linkage.

While a link expressing equivalence ideally results in the automatic retrieval of all the documents known by any of its terms, this should never be the case with the hierarchical and associative links. Their purpose is not to require but only to suggest that the searcher might expand the search to additional topics related in a particular way to the topic originally sought. The searcher follows up these links only if it seems worthwhile to do so under the particular circumstances of the search. Links of these two types must therefore be shown explicitly to the searcher, regardless of whether the search is manual or automated. Hierarchical and associative links cannot be hidden, or made transparent to the user, as an equivalence link can and ideally should be. It is also important not to overwhelm the user with these links. Hierarchical links can be kept under control by considering carefully what can and what cannot be considered to be a logical part of a more comprehensive unit and by linking only those levels immediately above and below each other. The associative relationship is much more difficult to keep under control. For example, if one links **STREETCARS** with **LIGHT RAPID TRANSIT**, should both these terms also be linked with **COMMUTING**? With **RAILROADS**? With **TRANS-PORTATION**? With [any other term]? There must be limits! These matters are discussed in relation to the principal current subject-indexing systems in chapter 7.

Authority Files

An authority file is the tangible expression of a controlled vocabulary. It is a list of the verified access points, both preferred and nonpreferred, along with those linkages relevant to the range of names/subjects considered in the vocabulary. It is maintained (now almost always as a computer file) separately from any bibliographic file; that is, it lists names, subject terms, etc. but not the documents bearing or indexed by these names/terms. An authority file has always been needed as a working tool of the cataloguer or indexer to keep track of the links even when they are also physically incorporated into the bibliographic file as cross-references. However, where the cost of maintaining links internally within a library's catalogue as cross-references or in some automated way means that they are inadequately represented in the catalogue or even absent, the authority file or some reasonable substitute must be made available to the public separately from the catalogue. This requires the thorough searcher not only to look under more than one access point in a single file but to search two separate files: first the authority file to decide what are the best access points, then the bibliographic file to see what documents are listed under those access points. No wonder library catalogue users get discouraged! Since both the name and the subject access points used in most North American library catalogues are subsets of those established at the Library of Congress, that library's subject authority file (published in large red volumes as *Library of Congress Subject Headings*) is a familiar and necessary searching aid beside the catalogue in other libraries as well. Similarly, *Library of Congress Name Authorities*, the microfiche authority file of the Library's name access points, is also appearing in the public catalogue areas of larger libraries. At present, name authority files are commonly kept separately from subject (that is, concept) authority files, but the Library of Congress plans ultimately to merge theirs. An increasing number of automated public catalogues have an authority-file component built into the catalogue's user-interface so that the searcher can see the nature of all the access-point links simultaneously with any use of the bibliographic file. That both Library of Congress authority files can be purchased in machine-readable form makes it possible for large local systems to use them directly as part of the interface.

The most complete form of an authority record maintained as a working tool of the cataloguer also mentions a record of all the steps taken in doing authority work and the discoveries and decisions made; for example, what pseudonym(s) were found? Where? Did any particular problems surface? When was the access point established or any part of the linkage last revised? One must document the processes of authority work if only to prevent the need to repeat some of the same work later. A typical record, complete in this respect, from a name authority file is shown in figure 14. Some from subject authority files are shown on pages 205, 214, and 314.

```
ACCESS UNDER:  York, Sarah Mountbatten-Windsor, Duchess of, 1959-
USED FOR:      Ferguson, Sarah Margaret, 1959-
               Sarah, Duchess of York, 1959-
Found in:      Burnet, A. The Book of the Royal Wedding, c1986: t.p.
               verso, etc. (Sarah Ferguson, b.10-15-59, Duchess of York)
Verified in:   BLAISE, 5/87 (York, Sarah Mountbatten-Windsor, Duchess
               of; ref. from Ferguson, Sarah, 1959-)
```

FIGURE 14. A record in a name authority file. The statements concerning where relevant information has been found or verified are normally not part of the authority record made visible to the public; they are for the information of those who maintain the authority file.

4

FILE STRUCTURE AND
ACCESS STRATEGIES

Technical, psychological, and economic factors have constantly refashioned the methods of storing and manipulating bibliographic data and of displaying selected data in response to searches. This chapter describes the major methods of organizing and displaying bibliographic data to users both before and since the application of computer techniques. During the past two decades, the computer has rendered obsolescent most manual practices of data storage and retrieval. This does not in itself signal the victory of paperless (or fiche-less) bibliographic lists. Those in book, card, and fiche form will not simply vanish from libraries. Indeed, they will continue to be produced for a long time to come, increasingly through the application of computer technology to data initially created in machine-readable form. During the century before the computer, methods of both displaying and searching bibliographic lists had become very standardized and therefore familiar to both professionals and end-users. Today, in advertising each new software package for storing, indexing, searching, and displaying bibliographic data, its creator claims to have established the new standard. But when so many of these packages are admittedly still being developed and tested while in actual use in library operations, how confident can one be of such claims? Paradoxically, although the computer demands an even more rigid adherence to standards in some respects (as documented throughout part II of this book), it has resulted in a sometimes distressing but ultimately desirable destandardization of the way bibliographic files appear to, and are searched by, their users (see pages 138–39).

The quantity and complexity of bibliographic information is quite extraordinary. A library or an A&I service of even modest size is easily comparable to any but the very largest business concern in its demands on a system to store and search separate pieces of information. However many reservations or stock items an airline or large retailer must deal with in the course of a year, they are constantly entering and leaving the active file so that the number of items requiring current processing grows slowly if at all. In contrast, a library collection or A&I database increases in size constantly and sometimes exponentially. Most librarians still consider the ideal to be a collection housed as a unit (remote storage is an evil) and, above all, revealed in a unitary catalogue. This creates technical and administrative difficulties well beyond those generally encountered in the world of business. A collection or file twice as large is more than twice as difficult to use and more than twice as expensive to maintain. In their printed publications, even the A&I services never attempted indefinite cumulation; a five-year period was about maximum until even that became too expensive. Now, most attempt no more than an annual printed cumulation or cumulate only the indices. It is worth noting that, because bibliographic lists can be so huge and are needed so quickly after their compilation, notable innovations in print technology were made precisely for their production. For example, a phototypesetter driven directly from a computer file was designed for the National Library of Medicine and first used to produce the July, 1964 issue of the A&I publication *Index Medicus*. Bibliographic needs have also occasioned some basic developments in computer technology, such as programming for the variable-length field and for repeatable fields in the same record, both discussed in chapter 8.

Although this book describes practices primarily in the library-catalogue context, it may be assumed that the same principles of file organization and management generally apply to the A&I publications and monographic bibliographies unless the contrary is specified. These three types of bibliographic list are intellectually and financially interdependent in meeting the common goal of bibliographic control. A century ago, when there were few of the other two types and interlibrary cooperation was rarer, a library's catalogue was more self-sufficient. It would, for example, include many analytic records for articles in otherwise unindexed journals (see page 261). By the time the A&I publication had emerged as a generally viable alternative to the listing of journal articles in individual library catalogues, it and the monographic bibliography were being bought and used not as natural extensions of the library's catalogue but as "reference tools" almost ignored by cataloguers and cataloguing teachers alike because their bibliographic practices had begun to diverge from those of cataloguers. More recently, the A&I services in the industrialized world proceeded with technological change independently of libraries and at least at first with different results, further emphasizing the unfortunate separation of these three parts of the bibliographic world. Now, as computer techniques encourage the linking of databases so that they can be searched in common in integrated systems, the library's catalogue and a variety of A&I publications can begin to be treated again by both user and bibliographic-systems designer as a single source of bibliographic information. As for the separately published bibliography of a person or topic—the so-called monographic bibliography—its relative economy of production by photographing computer output has given it a new lease on life with vastly improved internal indexing. There is no doubt that major bibliographies of this type will soon find their way into libraries' databases for end-user searching just as some encyclopaedias and dictionaries already have.

Manual versus Interactive Searching

Before the computer's involvement, a file could only be presented to the searcher as a visible whole whose individual records contained whatever data and whose access points were chosen and organized in whatever manner the file's compiler predetermined—once and for all. In the searcher's mind and on the searcher's notepad, data from the file might be excerpted and resorted, but the file organization itself was immutable by the searcher and in general could reveal only what the compiler decided to reveal (within the constraints of the limitations described on pages 71–72). Throughout this book, this kind of file, visible as a rigid cohesive unit, is called a *manual file*, and the process of searching it is called *manual searching*.

In contrast, nothing in a file of machine-readable data is visible to the searcher until its data elements have been called into visibility on a terminal screen, a printer, or any other output medium. This is never done by simply dumping the content of the file onto a terminal screen; it is done through the intermediary of a database management system, a set of computer programs which retrieve individual records from a database according to the access-point relationships designed into the system but, most significantly, also under some control by the person searching the file. When such a file is searched online, the searcher and the file are interacting continuously so that the search may be modified in any detail that the system permits until either a satisfactory result is obtained or the searcher gives up. Even though the file itself is not interactive, no better term suggests itself and these are sufficient reasons for calling this type of file an *interactive file*—or *interactive database*, since it is necessarily machine-readable.[1]

1. The term *online*, frequently still applied to this kind of file and/or search process, retains connotations of a wire link connecting the central processing unit of a distant computer with the user's terminal and keyboard. Now it usually means only that a task is begun and completed while the user is in direct control of its progress, whether the central processing unit is in a distant mainframe computer or in a desktop microcomputer in front of the user. In that sense, *online* is synonymous with the term *interactive*; for example, an online public access catalogue (OPAC) is an interactive catalogue. The term *interactive* is here preferred to *online* because it is more expressive of the essential difference under discussion and because the term *online* also has some specialized connotations, referred to on page 116. The converse of online/interactive processing is batch processing: in that mode, the user relays instructions to the computer which are processed outside the user's immediate control, the results being returned to the user at a significantly later time, for example, the next day. Most administrative processing of bibliographic records is done in

The terms *interactive file* and *interactive search* are used with the preceding connotations throughout the remainder of this book. An interactive file is therefore not the same thing as an automated one. At one time, a manual file had to be produced using only a pen, typewriter, printing press, or photocopier. Today, one can (and generally does) use a computer as a word processor or text editor to sort and print bibliographic records onto cards, pages of a book, etc.; that is, to produce manual files. This is unquestionably an application of automation but its *result* is another manual file: a product searchable only as determined by its producer as surely as is true of any list inscribed by a quill pen in the Middle Ages. One can even (and often does) use a computer to select and arrange bibliographic records interactively from machine-readable data compiled elsewhere in order to produce a new listing in book or card form. Again, although the method may be an interactive use of a database, the product offered to the searcher is a manual file. Interactive searching in its purest sense is an individualized reorganization of the elements of the original database accomplished by, or on behalf of, a particular end-user to answer a particular request—not to generate a list which may then be used by a variety of end-users seeking a variety of information. The present revolution in bibliographic control consists in the transition from a period when all files and searches were manual to a period when an increasing proportion of files are machine-readable and searched interactively.

The Database Management System

At the heart of any interactive file is the database management system (DBMS) under which it is organized and made searchable. In the technical literature, the acronym DBMS has only the very restrictive meaning of a set of programs which retrieves specified records from a file. There, the word *record* refers not to a bibliographic record but to a logical record, the smallest unit of the file structure managed by the DBMS, for example, a single access point or even a single word. Throughout this book, the word *record* has the broader meaning of a bibliographic record, and the term *database management system* means, in addition to the above, the application programs, communication links, operating systems, formats, etc. which together comprise a total operational package for storing, searching, communicating, and displaying bibliographic data. The word *file* also has a more specialized meaning in the context of a DBMS but continues to be used, as on page 16, synonymously with *list* to mean any organized collection of bibliographic records. Each database management system is different in some details. Exactly how any one of them is programmed to achieve its results is unlikely to be known to its users in technical detail: the owners of

batch mode, for example, the creation of overdue notices from a circulation file. This book focuses on the use of the bibliographic record for information retrieval rather than on its administrative uses in library management and therefore on searching as an interactive process.

such expensive proprietary software do not want its unique features copied. They also want to advertise good features and of course try to sidestep or downplay the limitations which every system has. It is too easy to suppose that a good system wipes away all practical limitations to access in interactive files. Both technical and local economic ones remain: a desired feature may slow down response time for multiple users; data may have to be recoded to meet the system's format demands; the amount of computer memory required may force a limitation of the number of access points allowed. It has been all too common for administrators purchasing library database management systems to underestimate seriously the amount of both computer memory and physical file space required to accomplish all that the users soon come to demand of the system.

A database management system may be thought of as something which indexes machine-readable data for interactive retrieval, but to do this indexing requires the explicit and unambiguous formatting of the data as separately coded elements by a human compiler. Formatting bibliographic data is discussed in chapter 8. Different database management systems can be applied to the same formatted database and each searcher can choose to make a different use of the various capabilities of the same database management system. It is this flexibility which differentiates the interactive file from the rigidly and immutably organized manual file. To the degree the searcher can decide which database management system to apply and which of its capabilities to use in a particular search, it is the searcher of the database as much as its compiler who determines what the file can reveal. To use an invisible file of electronically stored data via a database management system therefore requires the interaction of

1) the compiler of the file, who identifies its separate data elements for possible searching in a relevant format
2) the designer of the database management system, who determines how the formatted elements are actually to be made accessible using particular commands and
3) the searcher, who decides, ad hoc but within the parameters of the format and the database management system used, which elements actually to search for and how the results should be displayed.

This is another reason for calling the machine-readable file placed under the control of a database management system an interactive file.

The Closed Manual File

Interactive files grew out of the conventions of constructing and searching manual ones and must still be used alongside them. Their differences, which may not at first seem so great, are better appreciated after a study of manual files. There are two types of manual file. Although the terms *closed* and *expandable* are not sanctioned by convention, they are used here because they convey the essential characteristics differentiating them. The closed file, of ancient origin, began with libraries' and booksellers' lists. Before the invention of printing, each book, being a manuscript, was unique—written for and housed in a private or institutional collection—so the only listings were those made for inventory purposes. The lack of identical copies made standardized identification for any other purpose inconceivable. The inventory list consisted of one description of each book arranged in the order of shelving, of acquisition in a collection, or of topic or type; later more often in the order of authors' names. Since the descriptions were written or inscribed sequentially on the same medium (for example, clay or parchment) as any other writing, the catalogue itself took the form of a book and is called a *book catalogue*. The pace of bibliographic control must have been placid indeed when a very large library contained fewer than a thousand volumes, when additions could simply be included at the end or in the margins of the catalogue, and when the catalogue as a whole had to be recompiled only every few years or even decades.

The outpouring of new works following the invention of printing in Europe changed more than just the size of the typical bibliographic file. Because printing made it possible for identical (or almost identical) copies of a publication to exist in different places, it became desirable to list books that existed, rather than merely those available in a given library or from a given bookseller, and a bibliographic listing became much more than a mere inventory listing. Noble attempts like Gesner's in the mid-sixteenth century to list everything he knew ever to have been printed would have been inconceivable in the manuscript period. The flood soon became too great to be practicably encompassed within any one list, and specialized bibliographies have flourished ever since, alongside growing library catalogues. Both types of list continued to be produced in the old way (but now in print more often than manuscript), each being a snapshot of what existed at a given moment within the scope determined by its compiler. Such lists ranged from the few citations at the end of a chapter, book, or article to the multivolume comprehensive bibliography on a person, place, or subject. The form is now very familiar and easy to consult but, unlike its manuscript predecessor, a printed bibliography or catalogue cannot feasibly be updated by retrieving every copy and adding new items marginally or at the end: this would only be done with the library's master copy of its catalogue or with single copies of other bibliographies. To update the content requires either a recompilation and new printing or separate supplements, the latter necessarily compromising the unity of the list and making it more difficult to consult in its many parts. In this respect, the newest form of interactive file, that on CD/ROM, is also a closed (if not a manual) file since it is still impracticable to add records to an existing CD/ROM file and updating must take the form of recompiling and reissuing the disk.

The majority of closed files are never updated, whether for practical reasons or because of the permanent value of a list of those works someone considered integral to a topic at a particular time. Many lists, however, must be kept current, particularly catalogues of growing libraries and current journal indices. To establish the most serviceable and economical pattern of issuing cumulations and interim supplements for catalogues and A&I publications has always been a challenge. Users object to searching many separate supplements if they cannot predict which one might cover their needs, but both the A&I service and the library have better things to do with their resources than spend money and staff time compiling cumulations, each of which consists of a few new items among many transferred from the preceding one. After the Second World War, some large library card catalogues were photographed and issued in book format to support growing interlibrary loan services; few were ever kept up-to-date with published supplements. The largest bibliography ever printed was, however, so important that supplements continued to be manually compiled and cumulated until its complete automation in 1983. This is the *Library of Congress Catalog/National Union Catalog* sequence.

In the 1970s, many larger bibliographic tools, including library catalogues, national bibliographies, and publishers' trade lists, began to appear in microform (film or fiche) rather than, or in addition to, their earlier printed format. Eyestrain, although the subject of much discussion, is not a major problem if the list is to be used only intermittently for brief periods. It is a small cost for the convenience of portability through miniaturization (provided a reader is handy) and vastly cheaper reproduction costs through saving on paper. Computer technology made it possible to bypass the camera by fixing the product of a machine-readable file directly onto microform. Computer-output microform, or COM, is now the visible-storage medium of choice for large files of machine-readable bibliographic data and for its distribution in situations where interactive searching as described above is either too expensive or otherwise unnecessary. COM has also been a common form for the library catalogue as a bridge between the manually produced catalogue and the totally interactive one in libraries which could not make that transition in one step. Microform permits no additions, not even manuscript marginal ones, but it can be recumulated and reissued relatively inexpensively and the register format described on page 70 is ideal for it.

The Expandable Manual File

The related nineteenth-century trends of industrial revolution and compulsory education fostered a publication explosion the like of which had not been seen since Gutenberg's day and not again until after the Second World War. This significantly affected the production of the bibliographic lists which recorded that explosion. A much higher priority was assigned to methods of efficient updating, particularly for the catalogues of the new libraries of North America which were growing so rapidly. Listing each item on a separate card or slip to be interfiled among those already there made it possible, in theory, for a file to be updated the very moment a new accession was recorded. As usual, practice and theory did not match. In a larger academic library, it sometimes took months for a newly made card to find its way into the catalogue. Yet the possibility of dynamic updating became the raison d'être of the card file, which in this respect is much like a computer file. By the late nineteenth century, 7.5-by-12.5-cm. card stock became a standard medium around the world for the storage and display of bibliographic data. In the convenient unit-record system, identical records for an item were mechanically or photographically reproduced onto card stock, each to be filed into a different catalogue—or into the same one under a variety of access points.

In addition to the card stock, this technology came to involve the typewriter, the stencil printer, sometimes the printing press, and more recently xerography and even computer-driven laser printers for automated (not interactive) card duplication from machine-readable data. Following the initial cost of creating the records, the cost of the expandable manual file is far greater than that of the closed manual file: much wood or metal furniture, tons of card stock, and most of all the never-ending job of maintenance through manual filing. A card catalogue rarely exists in more than one identical complete copy because each would have to be separately filed and maintained. The A&I services used a mechanized variation of the card technique, keeping each record on a separate linotype slug or photographic negative to be shuffled about and interfiled for cumulations.

The expandable card file never totally replaced the closed file in book form. However superior it seemed in its heyday, roughly between 1900 and 1970, it is ultimately the least significant of the types of file discussed in this chapter. However, its hold on the habits of searchers and on the economics of library administration was such that advanced computer technology was used for nearly twenty years to continue printing cards for manual interfiling into existing catalogues. Frozen card catalogues still sit in some libraries, less and less used, beside their microform or interactive successors.[2] When all the records once only on cards have been converted into machine-readable form (see pages 124–26) to be managed by a database management system, the card stock can be recycled and the cabinetry disposed of to an antique dealer. As the computer pushes it aside, remaining practical uses of the expandable file in libraries are for the small, quick-reference file needing constant revision and for the temporary storage of data gathered from various sources and destined for transfer to machine-readable form. For these purposes, cards remain too handy ever to be entirely replaced.

2. A card catalogue is said to be closed if newly acquired items are not added to it, yet maintenance of what is already there is continued. It is said to be frozen if the library's policy forbids even the correction or deletion of any card in it.

On the other hand, the closed manual file is far from dead. Whether on papyrus, paper, or computer-output print or microfiche, this remains a convenient and inexpensive way to convey bibliographic information, likely to remain totally satisfactory for many needs. In almost every type of library, separate listings of the most current, the most used, and/or the most difficult-to-access material are constantly being prepared for distribution to users: neither a card catalogue nor an interactive file is a good publicity tool. The curator of any significant specialized collection, even when its records are part of an interactive catalogue, still aspires to a separately organized book-form listing where the collection's items can be described in depth and in more specialized context with prefatory material, etc.—a listing published for use outside the institution and in the study not yet equipped with modem and computer.

Coordinating Data Elements and Terms Interactively

The computer, a major cause of the third and present information explosion, also made possible the interactive file with which to manage it. To use the computer merely to produce manual files more quickly and cheaply seemed, in the 1950s and 1960s, good enough reason to plunge into automation; but even then the visionaries worked on perfecting its other bibliographic uses, including such technical ones as simultaneous access to the same database by multiple users and putting a million bibliographic records onto a five-inch aluminum disk. A century ago, the American bibliographer Henry Stevens suggested that a complete bibliographic record of a book should include a miniature photograph of its title page. This is now feasible in computer output. So is a floor-plan diagram showing the precise location where the item can be found. A catalogue that speaks to the visually handicapped user is no more out of the question than a talking automobile dashboard; it is already provided as an option by some libraries.

Without a very important conceptual advance, interactive searching as defined on pages 85–87 would not bring results significantly different from those obtained through skilful searching of a well-designed manual file. In the early 1950s, before the computer could have been thought of as a tool for the purpose, C. Dake Gull, Calvin Mooers, Ralph Shaw, Mortimer Taube, and other innovative indexers of technical documents in the applied sciences made the conceptual breakthrough of freeing a search for individual data elements from the inflexibility of any predetermined arrangement of them. The documents they dealt with in their special libraries fell between the two stools of library catalogues and the A&I services and were not being well indexed, so an innovative approach to them comes as no surprise. Searchers wanted to find single concepts within these documents but in various combinations not necessarily predictable by an indexer. To overcome the access limitations inherent in manual systems, these innovators sought a mechanical way to combine separate index terms at the moment of a request involving more than one such term. Thus a file might contain thousands of documents of which, for example, fifty dealt in some manner with ionization and a hundred with nitrogen. From the total file, the indexers wanted to locate easily the seven that dealt with *both* ionization *and* nitrogen. In a typical manual file of the time, this request would have been anticipated when the file was originally created by indexing those seven under the access point **NITROGEN—IONIZATION**. However, doing this makes it impossible to find everything about the topic of ionization in one location since descriptions of the other forty-three documents dealing with that topic have been separated in the file from these seven and the user must pursue many cross-references to find them.

There is an alternative solution, but it requires each access point to be duplicated as many times as is necessary to file it under *each* of its significant terms; that is, by adding **IONIZATION—NITROGEN** to the index for the seven relevant documents. While bringing more documents about ionization together in the file, this multiplies the number of access points required. When a single desired combination might involve not just two but many terms (say, **ELEC-TROLYSIS** and **HIGH-TEMPERATURE** in addition), this method breaks down in a manual file.[3] This is precisely why the method first described remained in common use for the preceding hundred years. Up to twenty-four separate access points are required in order to display fully the relationship to each other of only four terms which might be relevant to a document. This is illustrated in the following table using **A, B, C,** and **D** as the four terms. Furthermore, six possible access points begin with each of the four terms, introducing significant problems of complexity for the searcher, as follows:

A B C D	B A C D	C A B D	D A B C
A B D C	B A D C	C A D B	D A C B
A C B D	B C A D	C B A D	D B A C
A C D B	B C D A	C B D A	D B C A
A D B C	B D A C	C D A B	D C A B
A D C B	B D C A	C D B A	D C B A

That some of these twenty-four combinations make no sense in relation to the real topic is acknowledged, but how does one decide which—and would every indexer agree on which are valid and which are not?

The application of this principle to real topics is discussed in chapter 7. The file-management problem illustrated here is simply how to keep the access points for the different names, concepts, etc. to be indexed *separate* in the stored file but *combinable* at the time of searching. To do this, the innovators chose what now seem like very primitive storage media, including

3. Attempting it in the print form of the ISI *Citation Index* series, for example, is what makes the permuted index portion of that publication so large and cumbersome.

edge-notched cards to be manually sorted with modified knitting needles and punched cards to be sorted by passing electric current through the holes, both illustrated in figure 15. Each card stored one bibliographic record and its notched or punched subject code(s) enabled the searcher physically to extract from the whole file only those cards containing the requested combination of those codes. The original order of the cards does not matter to the searching process. After the search ends, the cards, unchanged and in any order, are ready for another search relevant to a different combination of concepts. This is exactly how a database management system separates the function of storage from the functions of searching and output which, in a manual file, are all fixed in relation to each other.

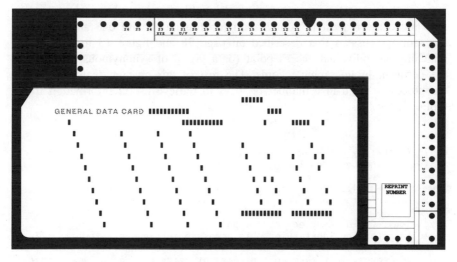

FIGURE 15. Two methods of the 1950s permitting the mechanical sorting of a group of records within extremely limited parameters. In the punched card, one or two holes punched within the same vertical column permit electrical contacts to cause the sorting of cards based on the code for a given numeral or letter in that column. Above and beside it are two edges of a simple edge-notched card. The notch at the *J* results in this card dropping out when a needle is passed through this hole in a deck of such cards.

Twenty years after the cumbersome mechanical techniques shown in figure 15 were first used on files of necessarily limited size, the computer finally had the storage capacity to do the same thing in nanoseconds with machine-readable files of virtually unlimited size. The interactive file, already quite old in theory, then became practical. In theory, only one copy of each machine-readable record exists in a database. Its access points are identified according to its formatting and the database management system applied. Neither the location of its data elements nor the order of the various records in the database is necessarily relevant to the search process. When the database is searched for, say, two particular access points, a copy is made of the record-identifier number of any record in which *both* access points are present. If none or only one of the desired access points is present in a particular record, that record is ignored. The copied record-identifier numbers are then used to retrieve the entire records for which they stand and the chosen output instructions are followed in order to select those parts (or all) of the record(s) for display on a screen, for downloading, or for printing on paper. The original records all remain unchanged in the database and therefore ready for the next request. Figure 16 illustrates the essential features of this process, the basis of all interactive file searching. The principal difference of this process from, and advantage over, manual file searching lies in how it brings together, for a particular request, those access points—or any other data elements—which are stored separately in a machine-readable file but have been identified as relevant to the request in combination (coordination) with one another. It is the same process as that described on page 78 and figure 13 in relation to matching an individual access point (or a group of synonymous ones) with the pertinent bibliographic records. The rest of this chapter deals with how the process is used in a number of ways to retrieve useful information from bibliographic files.

Child Psychology (subject access point)
   S10254   (number identifying this access point in the authority file)

   B17389, B35241, B68172, [etc.] (numbers identifying the
            bibliographic records given this subject access point)
. . . . .
Psychology, Child (subject access point)
   S10254   (number identifying this access point in the authority file:
            the same number as above because it is identified as an
            equivalent term on the same authority record; bibliographic
            records need therefore not be separately posted to this form)
. . . . .
School Environment (subject access point)
   S02718   (number identifying this access point in the authority file)

   B06121, B25713, B35241, [etc.] (numbers identifying the
            bibliographic records given this subject access point)

FIGURE 16. The database management system locates each of the requested access points in an authority file. The result is a separate set of record-identifier numbers indexed to each access point. These are matched. Only the number(s) (underlined in the figure) in common for the requested access points are matched with their document descriptions in the bibliographic file to be displayed to the searcher. Subject S10254 is located regardless of whether the searcher attempts access via **Child** or via **Psychology**. That record number B35241 is common to both subject numbers S10254 and S02718 means that it is retrieved when a request to match these two subject access points is made. The title on this record is *School Stress and Anxiety*. Many systems use a prefix to designate which file in the system contains the record in question; for example, an S for any record in a subject authority file; a **B** for any record in a bibliographic file.

Pre- and Post-Coordination

Gull, Shaw, and the other indexing innovators of forty years ago used the term *post-coordination* to describe the essential feature of this process. This reflects the fact that terms or data elements are being matched (coordinated) *after* (post-) being retrieved from their separate locations in the file in response to a request. Inevitably but unfortunately, the word *pre-coordination* came into universal use later in order to contrast the previous practice with the new one. Superficially it seems to be the perfect contrasting word, but it cannot refer, as *post-coordination* does, to repeatable processing involving the same data elements in different combinations. *Pre-coordination* can only refer to the one-time and irrevocable joining of separate concepts or data elements at the time the file is compiled, for example, **NITROGEN—IONIZATION**. It may help to think of pre-coordination as being a decision made *before* (pre-) receipt of any request for information involving any of the relevant concepts or data elements. Thus while there is such a thing as a pre-coordinate access point or a pre-coordinate index, there is no such thing as a post-coordinate access point or index. In post-coordination, there is only the momentary activity of combining what one might call free-floating access points or data elements available to be called into service as a kind of ad hoc task force to solve a particular problem.

It is not only subject terms, such as **NITROGEN** and **IONIZATION**, that are usefully combined, or coordinated, in bibliographic searching. Satisfying a request often requires the coordination of data elements of different types, for example, when the user wants

1) material in a particular form (say, statistics) issued by a particular agency (say, the Department of Mines) on a particular topic (say, sulphur) or

2) the text of a work (*Henry VI*) by an author (Shakespeare) as edited by a particular critic (G.B. Harrison).

In the first example, (a) any library has many books of statistics as well as some about statistics, (b) the Department of Mines has issued many documents, and (c) sulphur is a common subject. In the second example, (a) Shakespeare wrote a score of extant plays held in any library in numerous editions, (b) *Henry VI* is the title of some editions of his three-part play but also of some critiques of the play by other people and even of books unrelated to Shakespeare but about the historical king on whom the play was based, and (c) Harrison is an author or editor of many editions of Shakespeare's plays and of many other books and articles as well. The process of satisfying each of these two requests is the same as that of coordinating nitrogen with ionization; that is, in the second example, the access points for Shakespeare, for the title *Henry VI*, and for Harrison must be coordinated in the hope of finding one or more documents having all three characteristics.

Manual Pre-Coordination Using Subfiles.   Even in a completely manual file, it should not be necessary to scan every record indexed under Harrison's name to see whether a Shakespeare *Henry VI* is among them. Almost every manual file presents bibliographic data with some data elements pre-coordinated because they are so often wanted in conjunction with one another. It simply makes no sense to have all the Shakespeare items, for example, subarranged in the order in which they happened to have been added to the file. Yet many database management systems are still programmed so inadequately that this is exactly what happens: although the search process has ensured that every record retrieved is relevant to the request, the output display (which is a manual file from the point of view of the user) has the records arranged in the order of their record-identifier numbers, that is, in the chronological order in which the records were added to the file, not in the order of a more significant characteristic such as author's name or date.

Planned structuring of a manual file has always pre-coordinated the most useful pairs of access points according to either a cataloguing or citation rule (which determines the order of elements within a record) or a filing rule (which determines the sequence of records presented under an access point). Because an author's name and a title function in conjunction with one another to identify a work (see pages 169–71 and 270), both citation and filing rules usually require that items by the same author be subarranged by their titles and vice-versa. Either subject-date or subject-author also forms a useful pairing, so almost every filing rule requires that records with the same subject access point be subarranged by either author or date, but in this case there is not the unanimity of practice found in the case of the author-title pairing. In any case, the result is a series of subfiles; for example, the whole file under **Shakespeare** comprises a subfile for the work *Hamlet*, another for *Henry VI*, and so on.

Nothing prevents the same file (those under **Shakespeare**) from being subfiled instead by the names of editors. In that case, the subfiles would consist of the editions by Bradley, Harrison, Kittredge, etc. Might it be useful to have all the items listed under **Shakespeare** subarranged by their publication dates? By the languages in which they are printed? By the prices the library paid for them? By the date of their acquisition by the library? None of these can be dismissed as totally useless for some legitimate search request. The point is that, in a manual system, economics and file size dictate a practical limit to the feasible number of different pre-coordinations. One cannot, for example, conceive of a file in which all the Shakespeare records are subfiled first by title, then again by editor, then again by date, etc. If no pre-coordination established in the design of the file can help answer a given request, the searcher must scan a larger group of records under a relevant access point, item by item. A pre-coordination in manual library catalogues which is particularly troublesome to many users is illustrated by the request for a book *about* Shakespeare's *Henry VI*. This cannot be found in the subject catalogue under **H** (for Henry) because the cataloguing/filing rules of the past century have determined that the subject access point for a work takes the form of a pre-coordinated author/title pair: in this case, **SHAKESPEARE, WILLIAM, 1564–1616. HENRY VI**, filed only under S.

Subject Pre-Coordination.   This is a particularly troublesome aspect of subject access. It was introduced on page 72, and its analysis forms a large part of chapter 7, which is why name/title examples are generally used in this chapter. To introduce the coordination of concepts briefly in the present context, the example of **MICROWAVE OPTICS** may be viewed as a coordination of two different concepts in one access point. They are certainly not inseparable concepts: microwaves also heat foods, and optics is also the study of wavelengths. The designer of the controlled subject-access vocabulary decides when a single pre-coordinate subject access point should express more than one separable concept.

Techniques of Post-Coordination

Post-coordination is not restricted to interactive or computer-based searching. A searcher does it when browsing a manual file under each of two or more terms to see which items share the terms in common. This is tedious and only done when the number of items indexed under each search term is relatively small. Some types of term (for example, place names) are extremely valuable as search terms but are rarely indexed separately in a manual file precisely because the result would be too many items retrieved to be post-coordinated in the manual mode. To a database management system, no numbers are too great to use more than a fraction of a second in the actual search-and-match process.[4] It is now common to program the database management system to index not only certain data elements as whole entities but also to index every word (defined as anything with a space or a mark of punctuation immediately before and after it) in such elements as titles, subject access points, and notes. Anything so indexed in the system is separately retrievable and its retrieval may be made dependent on whether it occurs in a specified field in the record. Having been so retrieved, any two or more such words or data elements can be post-coordinated. This allows speedy response to such questions as:

1) Do both the word *law* and the word *family* occur in any title element in a record?
2) Does the word **Shakespeare** occur in any author access point and **fre** in any language code in the same record?
3) Does the word **SULPHUR** occur in any subject access point and the code for a state or provincial government publication occur as a type-of-document code in the same record?

4. Response-time problems cannot be ignored but they arise from other factors, for example, the number of users simultaneously attempting to access a library catalogue with complex requests.

This possibility is what ultimately distinguishes an interactive from a manual file. It has been developed along a number of different lines, the principal of which are described in the following sections.

Boolean Logic

Boolean algebra, boolean logic, and boolean operators are named after George Boole, a nineteenth-century English mathematician. They were first consciously applied in bibliographic searching by the innovative subject indexers of the 1950s named on page 91. The three commonly used boolean operators are (1) *AND*, (2) *OR*, and (3) *NOT*: each invokes a different type of post-coordination. In Boole's own time and even in the 1950s, no computer was involved. Today, boolean operators are inseparably linked with computer operations and one rarely hears mention of them when speaking of manual techniques of coordination.

The OR Operator.   Figure 17, called a Venn diagram (a type of diagram designed to show coordination graphically), shows the coordination desired in the request for documents about both Siamese and Burmese cats. It illustrates one use of the *OR* operator. The user wants any material concerning *either* of the two topics. This operator expands a search for what is named in the first term by adding to it everything named in the second. It provides an efficient way of retrieving information on a small number of separate topics which do not, when taken together, form a substantial part of the next more general unit that can be defined. For example, this request would not be efficiently answered if everything about pet cats had to be retrieved, even if it were practicable then to exclude all other breeds using the *NOT* operator.

FIND Siamese cats *OR* Burmese cats
RESULT: 30 ITEMS

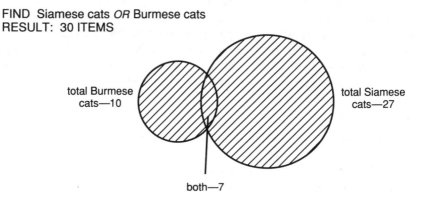

total Burmese cats—10

total Siamese cats—27

both—7

FIGURE 17. The *OR* operator retrieves everything shaded in the diagram: the twenty-seven records indexed under **Siamese cats** plus the ten indexed under **Burmese cats**. The number of *different* records is thirty, not thirty-seven, because seven are indexed under *both* breeds (twenty are indexed only under **Siamese cats**; three only under **Burmese**). In most systems, records indexed under each requested term are counted and displayed only once.

OR has a second useful function: to locate a single topic or name among access points not governed by vocabulary control; for example, to search for information about **Ceylon** *OR* **Sri Lanka** when either name for the island might occur in a title in the database. Similarly, one searches for **streetcar** *OR* **tram** because the subject is likely to be expressed one way in American titles and another in British ones. One might add the technique of truncation (see pages 103–4) as in searching for **Twain, Mark** *OR* **Clemens, Sam?** or for **LIBRAR?** *OR* **ARCHIV?**.

The AND Operator.   This operator, illustrated in figure 18, is the one most frequently used. The modern developers of post-coordinate indexing originally concentrated almost exclusively on *AND* in using their pre-computer techniques. It is a limiting, not an expanding, operator. The user does not want *all* the information available on Canada's external trade, but only what is *also* relevant to another topic: taxation. It is equally valid to look at this from the other point of view: the user does not want all the available information on taxation, but only that which is also relevant to Canada's external trade. As in any attempt at manual post-coordination, it is most efficient to make the first search under the access point likely to have the fewest records attached to it.

In a file which includes any natural-language access points, this operator should be brought into play after the *OR* operator has been used to comprehend the whole of each of the desired categories separately. Thus one might use *OR* to link the term **TAXATION** with one or more synonyms (perhaps **ASSESS-MENT** and **LEVY**) before using *AND* to combine the result with another term or combination of terms. The use of boolean *AND* is particularly desirable when:

1) the categories sought are broad but overlap each other in only a small number of documents in the file being queried
2) the terminology of a new field is not yet stable but particular single

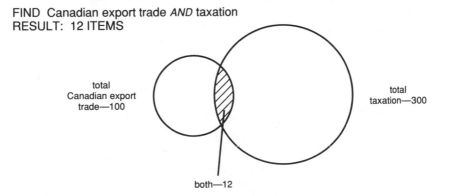

FIND Canadian export trade *AND* taxation
RESULT: 12 ITEMS

total
Canadian export
trade—100

total
taxation—300

both—12

FIGURE 18. The *AND* operator retrieves only those records whose indexing shares the specified characteristics; in this case only twelve documents from among the hundred indexed under Canadian export trade and three hundred indexed under taxation.

words can be expected to occur in some conjunction with one another in titles or

3)   the desired coordination involves a large number of terms.

The **A B C D** illustration on page 92 shows why few manual systems have ever made any attempt to facilitate the coordination of more than two or three names/concepts at a time, but traditional subject headings may add to these one or more form/audience elements as part of a pre-coordination (see page 217). Using boolean operators and truncation, it is relatively easy to express a complex request in a single statement, for example, *FIND* **CANAD?** *AND* **TRAD?** *AND* **TAX?** *AND* **COUNTERVAIL?.**

The use of *AND* can actually be enlightening to the searcher who combines concepts and retrieves unexpected material from different disciplines. It starts a train of new thinking when the particular combination of concepts does not yet represent a recognized independent field of investigation. This is precisely when no pre-coordinate access point representing those concepts could yet exist. New knowledge, occasionally startling and far-reaching in its implications, is often generated when ideas that had never previously been put together are thus associated. The first combining of **COMPUTER** with **INFORMATION** may have been one of this century's most significant uses of *AND*.

The NOT Operator.   The least frequently used of the three operators is illustrated in figure 19. *NOT*, the converse of *OR*, is, like *AND*, a limiter. After the scope of a broader search has been defined, this operator proceeds to exclude from that scope the specified concept or name. Thus it is useful when a large part but not quite all of a more generic whole is wanted, but only if the part *not* wanted can be clearly defined and simply named. This can be a dangerous operator; to forget that some concept is encompassed within another when using it is to risk eliminating from a search a component which is in fact relevant.

FIND diseases *NOT* viral conditions
RESULT: 150 ITEMS

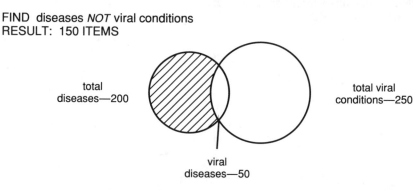

total
diseases—200

total viral
conditions—250

viral
diseases—50

FIGURE 19. The *NOT* operator excludes the fifty records indexed under viral conditions from the two hundred retrieved under diseases of various kinds, leaving the other hundred and fifty to be displayed.

Nesting Operators.   Most software permitting the use of boolean operators also permits the use of more than one of them in a single search command as mentioned in the discussion of *AND*. This is called *nesting operators*. Before   the searcher does this, it is necessary to know which of several possible sequences is intended and how to express it. The two results shown in figure 20 are very different although both could be expressed as **A** *AND* **B** *OR* **C**. The searcher must know the program's default sequence but can usually specify a different one by putting parentheses around whatever must be processed as a single unit.

FIND A *AND* B *OR* C
RESULT: 22 ITEMS

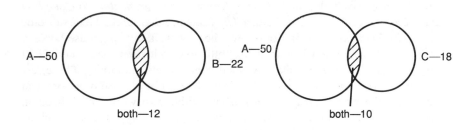

12 + 10 = 22

– – – – – – – – – – – – – – – – – –

FIND A *AND* B *OR* C
RESULT: 30 ITEMS

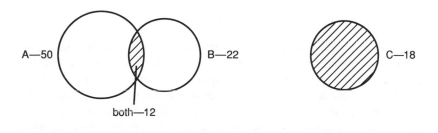

12 + 18 = 30

FIGURE 20. The upper illustration shows the situation properly expressed as **A** *AND* (**B** *OR* **C**). It retrieves a total of 22 items. The lower one shows the situation properly expressed as (**A** *AND* **B**) *OR* **C**. It retrieves a total of 30 items. Both results assume no overlap between **B** and **C**.

Proximity and Relational Searching

Searching for subject information among natural-language elements, such as titles, is particularly hazardous. To forget the possibilities for ambiguity in either the meaning of a single word or in the context provided by any requested combination of words is to risk retrieving what are known as false drops (that is, irrelevant items), lowering the precision of the search result. On the other hand, English word-order being what it is, one should not be too ready to exclude combinations which may be fruitful. The success rate can be maximized with careful thought and the application of the technique called proximity searching. This is permitted in many database management systems but not always with the same parameters. For example, a search for information about family law might request any title whose wording includes *family law* as a single, two-word term. This retrieves both *Family Law in Canada* and *Introduction to Canadian Family Law* but does not retrieve either *The Canadian Law of the Family* or *Law and Family Rights in Canada*. To retrieve these as well, one might use boolean *AND* to retrieve any title which includes both words wherever they occur: *FIND family AND law*. This brings the unwanted result of also retrieving *The Effect of Family Poverty on Canadian Social Law*. To avoid that false drop, one can require that the words *family* and *law* occur within two words of each other. This will still retrieve the two previous titles and presumably suffices to exclude any in which the connection between the terms is too tenuous to be relevant. In many systems, it is possible to request proximity of the desired words within any specified number of words of each other, from two to a dozen or more. Much experience with the vocabulary of the subject in question is needed to make a skilful user of this technique.

The relational operators *greater than* and *less than* are represented graphically as > and < when they appear before a number. For example, in searching a database which allows date as a parameter, these serve to limit retrieval to those documents published before or after the specified year.

Compression Codes

Manual searching offers nothing akin to the use of access points constructed (derived) by a computer program by combining specified parts of specified data elements. This technique combines truncation with post-coordination and can be useful in isolating a manageable number of records from a very large file, provided unambiguous data elements are available. It was the original basis for searching in the OCLC database (see page 120). The system designer determines the most useful type of code for the predicted uses of the file; there are no general standards. The database management system creates the code, or search key, for each new record from among its data elements as it is added to the database. The code's greatest value is in limiting input time and error by requiring the searcher to key in only a few characters. For example, the 4,4 author-title key

BOOR,AMER (the first four characters of the author's surname and the first four of the title excluding an initial article) retrieves

> Boorstin, Daniel J. *America and the Image of Europe*
> Boorstin, D. *American Civilization*
> Boorstin, D. J. *An American Primer*
> Boorstin, Daniel *The Americans*

A 3,1,1,1 title key is useful for isolating a book title; for example, **WIL,Q,R,G** can hardly retrieve much more than the *Wilsonline Quick Reference Guide*. It would make less sense to search a title code like **PRO,A,T,O** (*Proceedings and Transactions of* . . .), which would retrieve hundreds of different items. Precisely to avoid this, much-used words like *report* and *proceedings* are usually on the stop-list to be ignored when the program derives the search key. This technique is not widely used and is useful only for known-item (not subject) searching. A type of compression code, however, is generated by many database management systems which serve A&I databases. If names of authors are not subject to vocabulary control, the searcher may not rightly predict whether Cecil Heyward Johnson appears as Johnson, Cecil H.; Johnson, C. Heyward; etc. If the system reduces *all* given names to initials automatically, the user has more chance of retrieving the person sought, if at the risk of retrieving two or more persons who happen to share the same initials but not the same given names, for example, also Charles Henry Johnson.

Browsing, Truncation

In one respect not technically related to coordination, computer searching mirrors a much used manual technique perfectly. A common feature of modern retrieval systems is to allow the searcher to see successive access points in a file, or successive records associated with them, much as one browses backward or forward through the pages or cards of a manual file. This is done in one or both of the following ways:

1) A separate command, often *BROWSE* . . . , causes the program to display the file in sequence, beginning at the point specified and until told to stop.[5]
2) On finding a record or access point of interest, one can scroll ahead or in reverse to see succeeding or preceding records in the sequence, either one at a time or a screenful at a time.

5. The sequence is determined by the filing rule invoked in the construction of the search keys by the database management system. Chapter 9 discusses filing rules amenable to automation, but to save programming cost and running time, search keys are often filed by a very much simpler rule than would be acceptable for a library catalogue. The searcher must be aware of this possibility; filing rules embedded as system subroutines are rarely adequately documented.

A slightly more sophisticated version of the same technique allows one to specify boundaries for a browse. Not knowing whether what is wanted is accessible as **EMPLOYABLE** ... , **EMPLOYEE** ... , **EMPLOYER** ... , or **EMPLOYMENT** ... , one starts in a manual catalogue at **EMPLOY** and scans forward until reaching the title *Emplumada*. There one stops because nothing relevant can follow. The same result is achieved in a computer search by using a truncation code: *FIND* **EMPLOY?**[6] This is particularly useful when applied to access points, such as title words, which are not governed by authority control. The end-truncation (loosely called *suffix-truncation*) technique illustrated in this example is not expensive to program or to run and is now widely used. Allowing the search term to be truncated at the beginning (prefix) as well as the end is useful in some specialized fields with a highly structured vocabulary; for example, a request for **?GLYCER?** retrieves **MONOGLYCERIDE, NITROGLYCERIN**, etc. This technique, however, is considerably more expensive in terms of computer resources required and may affect response time adversely. Middle truncation, as in **ORGANI?ATION** to retrieve both *organisation* and *organization*, is also available at a cost, but the problem of variant spellings is complex enough that vocabulary control is a better method of dealing with it. Many systems, for example, cannot cope with internal truncation involving a variable number of characters, for example, *labor* and *labour*.

General versus Specialized Lists

Today, a very general bibliographic list is either a trade or national bibliography (one that lists publications of all kinds issued in a country), or it is the catalogue of a general library (a library whose collections cover all subject areas). Even in a modest public library, this is a complex file because its access points must be responsive to the needs of all subject areas, all types of documents, and all types of user requests. Yet it must retain its unity and should, where possible, not favour any one subject area or any one type of publication or request over another. Any changes of organization or access-point patterns must be applied with extreme caution because, if internal consistency is not preserved, the searcher loses confidence. These are also the types of list whose records are most often shared among libraries, as described in the next chapter. Their compilers therefore do not have the liberty to be idiosyncratic but must adhere to common standards for compatibility and economy. It is much harder to compile a well-organized general list than a well-organized specialized one.

An A&I tool or monographic subject bibliography operates within a more limited field of knowledge and/or type of document. Here, the right solutions to

---

6. The actual truncation code, the so-called wild card, varies from system to system: it is often a question mark (?) or a pound sign (#).

the issues of access are those which best meet the needs of the particular subject matter or form and the expectations of its more limited number of, and usually more knowledgeable, users. Their needs can usually be identified much more tangibly and clearly than those of all-purpose users (if this is not a derogatory expression). Subject access techniques are those most likely to differ markedly between the general and the specialized bibliographic file. For example, in the latter, the post-coordination of subject concepts is more likely to be desirable than in the more general lists where pre-coordinated access points are still quite effective even for interactive searches.

Too Much Access?

Clearly, interactive searching employing the variety of techniques made possible by automated post-coordination is vastly different from manual file searching. It is therefore useful to draw comparisons between them, without any prejudice that interactive searching overcomes every psychological, technical, intellectual, and economic drawback of manual searching. It does not. A basic difference is that in manual searching, the file's designer bears the responsibility for making it easy, difficult, or almost impossible to retrieve certain coordinations of access points or data elements (almost never are single words as such retrievable in a manual file). Post-coordinate searching thrusts the responsibility for good search technique much more heavily on the searcher since most database management systems are programmed to index a very wide variety of types of data elements and usually also single words in at least some data elements. However, one should not think that a manual file is necessarily a poorer searching tool, nor that it prevents the searcher from making good ad hoc choices among different ways of proceeding. A simple database management system may offer less scope for perceptive searching than a good manual system even though it inevitably processes a search more quickly. It has often been demonstrated in actual practice that using a manual file can be more productive of satisfactory results than using an interactive file, as well as vice-versa, regardless of how sophisticated each is in its construction.

The computer has caused a notable increase in the amount of indexing of all kinds being done. It has also increased the ease and lowered the cost of accessing this indexing. Even in print form, indices, especially to reference books, appear to take up a higher proportion of the books' pages every year. That this is an era of information overload is partly due to the fact that more of the information that was always there is being made a little more visible through an expansion of access possibilities. Does this represent the attainment, or even a closer approach, to the long-sought goal of perfect information retrieval? Full-text access to machine-readable copy being now commonplace, the reference librarian is bemused by the possibility of locating every instance of any single word in an entire encyclopaedia within seconds. Sometimes this is the only way to answer a query; sometimes it is merely a game of which one tires easily. How useful is it to be able to ascertain which twenty items out of the million described on a single CD/ROM disk contain exactly 93 pages?

Regardless of whether it is manual or computerized, a file with more access points is more complex to use than one with fewer access points and therefore a greater source of potential confusion to the untrained searcher. The more records a search retrieves, the more dross the searcher must sift out in determining what is most relevant, because an increase in response means a higher proportion of nonrelevant items recalled.[7] Is this an ultimate gain for the end-user? Does it diminish dependence on the costly interpretive services of a professional librarian? User-friendly interactive systems which make searching seem simple encourage the naive end-user to grope blindly without adequate definition of either what is really needed or what is the most appropriate access strategy. When this happens in using a manual catalogue, the only waste is of the user's own time: a currency invisible to the library administrator. In an interactive search, the cost can be real library dollars if the database being consulted is distant or commercial. It is no wonder that such considerations are pressed in defense of user fees for interactive searching.

Today's access practices are Janus-like: they try to look forward to the most effective use of interactive searching techniques but are still bound by the need of most users to continue to search manual files as well. The same databases and indices are often available in both print and CD/ROM forms. The availability of differing manual and interactive searching techniques is not yet always accompanied by any difference in the basic file structure in the two forms. This must eventually come about.

7. The issue of recall versus precision is taken up in its most complex form, in relation to subject access, on pages 197–99.

5
CREATING AND
SHARING RECORDS

Surely a model record for each publication need be created only once and copied into every library's various files. After all,

1) the copies of the item held in each library are all identical
2) each library's in-house records must be based on the same objective data elements described in chapter 2 which are relevant to that publication and
3) libraries subscribe in general to the same standards of both description and access.

Yet psychological, administrative, economic, and technological barriers have always stood in the way of the complete realization of this self-evident ideal: Who should create the model record? Who should be responsible for transmitting it to its potential user(s)? What is the best method of communicating it? Who should pay the costs involved? How can quality control be administered if responsibility for record creation is dispersed among different agencies? What priority should be assigned to pursuing the ideal in areas where it conflicts with local service and administrative considerations? None of these questions admits of any single or any permanently valid answer.

The computer and the high cost of human labour are diminishing the barriers to sharing, rather than endlessly recreating, bibliographic records, but they will probably never entirely remove them. This chapter deals with how systems for sharing records have been developed and how the problems of doing so are minimized. It must also deal with the politics and economics of how librarians interact in this sharing both among themselves and vis-à-vis other agencies and commercial firms engaged in compiling and distributing bibliographic data. There is never enough time, staff, or money to accomplish all the bibliographic work to be done. If more than one agency produces a record for the same document, other documents must be receiving less or no attention.

Commercial A&I services are market driven: their managers know that if two different services mostly duplicate each other in coverage and depth of indexing, only one is likely to survive; to be successful, each needs to define its own area of activity sufficiently different from the others'. Librarians who have long been sheltered from this commercial truth (in part by their public-sector financing) continued to repeat each other's work well into this century but can no longer afford to do so. So did colleagues in different departments of the same library: the record of an item made for acquisitions purposes would hardly be glanced at by the cataloguer in the next office. The history of modern bibliographic services is that of the gradual trend away from separate record creation toward shared creation and more efficient transfer. The exact effects of this trend in the practical management of any one library can only be evaluated locally. Sharing records does not eliminate the cost of hardware or software and all other expenses of interface with the local users. To suggest such costs for particular types of institution in the context of different institutional goals and users, system configurations, procedures, etc. is beyond the scope of this book. In any case, costs are always changing, often negotiable with suppliers, and dependent on local circumstances.

Practical reasons for isolation and redundant effort in the pre-computer era are easy to identify. When labour costs were not the overriding concern they are now, it could cost more to obtain and adapt a record from an external source than to begin afresh locally. Making a virtue of necessity, however, theoretical reasons were also proffered: each description of the same item was thought to meet the unique needs of a single function in a single library. The different data needed for order slips, in accounting, as catalogue records, in booklists for public distribution, as circulation records, etc. seemed irreconcilable. In general, the bibliographic record was considered as stemming not from the document itself (for which it is a standard description) but from the administrative functions of handling it (which are many and varied). In larger and smaller libraries, special and general ones, librarians defended the choice of different data elements and access points to meet local user needs. Moreover, the English-language cataloguing rules most widely taught in library schools until 1980 were not as widely adopted in practice as their originators might have hoped. They were not even addressed to the needs of all libraries but only to those supporting higher education and scholarly investigation (see page 137).

The Cost of Bibliographic Records

Bibliographic records are intellectual property created by people paid for their work by salary, by contract, or by claiming copyright and receiving royalties on sales. The cost of originally creating a record is largely a function of the time taken by these people to make professional judgements: time spent for results which may seem relatively intangible. This cost factor is high when compared with the more visible and certainly more directly measurable clerical operations involved in recording and communicating the result. The computer has markedly lowered the cost of the latter but at least temporarily increased the cost of the former by making the context of the required professional judgements ever more complex. To distinguish which exact functions and costs are professional and which are not is a difficult issue for administrators. Endless questionnaires and speculation over the years have failed not only to determine the average cost of the professional (as distinguished from the clerical) work involved in cataloguing; they have even failed to point to any agreed method of determining it because of the number of variables involved.

Very little bibliographic work can be made commercially profitable in itself. Almost all is highly subsidized. In modern times governments pay, in one way or another, the lion's share of at least the professional cost of creating bibliographic records, most of which is done in public-sector institutions. In less rich countries, the government is virtually the only possible source of money for the entire bibliographic enterprise of the nation. Librarians around the world have been spoiled by the generosity of the American taxpayer who throughout this century has paid most of the Library of Congress' cost not only of cataloguing publications from almost every country but also of sharing the resulting records with other agencies. The majority of A&I services are also academic societies or nonprofit companies receiving public grants and subsidies. Following these noncommercial models, it was once traditional for any library, private or public, freely to share the bibliographic records it created, even to the extent of bearing some of the cost of their reproduction and distribution. The present trend in many countries toward privatization is affecting public-sector bibliographic services by changing the attitudes of both librarians and their funding bodies toward bibliographic records as objects of commerce. While it is doubtful that any public-sector agency expects ever to realize a profit directly from record creation, a legal claim to copyright in the content of a bibliographic database at least gives its originator a means of protecting the integrity and proper use of its records.[1]

Cost-Control and Automation

Automation promised cost reduction in the clerical aspects of creating and using bibliographic tools. This occasioned the first major reassessment of the organization of these functions in libraries, A&I services, etc. in almost a century. While savings were quickly achieved in well-managed projects of updating, maintain-

1. The Library of Congress as a federal agency can only use copyright legislation to protect its records outside the United States. Proposed licensing arrangements are a different issue.

ing, and printing files, costs grew when the progress of automation reached the function of user access to information. Users quickly appreciated the benefits of the automated access techniques described in chapter 4. Satisfying their new expectations soon overtook the former costs of buying printed A&I publications, maintaining a single copy of the in-house card catalogue, and consulting a union catalogue in a neighbouring city by mail. Library administrators of the 1960s who aimed only at shrinking the typing pool made a serious error of judgement. Those with the foresight to press for in-house programmers, the installation of excess capacity in the hardware, cooperative software development, shared databases, and the continuing education of staff at conferences and workshops faced constant budgetary and management harrassment but ultimately served both their users and their staff.

Centralization and Cooperation

Administrators were aware of the budgetary implications of uncoordinated duplication of effort long before the computer began eliminating technical barriers to sharing records. Around 1850, two American librarians were addressing the issue almost simultaneously in practical ways which led directly to today's flourishing systems of (1) centralized journal-article indexing in the A&I services and (2) decentralized but cooperative library cataloguing.[2] While working in 1847 in a student-society library at Yale, William Frederick Poole made a list of the articles he encountered in its little-used journal collection which he thought would help classmates working on papers and debates. The value of his listing was so quickly evident that he published its 154 pages as *An Alphabetical Index to Subjects Treated in the Reviews and Other Periodicals to Which No Indexes Have Been Published*. Many college librarians bought it for use by their students even though their libraries might not contain all the same journals. Within five years, Poole produced a second edition six times larger and the work had to be put on a continuing basis. At almost the same time, Charles Coffin Jewett of the Smithsonian Institution proposed that each book be catalogued only once, the resulting bibliographic record to be distributed on cards for incorporation directly into the catalogue of any library in the nation owning the same book.

As in the mid-nineteenth century, so now, the practical success of any method of producing bibliographic data centrally or cooperatively depends on three factors:

2. Earlier efforts to compile union catalogues include the never-completed thirteenth-century list of all the manuscripts housed in British monasteries, the *Registrum Librorum Angliae*, called "the first co-operative catalogue" in Dorothy May Norris, *A History of Cataloguing and Cataloguing Methods, 1100–1850, with an Introductory Survey of Ancient Times* (London: Grafton, 1939), p. 30. Norris also notes that "Gesner [compiler of a comprehensive sixteenth-century bibliography] also marks another step in the history of co-operative cataloguing, since he suggested that his work . . . should be used by librarians instead of compiling author catalogues themselves" (ibid., p. 132).

1) adherence to accepted bibliographic standards (treated in part II of this book)
2) a means of getting records in usable form quickly from the place(s) where they are created to where they can be used and
3) agreement on some formula for sharing the work and/or the cost of creating and distributing the data.

The last of these factors is the one most fraught with difficulty. Poole's methodology led to the present A&I services; Jewett's to the present system of library cooperation: two paths to the same end. The following description of both manual and automated practices (and the strange mixture of the two in which we are at present immersed) emphasizes the common purposes of libraries and the A&I services in bibliographic control while recognizing their differences in implementing it cost-efficiently. Manual practices necessarily fostered centralization; automated ones favour cooperation.

Manual Technology and Centralization

Libraries and Derived Cataloguing

In the manual era, to catalogue an item only once demanded centralization or at least heavy dependence on one principal source. Jewett proposed to distribute unit records on card stock, that is, one identical complete description of an item on each card, to be filed under one access point in a catalogue. Each library would acquire as many cards per book as it needed for its various branch catalogues and the book's various access points. He proposed printing the cards to order from embossed metal stencils, a technique actually used a century later by some commercial firms. Jewett's concept lay fallow for decades but sprang to life in 1898 when the Library of Congress began selling copies of the unit-record cards it was printing for its own card catalogues. With this timely and subsidized source of records secured, Jewett's idea finally became an instant success. At the peak of card use in the early 1970s, the Library of Congress alone was shipping a hundred million printed cards a year to libraries all around the world by mail, each card picked by hand from a vast stock constantly replenished by new additions and reprintings. Commercial vendors of catalogue cards also flourished, their products often copied or adapted from Library of Congress cards. The receiving library had to tailor each card purchased from the Library of Congress to its own needs at least by adding at the top (or otherwise indicating) its particular access point, adding a call number according to the locally adopted shelving scheme, etc.[3] Libraries willing to pay for a

3. Later, when records existed in machine-readable form, the Library of Congress and some other agencies began printing cards to order, as Jewett had originally foreseen, using the computer and the laser printer. The Library of Congress is gradually withdrawing from the business of selling

customized product were the principal market of the commercial services which offered ready-to-file cards.

A library obtaining some of its records externally naturally adjusts its internal cataloguing practices to conform. A psychology of centralization thus took root through the early twentieth century. Perhaps making a virtue of necessity, the academic-library world in North America came to operate as if quality control requires a centralized product produced by the national agency. The force for centralization became even greater when, by January, 1947, the Library of Congress completed the publication in book form of a copy of every bibliographic record it had ever produced—then continued publishing its new records serially (see the brief description of the *National Union Catalog* in the next paragraph). While the original purpose of this publication was verification of interlibrary loan requests, soon every major library was using it as a source of records to be copied into the local catalogue by typewriting, photography, or xerography. Such copying gave rise to the term *derived cataloguing*, that is, cataloguing an item by copying or modifying a record obtained from an outside source. The preferred source being the national agency, records originating at the Library of Congress (and by extension other national agencies) are known as *source records* to distinguish them from records copied from other libraries. The opposite of derived cataloguing is original cataloguing, the much more expensive in-house creation of a record from scratch, which every administrator shies away from. A derived record is now almost always a machine-readable record downloaded into the local automated system either via a direct computer-to-computer link or more likely via an intermediate batch operation. It still needs editing, at least to add local housekeeping and location data, whether this be done in-house or commercially on contract.

Union Catalogues.   In 1902, the Library of Congress asked major American and Canadian libraries to send to it a copy of each new catalogue card they made. Interfiling these with its own cards, the Library began a union catalogue of a scope never previously attempted or since equalled. All the records created from the beginning of the century to today, and still continuing, are now available in the succession of print/microfiche/machine-readable publications entitled *National Union Catalog* (NUC). It is the largest single source of derived records for local cataloguing, both current and retrospective.[4] Regional union-catalogue projects also flourished through the first half of this century but most remained, like the NUC for most of its lifetime, only card files in a single location available to answer reference or interlibrary loan requests by telephone or post. They

records individually. It now sees its function as that of providing its total output of new and revised records as a package, whether on microfiche or tape. Selection and adaptation from this package are done by the individual library or by an intermediate consortium or commercial service.

4. By now, a large proportion of the manually created records in the NUC also exist in one file or another in machine-readable form, but it will probably be forever uneconomic to reassemble them all as a single machine-readable database.

remained of little practical use for derived cataloguing except perhaps at the library in which such a union catalogue was maintained.

Cataloguing-in-Publication. Until the 1970s, the greatest barrier to using derived records remained the difficulty of locating and obtaining a particular one when it was most needed, immediately when the library acquired the book it represented. The national (or source) agencies, whose records are considered of the highest quality and therefore most desirable, gave high priority to the quick cataloguing of new materials, but their records, issued in national and trade bibliographies, reviewing tools, etc., still had to be located and matched to the item manually. A new initiative led to printing at least a partial record within the very book to which it pertains (for an example, see the verso of this book's title leaf). Cataloging-in-Source was unsuccessful as a pilot project in the United States in the late 1950s because it could not be associated with a technology for its effective transfer to the local library's card catalogue. By the early 1970s, automation could provide technical support for this transfer; known as CIP, Cataloguing-in-Publication now operates in many countries. The publisher submits galley proofs and/or other data for a forthcoming publication to a designated library for speedy cataloguing. Controlled-vocabulary access points and certain formatted data elements are quickly submitted to the book's publisher to be printed within the book. They are also incorporated into various bibliographic and reviewing services, usually before the item's publication. Thus basic data in authoritative form can be copied into a library's bibliographic control system right from the point of selection or ordering. Although CIP does not provide a complete record, in most English-speaking countries it includes the controlled-vocabulary name and subject access points (including classification notations), which are the most costly elements to establish. A technician can usually complete the description when the book arrives; however, a professional check is desirable. In addition to the inevitable mistakes, errors of judgement can occur when cataloguing is done without the entire finished publication in hand. Publishers also occasionally make (and fail to notify appropriate agencies of) significant changes between the galley proofs on which CIP is usually based and the final publication.

A&I Services

Card indices of journal articles are not unknown but the quantities involved make them impracticable. A single large A&I service creates two or three times as many records per year as the Library of Congress does for books. Unlike a library catalogue, an A&I publication is not used in-house where it is created but is sold to many buyers. Which buyer would pay to interfile journal citations on cards or to extract from them only citations to articles in the journals to which it subscribes? A&I publications have always been more like union catalogues than like in-house library catalogues; a significant use is to obtain information for interlibrary-loan purposes. Poole's original listing (see page 110) quickly grew beyond his ability to continue it alone. Although production and distribution remained centralized, he chose the route of cooperative decentralization for creating new records. He hoped to get British volunteers to index British journals and American ones to index American journals, but finding competent people willing or able to spare the time was increasingly difficult. Eventually, the work had to be put on a commercial basis with paid staff. When the H.W. Wilson Company, formed in 1898, took over the work to stabilize it and provide more frequent cumulations, this century's explosion of A&I services was underway. There are now some fifty members of the National Federation of Abstracting and Indexing Services (NFAIS) in the United States representing hundreds of different databases. The listing of journal articles is not the only focus of these activities. Conference papers, literary works in anthologies, and other works issued as parts of larger publications also fall within the scope of these services (see page 261).[5] Librarians who once devoted much effort to the local cataloguing of individual journal articles and other such contents of larger publications were happy to vacate the field as much as possible by buying the products of the A&I services.

The Computer and Cooperation

The advances in communication brought about by automation encourage cooperation less through centralization than through decentralization, as illustrated throughout this section. But cooperation of any kind can be an inefficient luxury and automation is initially very costly. Centralization thus remains the only possible mode of operation in much of the developing world. Where a single national agency is responsible for all bibliographic control functions, it naturally seeks a single automated system under which to operate both library cataloguing and any locally based A&I service. While committees of IFLA and Unesco have helped set international standards, the technical expertise of libraries and associations in the wealthier countries tends to predominate. This is gradually resulting in adherence to technical standards which are sufficiently compatible to permit the exchange of records worldwide.

A&I Services

In the wealthy countries, however, differences are still strongly evident between library and A&I practices because of the multiplicity of independent A&I services and their organizational separateness both from libraries and from

5. This thumbnail history slights the projects of nonprofit societies, some of which antedate Poole (although not by much) and have been or remain volunteer efforts. Many are still flourishing.

each other. Unlike libraries, the A&I services of the developed world treat their records as proprietary: to be bought and sold, not shared. Only pressure from their users might make them consider cooperating in setting or implementing standards for citation, for the organization of printed products, or for software with which to search their machine-readable databases. While some small A&I services still use the computer for little more than word processing and sell only manual products, the largest ones have developed integrated in-house computerized systems and made these systems available directly to subscribers for searching. Such systems include WilsonLine, on which are mounted the many databases of the H.W. Wilson Co.; CAS, the Chemical Abstracts Service; and MEDLARS/MEDLINE of the U.S. National Library of Medicine, whose automation project began in 1958 and therefore antedates all others. While the Wilson Company still exercises the right of exclusive distribution of the information in its own databases, the latter two organizations also permit searching of their databases through other agencies as described in the next paragraphs.

Database Vendors (alias Database Brokers, Online Searching Services).   Most A&I services now produce machine-readable records but contract out some or all automated functions dealing with these records, in particular that of end-user interactive searching. This gave rise to a type of company, here called a database vendor, which acts as intermediary between the creator/owner and the searcher of A&I data in machine-readable form. Each vendor holds contracts with the creators/owners of various databases for a (usually exclusive) license to maintain the machine-readable databases and to permit subscribers to search them using the vendor's computer equipment and/or software. The usage fees collected from the searchers are shared between the vendor and the database owner. Databases of the A&I services are far from the only ones mounted by the vendors. Statistical, financial, and directory services are also prominent: it is immaterial to the database management system whether the data searched are bibliographic records or stock market quotes, provided all are compatibly formatted. With growing computer capacity, vendors seek databases to mount, even full-text ones, such as the content of newspapers and magazines. Anything made accessible only through natural-language access points (see page 74) needs no further reformatting.

The vendors' primary customers were originally libraries but their target market now extends to government agencies, businesses, and people in the professions—in fact, anyone with a microcomputer who is willing to pay for the service.[6] Vendors now exist in many countries in both the public and the private sector. Prominent American, British, and Canadian ones are:

6. The expected freedom of access to all the information contained in a public-sector library collection is not, however, to be taken for granted. Some database owners exercise their right to deny particular users or user groups access to such proprietary data as commercially sensitive statistics and financial information.

DIALOG, in Palo Alto, California, which originated with the Lockheed Corporation's searching software for defense information purposes; it is the earliest and still largest database vendor

BLAISE-LINE, *British Library Automated Information System* in London, an outgrowth of the British Library's production of the national bibliography which now incorporates both United Kingdom and foreign databases and

CAN/OLE, *Canadian Online Enquiry* in Ottawa, operated by the Canada Institute for Scientific and Technical Information, the country's national library in the science/technology disciplines.

Each vendor uses a sophisticated database management system which is the key to the services it can offer and which imposes on all the separate databases under its control a common standard of file maintenance, searching strategies, menu and/or command language, available output formats, etc. If the same database is available from two or more vendors, there will be some differences in how it can be searched and/or displayed, differences which may or may not be significant in practice to the user. Users express frustration over the lack of a common command language among the different vendors (see page 286), but the investment of each vendor in software, advertising, user training, etc. for its own version is too great for it to look favourably on any proposed change that would have little direct effect on the vendor's efficiency of operation. Because of the large number of vendors and such incompatibilities among their services, librarians have welcomed the appearance of the so-called front-end or gateway system, an intermediate communications/interface link between a searcher on the one hand and a number of vendors on the other. A gateway provides such services as a specially created unified command language, single billing, and a single service desk for troubleshooting.

Since a vendor's database management system is applied automatically to many databases, it can only apply those general access strategies described in chapter 4 (boolean logic, truncation, proximity searching, etc.) which the vendor chooses to support whatever database content is provided by the various database creators. Any vocabulary control over access points is applied to each separate database by its creator according to that agency's policies. One database creator may use a fully or partially controlled vocabulary while another may provide only natural-language text. Searching for a word or term which may or may not be part of a controlled vocabulary amounts in inexpert hands to groping or using a scattergun but at least guarantees some hits for almost any query in a large database. The effective searcher must become familiar with not only general access strategies but also how the access points of each different database have been established and which of them represent the use of a controlled vocabulary.

Many users still call these database vendors the online searching services because, from their origin in the 1970s through 1984, their product—the search and its output—was only available via connection with the mainframe computer at the vendor's headquarters. Among the first products in 1985 of the CD/ROM bibliographic revolution were the databases of several vendors. The database management software provided on the disk, a variant of that used on the main-frame of the vendor in question, remains both proprietary and largely secret. Although the searching process is totally interactive, the files on a disk are a batch product and must be replaced regularly with new cumulations, the cost and frequency of which are specified in subscription terms. Some services pro-vide for switching from the CD/ROM batch product to the vendor's mainframe computer during a search (provided a communication link is in operation) for more current information than is on the disk.

Library Networks

The start-up cost of automation, including hardware, software, and staff train-ing, was daunting in automation's early days. Uncertainty as to potential benefits made some administrators cautious and others aggressive. No desktop micro-computer had the capacity then for handling full bibliographic records in the quantities required, and mainframe hardware was far too expensive for any but the largest libraries to own or even lease independently. Hardware was there-fore typically shared with other departments of the library's parent organization, for example, a university computing centre or a municipal administration. Soft-ware had to be written from scratch or adapted from programs not originally intended for bibliographic purposes. Librarians who wanted to do this inde-pendently quickly discovered that competent programmers were few and that software development is a major and never-ending expense which it made sense to share with other libraries. The result was the formation of what are now called networks, some of which became the bibliographic utilities discussed in a later section. In their early stages, the term *consortium* was usually used to describe such a group of libraries working together to share the cost of automation.

Budgeting for shared costs was then totally new to most librarians. Besides fearing loss of control over local priorities to the demands of consortium projects, they had to devise complex formulae to take into account the differing value a shared project might have for each member institution. While such formulae are not new (some A&I services have long charged variable rates depending on the number of indexed journals the customer subscribes to), the greater complexity of consortium projects always seems to provide room for disagreement. The lack of operational models to imitate meant that early solutions to problems were invariably ad hoc, and even poor decisions could become entrenched in a consortium's structure. Networks remain very different from one another in what they require of, and what they do for, their members. These things depend on the network membership, which may consist of

1) libraries of similar type and/or size, for example, RLG, the Research Libraries Group

2) libraries of many types and/or sizes in a particular geographic area, for example, NELINET, the New England Library Network or
3) libraries which want to share only a particular function or functions, for example, a users' group providing liaison with a commercial equipment or software supplier.

Distributed Cataloguing.   The primary goal of most early networks was the creation of an automated union catalogue, both to support interlibrary loan services and to achieve for each member a higher hit rate of derived cataloguing than was possible by using only Library of Congress records. The combination of a cooperatively created database and a database management system developed to meet network members' requirements acquired the name *cataloguing support system.* Since Library of Congress source records are the natural and inexpensive base to which to add members' original records, the common record-formatting standard quickly became the Library of Congress MARC format, described in chapter 8 and the appendix. Members' demands govern what services a consortium supports through its database and computer system. At first, the product demanded was only cards to file into existing local catalogues and the networks became cooperative processing facilities. The resulting system in which each library adds some original records to a common database and each derives from that database some records it can use is called distributed cataloguing. It marked a major change from the psychology of centralized cataloguing described on page 112, but there were antecedents. In the 1930s, records created by a few large libraries in the United States were printed and made available as Library of Congress cards. In 1955, records created by cooperating libraries other than the Library of Congress began to be printed in the NUC for others to copy. In 1966, the Library of Congress began to accept current records from some two dozen foreign national bibliographies to be copied into its own catalogues with only the controlled-vocabulary access points edited to conform to Library practice. The feeling previously held by many that only the Library of Congress could catalogue to an acceptable standard was rapidly eroding. (A noticeable decline of quality control in revising and proofreading within the Library of Congress may also have been a factor!)[7]

Cataloguing backlogs, once considered inherently evil, are not so detrimental when a brief record can be made accessible as soon as the item is ordered. Some libraries did this even in a card catalogue, adding an order slip under either an author's name or a title. In an integrated automated system, a record input at the time of selection is searchable under natural-language access points

7. To complete this sketchy history, but outside the present context, the Library of Congress began in 1976 to accept authority records created by the National Library of Canada for all Canadian names as part of its own authority file. By 1985, it was accepting as its own, bibliographic records entirely created by a number of major United States academic libraries, thus coming full-circle to the project of the 1930s mentioned in the text. *Cataloging Service Bulletin* no. 42 (fall 1988): 4–7, describes the present National Coordinated Cataloging Program (NCCP).

until the item is fully catalogued and controlled-vocabulary access points are added. This permits a laxer attitude to backlogs but also increases the likelihood that complete original cataloguing is postponed in the hope that the Library of Congress or some other library will do it first and provide a derived record. However, distributed cataloguing is only effective if every participant does not wait endlessly for someone else to act. The consortium's fee structure may be used as an incentive for participants each to accept a reasonable share of original cataloguing, for example, by offering a credit for each newly input record. In the same way, consortia encouraged their members to share the conversion of older manual records to machine-readable form (see pages 124–26) so that each library's conversion project could both benefit from, and add to, the stock of records converted by others.

Bibliographic Utilities.   Consortia for distributed cataloguing were at first regionally based and several sprang up around North America during the 1970s. Four of these grew well beyond their original scope and are now commonly called the bibliographic utilities to distinguish them from other types of cooperative interlibrary arrangement—the term *cataloguing support system* became obsolete because of the far greater scope of the utilities' activities. A cooperative database is also necessarily a union catalogue, searchable as a unit regardless of how its file structure distinguishes the records of each individual member library.[8] It was inevitable that the cooperative database should come to be used also for interactive reference searching and, through an attached messaging facility, for interlibrary loan purposes.

The utilities are technically very similar to the database vendors described on pages 115–17, each with its own database management software, the key to its potential services. It is more in the contents of their databases that utilities differ from the vendors. The four have become more and more similar to each other in the services they offer, but their differing histories, administrative structures, and commercial interests give each a different niche to fill. A considerable volume of activity is needed to justify high expenses on hardware and software, product and service development, sales-staff and user training, etc. As with the database vendors, a huge database is what justifies their existence, but the competition for more users has an extra dimension for the utilities because their own member/users (and the Library of Congress) create their databases. Another notable difference between the utilities and the database vendors is that, while the latter are independently owned and operated, the former are, if no longer member-owned, still to a considerable degree influenced by member demands, which are now generally expressed through active users' groups. The following brief descriptions, arranged in the chronological order of their origin,

8. One model keeps the records of each member in a separate file; another permits only one record per item but it contains information on which libraries have that item.

highlight the four utilities' different history and organization but ignore their many similarities.

By 1970, Ohio State University had joined with publicly supported colleges in that state to make use of the university's computer for a cataloguing support system named the Ohio College Library Center. Following several name and organizational changes, the present nonprofit membership organization is named OCLC Online Computer Library Center, Incorporated. It has always been the largest utility measured by the number of terminals served by its database management system.[9] Its members are widely spread across the United States and several other countries. Most United States members participate in one or another regional group (for example, NELINET, mentioned on page 118), part or all of whose purpose is to offer liaison services with OCLC for training, standards interpretation, regional interlibrary loan management, etc. Similarly, the OCLC services are now marketed in Canada through UTLAS, the utility described next. The very large OCLC database consists of records from libraries of all types and sizes and is particularly rich in records for older materials converted to machine-readable form during members' data conversion projects. These factors, however, reduce confidence in the quality of records in the database. Once considered antiquated, OCLC's database management software has been upgraded to meet all the types of access needs described in the previous chapter.

The University of Toronto Library originally developed software only to automate its in-house technical services requirements. Named University of Toronto Library Automation Systems (UTLAS), it began to contract with other Canadian libraries in the early 1970s to permit them both to establish files of their own within the system and to copy records from the files of others. The system was eventually separated administratively from the university library, then later from the university itself by its sale to a private corporation. Its name is now Utlas International Canada, Inc., and its ownership and financial status are only as secure as those of other for-profit companies. Canadian libraries of all types and sizes remain its principal users, but it also serves some in the Far East and the United States. Through its present corporate parent, the utility has acquired proprietary rights to some very large databases, including the machine-readable form of the Library of Congress' pre-1968 shelflist, called REMARC.

Stanford University Library developed BALLOTS (Bibliographic Automation of Large Library Operations using Time Sharing), a library-oriented adaptation of the same university's general database management system named SPIRES (Stanford Public Information Retrieval System). In a manner similar to the University of Toronto, Stanford offered other libraries the use of its system. Ownership and administrative control of the system then passed to a consortium

9. Since it is impossible to tell how many records for *different* bibliographic items are in the databases of some of the utilities, record-counts are not a meaningful measure of their size or activity.

of those users, now some thirty libraries (mostly in larger universities in the United States), which incorporated under the name Research Libraries Group (RLG). The group gave BALLOTS a new name: RLIN (Research Libraries Information Network). RLG actively supports projects to input data into RLIN for types of material little represented in the other utilities, notably archival materials, exhibition catalogues, and nonroman-script materials.

The Washington State Library funded both the adaptation of Boeing Aircraft Corporation's database management system for library purposes and the compilation of a union catalogue of the holdings of libraries in the state, using the name Washington Library Network (WLN). The service then spread to neighbouring states, retaining the acronym but changing the name to Western Library Network. WLN pays considerable attention to quality control over both bibliographic and authority records. Uniquely among the utilities, it markets its database management software (without its database) to nonmembers. WLN was also the earliest utility to market its database on CD/ROM disks.

Compatibility: Character Sets and Interconnection. The purpose of communication is to get the content of a message unchanged from source to user. Linguistic or cultural differences may result in intellectual barriers but so may physical incompatibility hinder the transfer of the material document. A library choosing to use 4-by-6 in. catalogue cards is at no disadvantage in its in-house operations (except for their greater cost), but cannot effectively interfile them with those of a library using 7.5-by-12.5 cm. cards. In the same way, the intellectual content of two machine-readable records may be identical, but if their formatting codes needed for processing differ or if the libraries wanting to share them use incompatible hardware and/or software, it may be difficult or impossible to make the records jointly accessible. As another example, telephone companies are permitted to prevent the connection of incompatible equipment to theirs because it could interfere with reliable transmission. They also had to agree among themselves on technical standards for the transmission of signals among each other's equipment for intercompany (long-distance) calls. The utilities have contributed greatly to the establishment and maintenance of standards of technical compatibility in the communication and exchange of bibliographic records. The most important of these is the MARC format, described in chapter 8 and the appendix. The present section deals with two other requirements of cooperative database building: a common character set and the ability of one computer-based system to communicate directly with another.

Although the computer has become a primary communication device, intercomputer transfer of data was not at first foreseen or planned. Both the commercial nature of the industry and the diversity of computer uses continue to foster unique features. Like a letter of the alphabet, a byte has no inherent meaning. All the input/output and processing devices involved in a particular job must therefore accept the same imposed, or conventional, definition of what each byte should stand for. Whether for commercial or technical reasons, each computer manufacturer originally had its own unique way of relating bytes to alphanumeric characters. This situation could not continue. Now, when a key labelled *A* is struck, or an *A* is read by an OCR (optical character recognition) device in Vancouver in 1981 and the result stored on tape, it is expected that a phototypesetter activated in Chicago in 1990 by a different company's computer will display the same letter *A* when reading that tape. This is possible through agreement on a program called a character set, which translates a keystroke for a particular letter, digit, mark of punctuation, etc. into a byte and vice-versa. Agreement among manufacturers, programmers, and users on any particular character set is still not a foregone conclusion. Furthermore, once established, any character set is cloaked with the protection of vested interest in its continuation, as is the basic QWERTY typewriter keyboard, even if there are compelling arguments against its efficiency. This is totally contrary to the librarian's goal of complete freedom of information exchange with the greatest possible technical ease. It is not surprising that librarians dominate the development of means to prevent and/or circumvent technical, legal, commercial, and any other barriers to information exchange. With their help, worldwide standardization of character sets has been achieved to a degree.

The most familiar character set for English-language bibliographic uses is the American Standard Code for Information Interchange (ASCII), of which versions with extensions and minor variants exist. It is based on the requirements of languages written in roman characters. Character sets for other alphabetic scripts are being established. Standardization of input conventions for the nonalphabetic scripts of Chinese, Japanese, and Korean (CJK) remains elusive. These scripts involve the problem of how to input thousands of different characters using a manageable keyboard. One available system uses an extended keyboard for the segment-by-segment composition of such characters and for combining the Korean phonetic elements into graphic syllables. Another uses a numeric code for each different character. Still another calls for keying in a romanized form, whereupon a program displays all the possible original-script characters for that romanization and asks the operator to choose the intended one for input. Even graphic input (digitizing a drawing of the character) can be accommodated. These methods all rely on complex software associated with the input terminal, making that terminal a sophisticated computer dedicated to a single purpose.

Some codes, formats, instructions, etc. required for the operation of one system may be incompatible with the hardware or software of another. A translation program can usually be written to change the inoperable codes, etc. into something that will work without affecting the intellectual content of the file. It is much more difficult to write a program that can reliably determine from the content of a file what codes, etc. are needed for processing if they are absent. A package of translation and other programs called a communication protocol ensures that the hardware and software of an integrated system can sustain usable data transmission among themselves. Such an integrated system, often called a local area network (LAN), connects compatible input/output devices and processors within a single institution or among the libraries of a geographic region or even a national or international consortium. The word *local* refers to the system; the number of, and the distance between, its processing units, terminals, printers, etc. is irrelevant. An international standard now exists for open systems interconnection (OSI) protocols which can transfer any kind of data (programs or data files) from one system to another regardless of equipment and program incompatibilities.[10] Whereas a translation program deals ad hoc with specific single-operation or single-database problems, it takes up to seven levels of adjustment for OSI protocols to get around all the possible technical problems, but the result is dependable computer-to-computer communication of data regardless of file structure or function.

Cooperation and Local Processing

The original consortia and the three earliest utilities (described on page 120) produced manual card or fiche catalogues as batch products for member libraries from the joint database. Later, each developed software to support other technical service functions of member libraries in-house, for example, serials control, circulation, acquisitions, and interactive catalogue searching. Today, a library need not rely on a distant mainframe computer for its local processing because in-house microcomputers have the capacity to do it. This gives the local librarian increased control over the user interface and other local priorities. Increasingly, therefore, a member uses the utility not as a production facility but only as a communication system for interlibrary loan messaging and as a source of records for downloading into the local system. This development required an adjustment of utility functions and fee structures. Any utility will now negotiate a package of bibliographic services tailored to a library's request-for-proposal. Some utilities now market their complete databases on CD/ROM in the same way as some database vendors do (see page 117). Like all competitive enterprises, each utility constantly redefines its services in relation to the market.

Integrated in-house processing is supported by software packages some of which were developed by or in conjunction with a utility, others entirely within the library in question. Most, however, are the product of a different group of entrepreneurs who have undertaken such software development and servicing as their only function. Names particularly prominent in this area are CLSI, GEAC, and NOTIS. Such systems use records downloaded from the utilities

10. See the standards in ISO group 2370. See also *Standard Network Interconnection Protocols: Specification of the Protocol Layers for Open Systems Interconnection*, SNI.30 (Washington: Library of Congress, Network Development and MARC Standards Office, 1986) and *Open Systems Interconnection: The Communications Technology of the 1990's: Papers from the Pre-Conference Seminar Held at London, August 12–14, 1987*, ed. Christine H. Smith, IFLA Publications 44 (München: Saur, 1988).

as well as those locally input and support all in-house functions based on the bibliographic record. Chapter 10 deals with aspects of the user-interface for interactive searching. The ideal system for libraries of similar size and type—a so-called turnkey system whose tank could be filled with the library's records, the ignition turned on, and which would function satisfactorily ever after— proved to be a chimera. This has become a very competitive field and libraries differ from one another greatly in what they demand of an integrated processing system. Each company offers a model which it hopes might match the library's budget and stated requirements, or can be modified to do so. To describe these in any detail is beyond the scope of this book. The significant issue here is the relationship of the local processing system to the bibliographic records it uses and where they come from. A processing system must be capable of receiving a record in the now-standard (MARC) format and of interactive searching using the techniques discussed in chapter 4. Systems which do neither are still being sold, but retaining a card catalogue may be preferable to installing such a low-quality isolated system.

Data Conversion

Automation's early goals were more administration- than searcher-oriented, giving priority to economy and speed of updating rather than to completeness of data or intellectual access. Public access to an interactive catalogue is so complex a matter that it has often been a library's last, not first, step in automation. Beginning with a circulation system is more immediately cost-beneficial. It is also much simpler because it requires only a very brief machine-readable record for every publication and only one access point for each physical item, ideally just a number-code. Many administrators starting automation with a circulation control system rushed to make the system's truncated data elements and few access points (usually only natural-language ones except for the call number) available as an interactive catalogue for the public. A generation of users, especially in public and school libraries, got a very restricted view of what an interactive catalogue can do from the limited access provided by such a circulation-system-turned-catalogue. To provide *full* bibliographic records for everything in the collection under a single state-of-the-art database management system is an inevitable goal. It is usually the most costly part of an automation project and can take years to complete.

The A&I services are not troubled by the need to go back and produce machine-readable records for what had previously been listed only manually. They do not operate circulation systems. People generally search for journal articles, particularly in the sciences, only in limited and usually recent time spans. Many automated A&I databases, like their former manual cumulations, are still segmented into separate time periods so that a whole database need not be searched for each request. A library collection is different. Few users are interested in knowing what was acquired between, say, 1980 and 1984. Particularly in a search in the humanities and social sciences, it is just as important to be able to find books of a century ago as to find current publications. A library buys old as well as new publications and constantly discards items, adds copies and new editions of items already listed, changes access points and locations, etc. Its interactive catalogue must provide access to a complete but ever-changing collection. This is why the card catalogue was the ideal manual file.

The conversion of existing manual records to machine-readable form is usually called, redundantly, retrospective conversion or recon. This is more than just a matter of copying the words on the manual record; much additional coding is needed as detailed in the appendix. Any conversion project should be preceded by a re-evaluation of the collection and weeding so that more time is not spent on useless material. The databases built up for some twenty years now by the consortia and utilities are a major source of converted records for whatever conversion projects remain to be completed (see page 120). The Library of Congress' manual shelflist of some five million records created from 1898 through 1967 was converted in the largest single conversion project ever. It was done using very little professional help, so the data were sometimes distorted and/or inadequately coded; yet this database, named REMARC, is a valuable source of derived records for very old material. The CD/ROM revolution has made conversion projects more feasible by providing the entire databases of several of the utilities for in-house searching and downloading. Alternatively, it is possible to contract with one of several external agencies to do the work of matching, downloading, adapting, and uploading the final product into the library's processing system.

Careful systems analysis should try to predict future uses of the data before they are keyed the first time or converted from existing manual records in order to match the data to the capabilities of the new system. It is not usual to revise the descriptive part of a converted record to conform to current cataloguing rules because differences are rarely worth the trouble of individual review by professional staff. Controlled-vocabulary access points are another matter. These must remain consistent within the catalogue. Both name and subject access points have undergone considerable revision in recent years. When records for older material are converted, therefore, they may be passed through an authority-control program, whether in-house or, more likely, by contract with an outside agency. This identifies any controlled-vocabulary access point which does not match a currently authorized one and may even automatically change it to its current equivalent—if one has been identified as such—but the result is usually a very large number of snags to be reconciled one-by-one by a cataloguer.

Some notable cooperative conversion projects have been fostered by utilities to enlarge their databases; many are funded by governments and foundations. Because of the complexities of serial records, the ongoing CONSER (CONversion of SERials) project requires either the Library of Congress or the National Library of Canada to authenticate every record input by other cooperating libraries before it is identified as up-to-standard. By 1988, the Association of Research Libraries could announce a final assault on the records still only in card catalogues in its member libraries, so after a quarter century of automation, the prominence of data conversion as an issue in bibliographic control is finally waning.

Quality Control

Quality control as an issue, on the other hand, is increasing in prominence. Centralized cataloguing, particularly that done by source agencies (the national libraries, CIP agencies, etc.) has always brought with it assurance of relatively high quality control standards. A principal function of such an agency is to prepare a definitive bibliographic record for each document published in its country. (Only the Library of Congress accepts the broader mandate of preparing records for huge numbers of documents from outside its country.) National agencies also subscribe to, and in many cases help write, the relevant rules of practice. When other libraries contribute to a cooperative database, standards are put at some risk. The administrators in some contributing libraries exert pressure for greater productivity by cutting corners. A smaller library has fewer reference tools for checking names, subjects, etc. Any cataloguer is bound to forget an obscure rule or just to be careless from time to time. Who guarantees the quality of investigation, rule application, subject knowledge, or simply judgement? It cannot be left entirely to good will; it is too important. Yet it is impracticable to hire a staff of revisers to vet the content of every record as it enters a cooperative database. Even if possible, this would doubtless be resisted as interference. Peer pressure is a help: it becomes known very quickly which libraries often input substandard records, but is it possible or even desirable to reject their input, some of which is perfectly acceptable?

Before creating a new record for a publication, it is always necessary to determine that no record for that publication already exists in the same file. Yet if a library with a large cataloguing staff acquires two copies of the book shown in figure 1 on page 28 at different times, a cursory search under only one access point might well miss the fact that a copy is already listed in the file when the second one is searched by someone who has not seen the first. It should therefore be no surprise if each of the two different records in figure 1 find their way into that library's catalogue. No human check is possible of every record entering a union catalogue and in any case any check would be far from reliable if done without the books in hand to be visually compared if necessary. The professional editors of the NUC in Washington wrestled with the problem of whether two records represent the same item on a record-by-record basis through most of this century without always resolving it to their satisfaction. When different libraries input records for the same item into a machine-readable database and when the records can vary in some details either within the acceptable limits of the cataloguing rules' flexibility or because of outright cataloguer's error, it is impossible to write a computer program which can match the records and remove duplicates reliably without some objective identifier. This is one reason why libraries encourage the use of exact identifiers, such as the ISBN, the serial key-title, or the Library of Congress record-identifier number. Because most identifiers cannot distinguish every possible edition or state a cataloguer might wish to describe, they are imperfect for the purpose but are still better than nothing. All cooperatively built databases therefore contain unrecognized duplicates: unmatched records for what are in reality copies of the same publication. When two records are identified as relating to the same publication, some databases are designed to retain only one and append all holdings to it (see footnote 8 on page 119). A source record from a national agency is almost always preferred but if it is not available, it is again difficult to trust a computer program to judge which is the better record.

Levels of Cataloguing; Options

Much corner-cutting in cataloguing involves nothing more serious than ignoring some minor descriptive data element which another cataloguer would include in the record. Over a century ago, Charles Cutter recognized the viability of different levels of cataloguing, to which he not surprisingly attached the descriptions *short, medium,* and *full*.[11] He was not being whimsical when he cautioned "that the Short Family are not all of the same size, that there is more than one Medium, and that Full may be Fuller and Fullest."[12] AACR2 now permits the same kind of latitude in rule 1.0D and in making the inclusion of many data elements optional, for example, a second imprint, most notes, and multilingual repetitions of information on a title page. Typical guidelines for input to a common database also specify whether a code or data element is (1) absolutely required, (2) required if it applies to the particular item, or (3) entirely optional.

Even the standard-setter, the Library of Congress, creates abbreviated records for what it considers to be less important or less used material. It did what it called Limited Cataloging for many popular books between 1948 and 1963. Since 1981, the Library applies Minimal Level Cataloging to some categories of material; their records in the NUC are identified by the code MLC.[13] MLC records are in general conformity with the so-called National Level Bibliographic

11. Here, the word *levels* refers to degrees of completeness of the bibliographic record. This is totally distinct from the meaning of different levels of identity within a publication itself. The latter are discussed on pages 249–62.

12. Cutter, *Rules for a Dictionary Catalog*, p. 11.

13. *Cataloging Service Bulletin* no. 36 (spring 1987): 40–53, defines this level in detail.

Record whose "specifications are designed only for records to be contributed to a national data base, not necessarily for records for local use."[14]

Nor should the same level of detail be expected among different files maintained in the same library. Different data elements may suffice in the records of a departmental file, for materials considered ephemeral, or for items destined for storage. Within the bounds of cataloguing codes and local policies, the professional cataloguer must also be allowed to decide what bibliographic information is or is not essential in an individual case, considering the nature of the item and its local users' needs. Two records for the same item need not, therefore, be identical for both to be applications of the same standard. At one time it was quite simple to keep standard and nonstandard (never substandard!) cataloguing separate from one another: standard records went into the library's catalogue while nonstandard ones went into other physically separated files. Today, all records are more commonly loaded into linked files in a single master database for access by the same database management system. This makes it desirable to specify for each record what level of cataloguing is being applied, but this is in fact rarely done: what, after all, distinguishes "Fuller" from "Fullest" cataloguing?

Error Detection

Errors adversely affecting access are inevitably made when humans create, code, and input so many separate data elements for so many items. Some errors are caught and corrected by human proofreaders and/or by automated error-detection programs. Automated input processes, such as optical character recognition, are being developed as much to avoid human input error as to reduce labour costs. Manual filing into a card catalogue constitutes a final exercise in proofreading, especially when the filer is observant of the entire record, not just the access point being filed. Experience shows this final check to be desirable but it is not possible in an automated system. A particular problem in proofreading machine-readable bibliographic data is that the many codes it must include are not in a human language and are therefore difficult for humans to proofread. A look at the first and last records in an unrevised version of any machine-sorted file demonstrates how errors in these codes tend to cause records to display at the beginning or end of a file rather than where they belong even if the linguistic text of the record is entirely correct. At worst, a coding error can cause a program to abort a computer process and damage the file.

A good proofreader knows the types of error common in a given kind of text and where one is most likely to occur. Errors of types that can be tangibly defined can also be detected and corrected by a well-written computer program. Some help may be needed in the form of additional input; for example, a check digit is input as part of many number-based identifiers, such as the ISBN and ISSN, to

14. *National Level Bibliographic Record—Books* (Washington: Library of Congress, 1980), iii. A national-level standard has been published for books, maps, films, music, and serials.

help detect inadvertent mistranscription of numerals, (keying 12435-1 or 12245-1 instead of the correct 12345-1, where the final character is the check digit). An error-detection program then performs a mathematical calculation involving all the other digits of the number; if the result of the calculation matches the check digit, one can be about 95 percent certain that the number has been correctly transcribed. Another type of error-detection program checks that all the required areas, elements, and codes are present in a record even if it cannot ensure that the content of any of these is correct.

Authority control (see pages 76–82) is the most important form of error detection in any bibliographic system. It can be overridden; that is, a cataloguer can deliberately insert into the authority-control system an incorrect or improperly linked access point. It is also possible to apply an authorized access point to an item for which that access point is irrelevant or a poor choice. However, authority control at least ensures that any attempt to key in an access point not already accounted for by the system results in an error message, which makes the cataloguer do further checking as to what the access point should be. The name **Twaim, Mark** and the topic **HISTROY** are unlikely to appear in a file with authority control; they are all too likely to appear in a file without it. In a manual search, where the user sees many records at a glance and almost inevitably browses a bit, errors of this kind are actually less serious than in an interactive one where only what is asked for is presented on the screen. It is ironic that the manual file received that final filer's check which is impossible in the machine-readable database.

Cataloguers are not the only people who make mistakes; users make them too. Neither a person nor a computer can adequately deal with a user's totally mistaken notion of a name, title, or subject term. Every reference librarian has a stock of users' bloopers, such as the patron who asked for Norman Ward's book of humour as *My Sin, the Beer* (its actual title: *Mice in the Beer*). One cannot clutter error-detection programs or authority files with possible goofs, only with probable ones.

Revision

After all the automated systems have had their chance, it remains necessary for trained, perceptive, and experienced librarians to judge when something is going wrong and to correct and revise files constantly. Not only are there inaccuracies in every bibliographic file; a record of impeccable quality when it was created may fail to be adequate in the future because of the discovery of further facts about the item or a change of cataloguing rules. The most labour-intensive clerical operations of the pre-computer era were devoted to changing and correcting existing records. This task is never faced with much enthusiasm. It adds nothing to output statistics except those which leave an uncomfortable feeling that the work was not done properly the first time. The cost and practical difficulty of changing individual records in a large manual catalogue was long considered an insuperable barrier to accepting some rule changes even when it was acknowledged that such changes were very desirable. It is no wonder that so many rules in older cataloguing codes were written more with a view to creating a record which could stay unchanged in the catalogue forever than with a view to the user's greatest benefit (see, for example, page 172).

Automation has drastically reduced the cost of the clerical operations involved in correcting and revising. A few keystrokes take the place of (1) searching for and removing the records affected, (2) using erasers, scissors and paste, etc. to make the corrections, and (3) refiling the revised records. Computer programs that can "find and replace" in an entire file make it possible to change a character string in many records without the need to retrieve and edit each one separately. Using automated authority control, as described on page 94, makes it possible to revise an access point attached to thousands of individual document descriptions by changing one copy of that access point in a single authority record. Few changes ever require re-keying an entire record and, if they do, one might expect a revised derived copy for it to be available. Perhaps the most drastic possible revision ever required would be a change in processing systems, requiring the reloading of the entire database into a different database management system. That too is possible without re-keying much if any of the original data. Finally, in an interactive file, any change is visible to all users as soon as the file's indices have been updated.[15]

That substantive changes in cataloguing rules, subject heading practice, etc. have been particularly numerous since about 1975 is therefore no coincidence. By then, the automated methods of file maintenance briefly sketched here were available in most larger libraries: those where the resistance was the greatest when changes had to be effected manually. Today, outright hostility to rule changes comes only from those who choose not to differentiate between an error to be corrected and a new form of access point which might make the file more user-friendly or more effective. However, it is possible for two libraries to be in such different automated environments that implementing a particular change is a simple matter for one but an intractable problem for the other.

National Databases

The trendy word *networking* is applied by librarians to any kind of computer-based communication of bibliographic data, messages, etc. Its technology being

15. Any change or addition to a machine-readable file is theoretically available for output instantly, but to make it accessible, the database management system must derive from the data all the access points called for and incorporate them into the indices. Because the job of recompiling an index makes great demands on the computer's central processing unit, it is generally done overnight or on a weekend when it will not interfere with the response time for end-user searching.

now well developed, the economic and administrative implications of networking appear to be at the centre of current developments in the information professions. The emergence of every cooperative bibliographic project discussed in this chapter has helped increase librarians' awareness that financial resources for bibliographic control are not best deployed as separate, single-institution budgets but as a common, yet finite, fund with which cooperatively to establish an integrated group of databases. That there are many database vendors, several utilities, and many consortia, each a bit different in purpose and organization, is a trend toward fragmentation and therefore inefficiency. However, this historical and probably irreversible reality need not preclude exchange of data among them or the receipt of data from many by using one search command. Gateway links to the database vendors are mentioned on page 116. The three United States utilities and the Library of Congress propose to use the software of the Open Systems Interconnection (described on page 123) in the Linked Systems Project (LSP) to permit the searching of any or all of their databases from the same terminal. The Library of Congress is experimenting with allowing other institutions direct computer access to its own internal systems. It is therefore not impractical to consider the many large existing databases as together constituting a single national bibliographic database. Similar links, both technical and administrative, are being developed among the systems of different national agencies, the relationship between the Library of Congress and the National Library of Canada being a particularly close one. The national agencies of Australia, Canada, the United Kingdom, and the United States accept so many standards in common that they meet under the unlikely acronym of ABACUS to make joint policy decisions on implementing them. Such wide-ranging integration is facilitated by a fact which distinguishes the practice of libraries from that of the private A&I services—the acceptance by the former of a single standard format for their machine-readable records, namely, the MARC format (analyzed in chapter 8 and the appendix).

Centralization and cooperation thus look increasingly like two faces of the same coin. Poole's and Jewett's proposals are coming to fruition jointly and in reasonable harmony with one another. This is not a happy state of affairs for those whose livelihoods depend on the endless retyping of previously typed bibliographic data and the cataloguing anew of previously catalogued items. However, their dis-employment (or, more happily, re-deployment to other bibliographic functions) lowers the cost of creating, transcribing, and proofreading bibliographic data. More significantly, it reduces the incidence of error in the final product and makes a more comprehensive bibliographic file available to the end-user. The administrator is charged with giving higher priority to these matters than to the evils of unemployment.

II Library Standards

Part I of this book deals with principles. However specifically and practically these may have been elucidated, the reader is likely to reach this point frustrated by uncertainty about which keys to hit at the input keyboard when creating or searching for a single real record in a single real file. This may stem from the fact that part I deals with the construction and use of records in *all* types of bibliographic file: the A&I publication and the monographic bibliography as well as the library catalogue. While the basic principles are the same for all, their specific implementation differs, from very little to considerably, among these types of file.

The least degree of standardization is to be found among the monographic bibliographies. As often as not, the compiler of one of these adheres only selectively to pre-existing standards for selecting and arranging data elements, for formulating individual access points, for dividing the database into subfiles, or even for alphanumeric arrangement. The full records in these bibliographies are most often arranged according to a classification scheme, but rather than use an existing one, such as the Dewey Decimal Classification, it is most common for the compiler of such a bibliography to create a new one ad hoc. This does not mean that monographic bibliographies are either poorly constructed or hard to use—provided each is internally consistent—but it does mean that the user cannot unthinkingly transfer a known searching procedure from one list to another. There is somewhat greater similarity among the A&I publications. The user may expect those published by the same firm (for example, the H.W. Wilson Company) to be much like one another. Similarly, the tools produced by different A&I services are likely to be organized in much the same way and to use similar access-point terminology when they cover the same subject field. The database vendors described on pages 115–17 also impose common search commands and output formats on the different databases they service even when the print versions of those databases differ considerably.

It is in the construction and use of library catalogues that adherence to national and international standards is pursued most actively and has been so pursued for the longest time, largely for the reasons of cooperation discussed in chapter 5 and implicit throughout this book. A notable peaking of interest in library-catalogue standardization in the last quarter of the nineteenth century resulted in the adoption of a common technology (the file of unit records on cards), a common basic arrangement (the single-sequence dictionary catalogue), common cataloguing and filing rules (in North America, those of Charles Ammi Cutter), a common classification scheme (that of Melvil Dewey), and a common philosophy of bibliographic service. The latter is perhaps best shown by the establishment within a year of each other in 1876/77 of national library associations on both sides of the Atlantic whose primary focus of interest for the remainder of the century was the cataloguing function, broadly interpreted.

The chapters of part II and the appendix explore in some detail the standards and practices now widely followed by libraries in creating and communicating their catalogue records. These standards and practices deal with: controlled-vocabulary name access points (chapter 6), subject access points in both words and classification symbols (chapter 7), description and formatting (chapter 8), and the alphanumeric arrangement, or filing, of access points (chapter 9). Chapter 10 on the user-interface is less a description of practice than a description of the search for some common practice. This is at present the least standardized part of the provision of bibliographic services in libraries. The technical description of the MARC format in the appendix arises out of all the preceding since that format is the basis for automating the entire record. Because these chapters are based on the principles analyzed in part I, some repetition or rephrasing of those principles is unavoidable in sketching the context of the topics raised in this part. The connection with chapters 3 and 4 is particularly close since so much of part II deals with access.

For up to a century, the practices described in the following chapters have been carefully thought out, integrated, and continuously revised both to meet users' needs and to match the technologies available at any given time for file maintenance, searching, and communication. Those other than librarians who compile bibliographic tools are also intelligent enough not to reinvent the whole wheel if only a new spoke design is wanted. They copy and/or imitate established library practices in whole or in part as they find them relevant and affordable.

What Is a Bibliographic Standard?

Library practices are based on standardized methods of description based on the data elements described in chapter 2 and the provision of access points as described in chapter 3. The use of the computer has made standardization even more important than before. Human nature being what it is, however, there is never only one accepted way of doing anything that can involve different purposes, processes, costs, or historical antecedents. Bibliographic standards do not even have the compelling force of the standard that requires a current of 110 volts (more or less) to run the electrical appliances in a North American home. Using a bibliographic file that departs from recognized standards occasions neither physical disaster nor, in a stable person, emotional trauma. A catalogue card measuring 3-by-5 inches is functional despite its slight departure from the standard measurement of 7.5-by-12.5 centimetres. It is not hard to recognize a series statement that precedes an imprint in a citation even if library cataloguing rules would locate it after the collation. One can write a program in a number of ways for an independent computer-based system and still achieve the desired result. However, if common basic practices are applied in producing different files or in using different systems to maintain and search them, then

1) records can be interchanged among them
2) a person consulting more than one such file becomes familiar with the pattern and can more easily find and interpret the relevant data and
3) the same programs can be used to process records coming from various sources.

Reasonable people are persuaded that there are more advantages than disadvantages to standardization and eventually one particular practice gains overwhelming favour while its competitors wither from disuse. When consensus is well enough advanced in a particular area, the prevailing practice is usually codified formally by a representative committee of practitioners who ensure that it is stated as clearly and comprehensively as possible. This codification is a standard, whether it is formally ratified by an officially recognized body or only informally but widely implemented in practice.

National and International Standards

Variations in bibliographic practices in different countries or among quite separate user groups (for example, school librarians in Indonesia and medical-journal editors in London) are tolerable to the degree that their worlds remain separate. However, the integrating computer has made a global village of the whole bibliographic world. The sheer cost of redundant programming would have imposed common standards and practices even if record sharing were not imperative. In every field it touches, computerization has the salutary effect of demanding an answer to the question "Why is *this* done differently from *that*?" Idiosyncratic variants tend to disappear for the sake of closer compatibility when the answer is "I don't know." The development of international standards for manual library catalogues took about a hundred years; for computerized ones, it took about ten.

Being relatively rich, libraries throughout the English-speaking world have been able to devote much professional staff time to the formal codification of bibliographic practices. Active Anglo-American cooperation is almost a century old although interrupted by periods of apathy and by the inactivity imposed by two wars. This cooperation formed the basis for broader-based international cooperation after the Second World War when existing Anglo-American initiatives were expanded, notably under the aegis of IFLA (particularly its programme now named the Universal Bibliographic Control and International MARC Programme) and by Unesco (particularly its General Information Programme (PGI) and its role in the United Nations Information System in Science and Technology (UNISIST)). The projects of IFLA in particular are forwarded largely through the volunteer work of committee members from many countries who have the vision, political acumen, and fund-raising ability needed (Unesco often provides the funding for IFLA projects). Even where a particular standard is developed under other auspices, its approval by one or another of these bodies can help foster widespread adoption.

The ultimate international standard-approving organization is the International Organization for Standardization (ISO). Both the original initiative for a new standard and the ultimate responsibility for announcing it and persuading people to implement it rest with ISO's component national bodies, for example, the British Standards Institute (BSI), the Canadian Standards Association (CSA), and the American National Standards Institute (ANSI). Each national body activates a technical committee to deal with a particular issue, be it the pitch of a screw thread or how to cite the publication facts of a book. The ANSI subcommittee formerly known as Z39: Library and Information Sciences and Related Publishing Practices was renamed the National Information Standards Organization (NISO) in 1985. This is the agency whose publications are best known in North America in this field. It is a grass-roots organization composed of representatives of various library associations, library consortia, the association of A&I services, the database vendors, the bibliographic utilities, etc. NISO and its counterparts in other countries have taken a number of prevailing bibliographic practices through the rigours of adoption by ISO Technical Committee 46 (Information and Documentation) or Joint Technical Committee 1 (Information Processing Systems), and to eventual publication as ISO standards.[1]

Bibliographic practices, however widespread, are not necessarily ratified as standards in this fullest sense of the word; many have not yet been, and may never be, subjected to ISO scrutiny. The following chapters are based on existing ISO standards and on Anglo-American, or even just North American, de facto standards; in other words, on what tends to be done in libraries. The author's nationality is the only justification for the frequent choice of Canadian examples, including the detailed tabulation of the Canadian version of the MARC format in the appendix.

---

1. These are the many bibliographically related standards consolidated in *Documentation and Information*, 3rd ed., ISO Standards Handbook 1 (Geneva: ISO Central Secretariat, 1988).

Compatibility

A standard should provide (1) a unified structure, (2) a statement of minimum expectations, and (3) guidelines to determine when absolute uniformity in execution is essential and when it is not. The most frequent reason for ignoring a standard is the perception that it is too difficult or costly to adopt or that it is unnecessary. It is therefore desirable for a standard, particularly one ratified at the international level, to be as flexible as its purposes permit. The larger and the smaller, the richer and the poorer, the general and the specialized institutions of the world can then reasonably aspire to adhere to it instead of simply ignoring it. What is needed is compatibility, not necessarily uniformity of a product down to the last comma. The 1949 cataloguing code set out to "meet the present day needs of the cataloger in the large scholarly or specialized collection." Its 1967 successor, in operation until 1980 in a large part of the library community, was "drawn up primarily to respond to the need of general research libraries." In effect, these codes prescribed one way of making a catalogue record: the way of the Library of Congress. Even if such rigid uniformity were desirable, it is simply an impossible goal and a majority of libraries could, at least in some details, legitimately ignore those rules as being irrelevant to them. AACR2 more closely matches the characteristics of a good standard; for example, it permits the use of any of three levels of descriptive detail in rule 1.0D and allows different script- and language-forms of name access points in rules such as 22.3C2 and 24.3A. It can claim to be practicable in "general libraries of all sizes and types" while still leading to the formulation of compatible records. In the same way, not every library using the MARC format for machine-readable records fills in every possible processing or searching code. The resultant record may not be as complete but different database management systems can accept and process it satisfactorily.

Most bibliographic operations are relatively free of controversial political, linguistic, racial, and cultural implications. In the area of subject analysis treated in chapter 7, this is not possible. There can be no totally objective view of the subject of any document because it is seen differently in different cultures, in different contexts, and when approached for different purposes—or even for the same purpose by different people. All the natural problems of intelligent communication interfere with the unambiguous expression of subject content, whether through words as subject access points or through the logical juxtapositions of a classification scheme. While it is possible for chapter 7 to discuss internally consistent and compatible systems of producing effective subject indices, it is not possible to ensure that two different indexers will approach the content of a particular document from the same point of view and therefore come up with the same subject-indexing terms for it. This ultimate impossibility of uniform subject analysis for all purposes is reason enough for the same item to be indexed over and over again in different ways in different subject-oriented lists. It is also the reason why people accessing bibliographic records for interlibrary-loan and any international purposes rely on name/title and code-number access points rather than on subject/classification access points. The former are all objective, the latter highly subjective, in their application.

Libraries versus A&I Services

Libraries and the A&I services have remained as separated in how they use and prepare bibliographic standards as in how they create and disseminate bibliographic records as described in chapter 5. Of the two international bodies named above, IFLA's focus of attention is libraries, while Unesco also pays considerable attention to the A&I services. It may not be possible or even desirable to merge the functional aspects of the two types of bibliographic service, but efforts to do so through standards flexible enough to meet their differing needs are having some success. Examples are: (1) the Common Communication Format described on page 249 and (2) the Guidelines for the Application of the ISBDs to the Description of Component Parts described on page 236.

De-Standardization

For a hundred years, every informed user of a manual library catalogue knew what a unit record should look like and which few of its data elements could be accessed directly. The interactive catalogue revolutionized access techniques as described in chapter 4. Rather than foster a new standardization, the (perhaps temporary) effect has been the opposite. Libraries have been experimenting for the past decade to determine what is both economically practicable and sufficient to meet user needs in searching the interactive catalogue. For example, while everyone agrees on providing access to any title-word (other than words such as articles, on a stop-list), just what *is* the title for this purpose? Is it enough to make the title proper accessible in this way or should subtitle(s), parallel title(s), title(s) in notes, etc. be included? When a date is made searchable, should it only be to qualify a term from another field or fields using a boolean or relational operator? But which fields? The *total* access now possible is usually considered impracticable and probably undesirable. If a library offered full-text searching of the entire record, the user would be able to determine which items are written by persons who use the given name John: perhaps a waste of resources. Is it also a waste of resources to make single words of the unstructured fields of general cataloguers' notes accessible? A system might pass the buck by giving the user the option of designating, for each particular search, which specified fields are to be searched word by word. At the same time, most of the old manual conventions of designating only certain data elements as accessibile have been carried over into the formatting and coding of machine-readable library records for interactive files because such conventions are still sensible ways of choosing and displaying access points when a whole interactive file is output in batch mode onto microform or the printed page.

Each database vendor, bibliographic utility, and individual library makes its own decision as to what functions it is willing or able to support using its chosen database management system. Once the decision is made, however, it is very costly and disruptive to change either that decision or the whole system. As interactive systems are newly designed with an unprejudiced attitude toward the needs and reactions of both end-users and librarians, almost every access possibility is being tested somewhere. Thus the user who has finally mastered the new interactive techniques in searching one file must alter the search strategy when approaching another. The library catalogue in particular, which was once virtually the same in every library, now differs, sometimes considerably, from library to library. Even different databases within the same library often have different access parameters, a difficulty more likely to affect the librarian who has access to all of them than the end-user who is given access only to some. A written description of the system's features clarifies the simpler aspects of searching to end-users but the more sophisticated ones often remain a mystery to all but the most determined or frequent user. The library upgrades the access capabilities of its system when and as it can afford to do so; to its users this is yet another confusing change, particularly when clearly written documentation of changes lags behind their implementation, as it so often does. In summary, both the appearance of, and accessibility to, bibliographic records in files have become de-standardized. There is at present no recognized standard for interactive searching analogous to the one implicit in the rules and practices of constructing manual catalogues. Although there is no compelling need for the same degree of uniformity familiar in manual catalogues to obtain in a more flexible technology, users have a right to *some* greater degree of common expectations in the future.

6

CONTROLLED-
VOCABULARY
NAME ACCESS
POINTS

A name uniquely identifies

1) a person
2) a corporate body, for example, a society, an institution, a business, government, or a government agency
3) a place: a definable geographic location or feature or a jurisdiction known by a place name
4) a work or
5) a publication or document.

This chapter deals with issues of vocabulary control in establishing access points for individuals in the first four categories: persons, bodies, places, and works.

The fifth category, the name of a publication or document per se, is *not* subject to authority control. The implications of this are discussed in this paragraph and are then taken for granted throughout the chapter. The practical difference between a work and the document (publication) which embodies it was first discussed on page 11 and has arisen at several subsequent points. The name of a document is its title proper, something imposed by its author, editor, printer, or publisher. Whether that title proper is accessible only by its first word other than an article (as in the traditional library card catalogue) or by *any* significant keyword (as in some older manual lists and generally now in interactive files), its wording cannot be tampered with. A title is a title is a title. However, publications with different titles may contain the same *work*; for example, *Matthew's Good News*, *The Life and Work of Christ as told by Matthew*, and *L'Evangile selon Mathieu* are all differently titled versions of one work: St. Matthew's

Gospel.[1] When two or more publications bearing different titles proper but containing the same work exist, some users want only one particular version of the work; in that case, its publication-title or some other data element identifies the desired one. More often, however, *any* version of the work (in a language the user can read) will serve. The user is assured of finding them all in a single file location or by a single search command only when a work-title is imposed on all of them and is linked to all the different publication-titles. This work-title is known to cataloguers as a uniform title. Being constructed by the cataloguer according to a rule, it *is* subject to vocabulary control; for example, **Bible. New Testament. Gospels. Matthew** is the uniform title for the above work according to AACR2 (see pages 167–68). In other words, using a publication-title access point retrieves one document; using a work-title access point retrieves all the documents containing one work regardless of their publication-titles.

Any name may be a subject access point as well as an access point of another type; that is, any person, corporate body, place, work, or publication can be the topic of another document. Someone may write a book about Mother Teresa, or about the Sony Corporation, or about the United States Presidency, or about the Loire Valley, or about Homer's *Odyssey*, or about a single copy of the First Folio (the 1623 printing of Shakespeare's plays). When a name is used as a subject access point, it is reasonable to expect to find it in a subject index in the same form as when it is used in a name or author index. It makes no sense, for example, to use **Twain** as the authorized access element for books *by* the writer of *Tom Sawyer* but **Clemens** for books *about* the same person, regardless of whether authors and subjects are interfiled in a single sequence in a dictionary catalogue or are kept in separate indices. This chapter therefore deals also with the establishment of names as subject access points. Since users are also better served if the same form of a name is used in different catalogues, bibliographies, and A&I publications, librarians are at some pains to encourage the use of their standards and rules of name-identification in other bibliographic sources.

Names are as objective as are numbers. References to James Earl Carter, Jr., to Jimmy Carter, to the 39th President of the United States, or to the Governor of Georgia in 1975 all point to the same man; but if one gets a detail wrong and says Jack Carter, or the 38th President, or the Governor of South Carolina, the message is garbled. A user may or may not know whether the surname of a particular person is spelled Smith, Smythe, Smithe, or Smyth, or recall whether the corporate body wanted is the Department of Education, the Ministry of Education, or the Education Department; but like a publication with its explicit and fixed title, so a person, body, or place does not have some vague name whose form may be this or that depending on the user's whim. Even if there is more than one name, each is precise and objectively determinable like the title

---

1. That this work is also part of a larger work, the Bible, is a separate issue (see page 167); because this one Gospel may reasonably be sought independently in a file, it warrants its own access point just as if it were an independent work.

on a title page. These objective forms must be respected when access points are established even if it is desirable also to include some additional forms as cross-reference links.

Name Authority Work

Name authority work involves the processes introduced on page 76:

1) determining all the names, including all their variant forms, which have actually been used in documents to identify the individual person, body, place, or work at issue
2) choosing one of these (if more than one exist) as a preferred name or form to act as the primary identifier of the person, body, etc.
3) presenting the preferred name or form in such a way that it can be most readily located in an alphanumeric file and most surely distinguished from all other names in the same file and
4) either
   a) (in a manual file): linking all other names or forms under which a user might reasonably look for the person, body, etc. to the preferred form by means of visible cross-references (see page 78)

   or
   b) (in an interactive file): linking all relevant access points for the same person, body, etc.—preferred and non-preferred—directly to each bibliographic record involving that person, body, etc., as shown in figure 13 on page 79.

The last three of these functions require the application of cataloguing rules but are not the costly and time-consuming ones. Only when the first function is complete can the cataloguing rule be applied to the facts discovered; it is the discovery of those facts that takes time. The search for them, although theoretically exhaustive, is necessarily limited in practice. The reasonable cataloguer searches for any clue to the existence of a problem with the name in question in biographies, directories, gazetteers, etc. but must sense when to give up if no problem surfaces. If the name appears in an existing authority record known to have been compiled according to the same rules, it is accepted and copied (downloaded) into the local authority file just as derived bibliographic records are downloaded into the local bibliographic file. Not surprisingly, the Library of Congress and other national agencies do most of the world's authority work and are the prime sources of authority records for others to use.

Scope of the Problem

Although some investigation must be done on every name encountered, only a small percentage of persons and works offer any real problem in vocabulary control. Counts of random samples have consistently shown that more than 60 percent of the persons whose names appear in a library catalogue as authors are so represented for only one work each; the chance of any problematic variation, although always present, is therefore small. Similarly, the vast majority of all published works have appeared only once and under only one title. The potential for conflicting or confusing title citations in such cases is reduced to instances of outright error either in the cataloguer's transcription or the searcher's recollection. No amount of vocabulary control can guarantee against confusion if the user asks for *My Sin, the Beer* (see page 129) or if the cataloguer has absent-mindedly keyed in *The History of England in the Middle Ages* when the title page reads *The Story of England in the Middle Ages*. Corporate bodies and works which are translated and/or frequently republished are found at the other extreme in the scale of difficulty. These are a magnet for bibliographic problems. Special precautions are wisely taken when dealing with any instance of one of their names or titles.

On first encounter with the name of a given person, body, place, or work, it is possible to investigate other names or name forms by which that person, etc. is known now or has become known in the past. This is the extent of the concern of those A&I services which pay any attention to authority control. In a unified and dynamic file like a library catalogue, however, an access point established today may affect one to be established years later. The catalogue of a general library typically includes names of all periods and cultures. Its records are also created cooperatively over an indefinite time period by many different cataloguers in different libraries. Library cataloguing rules are therefore particularly complex; they must deal with problems in this area which are present only to a lesser degree, or are ignored, in other bibliographic tools.

Vocabulary Control and Computer Searching

Personal name forms have been subject to authority control for centuries, and not only in library catalogues. Chinese, Hungarians, Japanese, and some others speak and write their names as they access them in an alphabetic listing, that is, beginning with the most significant (but not necessarily most clearly identifying) element: the family or clan name. The development of surnames in the West many centuries ago led people to become accustomed to looking for Hector Smith's name among the Smiths, not among the Hectors, however much more distinctive and easily searchable Hector might be than Smith. Interactive files and post-coordinate access do not change this. The structure of personal names is commonly known to end-users and name access points are formalized according to that structure precisely to make their location simpler regardless of whether manual or automated techniques are used. It would simply not be efficient to post-coordinate the surname **Cooper** with the given name **Richard**, making the computer locate a few hundred Coopers in the file, and some thousands of Richards, then sort through them all to find the two or three different Richard Coopers in the file. A controlled-vocabulary personal-name access point is intended to be used as a pre-coordinate unit.

The typical corporate name is more complex than personal names, its structure not always so predictable by the end-user. It can be a great help to be able to search for any significant word in it, singly or in combination, particularly when

1) the user is likely to remember only one or a few words within the full name

2) the access element for the name of a subordinate body is the name of its parent body (see page 157) or

3) a corporate name begins with a term so frequently used in the file that browsing, or even understanding the filing sequence, under that term is difficult, for example, **United States**.

A combination of truncation and post-coordination enables the user to search, for example, for any access point which includes **Canad?** *AND* **Environ?**, thus retrieving the access points for the (hypothetical) government agencies **Canada. Department of the Environment** and **Canadian Environmental Pollution Study Group** and for the nongovernmental body **Canadian Association for the Protection of the Environment**. Retrieving a conference name is simplified if one can, for example, *FIND* (**Confer?** *OR* **Sympos?** *OR* **Workshop?**) *AND* (**Astronom?** *OR* **Astrophys?**) *AND* >**1985**. Despite all these benefits of keyword access to corporate names, satisfactory results from a search of this type are much more likely when the terms being post-coordinated are themselves part of controlled-vocabulary access points than when they are only part of the natural language of titles, abstracts, text, etc. This is because invoking any part of a controlled vocabulary also brings into play its cross-reference links, which are absent from natural-language searching. Vocabulary control is therefore the key to efficient name retrieval from any file and is taken for granted in the rest of this chapter. What follows may at first glance seem to apply more to the manual catalogue (where the user finds item-descriptions attached only to the preferred form of name) than to the interactive catalogue (where all access points, preferred and other, are attached automatically to those descriptions). Nevertheless, a preferred form is still required in an interactive system as a basis for the required links in the authority file.

Cataloguing Rules for Name Access Points

Common rules for establishing name access points have been followed in libraries throughout the English-speaking world for a century. These rules, developed through United States/United Kingdom cooperation, have spread to many non-English-speaking countries. At the same time, somewhat differing cataloguing traditions were also being developed, for example, those in France and Germany. All rules must be re-examined and some changed from time to time because of changing purposes of the catalogue, changing technologies, and changing conventions in how people, corporate bodies, and governments choose to name themselves. After a long period of only minor tampering with the late-nineteenth-century English-language rules, a major change was promulgated in 1967. The pre-1967 practices are based on Charles Ammi Cutter's 1876 *Rules for a Dictionary Catalog*. Every reference librarian must still learn its salient features because they remain embedded in older published bibliographies and library catalogues. The English-language codes in direct descent from Cutter's are (1) the so-called Joint Code of 1908, (2) its 1941 preliminary second edition, and (3) its 1949 second edition. The 1908 rules, called Joint because of formal consultation between cataloguers in the United States and the United Kingdom, largely represent the Library of Congress' adaptation of Cutter's rules to a large academic collection. As these rules were used over the next three decades, the Library of Congress made many changes recorded only in its in-house files. When the need for thorough revision became urgent, the United Kingdom had gone to war, so both the 1941 draft revision and the 1949 completion of a second edition were published and widely adopted only in North America.

In October, 1961, the International Conference on Cataloguing Principles (ICCP) in Paris successfully reconciled many of the differences among Anglo-American, French, German, and other cataloguing traditions inasmuch as they affect name and/or title access to records in library catalogues. The resulting twelve so-called Paris Principles form the basis of the English-language code named the Anglo-American Cataloguing Rules (AACR) whose first edition (AACR1) appeared in 1967, followed by a considerably refined second edition (AACR2) in 1978 and a revision of the latter in 1988 (AACR2R).[2] Among the rules to appear in languages other than English based on the Paris Principles, some (for example, the Regeln für die alphabetischen Katalogisierung (RAK)) were independently written, but the majority are direct translations or adaptations of AACR. IFLA, which sponsored the Paris Conference, has also issued a num-

2. All editions of AACR as well as Cutter's code and the 1908 and 1941 ones include rules for description whose history is sketched in chapter 8. The 1949 code deals with nothing more than the choice and form of name and title access points, the topics of this chapter. Only Cutter's code deals also with subject access points and filing (see chapters 7 and 9). To locate full citations, the titles of the codes since Cutter's are: 1908 (American edition): *Catalog Rules, Author and Title Entries*; 1908 (British edition): *Catalogue Rules, Author and Title Entries*; 1941: *A.L.A. Cataloging Rules, Author and Title Entries*; 1949: *A.L.A. Cataloging Rules for Author and Title Entries*; 1967 (American edition): *Anglo-American Cataloging Rules*; 1967 (British edition): *Anglo-American Cataloguing Rules*; 1978 and 1988: *Anglo-American Cataloguing Rules*. The proceedings of the Paris Conference were published in 1963 by the Conference Organizing Committee with the conference name as title. The Paris Principles are in *Statement of Principles Adopted at the International Conference on Cataloguing Principles, Paris, October, 1961*, annotated edition with commentary and examples by Eva Verona [et al.] (London: IFLA Committee on Cataloguing, 1971).

ber of both general and more specific guidelines for the formulation of difficult name access points conforming to the Paris Principles in the hope that they will foster increasing international standardization.[3]

Conformity with the Paris Principles and particularly with AACR has become the cornerstone of the standardization of name access points in the world's major libraries and national bibliographies. However, it took time for the sometimes radical changes brought about by the ICCP to replace older practices. In existing catalogues, this could usually be done only piecemeal if at all. In the Anglo-American library world, the period from 1967 to 1981 was therefore one of major turmoil in the maintenance of library catalogues as the 1967 and 1978 stages of AACR development and the policy known as superimposition (see page 173) mingled these problems with the upheavals of catalogue automation.

In the remainder of this chapter, each of the four categories of controlled-vocabulary name—of a person, a body, a place, and a work—is treated separately. In discussing the principles and rules involved,

1) a problem is identified
2) examples are provided to show something of the range of situations encountered
3) valid criteria on which to base a solution are evaluated and
4) both the pre-1967 and the current English-language library cataloguing rules related to the problem are briefly described and, where relevant, contrasted with each other.

Personal Names

Many women still change name on marriage. Other legal changes of name are common. People may not only acquire but also renounce titles of nobility or be entitled to use terms of honorific address. Many writers and performers use pseudonyms, sometimes more than one simultaneously. By far the most common variant from use of the full official name is the use of a form in which some part is omitted or reduced to an initial letter. Thus a person may be identified by one or more of the following types of name:

1) the complete personal name given by the parents and legally registered in an office of vital statistics, for example, Mary Roberta Smith
2) any title bestowed by a monarch or the state, or inherited, for example, The Marchioness of Bucktooth; Prime Minister of Lower Slobbovia

---

3. For example, *List of Uniform Titles for Liturgical Works of the Latin Rites of the Catholic Church*, 2nd ed., 1981; *List of Uniform Headings for Higher Legislative and Ministerial Bodies of European Countries*, 2nd ed. rev., 1979; *Anonymous Classics, a List of Uniform Headings for European Literatures*, 1978. All are published in London by the former IFLA International Office for UBC whose publications are now handled by the British Library.

3) any kind of abbreviation of any of the above, for example, Mary R. Smith; M. Roberta Smith; M.R. Smith; Lady Bucktooth; The P.M.
4) any nickname, known to many or to few, for example, Bobbie; Buckie; Cuddles
5) any pseudonym (a name designed to conceal identity), for example, Agent 009; M.R.S.; Jane Doe
6) any name which represents a formal change from a previous name or title, for example, Mrs. John Young; The Duchess of Worcester.

A significant number of persons identified in bibliographic lists appear in their own works or in reference sources under more than one name and/or form of name. In the course of an ordinary lifetime, almost everyone uses and/or is known by quite a number of different names. There is a time and an occasion for each.

Choice of Name

To choose a preferred name or name form from among the different ones available, it is equally reasonable to apply either of two principles. Which is better depends on the purpose of the list in which the name appears and on other circumstances. According to the principle adopted for cataloguing rules before AACR, the access point should be based on the full official personal name as it would appear on the person's birth certificate or most recent passport, preferring the latter if there has been any formal change of name. If the person possesses a legally conferred title, this principle calls for the use of the most recent title along with the personal name. The advantages of adopting this principle are stability and objectivity. There can be no doubt as to what the full official name is once it has been found, and it is rarely formally changed. The chief disadvantages are that (1) it can be difficult to discover the full official name of, for example, Dr. X. or J.L. Smith, and (2) the average searcher may not readily recognize a person by that name, for example, Thomas Edward Lawrence, George Herman Ruth, and Friedrich Hardenberg. This principle is still valid for indices where stability of naming and legal identification are prime requirements, for example, in archival finding aids.

A contrary but equally reasonable principle was adopted by the ICCP and is embodied in AACR. It requires the access point to be based on the name encountered commonly or most frequently, be it a name given at birth or acquired late, a title, a pseudonym, etc. Principal evidences of such common usage for authors are the formal statements of responsibility in publications of the author's work issued in his or her own language. For persons not known as authors, what prevails is the cumulative evidence of how the person is referred to in other publications in the person's language or place of residence. The advantages and disadvantages of this solution are the converse of the preceding. This principle works best for the user who approaches a name index from a footnote citation, from a title page of a publication, or from a newspaper article or magazine story. The name form found in these places is also the one most likely to reflect the preferences of the person in question and therefore to be perpetuated on title pages, in reference books, and in general usage, for example, T.E. Lawrence (or Lawrence of Arabia), Babe Ruth, and Novalis for the three persons whose official names were given in the previous paragraph.

The chief disadvantage of this new approach is the instability of the resultant access points in the case of living persons, who are notoriously fickle in their use of different name-forms at different times of their lives. Consider the following not improbable situation: A first work of an author bears the name John L. Smith on the title page. The same person is identified in his next two works as J.L. Smith while the title pages of his fourth and fifth works once again identify him as John L. Smith. He dies, and his second work is reissued using his full name, John Llewellyn Smith. If a library acquires each of these publications in the order in which they are published and follows the AACR rule literally, the preferred access point for Mr. Smith's name must be reformulated three times. The first book generates the preferred form **Smith, John L.** After the third book has arrived, the preferred form must be changed to **Smith, J.L.** The form **Smith, John L.** is once again the correct form on the arrival of the fifth book. If the library does not acquire all six publications, it is still necessary to discover what form of name appeared on the ones not acquired in order to apply the current principle. Prior to 1967, the only preferred form from the arrival of the first book was **Smith, John Llewellyn**, a form the cataloguer would have had to discover externally and a form not sanctioned at any time by the current rules. Fortunately, this example illustrates an exception, not the norm: most persons identified in library catalogues are obscure authors of a single work, persons not readily found in biographical sources. For these, the current rule, which does not require a reference search for the full official name in every case, is a great economy as well as a more adequate answer for most user needs. However, enough investigation is always needed to satisfy that no pseudonym, etc. is involved.

The preceding assumes that a person known by more than one name remains the same person and should therefore be identified by only one preferred access point. The possibility of computer linkages diminishes the importance of this and public libraries have long urged that a person clearly identified differently for different writings should be permitted to have more than one preferred access point, for example, **Carroll, Lewis** for fantasy writings and **Dodgson, Charles L.** for mathematical writings. The 1978 AACR2 opened the door to this by permitting it as an option, the 1988 revision requires it if, in the cataloguer's judgement, the person intends to hold two different identities simultaneously.

Formal Change of Name. Notwithstanding the above, both old and new rules require the preferred access point to be changed immediately on a deliberate formal change of name, for example, from **Clay, Cassius** to **Ali, Muhammad**. No matter how well known the former name, and even if it continues in occasional use, its owner intends a different name to replace it. The same is also true in case of acquisition of a title, assumption by a woman of her husband's surname on marriage, etc. Rules have always left the cataloguer some latitude for judgement, providing for the retention of an earlier name if it appears likely to remain the common identification of the person. Thus John Buchan's title, Lord Tweedsmuir, would not be adopted as the basis for an access point under either old or new rules since he continues to be best known as an author who used his personal name, not his title, on the title pages of his works.

Language. When the community of European writers was more international, a personal name might appear on title pages in any of several languages; for example, the seventeenth-century Flemish Scripture commentator Cornelius van den Steen published principally under the Latin form of his name (Cornelius a Lapide), but is also known by the Greek one (Cornelius Petros) and the French one (Corneille de la Pierre). Old rules never allowed translation of any element of a personal name, preferring the use of the person's vernacular, for example, Juan de la Cruz; Quintus Horatius Flaccus. AACR makes an exception for (1) Romans of classical times and (2) persons not identified by a surname. If a name in one of these two categories commonly appears in English-language reference tools in an English-language form, that is preferred, for example, **John, of the Cross**; **Horace**. The language-related problem of romanization, or transliteration, which may occur in any kind of name access point, is discussed on pages 275–79.

Choice of Access Element

By almost universal convention, a name of modern times appears in an alphabetic list arranged under the surname or family name regardless of where that appears when the name is written in direct order. Any given name(s) and/or initial(s) follow after a comma, for example, **Rogers, J. Eliot**; **Deng, Xiaoping**. However,

1) a compounded or prefixed surname consists of more than one unit, perhaps leaving uncertainty as to which should serve as the access element, for example, Richard Dennis Hilton Smith, Karel ten Hoope
2) the preferred name chosen according to the preceding criteria may not contain a surname at all, for example, Saint Catherine of Siena.

In these two cases, old and new rules are almost identical. If no surname exists, the name is filed under its first element as it is spoken, for example, **Catherine, of Siena**; **Leonardo, da Vinci**. In the case of a compound surname or a surname involving a prefix, the access element is that under which the surname normally appears in alphabetic lists in the person's own language, for example, **De la Mare, Walter**; **Gaulle, Charles de**; **La Fontaine, Jean de**. Acquaintance with different linguistic and national usages is needed to apply this principle.[4] When a title of nobility is part of the chosen name, the proper word in the title is the access element and the personal name is given between it and the rank, for example, **Devonshire, Spencer Compton Cavendish, Duke of.**

Qualifier(s)

Cataloguing rules are based on the assumption that a unique access point should identify each individual person, body, etc. A qualifier of some kind is therefore needed if the access points for two different entities would otherwise be identical. Qualifiers available to distinguish persons include birth and/or death dates, occupation, place of residence, and academic degrees. Dates, the most objective and stable qualifier, have always been preferred in cataloguing rules, but when it is known what the initials in a name stand for, new rules allow these to be added as a qualifier; for example, if two persons are commonly known as T.S. Eliot and their full names can be determined, the appropriate access points are **Eliot, T.S. (Terence Stephen)** and **Eliot, T.S. (Thomas Stearns).** This separates their two access points and identifies each person yet ensures that both are accessible under the best-known form—the one containing initials. Since names which lack a surname are very likely to be common to many people, both old and new rules require a qualifier stating an office, epithet, rank, status, etc. to be added to the access element, for example, **John, King of England; John Paul I, Pope;** and **John, the Baptist.**

Nongovernment Corporate Bodies

A corporate body is a person or group of persons which chooses to act as an entity under an identity and a name other than that of any one person. Thus John Smith is a person but John Smith, Inc. is a corporate body. A modern, nongovernment, legally incorporated body is easily recognizable because a government registrar has ascertained that its proposed name is distinctive and unambiguous for its purpose and has caused it to be officially gazetted. In bibliographic files, it is not possible to restrict the notion of a corporate name to one thus legally authorized in at least two areas:

1) Corporate bodies breed separately identifiable subordinate units. If all the materials produced by the American Library Association were subfiled by title without grouping items emanating from each separate

4. A number of reference sources exist to provide this acquaintance, for example, *Names of Persons: National Usages for Entry in Catalogues*, 3rd ed., compiled by the IFLA International Office for UBC (London: The Office, 1977), and its 1980 Supplement; also *Naming Systems of Ethnic Groups: a Language Guide for Departmental Staff* (Canberra?: Department of Social Security, Migrant Services Section, 1987).

component association, section, committee, discussion group, etc., the resulting arrangement would not adequately serve the user who identifies a topic or report with one of these subunits. In other words, even if the Subject Analysis Committee is not a separate legal entity, it must be separately identifiable in an access point. Similarly, in referring to a publication by or about the Library of Vancouver Community College, it is the library which must ultimately be identified, not the college as a whole, and not the college's hierarchical superior, the provincial government's Ministry of Advanced Education.

2) A catalogue must also provide access points for ad hoc bodies, such as conferences, fairs, or projects, despite the problems of doing so. The world's fair known as Expo 67 is in this sense a different corporate body from the Canadian Corporation for the 1967 World Exhibition, the legally recognized body which signed contracts and paid bills on behalf of the fair.

What Is a Corporate Name?

Whether a corporate body exists for cataloguing purposes therefore depends not on what the body can do or what its legal status is but on whether it bears something recognizable as a name. Isolating a name as such from the rest of the wording on a title page, etc. is a matter of interpreting both graphic and linguistic style and intent, much like isolating a title as such as illustrated in figure 1 on page 28. Names of corporate bodies commonly consist of a mixture of subject words, generic terms, proper words (that is, personal or geographic name elements), grammatical links, articles, etc., for example,

> College of Physicians and Surgeons of British Columbia
> 5th Annual Symposium on the Effects of Air Pollution in Coastal Areas
> National Council for Educational Technology.

When a corporate name is embedded in prose text, the casual searcher may not be conscious of where it begins and where it ends, particularly when it contains no proper words, as in the last two of these examples. Formal presentation in grammatical or typographic isolation from other data, as is usually the case on a title page, is an aid to identifying a name as such. However, even a title-page presentation is not always unequivocal: in this age of graphic imagery, a corporate name is often presented within a graphic design which obscures its identity or parts.

A name must be a specifying appellation, not merely a generic reference to the existence of something. Clues to this are the use of full or initial upper-case letters, definite articles, etc. Just as Mary Smith is a name but "the girl who lives next door" is not, so Bureau of the Budget is a name but "the office that looks after budget preparation" is not. The dividing line becomes very subtle in the case of conferences, meetings, etc. The formally presented wording "Conference on the Analysis of Brain Waves" is accepted by AACR as a name, but the wording "a conference on the analysis of brain waves" is not, especially if presented only in grammatical connection with other text. An individual corporate body may be identified by one or more of the following types of name:

1) the name under which it is officially incorporated by letters patent or other legal means, for example, The Canadian-American Railway Corporation

2) any abbreviation thereof, including any acronym however fanciful, for example, CanAmRail; CANARY (some of these have legal or quasi-legal status while others are only used informally)

3) any translation of one of the above types of name whether the other-language form has legal status (as is true if the body is officially bilingual) or is merely used for convenience in referring to the body in foreign places; for example, the Frankfurt sales agency may use Kanadisch-amerikanischc Bahnlinie (KAB) in local advertisements

4) any name which represents a formal change from a previous name (as distinct from one of several variant forms used simultaneously), for example, North American Railways, Inc.; Interail.

Choice of Name

Cataloguing rules have always attempted to apply the same criteria whether the name identifies a corporate body or a person. Thus the old rules called for the access point **European Atomic Energy Community** (the full official form) while **Euratom** (the form commonly found in publications of the body and reference sources) is now correct. The commonly found name is more and more frequently an initialism or acronym. The perception that any of these must "stand" for some full name which should be the "real" access point greatly complicated older filing rules by requiring that an abbreviation (for example, U.S.) be filed as if it were spelled out (in this case, as United States). It took more than one stage of rule-making to overcome this habit. In AACR1, an acronym commonly written in upper/lower case (for example, Unesco) is permitted as a preferred access point, but an initialism as such (for example, AFL/CIO) is not. In AACR2, any initialism, acronym, etc. is acceptable as a preferred access point provided it predominates in the body's own usage. Filing rules also had to catch up with the implications of this in stages. Public perceptions are often behind the times: many think that IBM and Utlas, for example, are still abbreviations for some longer wording which they expect a cataloguer to prefer; in reality, these and many other initialisms and acronyms are now the full corporate names of the bodies in question as well as the forms commonly used in their publications. Perhaps the examples in this paragraph are respectable, but librarians wish the use of catchy acronyms had not gone quite out of control, confusing both the identification and the file location of many corporate bodies.

Language.   Two or more different language-forms of the same corporate name, each equally official, exist in the case of a bilingual or multilingual body. Which language-form should be the basis for the preferred access point: That of the jurisdiction where the body is incorporated? That of the cataloguing agency? The name which happens to occur first, or most frequently, in the body's publications or in other sources? The solution of both old and current rules is that, if a body *officially* uses a name in English as well as one or more in other languages, the English name is preferred for use in an English-language catalogue. Otherwise, the vernacular form as determined from the body's publications is preferred. Two exceptions exist favouring the additional use of English. One requires the use of an English name commonly found in reference books for an old and international body, such as the Catholic Church. AACR2 permits, as an alternative intended to be applied only in unilingual school and public libraries, the use of a translation, for example, German Federal Railway instead of what is found in the body's publications—Deutsche Bundesbahn.

Change of Name.   Corporate name changes, which are increasingly frequent, present a very different problem from personal name changes; the solutions must therefore also differ. While sometimes a change reflects nothing more than a desire to project a different image, many name changes result from a change of purpose or constitution or from a merger with or a split from another body. When a name change results from one of these more radical reorientations of the body, attempting to preserve the continuity of the body under a single access point is less than relevant to the situation, although it was attempted in the old rules. Pragmatically, there is no way of judging objectively how much change has taken place in the nature of the body, so this cannot be a valid criterion in deciding whether one heading or two should be used. AACR arbitrarily dictates that, upon any deliberate change in a body's name, a different corporate body has come into existence. Thus both the old and the new names are established as preferred access points linked to each other in an associative, not an equivalence, relationship (see page 77), that is, in a manual catalogue, by *see also* (not *see*) references. For example, although the name of Long Beach State College was changed to California State University, Long Beach, the former name remains valid as an access point for all documents relating to the institution before the name change. The latter name is used as an access point only for materials pertaining to the institution after the name change. This leaves the problem of what *subject* access point(s) to use for a work describing a body's history both before and after a name change. The usual solution is to use only the latest name borne by the body during the period covered by the work being catalogued. In practice, this means that a search for material about a body should begin with its latest name and the links with earlier names should only be pursued if noncurrent information is specifically wanted.

Choice of Access Element

The problems of choosing an access element for a personal name are few compared with those involved in corporate naming because a corporate name contains no obvious conventional analogy to the personal surname. It might seem easy to let each cataloguer decide, ad hoc, which word in a given corporate name is the most useful for the purpose but this is the one unacceptable approach because it precludes standardization. For generations, rule makers therefore sought some method which could be phrased as a general rule for predicting the most memorable word of a corporate name under which most searchers would think to look for it. In the very earliest attempts, an access word in the name might be chosen for its subject value but this is an extremely ad hoc type of approach. By the nineteenth century, nobody seriously thought it best to find, for example, the National Education Association under **E**. To preserve its objectivity as a finding device, a name must be treated as a name, not as a topic. Yet the more the rule makers tried to find a method both applicable over the whole range of corporate names and as simple for users as finding a person under a surname, the more it eluded them. As they tried various approaches, the ground was shifting under them because the patterns of corporate naming were themselves changing, as illustrated on page 153 in the recent development of acronyms and other abbreviated forms. If corporate bodies refuse to adopt a simple naming pattern, it should be no surprise that attempt after attempt at a simple solution to locating their names in alphabetic files has foundered.

The solutions incorporated into successive cataloguing rules have always admitted two possibilities depending on the type of body and/or name:

1) accessing the name of the body in its direct order by its first word other than an article and
2) accessing the body not under its own name at all but under the name of a hierarchically superior body or under a place name, with the name of the body actually being identified treated as a subheading rather than as the access element.

The first method may seem simple, even inevitable; the second, devious and convoluted. Yet although the first is becoming more and more prevalent, it has never been accepted as desirable for every corporate name or type of corporate body. The amount of detail given below to illustrate the use of these methods cannot replace close study of the quite complex rules of the cataloguing codes.

Direct Order.   Both old and new rules establish the names of most independent private-sector bodies as access points in direct word-order, for example,

American Association for the Advancement of Science
Council on Library Resources.

If the body being sought is not connected with a government, this appears to be the natural approach of most users to today's typical distinctive corporate name. Even so, the feeling that the average user would not naturally search under certain types of words, such as a given name or an initialism, persisted as late as AACR1, where the access point for The Richard J. Young Tractor Company was still established as **Young (Richard J.) Tractor Company.** AACR2 finally abandoned as unworkable any further attempt to define acceptable versus unacceptable access elements which could be defined over the broad range of corporate naming. Direct order is a simpler rule to follow and to explain even if the result is an access point like **R.J. Young Tractor Company,** which must be found among the initials at the beginning of a letter sequence.

As noted on pages 151–52, a hierarchically subordinate body must be allowed its own access point; its identity cannot simply be merged with that of its superior body. Many subordinate-level bodies have entirely distinctive names which contain no hint of a hierarchical relationship, for example, the Bodleian Library (a part of the University of Oxford) or the Vancouver Vocational Institute (a part of Vancouver Community College). In searching for a policy statement of, for example, the Library and Information Technology Association (LITA), it would hardly occur to the average user to look under the letter **A** (for American Library Association), even though LITA is wholly a part of ALA and can legally bind, and be bound by, some activities of the parent body. Whatever the function or corporate status of the body, in each of these cases its name is distinctive. Old rules often, and new rules almost always, establish such corporate names directly as preferred access points. An equivalence link may direct the searcher who first approaches the name of the hierarchically superior body, for example,

American Library Association. Library and Information Technology
Association *see* **Library and Information Technology Association.**

Alternatively, a hierarchical link may suggest the names of related/subordinate bodies to be found elsewhere in the file, for example,

American Library Association
see also **Library and Information Technology Association**
Public Library Association
[etc.]

However, old rules prescribe subordinate access as described in the next section for a significant proportion of subordinate and related bodies which under AACR are to be accessed as shown in the preceding under their own names; for example, the reference librarian must be prepared to find such preferred access points as the following in older bibliographies and catalogues:

Smithsonian Institution. Renwick Gallery.

Accessing the Name of a Subordinate Body as a Subheading.   In the majority of cases, a subordinate body's name is not as distinctive as "Bodleian Library," which contains a proper noun. Most are only nondistinctive strings of generic terms; for example, another subordinate unit of Vancouver Community College is simply named The Library. Nondistinctive naming implies dependence because it tends to occur only when the subordination is total (that is, when the higher body entirely controls the lower) and/or when the relationship is single-purpose and very close. This type of naming also focuses attention less on the lower-level body with the nondistinctive name than on the related higher-level body whose more distinctive name helps establish the lower-level body's identity. This is partly because nondistinctive names are typically shared by many different bodies; for example, not only General Motors but also the University of British Columbia has a subordinate body named Department of Finance; not only Vancouver Community College but also the accounting firm of Wood, Gundy has a subordinate body named The Library. Who thinks to search under N for a Nominating Committee or under F for a Faculty of Law or for a Friends of the Library group? The instinctive reaction is to precede the search by a question: *Whose* Nominating Committee? *Which university's* Faculty of Law? *What library's* Friends? As a result, the searcher tends to go first not to the name of the committee, the faculty, or the friends group even though that name is clear and well known, and would be easily locatable in an alphabetic list, but rather to the name of the superior or related body. The preferred access point therefore consists of what is called a main heading[5] (the name of the superior or related body) followed by a subheading (the name of the body for which the entire access point is being established), for example,

Queen's University. Faculty of Law.

The corporate names Yale University Library and Bibliothèque de l'Université de Montréal are distinctive. According to the preceding criteria, they should appear unchanged as access points, under Y and B respectively. However, such names often occur in both text and formal presentation in a way that separates the name of the higher body from that of the lower by typography or spacing or by sometimes omitting grammatical links within the name (for example, de; of) so that the searcher may not easily know whether to look for the name of the lower body directly or as a subheading under the name of the higher. For this reason, even AACR requires the latter treatment, namely,

Yale University. Library
Université de Montréal. Bibliothèque.

5. A main heading is simply the first part of an access point which includes a subheading, as shown in the examples. This term has absolutely nothing to do with the concept of a main entry heading, or principal access point for a work, for which see pages 169–71.

The Yale example may seem like the silliest hairsplitting: what possible difference does the presence or absence of a period make? Why not just **Yale University Library**? Furthermore, if subordination is the issue, why is the access point not **Yale University. Yale University Library**? The answer to the latter query is that the rules have always removed redundancy in an access point unless objectionable distortion of the name would result. The answer to the former is that some, but not all, filing rules *do* make a distinction based on whether a period exists in an access point (see page 265).

More than one level of hierarchical subordination may be involved. For example, the subordinate body named School of Library, Archival and Information Studies is a part of the Faculty of Arts of The University of British Columbia. AACR prefers the access point

> **University of British Columbia. School of Library, Archival and Information Studies**

omitting the middle element, the faculty's name, because the latter cannot in any case be the access element and is not needed to identify or to distinguish the school's name as a part of the university. In the following example, however, all three parts of the hierarchy must appear in the access point because there are many Admissions Committees within the same university:

> **Queen's University. Faculty of Law. Admissions Committee.**

Old rules consider not only the distinctiveness of the name but also the reality of the body's organizational function in determining whether the name of a body should be made accessible directly or subordinately. Concentrating thus on function, they also tend to make more levels of a hierarchy explicit in the access point for a lower-level body than is now permitted. Over the years, many ad hoc exceptions made Cutter's original rule based on organizational function almost unworkable. AACR2 takes account of a body's function only in the case of certain types of government bodies as described on page 165. Fortunately, the way subordinate bodies are actually named tends to ensure that, in the great majority of cases, nongovernment subordinate bodies are identified by the same preferred access points regardless of whether old or new rules are used.

Access under a Place Name. Some corporate bodies are closely identified with permanent structures in a locality whose population constitute their primary supporters or users. Such a body is often called an institution to distinguish it from a society, business firm, or association whose activities are not so geographically fixed. Educational institutions, galleries, theatres, museums, churches, hospitals, prisons, and libraries are examples fitting this general description. In English, the name of the place served is often the first word of an institution's name. Even if not, it may still be the only proper word in the name and therefore the one memorable element to use in searching an alphabetic file. Public libraries provide good examples of this issue. The following, alphabetically listed, are some names of public libraries in the predominant forms found in their own publications:

> The Borough of Etobicoke Public Library
> Carnegie Library of Pittsburgh
> The Fraser-Hickson Institute
> The Free Library of Philadelphia
> Greenwich Library
> Indianapolis-Marion County Public Library
> Kirn Memorial Library
> The Library Association of Portland
> Portage La Prairie City Library
> Prairie Crocus Regional Library
> War Memorial Library

Only three of these names begin with the name of a jurisdiction (Greenwich, Indianapolis, and Portage La Prairie). Another implies a geographic area (Prairie Crocus Region). Three name people, not places (Carnegie, Fraser-Hickson, and Kirn). The last consists solely of generic words. The third does not even designate the function of the body.

Someone who knows enough about a particular public library to seek its name in a directory or other list probably knows where it is but may not remember, and may never have consciously known, its precise name. Does the average searcher consciously consider whether the name of a particular gallery takes the form [Place] Art Gallery or Art Gallery of [Place] or even [Name] Art Gallery of [Place]? As with the naming of subordinate units, linguistic patterns strongly influence the structuring of such a name but do not ensure a uniform sequence of elements. For example, the first of the three word sequences in the hypothetical art gallery example is more common in English while the second is more common in French.

Cutter's code, its direct descendants, and certain holdovers in effect in AACR1 right up to 1980 made the relevant geographic place name the access element for the names of many (but not all) such institutions regardless of whether that place name appears in the name of the body or is only implied. The basic old rule is that if the name of the body begins with a proper noun other than a place name, it is to be established directly, for example,

> **Yale University**
> **Enoch Pratt Free Library**
> **Mendel Art Gallery.**

Otherwise, the name of the body becomes a subheading after the name of the place (municipality) where the body functions, for example,

London, Ont. University of Western Ontario
Paris. Musée nationale du Louvre
Akron, Ohio. Public Library.[6]

When Cutter devised the above distinction between a society and an institution and established this pair of basic rules for the latter, they made good sense. The boundaries of a municipality's jurisdiction were clear both geographically and functionally; an institution was likely to be known and named by its municipal location even if its functions were broader; in general, only one institution of a particular type existed in any one municipality. These reasons for using a municipal place name as the access element have, however, become less and less relevant. As they grow, institutions now tend to drift to suburbs and/or disperse their activities among several locations. Their naming has also changed: they are less likely to adopt a name with the simple structure of Place-Function or Function-of-Place.

It took a long time for Cutter's rules for geographic access to institutional names to be recognized as inadequate. In the meantime, they were bolstered by more and more exceptions in an attempt to ensure that their basis would still operate while their most undesirable side effects were minimized. There were, in the end, exceptions to exceptions and even one exception to an exception to an exception! The process became a case study in how *not* to write a cataloguing code. The resulting mess left in catalogues by the 1970s may be illustrated by a single example. Although the University of Oxford's name was established as a subheading using the name of the city (Oxford) as the access element, the University of Michigan's was established using the name of the state (Michigan), not the city (Ann Arbor), as the access element. This makes some sense, but the consequence of defining a state/provincial institution as an exception in order to put the University of Michigan's name in the catalogue under **M** was to locate the University of Victoria under the letter **B** for its province: British Columbia. Tossing a coin in each case might have produced more rational results. What this is intended to illustrate is that some ingenuity and willingness to suspend disbelief may be needed in searching for corporate names in older bibliographic files. Yet explicit case-by-case cross-references in these older files are rare: the professional was expected to know the rule!

After all the preceding confusion, the rules in AACR2 appear clear and simple: there is no longer any distinction between societies and institutions and only a government agency's name can have a place name as its access element, followed by a subheading naming the agency (see pages 163–66). The preferred access points for the above examples are therefore now

---

6. The name of this body is Akron Public Library, but as with the Yale University Library example on page 158, the redundancy is removed. The place names forming the main headings in these examples are given as prescribed by the old rules: current practice encloses the larger jurisdiction in parentheses, for example, **Akron (Ohio)**.

University of Western Ontario
Musée nationale du Louvre
Akron Public Library.

Qualifier(s)

Two or more corporate bodies, like two or more persons, may bear the same name, requiring qualifiers to distinguish their access points. The choice of qualifier depends on what makes most sense as a distinguishing characteristic but should be of the same type for any pair of names which would otherwise be the same, for example,

Newman Club (University of British Columbia)
Newman Club (York University)
National Portrait Gallery (Great Britain)
National Portrait Gallery (U.S.).

A qualifier may also help identify the body or simply clarify that an otherwise ambiguous name does represent a corporate body, for example, **Guess Who (Musical group)**.

Conferences. In the case of a conference name, a qualifier is always required. Many conference names are unique but this cannot be predicted: a successful Symposium on [Topic] is quite likely to be followed by a Second Symposium on [Same Topic]. In addition, a searcher is as likely to recognize a conference by its number, venue, and/or date as by its name alone. These are therefore useful parts of the access point, for example,

Ferring Symposium on Brain and Pituitary Peptides (3rd : 1979 : Munich)
Bibliographical Society. Annual Meeting (93rd : 1987 : University College, London).[7]

Old rules use commas instead of the colons shown here, and locate the date after, rather than before, the place name.

Places

A place name may no longer be the access element for the name of an institution but it still serves to identify

1) a geographic location as a subject and
2) a political jurisdiction, that is, the government which exercises jurisdiction over the geographic territory

7. Here, the name of the conference (*Annual Meeting*) appears as a subheading following the name of the society because it is a subordinate body without a distinctive name, as described on page 157.

In the latter case, place serves as the access element in the names of many government agencies. A place may be identified by one or more of the following types of name:

1) the name assigned to it by tradition or by an official agency in the jurisdiction in which it is located, for example, by the Canadian Permanent Committee on Geographic Names in the case of a Canadian place
2) any name assigned to it by an official agency in some other jurisdiction, for example, by the United States' Board on Geographic Names, which prescribes geographic names for locations the world over for use in the United States civil service
3) any translation of an official or traditional name as found in a gazetteer or other reference source in any language, for example, Londres (London); Munich (München)
4) any name which represents a formal change from a previous name, for example, Hồ Chí Minh Thành (formerly Saigon).

The third kind of naming produces problems for standardization. On pages 150 and 154, the practice is described of using a name in the language of the catalogue user (English is used in the examples) rather than in the vernacular but only in certain limited circumstances. However, people have a different attitude toward translating place names than toward translating the names of persons or bodies. English speakers who would never dream of translating the name Mr. Schneider into Mr. Tailor (or Taylor) or even the name NHK into Japanese Broadcasting Corporation have no qualms about translating the name Huanghe (a romanization of 黃河) into Yellow River or the name Venezia into Venice or the name Svizzera/Schweiz/Suisse/Confoederatio Helvetica (take your choice: they are all official) into Switzerland. While a place of little significance beyond its immediate region is likely to be identified everywhere and at all times by only its vernacular name, many places are referred to internationally and over a centuries-long time span by conquerors and colonizers using many different languages. Bombay is only a war of occupation away from the Portuguese city Bom Bahía (Beautiful Bay) and has now reverted to a more indigenous name, Mumbai. Looking at it from the point of view of speakers of other languages, who is to say that Atlantisches Meer is less legitimate than Océan atlantique, Mar atlantico, or 大西洋 ? Some geographic features belong to no single jurisdiction or language-group authorized to establish an official name. Increased travel and familiarity with foreign place names mean that fewer geographic names are translated now than in the past, but this is an area where international uniformity of access points can never be achieved and where equivalence links in large numbers will always be necessary in internationally maintained databases. In both old and new English-language cataloguing rules, a predominant English form of a place name found in English-language gazetteers is prescribed for use as the preferred access point.

It may seem redundant to use a qualifier when one London is so much better known than any other, but to distinguish places of the same name and simply to identify where a place is located even if it has a unique name, the 1988 AACR2R removed the last remaining options regarding geographic-name qualifiers and made it standard practice to include a qualifier in the access points for names below the national, federated state, or provincial level. The name (often abbreviated) of the next larger jurisdiction in which the place is located is the natural, if not entirely trouble-free, qualifier; for example, **Victoria (Tex.)**. Changes of geographic name and changes of the jurisdiction in which a locality exists are treated generally the same as changes of corporate names, for which see page 154.

Governments and Government Agencies

Governments have official names found in their constitutions and other documents, for example, République française, State of Rhode Island and Providence Plantations, City of El Paso de Robles, Corporation of the Municipal District of West Vancouver. It is rare to find such a name used as an access point in a name index. Rather, the access point for the government is formulated as the geographic name of the territory governed as described in the previous section on places; in other words, a location and its government are not normally distinguished. The access points for the preceding governments are therefore **France**; **Rhode Island**; **Paso Robles (Calif.)**; and **West Vancouver (B.C.)**.

This solves the problem of naming but not that of deciding what *is* the government in question. International wars change boundaries and civil wars change governmental forms. Even within peaceful states, the geographic extent and the naming of local jurisdictions are not as stable as they once were. In the United States, counties and municipalities are fairly autonomous and over two centuries only a few changes have radically affected their access points. The need for regional and other larger-base services has been answered generally by single-purpose corporate bodies responsible to two or more jurisdictions, for example, the Twin Cities Metropolitan Planning Commission composed of members from St. Paul and from Minneapolis. The names of such agencies are treated as names of nongovernment corporate bodies.

In most jurisdictions, however, municipalities are the creatures of a higher level of government. The United Kingdom and several Canadian provinces have in recent years radically revised municipal naming, boundaries, and functions. For example, the new Welsh county named Dyfed covers much but not all of the territory of the old Cardiganshire plus some territory formerly in other counties. The pattern in Canada has been to impose an additional supra-municipal level of government on the existing levels. In some instances all the previous jurisdictions have remained intact (although with changed powers) within the new framework; for example, the Municipality of Metropolitan Toronto is a political entity additional to its component parts, the City of Toronto and several surrounding municipalities, all of which retain their old names and political existence. On the other hand, the creation of the neighbouring City of Mississauga obliterated the political existence of the former villages of Malton, Streetsville, etc. Although the latter words may remain as geographic names on old maps, they no longer correspond to any present governmental reality.

As new jurisdictions come into existence today, they are not always assigned names conforming with the old traditions of using words describing natural features, names of explorers, names brought by immigrants from a home country, etc. To anyone, the new name Mississauga has the ring of a geographic name of a precise area. The name Metropolitan Toronto was established earlier than Mississauga and for an equally precise jurisdictional area, but many people still think it connotes merely a vaguely defined market- or population-area, as the term *metropolitan* implies in the United States. Gazetteers record place names, not those of governments, and have been slow to recognize new kinds of jurisdiction-naming. Metropolitan Toronto is now listed under **M** in the Ontario volume of the *Gazetteer of Canada*, but Capital Regional District (an equivalent new political jurisdiction in another province) is not yet to be found under **C**, or anywhere, in the British Columbia volume.

Government Agencies

Most governments list and describe their agencies in a directory called a government organization manual. If carefully edited and frequently revised, such a directory is an indispensable guide to anyone who indexes or searches for government names. Hierarchy in a bureaucracy is the basic organizational principle of government; autonomous and arm's-length public agencies complicate most government organization charts. Name and function changes are frequent. The first difficulty in providing access points for the names of government agencies is therefore to decide which of them should be established as subheadings (see page 157) with the name of the jurisdiction (country, province, city, etc.) as the access element and which should be established directly under their own names. For example, should the preferred access point for the Smithsonian Institution, a government-owned museum, be under **U** (for United States) or under **S**? Differences in attitudes toward this issue can be expected as between free enterprise societies and more socialized systems, but a deep penetration of government into areas of corporate activity is a fact of modern life everywhere. Old rules make an agency's *function* the primary determinant of whether the access element is the name of the jurisdiction: they treat the names of agencies which directly exercise executive functions of government as subheadings, for example,

> United States. Federal Bureau of Investigation
> United States. Southern Forest Experiment Station
> Canada. Royal Canadian Mounted Police.

However, old rules, like the current ones, establish the access points of arm's-length agencies, such as crown corporations and quasi-commercial boards, as if no government were involved. In the case of institutions (universities, museums, etc.), this means that the provisions described on pages 151-61 take precedence; the Smithsonian Institution has always appeared in a library catalogue under S.

AACR continues to specify some government functions whose agencies' names are always to appear as subheadings following the name of the jurisdiction. In AACR2, these are restricted to only the most basic legislative, judicial, military, and highest-level executive functions, no matter how distinctive their agencies' names may be, for example,

> Alberta. Alberta Culture (a major cabinet-level agency)[8]
> Israel. Knesset
> Canada. Royal Canadian Air Force.

For the general run of executive agencies of government, nondistinctive naming prevailed for centuries (for example, Department of Cultural Affairs; Real Estate Commission; Home Office). It was, and remains, natural to access these under the name of the jurisdiction just as any private-sector body named nondistinctively is best located under the name of its parent body. However, there is now a very strong trend toward giving government agencies distinctive names, usually made unique by the incorporation of the name of the government in question, for example, Canadian Wildlife Service; Telecommunication Authority of Singapore. As part of this trend, the nature of organizational dependency is being obscured (as, no doubt, agency workers prefer); for example, first the Dominion Bureau of Statistics became Statistics Canada, then that agency's Health Division became the Canadian Health Information Centre. Such name changes, taking place in more and more jurisdictions, are having a profound influence on the way the average person identifies what is in fact a government agency and where it is most naturally sought in an alphabetic file. For this reason, AACR and AACR2 successively limited the proportion of names of government agencies for which the name of the jurisdiction is the preferred access element. Now, except for agencies exercising the most basic functions mentioned at the end of the previous paragraph, if the name of a government agency meets the test of distinctiveness given on page 156, its preferred access point does not begin with the name of the jurisdiction; for example;

> Royal Canadian Mounted Police
> Southern Forest and Range Experiment Station (New Orleans, La.)
> Telecommunication Authority of Singapore
> Canadian Health Information Centre.

8. Here, the redundancy of two Albertas is required because **Alberta. Culture** would be ambiguous.

Logically, but perhaps to a searcher's surprise, the name of the FBI remains a subheading of **United States** because the word *Bureau* implies subordination. The word *Station* in the above example does not.[9]

The second issue in naming government agencies is whether much or all of the hierarchy should be explicit in the access point for a subordinate agency (so that agencies are grouped according to their bureaucratic organization) or whether the access point should be kept as brief as possible (so that the naming of one particular agency is clear and unencumbered by its relationships with others). For example, is **Canada. Egg Unit** a useful access point for the agency at the bottom of the following hypothetical hierarchy?

> Canada
> Department of Agriculture
> Production and Marketing Branch
> Poultry Division
> Turkey Section
> Egg Unit

If not, how many and which additional levels of the hierarchy should appear in the access point naming the Egg Unit? Since there are normally many names of subordinate agencies to be accessed under the name of a jurisdiction, the filing order is very much affected by this decision. As with nongovernmental subordinate bodies, old rules tend to include more elements of the hierarchy in the access point than new rules permit, for example, **United States. Dept. of Agriculture. Dairy Division.** Since there is only one body named Dairy Division in the United States federal government, this body is now filed as **United States. Dairy Division.**

Works

As illustrated with St. Matthew's Gospel at the beginning of this chapter, one cannot rely on the words of the title proper of any one *document* to retrieve all the documents containing a particular *work*. As a corollary to this statement, there is no guarantee that any title borne by a particular document will correspond to a particular user's title-approach to the sought work. The many works published only once, in only one form, and under only one title offer no problem with regard to the issues raised in this section. The few works republished, adapted,

9. These illustrations may help explain why another type of alphabetic name-list, the telephone directory, now usually treats names of government agencies in isolation from all other names by some means, such as putting them all in a separate section on coloured paper or subfiling them all under G for Government. Although this may seem to be the exact opposite of the trend in library catalogues, it serves the same purpose: to define that group of government agencies which users would like to find together in one file location. The actual agencies grouped in the two types of list differ because catalogue users focus on names as found in citations, etc. whereas telephone-directory users focus on administrative functions.

translated, etc., under various titles proper present major problems for users. A work may be known to someone searching for it in a file by one or more of the following types of title:

1) the title proper assigned to the work's first published form by its author and/or original publisher, for example, *Ten Little Niggers* by Agatha Christie

2) any title given to any subsequent publication of the complete work whether in the original or in any other language, for example, *And Then There Were None*; *Dix petits nègres*; . . . *e poi non rimase nessuno*; *Letztes Weekend*

3) any title given to an adaptation or other modification of the work, for example, *Ten Little Indians* (the title of a dramatization)

4) any wording by which the work is referred to in reference sources but which is not necessarily the title proper of any particular publication of it—this is more likely to be an issue in the case of works originating before the advent of printing and formal titling (see pages 59–60).

A work may later be re-created or otherwise modified by someone other than its original creator: such an adaptation often bears a different title proper from the original; for example, Ivor A. Richards' *The Wrath of Achilles* is Homer's *Iliad* in an adapted translation which does not state its origin on its title page. In the case of a translation, the title almost always differs from that of the original. A work created separately and still known by its own name may also come to be thought of as part of a larger work; for example, *Saint Matthew's Gospel* later became part of the canon of *The Bible*; a poem or article with its own title often appears only as part of an anthology or a periodical. Like a corporate body, a work may have parts (arias, chapters, sections) known by and/or separately published under their own titles.

Using one preferred title as a controlled-vocabulary identifier for a work is the same as using one preferred form of name as a controlled-vocabulary access point for a person, corporate body, or place. It is called a uniform title (prior to 1967, a conventional title). This is usually the title borne by the original published version of the work but may be a title commonly adopted by later critics. The function of a uniform title, used in association with the name of the author if one can be identified, is to ensure that there is one location in the file where all the documents containing or otherwise related to the same work can be found.

Using a Uniform Title Alone to Identify an Anonymous Work

Using a uniform title is clearly essential when the many versions of a work bearing different titles proper cannot be grouped in a file under an author's name. Without the application of a uniform title, access points for editions of the *Chanson de Roland* are scattered throughout a file under that title, under *Song of Roland*, under *Rolandslied*, etc. Uniform titles were first used for such anonymous classics. To list every version under one uniform-title access point does not mean that the titles proper of the different versions are lost to the searcher. They appear in a multiple-access file as additional access points, each for the one document bearing that title. They should also appear as equivalence links in an authority file, for example,

> **Song of Roland**
> *for editions of this work, search under* **Chanson de Roland**.

Using a Uniform Title Together with an Author Access Point

When an author's name is available, it may seem less important to use a uniform title as a grouping device. Agatha Christie's mystery cited previously is, after all, accessible under her name no matter which title appears on the edition the library owns. However, she also wrote other books, so the several titles proper on editions of *this* work will be interspersed among the titles proper of the many editions of her other works rather than appear in a single location in the alphabetic sequence. An author's name followed by the uniform title of a work together form what is called a name-title access point, *both* of whose elements, not just the author's name, are subject to authority control. This two-part access point identifies one work uniquely and provides a single predictable file location where all its editions, translations, adaptations, etc. can be located. The need for this has long been acknowledged in the case of scores and recordings of serious music. Their publishing is international in scope. The concert goer, score reader, or listener is unconcerned about the language of the title: the same Mozart opera is almost equally well known as *The Marriage of Figaro*, *Le Nozze di Figaro*, and *Figaros Hochzeit*; a recording of the same Shostakovich quartet may bear a label reading *Quatuor no 1*, *Erste Streichkvartett*, or *String Quartet no. 1*. Without organization by uniform titles, the lengthy list of Mozart's compositions subarranged under his name, or even the more modest list under Shostakovich's, would be a disorganized grab bag. Figure 21 shows how a uniform title is associated with an author's name as an access point in the traditional unit-record format. In a smaller manual catalogue and when an author's name is available for access, a uniform title is usually used as a grouping device only for music and for the works of a few prolific authors whose publication titling is variable. The assumption is that in other cases, the user will browse through all the records under the author's name.[10] In the interactive catalogue, however, the searcher normally first selects from an index of access points and only later

---

10. In the past, it was not uncommon for the filer of the catalogue cards, not the cataloguer, to decide whether the file organization required uniform titles and to pencil them in as needed on an ad hoc basis. The use of uniform titles is still treated as optional in current cataloguing rules but the cataloguer, not the filer, makes the decision.

sees the bibliographic descriptions with their titles proper; uniform titles are therefore now usually applied wherever applicable because they are an essential part of access points identifying single works.

(3)
```
        SWIFT, JONATHAN. GULLIVER'S TRAVELS.
        Carnochan, W.B.
          Lemuel Gulliver's mirror for man / W.B. Carnochan ...
```

(2)
```
     Swift, Jonathan.
       [Gulliver's travels]
       Travels into several remote nations of the world / by
     Lemuel Gulliver ...
```

(1)
```
   Swift, Jonathan.
     Gulliver's travels / by Swift ...
```

FIGURE 21. Record 1 shows an author's name followed by a title proper indented on the next line. A combined name-title access point in which each of the two elements (name and title) is standardized makes *all* editions, critiques, etc., of the work accessible via that same access point. In record 2, these two elements are displayed on different lines, the latter within brackets to distinguish it from the following title proper. The old card-style display uses this style for editions of the work (the uniform title in brackets was also printed in smaller type). Record 3 shows the name-title combination as a subject access point on a single line, the two parts separated only by a period. This style, always adopted for additional and subject access points, is becoming more common for *all* access-point display involving uniform titles at a computer terminal. Record 1 does not require a uniform title in addition to the title proper because the two would be identical and file in the same location.

The Principal Access Point for a Work: Its Main Entry Heading

In dealing with access points in general, chapter 3 describes many types of both natural-language and controlled-vocabulary access points which can serve to locate a document by its subject content, by such data elements as titling and code numbering, by any name associated with the document or work, etc. All modern cataloguing codes presuppose the existence of multiple-access catalogues, including the links as well as the preferred access points of a controlled vocabulary. In such a catalogue, no one access point has any essentially greater value than any other in making it easy to locate a publication. Yet cataloguing codes continue to devote many complex rules to defining which one record for an item is its *main entry*, a term used in all the English-language rules from Cutter's in 1876 to the 1988 version of AACR2.

Cutter and the 1908 Joint Code define the main entry as "the full or principal entry; usually the author entry." All editions of AACR define it as "the complete catalogue record of an item, presented in the form by which the entity is to be uniformly identified and cited." AACR2 elaborates this in rule 0.5: "the concept of main entry is considered to be useful in assigning uniform titles and in promoting the standardization of bibliographic citation." In other words, before AACR the emphasis is on a main entry (that is, a full record) which provides more bibliographic information than does an added entry (that is, a briefer record for the same document). In those earlier days, rules were written in anticipation of their use in compiling book catalogues and single-access files, for the latter of which it is essential to define a predictable access point where the one record for an item can be found; the reason why this is normally an author's name is mentioned on page 68.

AACR shifts the emphasis away from defining the word *entry* as a record and toward defining it as an access point or heading. Its purpose is now to provide for the standardized identification and citation of what the definition calls "the entity." What is meant here cannot be the document or publication because that is the "item" of the earlier part of the definition. As rule 0.5 makes clear, the so-called main entry now refers to identifying the *work* by means of a standardized uniform-title or name-title access point as described in the earlier parts of this section.

All the cataloguing rules from Cutter through AACR2R are written in the context of the production of a manual catalogue, in which a bibliographic description and the access point under which it is to be filed are physically inseparable from one another. In that context, no practical distinction exists between the entry (something this book calls a record) and its heading (something this book calls an access point); in fact, those two older terms are treated as synonymous in the texts and glossaries of the rules prior to AACR! In contrast, this book is written primarily in the context of the searching of an interactive catalogue, in which an entry (record) is often not seen by the searcher until a selection has been made from among the available headings (access points) which are usually initially presented in isolation on a terminal screen. The distinction is therefore now vital. Cataloguing teachers have tended to use three words, *main entry heading* (a combination not found in the rules themselves), to emphasize the distinction: a main entry heading is only the access point of the main entry, not the entire entry, which also includes the descriptive data elements.

This explains why this issue arises in the present context of the standardized identification of works. It is the purpose of any type of controlled-vocabulary access point to lead to precisely the "entity" wanted. The user searching for all items about the person William Shakespeare properly looks in the subject file for the standardized personal-name access point **SHAKESPEARE, WILLIAM**, but the user searching for anything about the play *Hamlet* properly looks in the subject file for the standardized access point for the *work*, which is its main entry heading, the name-title combination **SHAKESPEARE, WILLIAM. HAMLET.** A work's standardized access point, its main entry heading, therefore serves as a most important link. It is the one form under which a user can find a work's text in the author file or a critique of the work in the subject file. It is also used to relate one work to another. Thus to state on the catalogue record for Ivor Richards' *The Wrath of Achilles* that it is an adaptation of the *Iliad*, the appropriate linking note is best phrased using the structure of the related work's main entry heading: Adaptation of: Homer. *Iliad.*

Since the main entry heading preferably begins with the name of a work's author or principal author, the history of library cataloguing rules for the past three centuries is largely the history of the attempt to define the functions of authorship and to establish an order of priority among them so that a principal author can be identified when a work has more than one author or more than one authorial function. Jewett extended the concept of authorship to include corporate bodies as authors but the rules for dealing with the latter became very complex and eventually so counterproductive that corporate authorship was finally abandoned as a general principle, to be replaced in AACR2 with pragmatic rules outlining a few restricted circumstances in which a corporate body's name serves a useful function as a main entry heading. A title, or uniform title if it is different from the title proper of the item being catalogued, is always a part of the work-identification intended in the choice of a main entry heading. Similarly, when the rules provide for a title alone as the main entry heading because no person or corporate body can serve as its first element, they always imply the use of a uniform title if one is relevant. If an author and title alone cannot serve uniquely to identify a work, as is true in the case of the existence of different editions, translations, etc., a date or some other appropriate data element becomes a part of the function of the main entry heading. In a manual catalogue, it is generally filing rules rather than the visual appearance of the record which effect this, but in an interactive one, the display of the parts of an access point may include such additional elements.

Because this subsection deals with an issue for which older terminology is very familiar and still found in current cataloguing rules, the words *entry* and *heading* have been used even though they are replaced by more modern terminology throughout the rest of the book. The separation of the descriptive portions of a record from its access points has led to misunderstanding and controversy concerning the concepts of the main entry and the main entry heading. Perhaps a clearer understanding is possible if they are thought of as, respectively, the principal record (for an item) and the principal access point (for a work). The latter, the principal access point for a given work (not publication or document), is an essential part of the catalogue's system of controlled-vocabulary access points.

Rule Changes for Name Access Points: Why and How?

The practices described throughout this chapter as "old" had been in effect without basic change for almost eighty years when they were first seriously challenged in Seymour Lubetzky's *Cataloging Rules and Principles, a Critique of the A.L.A. Rules for Entry and a Proposed Design for Their Revision.* Although this was published in 1953 by the Processing Department of the Library of Congress, it should be no surprise that the most immediate and strongest resistance to Lubetzky's proposals came from the reference divisions of the same library. Once a pattern of rules for access points, or even a single access point, is established for a file, the habits of the users of that file become ingrained and are not easily altered. All the benefits of record sharing and of standardization referred to in chapter 5 and in the introduction to part II also reinforce the desirability of maintaining the status quo. Changes as widespread and radical as those outlined in this chapter between old and new name access points are of traumatic consequence in a living tool like a library catalogue. They cannot be undertaken lightly. The following arguments proved effective in the ultimate adoption of the changes Lubetzky began.

1) Old rules led to practises often less beneficial to the end-user than to the professional librarian (who had the knowledge to understand and use a more complex tool) and to the library administrator (who saw stability of existing access points as economically efficient).
2) Names themselves, particularly corporate names, have undergone significant change in patterns and usage during the twentieth century: rules for old-style names do not necessarily apply as well to new-style ones.
3) A greater degree of standardization, and therefore international cooperation in sharing records, is possible if varying national practices can be more closely aligned.
4) Automation makes the changing and updating of files relatively easy and their searching more effective, but its efficient use requires internally consistent rules, which the old ones were not.

It took almost three decades for Lubetzky's initial proposals to be (1) added to and amended by the many others who took up the challenge, (2) discussed and vigorously debated, (3) brought to the international stage, (4) drafted into a code of rules (AACR1) published in 1967 for testing in practice, (5) once again revised and published as AACR2 in 1978, and eventually (6) put into international practice fully on January 2, 1981. Cataloguers and reference librarians had to adjust to the new rules at these several stages and explain them to end-users. Some did so with enthusiasm, others not; in either case, programmes of re-education occupied the entire period. The process of rule revision spawned offshoots not originally envisaged, the most important of which, the International Standard Bibliographic Description, is discussed in chapter 8. The simultaneous development of bibliographic automation from the stage of primitive experiment to that of sophisticated linked network was both a help and a hindrance to rule revision. It was fortunate that automation merged with other reasons for change during the 1960s and 1970s. In addition to being an indispensable tool for effecting the changes in practice, automation provided defensible reasons for change which perhaps convinced some foot-draggers. The magic word *computer* also generally made money available to pay that part of the cost of change which could be attributed to, or hidden under the guise of, automation. By 1979, the original proposed date for the sixth and final stage of implementation mentioned above, money for both special projects and automation was becoming scarcer in many major libraries and considerable resistance to the final proposed changes again surfaced. Their implementation by the national agencies was therefore delayed until 1981 in order to give local libraries more time to plan for the phase-out or freezing of manual catalogues containing old-rule access points. The conversion of their records to machine-readable form with new-rule access points is discussed on page 125.

There is no best moment to make a major change in any ongoing bibliographic system. Travel on the lengthy road described in the previous paragraph was far from smooth. The major road block was a policy called superimposition, in effect at the Library of Congress from 1967 through 1980 and therefore automatically followed in the large proportion of the English-speaking world's major libraries dependent on the Library's source records for derived cataloguing. During those fourteen years AACR1 was nominally in effect but superimposition took precedence. It required that an old-rule name access point existing in the file prior to 1967 continue to be applied to newly catalogued materials; for example, if the access point **Los Angeles. University of Southern California** existed in the Library of Congress catalogue on January 20, 1967, that same form continued to be applied to newly catalogued books by or about that university until December 31, 1980, even though the correct form according to AACR1 is **University of Southern California**. In addition to this policy, the resistance to wholesale change in the pre-automated 1960s was such that when AACR1 was written, its North American version (but not the British one) preserved some aspects of place-name access for corporate bodies which were inconsistent with its own principles. These gradually disappeared from the rules through the 1970s and were finally cleared out in the 1978 AACR2. The result of this and of superimposition was a very messy situation in single catalogues, in union files, and in bibliographic control in general between 1967 and 1980. The ability of most libraries to use computer programs to revise older records in accordance with new-rule authority files is rapidly diminishing the problems, but any reference librarian consulting older published bibliographic lists must be cautious about approaching records created during the 1967–1980 period: they may contain old-style or new-style access points in any mixture.

Sharing Name Authority Records

When bibliographic records are shared, so are the preferred access points appearing on those records. However, a bibliographic record does not show the reasons for, or the sources of, decisions made in establishing the preferred form of an access point. Nor does it show any of the links involving that form, and it is impossible to track down the links *to* a particular access point in a catalogue containing cross-references. To know all the name authority work done at the Library of Congress—the reasons and links as well as the preferred forms—is very important to the work done in other libraries, yet until 1974 this could only be found in the Library's in-house files in Washington, D.C. In that year, the Library of Congress began to photograph and print for distribution its ongoing production of authority cards. This initiated the practice of publishing authority files in addition to bibliographic files. Soon its authority file was automated and publication on paper was abandoned in favour first of a regularly cumulated COM product and now also tape and CD/ROM products containing all the name access points established or revised since 1968. Other national agencies such as the National Library of Canada and the British Library have followed suit.

It is a principal tenet of IFLA's programme of Universal Bibliographic Control that a national bibliographic agency in the country where a name originates is the ideal locale for that name to be investigated and established as part of a controlled vocabulary according to an accepted cataloguing code. With cataloguing codes becoming more alike, national agencies are working toward a common name-authority system. This is already in partial operation among agencies using AACR2; for example, since 1976 the National Library of Canada establishes every name form for a Canadian person, body, and place, not only for its own authority file but also for that of the Library of Congress. Below the national level, individual libraries in networks are also beginning to share authority records as well as bibliographic records.

7

SUBJECT ACCESS

The names discussed in chapter 6 form a large proportion of the access points in most subject indices and subject-classified arrangements. When one thinks of access by subject, however, what comes first to mind is more likely to be a non-name concept or topic: psychiatry rather than Carl Jung; dog-training rather than Barbara Woodhouse. This chapter deals with the access points under which such concepts can be indexed and searched. The title and scope of chapter 6 restrict it to *controlled-vocabulary* access points. This cannot be the case with this chapter. Controlled vocabularies of the several types discussed later in this chapter are available for identifying the topical content of a document, but the natural language of titles, abstracts, etc. is also used and the two types of access, controlled and uncontrolled, are often mingled during a single search. Furthermore, this chapter must deal with rather more than just subject access *points*, hence the more general title.

While the philosopher might distinguish, define, name, and categorize a separate concept as an abstraction, the librarian—whether indexer or searcher—must be more pragmatic and think of it as something a creator has chosen to write (paint, compose, etc.) about or something an inquirer is searching for. Sound is a subject. The means of producing sound is a subject. The electronic production of sound is a subject. Music is a subject. Contemporary music is a subject. Popular music is a subject. Rock music is a subject. The use of electronic mixing boards in rock music recording is a subject. The music of John Lennon is a subject. The relationship of rock music to serious music is a subject. The influence of Lennon's music is a subject. There is almost no end to the proliferation of subjects which consist of levels of, ramifications of, or combinations of other subjects.

It is hard to conceive of a work so intellectually shallow that it deals with only one subject. A book's internal index typically isolates dozens, if not hundreds, of topics. The subject-oriented component of a library catalogue, an A&I publication, or a monographic bibliography does not attempt to duplicate that internal book-index. It only directs the searcher to the principal subject focus or focuses of the document *as a whole*. Put another way, the subject of a book or article, the subject of one of its chapters or sections, the subject of a group of paragraphs, and the subject of a single sentence are each likely to be different. In principle, the bibliographic files discussed in this book are concerned with access to only the first of these. Practice is, of course, a little more ambiguous.

Knowing the principles discussed in chapter 6 gives a searcher some confidence in creating a standard access point for an individual person, body, place, or work and in locating the name of any one of these in an index. Providing or locating an access point to identify a topic or concept is, on the contrary, fraught with all the ambiguities, inconsistencies, and problems of definition inherent in communicating in any living language. While a few of these problems are also encountered in dealing with names, even those are generally more difficult to resolve in the case of concepts, as may be seen in a number of examples:

1) A person or corporate body can undergo a change of name, giving rise to a new (or additional) access point. However, there is no ambiguity about what the new name is or when it takes effect, even if in practice some weeks or months may elapse before indexing catches up with reality. Is it ever as clear precisely when a subject term (for example, **MOVING PICTURES**) should be replaced, or precisely what new term should replace it?

2) A controlled-vocabulary name access point identifies one, and one only, person, body, place, or work. A single subject access point may identify more than one topic; for example, both the topic *libraries* and the topic *automation* are explicitly identified in the single access point **LIBRARY AUTOMATION**, whether it is expressed in that way or as **AUTOMATION OF LIBRARIES** or as **LIBRARIES—AUTOMATION**. How many topics belong in one subject access point?

3) Except in such fields as genealogy or organizational studies, it is not a common concern of an alphanumerically arranged name index to link related persons, bodies, etc.; for example, most people searching an index do not expect the names of Judy Garland and her daughter Liza Minelli to be linked by cross-references to each other. In contrast, only a very incomplete and less-than-useful subject index fails to relate the terms **MOTORCYCLE** and **MOPED** somehow, whether this is done by
   a) using a *see also* cross-reference in a manual file
   b) using a link in an interactive file which may shunt the user auto-

matically from either term to the other or may simply display the other term as a suggestion

c) showing the relationship of indexing terms to each other in an authority file maintained separately from the bibliographic file so that the conscientious searcher can plot out a search strategy for using the best ones in the best sequence *before* consulting the actual catalogue, etc. or

d) collocating the access points for related concepts in a subject-classified arrangement.

Doing what is outlined in (a), (b), and/or (c) fulfils what Cutter called a syndetic catalog.[1] The possibility described in (c) introduces a preliminary step into a subject search and does not appeal to the user who lunges at an index expecting instant results. It is, however, increasingly necessary in using an interactive file because the contents of that file are essentially invisible to the searcher in the sense discussed on pages 85 and 281. Interactive searching begins in this way whenever only index terms, not complete bibliographic records, are displayed as the first response to a query.

Assigning or using subject access points cannot be as straightforward as assigning or using name access points. It is always clear what constitutes an individual person, and fairly clear what constitutes an individual corporate body, place, or work. Can anyone define unambiguously what constitutes any given topic? Woody Allen lives and acts in particular time and space regardless of the perceptions of others or any external circumstance. Despite his use of a pseudonym, he cannot be mistaken for any other person. The geographic boundaries of the city of Geneva, Switzerland, are clearly drawn on a map and make it impossible to mistake this city for its namesake in New York State or for Carouge, its adjacent suburb in Switzerland. Linkages among various forms of name for the same person, etc. therefore express only an equivalence relationship, for example, Clemens-equals-Twain and Twain-equals-Clemens. On the other hand, what constitutes a particular concept is not definable objectively but only in relation to how someone wishes to use it for a given purpose: the communicator of topical information has an agenda and posits a context which the recipient may not hear, wish to hear, or understand. What the recipient of information understands as the scope and focus of any topic is affected both by fashions of time and place and by the emotional charge which surrounds many terms and topical juxtapositions. When a topic is defined and named as **HANDI-**

1. Cutter's definition of syndetic is "connective, applied to that kind of dictionary catalog which binds its records together by means of cross-references so as to form a whole, the references being made from the most comprehensive subject to those of the next lower degree of comprehensiveness, and from each of those to their subordinate subjects, and vice versa. These cross-references correspond to and are a good substitute for the arrangement in a systematic [that is, classified—see pages 187–88] catalog. References are also made in the syndetic catalog to illustrative and coördinate subjects, and, if it is perfect, from specific to general subjects." (*Rules for a Dictionary Catalog*, p. 23.)

CAPPED PERSONS, for example, is it precisely the same topic as the one defined and named as **INVALIDS**? If not, on what objective grounds does one distinguish these concepts? Which type of link between these terms—equivalent, hierarchical, or associative—is the most appropriate? Subject identification is a messy and often indeterminate business. After everything else in bibliographic control has been programmed into a computer, this area will remain in the domain of human judgement.

Concept versus Word(s)

When a topic is expressed in words, it is tempting to equate one word with one topic for purposes of indexing. In English, the single noun and gerund (for example, architecture, fishing) are ideal parts of speech to use in expressing topics in an indexable fashion. They predominate in any topical index, whether in the back of a book or in any type of bibliographic file. But a topic as the equivalent of a word in a dictionary is the philosopher's abstraction, not what a searcher and an indexer deal with. Their task is first to define the scope and boundaries of the topic in the particular context of the documents likely to deal with it and the users likely to search for it. Only then do they seek the best means of expressing it. Searching and/or indexing using a computer focuses attention on single words because a word, defined as anything with a space or a mark of punctuation immediately before and after it, is the easiest thing to input cheaply into, and to retrieve automatically from, a database.

A single word often suffices to identify a topic (for example, **COSMETICS**; **USURY**). In English and most other languages, it is natural for a new topic eventually to be communicable using a single word (for example, needlework is work done with needles; xenophobia is the fear of foreigners), but this is not always the case. When more than one word is needed to express a concept, each of them may or may not carry its original context(s) and/or meaning(s) into the combination. Each of the two words in the term **PRESSURE BROADENING** is used in the same sense it has as an independent word, but only in combination, and only in this order, do they identify a single topic in the discipline of astrophysics. In isolation, *pressure* connotes mechanics to most people. *Broadening* might relate to anything from subject analysis to tailoring. It is irrelevant that a non-astrophysicist might not know what pressure broadening is; what matters is that anyone who speaks English and is informed about the topic knows it best by that term. It also matters very much to an indexing system that if the word *pressure* appears outside this context, the average searcher legitimately assumes a different context: that of physics. The term *black hole* also has a specialized meaning in astrophysics, but here each word in the pair has been totally and very obviously divorced from any but allusive connection with its original meaning. Since one subject often cannot be equated with one word, any system relying on single words (for example, **PRESSURE** or **HOLE**) as search keys in a topical index must be used with great caution because it ignores the integrity of subjects. Further examples of this point are given on pages 182–83.

Natural Language

Uncontrolled, or natural-language, words and terms are distinguished from words of a controlled vocabulary on pages 74–76. The former can be of considerable value as subject access points when they come from such sources as the titling of a document, a cataloguer's note on its record, or an abstract. Such a word, thought of by a searcher or used by an indexer as a subject access point, is often called a keyword or a derived keyword—derived, that is, from the document or its record rather than from a controlled vocabulary.[2] In the title *Should America Go to War?*, there can hardly be any disagreement that *America* and *War* are words with some subject-retrieval value and that *Should*, *Go*, and *to* are not.

The use of natural language for subject indexing is sometimes thought to have originated in the keyword-in-context (KWIC) and keyword-out-of-context (KWOC) indices which inaugurated the automated (but not yet interactive) bibliographic file just after the Second World War (see figure 12 on page 73). In fact, it is much older. In the nineteenth century, before Jewett and Cutter developed the practice of controlled-vocabulary subject indexing, the multiple access points for a book in a subject index were typically permutations of its title's significant words and looked exactly like those in a modern KWIC index, for example,

> Federal Policymaking, How the Press Affects
> Policymaking, How the Press Affects Federal
> Press Affects Federal Policymaking, How the

Similarly, a typical access point in a back-of-the-book index of the late nineteenth century consists of the parts of a phrase or clause taken from the text being indexed and rotated around the word within it chosen as the access point. Adjustment of the word order may be needed to preserve the sense, for example,

> Cross-references, system of, in the British Museum catalogue
> Names, transformation of, for use as catalogue headings

2. Especially when used alone, *keyword* is an unfortunate term and is used very loosely. A keyword is not necessarily just one word. To imply that it is the key to subject searching inflates its value: it is a key only in the sense that it unlocks the door behind which some information of value might be found, not in the sense that it is the best guide to information. Furthermore, a single word from a multi-word controlled-vocabulary term is not uncommonly called a keyword. For clarity, therefore, the word is avoided in the remainder of this chapter and *natural-language access point*, although more awkward, continues to be used as in chapter 3 to mean a word or words made an access point but not derived from a controlled vocabulary.

From these old types of indexing come the terms *rotated index* and *permuted keyword index* seen in the modern literature of subject analysis. Before automation was applied to this technique, the human indexer made a conscious decision as to whether each separate word would serve usefully as a lead term and sometimes adjusted the other parts of the resulting access point. Constructing each index entry was therefore labour-intensive although no separate indexing vocabulary had to be constructed.

After the giants of the late nineteenth century—Jewett, Cutter, and Dewey—developed and focused attention on controlled vocabularies, librarians shunned natural-language access points for subject retrieval for almost a century. This meant that in the preceding example, the concepts implied by the title words *America* and *War* had to be approached through controlled-vocabulary subject access points beginning, respectively, **UNITED STATES** and **WORLD WAR** or through a cross-reference to one of those. The first word of a title other than an article (here, *Should*) continued to be made accessible, but not as a subject-retrieval term per se. Its purpose was only to provide access to the publication as such via its *name*, the title.

Using the computer, indexers not only restored the KWIC/KWOC type of index but expanded the potential of natural-language access points in subject searching. If a database mounted by a database vendor is not provided with a controlled-vocabulary index, natural-language searching is not a choice but a necessity. Scientific databases were typically the first to be mounted; the precision of much of their terminology and writing gives their natural language many of the characteristics of a controlled vocabulary. As databases in other disciplines are increasingly included in the vendors' services, more and more authors, editors, and publishers appreciate how citations to their books and articles are retrievable from computer-based subject indices using natural language. This is an incentive to choose title wording carefully. Since many vendors also make the text of abstracts searchable on the same basis as titles, etc., professional writers and editors of abstracts are in effect beginning to exercise a kind of vocabulary control by choosing terms consistently even if these terms are not linked as they would be in a controlled vocabulary. It is increasingly hard to draw a sharp line between the actual words of natural language and those of controlled vocabularies when dealing with academic and scientific writing and abstracting in the better journals. However, the links, the most costly aspect of both constructing and applying a controlled vocabulary, have not been applied to the former. In a search using only natural language, the responsibility for intelligently identifying the need and matching it with the available documents is shared between the documents' creators and the searcher; in a search using a controlled vocabulary, the creator of the vocabulary and the documents' indexer(s) are also intelligent participants.

Automated Natural-Language Indexing

In both library catalogues and A&I databases, it is now considered very useful, even indispensable, to be able to search for natural-language words at least in titles and subtitles. Indexing these is no longer the labour-intensive work it once was, provided each word does not have to be separately considered for its indexability value by a human indexer. Automated indexing depends on the availability in machine-readable form of the database to be indexed. This was once an expensive proposition requiring the keying of existing typed and printed documents anew. With the entire content of so many bibliographic tools, issues of newspapers and journals, and even books now already in machine-readable form for their own production, the issue is no longer cost but only format compatibility and ownership clearance. Programs written to make the necessary indexing decision for every word in a database (whether of titles, of abstracts, or even of full text) range from the simple-minded to the extremely sophisticated; the cost of running them varies accordingly. At the simpler end, the computer may be asked to count the number of bytes per word and exclude all very short ones from the index to eliminate prepositions, articles, conjunctions, etc. Compiling a stop-list to identify those words of natural-language text which the program is *not* to make accessible in an index involves a little more judgement. It is a one-time cost to the indexing operation. In theory, automated indexing using a stop-list makes accessible only those words which are highly significant for retrieval purposes. To be effective, the stop-list must take into account the topic(s) of the particular material being indexed and its users' searching habits. This may be fruitful in limited subject areas with precise terminology; for interdisciplinary searching by generalists, using a stop-list is not an effective indexing technique.

More sophisticated automated indexing programs represent an attempt to identify intelligent human indexing and searching decisions as algorithms, bypassing the need for a human to make the same decision over and over in the face of different documents and requests. The basis of the decision is often the frequency of use of a word or word-group in the natural language of the material to be indexed or searched: at a certain threshold of use in a certain context, sentence pattern, etc., the program determines that a word or group of words is important enough to index or retrieve. A programmer can even use the morphological patterns of a language to determine what truncations will best leave only the meaningful roots of words to be searched. Investigating thought/language patterns with a view to automated translation and indexing is at the forefront of information retrieval studies. The most advanced computers able to modify a search while it is in progress on the basis of complex feedback information hold out considerable hope that what is still theory may someday be turned into practice on an operational scale in limited subject areas where the terminology and the information-seeking patterns of users are predictable. Whether this will constitute artificial intelligence is still debatable. At the moment, these studies are a bit distant from the practice of searching the average library catalogue or A&I database.

Natural-Language Access Points and Coordination

Every subject-indexing technique must find some way of pairing terms which can add to each other's meaning and precision by providing the most relevant context. Every controlled vocabulary does this in part by pre-coordination, at least to the extent of bonding the words of a term like black hole. Natural-language retrieval must rely heavily on the techniques of post-coordination described on pages 97–104 and therefore on the common sense and terminological awareness of the searcher. The title *The Reign of the Theatrical Director: French Theatre, 1887–1924* contains three nouns. The first might be useful in accessing material about political history, but not theatre. The second and third are also less than useful when isolated from one another, but in combination, *Director* and *Theatre* pinpoint the conceptual focus of the book well. If the geographic context is also wanted, the searcher must always be aware of the need to use both the substantive and the adjectival forms (France/French) if the same truncation will not do for both as *Canad?* will for Canada/Canadian.

The social worker wants some current data on marriage breakdown (not divorce); the interior designer knows that the venetian blind is something to consider for a particular job. Like pressure broadening and black hole, neither of these topics can be expressed in a single word. Post-coordination using proximity searching can retrieve any record containing the word *blind* provided that word immediately follows the word *venetian* (since neither a blind Venetian nor a Venetian bas-relief in a hospice for the blind is the desired topic). Post-coordination using the boolean operator *AND* retrieves any title, etc. in which both the word *marriage* and the word *breakdown* occur, thereby catching such phrases as "breakdown and dissolution of a marriage." To use post-coordination effectively with natural language, the searcher must be aware of whether a group of words denotes a single topic or more than one topic. This can usually be determined easily but it takes a moment's thought since meaning is not always revealed by the mere forms of words; for example, press law is a combination of the topic *press* (or its synonym, journalism) with the topic *law*; on the contrary, a press release, despite its connection with journalism, is hardly about either that topic or about most meanings of the verb *to release*. Experienced indexers may disagree at times whether a pre-coordination of separate topics or a single multi-word topic is at issue; for example, whether juvenile press should or should not be closely associated with journalism probably depends on the indexing context. As another example, a pressure group is a group (of people) which exerts pressure (on politicians, etc.) and a pressure gauge is a type of instrument for measuring pressure. Both might seem to be post-coordinations of separate topics but it is probably better to consider the first (pressure group) to be a two-word single concept since neither the word *pressure* nor the word *group* is used in its most unambiguous sense in this combination: both are used allusively.

The topic of life on other planets illustrates limitations of the available techniques of post-coordination when used with natural language. The terms *life* (in the broadest biological sense) and *planets* (we think we know precisely how many there are in this solar system) are unambiguous; yet their post-coordination to retrieve the above topic can produce only poor results. Other planets can be expressed negatively (*FIND* [planet] but *NOT earth*) or positively (*FIND mercury AND venus AND mars AND* . . .). Yet post-coordination using *NOT* will not produce a satisfactory result because Earth is virtually always implicit, not explicit, in writings on the subject. Using *AND* works no better because individual planets (except perhaps Mars) are rarely named explicitly in the literature on this topic. Using a pre-coordination in a controlled vocabulary is the only sure way to index this concept.

Natural-Language Access Points and the Larger Database

How effective is it to combine natural-language words from many sources into a single database? A number of indices appeared in book form in the early 1970s to test this. The publisher's series name for them was CumIndex. Each was a single-alphabet mechanical combination of all the back-of-the-book indices of a number of the most reputable publications in a broad but clearly defined field. One CumIndex originated in almost a hundred books in the field of librarianship, over eighty of them published during the previous decade. Although the subject and time contexts were limited and although each separate book-indexer, presumably a librarian trained in subject analysis, probably used a degree of vocabulary control in choosing indexing terms, the differing techniques and vocabularies of a hundred different indexers are painfully evident when their work is cumulated into a single alphabet. The CumIndex series achieved neither wide sale, use, or respect and soon vanished. Its potential virtues did not balance the negative account. In a technical subject area with a more fixed terminology, consistency might not have been such a problem as in librarianship during a period of radical change. Still, the series demonstrated a more fundamental impracticality of combining uncontrolled vocabularies.

There is no doubt that natural-language access provides answers to some questions better than a controlled vocabulary can. It is, at first, even exciting to discover that the computer can find, in under half a second, the truncated word *environ?* 1,675 times in the titles of a library's books and 5,236 times in the texts of magazine articles published last year. Does the promise of so much more information than one could previously discover also bring the motivation to pursue it all? When a check of the result reveals such titles as *The Work Environment in the Civil Service*, it dawns on the searcher that more unpleasant surprises may be in store. However accustomed we are to being deluged with, and sifting through, irrelevant information of all kinds, most users become discouraged on finding a high proportion of only distantly relevant material retrieved in what they thought would be a precise search. They are even more discouraged when they realize that the material most relevant to their needs can elude that search, for example, *Man and Earth: Their Changing Relationship*. Because a book's title is not necessarily the best source of relevant natural-language access points, tables of contents might be added to a bibliographic database for natural-language searching. There is no guarantee that this would make *Man and Earth* . . . retrievable under the word *environment*, but it does guarantee a vast increase in the number of items which would be retrieved under that word. Is this what the searcher wants?

The limitations of a natural-language access system are at first less visible than its ease and copious results. They are certainly underemphasized by commercial vendors of computer-based title- and full-text-indexing services. That these provide no cross-references linking variant terms for the same concept is taken for granted: one must search synonyms separately. It is a greater disadvantage not to have links among related concepts. At their present stage of development, the techniques of both automated indexing and natural-language searching, which are two faces of the same coin, are excellent tools for *document retrieval*, that is, for locating a particular document known to exist or just any relevant document. They are very blunt tools to use for *information retrieval*, except possibly in a limited subject field whose natural language approximates a controlled vocabulary. Their primary virtues are low cost and a sense of immediacy in the user's approach to the database.

Controlled Subject Vocabularies

A controlled subject vocabulary does not permit this sense of immediacy. It is, rather, a mediator—some would say a barrier—between the searcher and the database. It is a greater help to the person who is less well informed about the subject under investigation than to the person who knows the subject intimately. Yet the person who feels uncertain about the subject's exact scope and about how to express exactly what is needed is paradoxically also the person most likely to be impatient with having to cope with an intermediate and seemingly unproductive step in a search. Both making and using a controlled vocabulary demand the conscious exercise of judgement about the nature, naming, and relationships of concepts in both the context of a particular need and the context of the documents available to meet that need. The goal of a controlled vocabulary is not merely information retrieval; the previous section shows that that is possible using natural language. The goal is, rather, *efficient* and *thorough* information retrieval which is unattainable using only natural-language access techniques.

However helpful a name authority file is, a cataloguer can apply authority control to names independently of other cataloguers by using generalized rules such as those discussed in the previous chapter. This is not possible in subject analysis. Internal consistency is difficult enough to achieve even in a subject index or classification for a specialized topic and when only one person creates it. When there are many indexers/classifiers of many subjects over a long period, they cannot operate without a well-edited term-by-term list of all the approved access points and links and/or a minutely itemized classification scheme. This is why Cutter's rules on establishing and applying subject access points, last revised in the earliest years of this century, still have no successor and why there is no recognized set of rules on how to construct or update a particular classification scheme. But there are many lists and classification schemes designed for particular purposes: some compiled by individuals, others by committees. Some are created outside the context of any particular collection of documents; others reflect the indexing and arrangement of a particular collection, closely reflecting both its intellectual content and the perceived needs of its users.

Classification: Dewey et al.

The oldest type of controlled subject vocabulary by far is a classification scheme. In one such scheme, the subject access point for the topic baseball is the number **796.357**, an access point familiar to tens of thousands of Americans who use public and school libraries and who head directly to that numeric location in the shelf arrangement every spring. The three types of controlled subject vocabulary described in the following sections use words to name a topic and arrange these alphabetically. A classification scheme is a fourth type of controlled subject vocabulary which arranges topics according to how they are logically related rather than how they are verbally named. It places the aardvark closer to the zebra (because both are animals) than to the abacus. The resulting arrangement is expressed as a notation, a sequence of numeric, alphabetic, or alphanumeric codes which makes it possible to arrange the classified (logical, systematic) sequence as easily as (indeed, usually more easily than) one can file subject access points in word form.[3]

Centuries before people retrieved subjects from documents via indices of words, whether words of any natural language or of a controlled vocabulary, they were devising classification schemes for both the direct subject retrieval of

3. It is not redundant to describe the access point **796.357** as a classification *notation* or a classification *symbol*. A classification, or a classification scheme, is a particular ordering of concepts. What numbering is attached to the sequence expressed in that order is a separate issue. Just as each classification scheme differs somewhat in its arrangement of concepts, so each has a unique notation. To use examples from some classification schemes used in libraries, the dog, classified as a biological species, is designated **K[5791]** in the Colon Classification, **TUS** in Rider's International Classification, **QL795.D6** in the Library of Congress Classification, and **599.74442** in the Dewey Decimal Classification.

documents in collections and for the listing of those documents in bibliographic files. In a majority of all printed monographic bibliographies, and in the print versions of a significant proportion of all A&I publications, classification remains the primary subject-access method and it is only at the filing position of a classification notation that the full bibliographic information is printed. Users may become familiar with the intellectual organization of such a bibliography but few pay much attention to the actual notation applied. A formal notation, rather than simply numbering the logically organized citations in a single numeric sequence beginning with 1, is more common in an A&I publication where it serves to identify the same topic to searchers in each of many issues and cumulations. The specialist in international trade who frequently consults the *Index of Economic Articles* . . . gets to know that the relevant section is the 410s and looks for that section without needing to consult the alphabetic word-index first (see figure 22), just as the baseball fan heads directly to **796.357** in the public library. Although the earliest interactive files tended not to provide access to their classification notation (if indeed they use one), such indexing is now more common.

Classification System

```
400   International Economics
              4000    General
                      Most articles pertaining to the New International Eco-
                      nomic Order are classified here.
      410   International Trade Theory
            411   International Trade Theory
                  4110    General
                          For theory of international investment see 4410; for bal-
                          ance of payments theory see 4312.
                  4112    Theory of International Trade
                  4113    Theory of Protection
                          For theory of protection in relation to development see
                          also 4114; for commercial policy see 4220.
                  4114    Theory of International Trade and Economic Develop-
                          ment
                          For agriculture and development see also 7100; for multi-
                          nationals and development see 4420; for international aid
                          see 4430; for international investment see 4410.
```

FIGURE 22. A small part of the classification scheme and notation from *Index of Economic Articles in Journals and Collective Volumes* (Nashville: American Economic Association), showing both the classified arrangement (expressed by both indentation and a hierarchically expressive notation) and links (expressed by cross-references in italics).

With their different interests, viewpoints, purposes, and linguistic usages, different people who use the same language often name the same subject in different ways. It is only natural that they should also differ about what logical grouping best encompasses a particular topic. There are at least as many different classification schemes as there are different word-indexing vocabularies. As is true of the latter, most classification schemes are not ones like Dewey's which cover all of knowledge; they are ones covering a limited subject field. New ones are constantly being invented. Merely to put ideas into prose is to invent a classification scheme, a scheme whose notation is the table of contents of the resulting book or the captions of the article. The hardest part of writing anything is the usually lengthy process of deciding what is the best possible order of concepts and the best notation for that order, the latter being the chapter, section, and subsection numbering and/or captioning (heading) which makes the content of the writing clearer to the reader.

A classification scheme and a controlled vocabulary using words are not as different as they might at first seem; they are mirror images of one another. The primary sequence of a word-based vocabulary is the verbal index to the classification scheme; the secondary structure of a good word-based vocabulary, which is its term-linking system of cross-referencing, is the primary structure of a classification scheme. Thus a classification scheme puts baseball near football by making their access points appear near each other in the prescribed sequence—in Dewey, **796.357** and **796.33**, respectively, both of them part of the sequence of sports/games/ball-games/etc. A verbal controlled vocabulary collocates them by making them common cross-references under the same terms: sports, games, ball games, etc. The difference between a classification scheme and a controlled vocabulary of words is very small indeed if *all*, not just the most obvious, indexing techniques of classification and of words are considered. Both classificatory and verbal aspects are necessary in either type of controlled vocabulary: a classification is less than fully effective if it lacks a good word-index and a word-vocabulary of subjects is less than fully effective if it lacks a good classification scheme evident in its linkages.

A searcher does not always have to take full advantage of both methods of subject retrieval to arrive at the needed documents or information. If either verbal or logical sequencing suffices, to use the other would be redundant. One may be used only as a path to the other; many end-users consult a library's subject catalogue only to get a call number where they can browse the classification sequence on the shelves. However, each of these approaches can best supply a different type of the needed insight into subject relationships and the two ideally work as a pair in the formulation of a search. Why else do libraries spend so much money maintaining two parallel subject-retrieval systems? If libraries are being wasteful in doing so, is the same true of the A&I services and other commercial publishers of bibliographic lists whose products embody both a logical classification of bibliographic records and one or more alphabetic subject indices to the same records?

Most users think a library uses a classification scheme only to give a subject-based shelf location to the physical items, but every library also maintains a catalogue whose records are arranged in the order of the library's classification scheme. It serves to keep track of the call numbers assigned to avoid their duplication and to take inventory unless automation provides a different method.

It is called a shelf list because it theoretically lists items in the order in which they appear on the shelves. Through most of this century in North American libraries, the verbal approach was in the ascendency for subject retrieval and the shelf list was rarely located where the public could consult it. In Europe, where closed-stack libraries and multilingual users are more common, classification has always served a more fundamental subject-retrieval function within the library's catalogue system. The shelf list was developed there not as merely a single-subject-access list (each item listed only once under its call number) but as a multiple-subject-access list (each item listed under as many classification notations as are appropriate to its content). In this way, classification for information and subject retrieval becomes separate from classification for physical shelving and document retrieval even if *one* of the classification notations attached to an item's record is identified as its shelf location. This multiple-access version of a shelf-list arrangement is known as a classified catalogue. It can only be the subject portion of a library's divided catalogue; the author/title, etc. part(s) must remain separate and arranged by words. As North American librarians value classification more, they are at least making the single-access shelf list available to the public, whether as a manual file or by indexing call numbers in an interactive catalogue, so that a user can browse the entire collection, not just what happens to be on the shelves of a given branch at a given moment.

Devising an ad hoc classification scheme to organize some prose writing or a subject-specialized bibliography is commonplace. Devising a general scheme which classifies all of knowledge is among the most intimidating possible tasks for either philosopher or librarian; few will ever undertake it. Only two such schemes are in widespread use in English-language libraries:

1) the Library of Congress Classification (LCC), adapted for shelving that library's own collection from Cutter's *Expansive Classification* of the late nineteenth century and
2) the Dewey Decimal Classification (DDC), devised by Melvil Dewey in 1876 for a particular library and now in its 20th edition.

An offshoot of the latter, the Universal Decimal Classification (UDC) is used more for classified catalogues than for library shelving and more outside North America than within it; in many ways, it is more a collection of specialist schemes than a unified general scheme.

Classification by Discipline.   Any topic written about can be located within the notation of any general scheme. While a subject-specific classification scheme looks at everything from the point of view of that subject, a general scheme must maintain an impartiality of viewpoint toward all subjects. Perhaps a theoretical impossibility, this is accomplished in practice by treating every subject in the context of the discipline(s) toward whose point of view the document in question is directed. The classifier cannot classify the subject *the cat* as such but is forced by the scheme to decide whether the document being classified deals with cats primarily as subjects of artworks; as symbols in religious ritual; as pets; as inspirers of poetry; as an amount of living (or dead) tissue and bones; as controllers of rodents and other pests; or even as bystanders at historical events! The location of the document within the classified arrangement depends entirely on which of these is judged to predominate as the document's viewpoint. This emphasizes that all library subject-indexing schemes must be based at least as much on existing documents as on abstract concepts. Although they differ in the details of how they divide and arrange the subdisciplines, all subject-indexing schemes tend to follow closely the way in which subjects are treated from the point of view of academic study since, for the most part, serious writing on most topics also respects the academic disciplinary framework. This helps explain why books written from many popular viewpoints, subject-oriented visual materials, etc. are harder to fit into the existing general classification schemes than is academic nonfiction. The schemes were essentially tailored to the contextual presentation of the latter.

Despite their age, LCC and DDC are not antiquated. They are subject to continuous revision while being put to practical use, an advantage they share with few other classification schemes. DDC's original popularity probably stemmed primarily from the simplicity and memorability of its decimal notation and its easy-to-grasp division of topics. What promoted LCC to widespread use is the same economic factor that made all Library of Congress services de facto models: LCC notation appears on Library of Congress source records for derived cataloguing. In view of the entrenchment of DDC among American public, school, and at that time college libraries, the Library of Congress began to add DDC numbers to its records in 1930 and now does so for a high proportion of what it catalogues. This makes the Library of Congress one of the biggest users of DDC, so when the ability of the DDC copyright owners to finance further revision was threatened in the mid-1950s, the editorial office of DDC was transferred to, and is still at, the Library of Congress. Editorial policy decision on LCC revision is the sole responsibility of the Library of Congress although it heeds the suggestions of other users. In the case of DDC, an international committee governs revision policy.

Controlled Subject Vocabularies Using Words

The four functions of a vocabulary are:[4]

1) to standardize which of two (or more) synonyms to prefer as the access point for a given topic, for example, **COURTSHIP** or **WOOING**

---

4. For convenience and brevity, the single word *vocabulary* hereafter stands for "controlled subject vocabulary using words." It implies both authority control (including all links) and the use of words, not classification, for subject access. Where classification as a controlled vocabulary is relevant to any discussion in the remainder of this chapter, that is stated explicitly.

2) to determine the preferred lead term, or access element, when a single topic can only be expressed as a multi-word combination; for example, should it be **VENETIAN BLINDS** or **BLINDS, VENETIAN?**

3) to provide explicit links among equivalent terms (for example, **WOO-ING** *see* **COURTSHIP**) and among both hierarchically and associatively related terms (for example, **MATE SELECTION** *see also* **COURTSHIP**) and

4) to determine whether and how two or more conceptually separate topics should be linked in a single pre-coordinated access point, for example, **ZEN BUDDHISM AND SCIENCE.**

Not every vocabulary accomplishes or even undertakes all four functions. The first is the most obvious one. It illustrates the very fine line between natural-language indexing and the use of a vocabulary. When writing abstracts of material in the same or related subject fields, an experienced abstractor tends to exercise this function without conscious attention to vocabulary control, without making any permanent record of the decisions taken, and without thinking of any of the other three functions described here. To think of the second function comes as naturally as thinking about which element of a personal or corporate name should be its access element. The third and fourth functions, linking and coordination, deal with the processes of logical arrangement described in the previous section on classification. The third function produces Cutter's syndetic catalogue described in footnote 1 on page 177. It is usually the most time-consuming function and, perhaps because of that, the one usually done least well. Vocabularies fall into two major groups depending on whether or not the fourth function is undertaken. These groups are called (1) lists of subject headings (which pre-coordinate separate concepts) and (2) thesauri (which do not).

Subject Headings.   Jewett and Cutter were instrumental in introducing the vocabulary to index libraries' bibliographic records

1) to replace the use of rotated or permuted natural-language words illustrated on page 179 for subject retrieval (because a vocabulary produces more relevant results) and

2) to supplement the only controlled-vocabulary subject approach then prevalent, the classified catalogue described on pages 187–88 (because vocabulary is more direct and therefore quicker to search).

They carried over some aspects of those other approaches, a fact quite evident in the oldest of the vocabularies still in use, the *Library of Congress Subject Headings* (LCSH). Like access points consisting of rotated phrases or permuted title words, those of virtually all vocabularies up to the 1950s admitted pre-coordinate access points. Not only is it inefficient to do a separate manual search for both **ZEN BUDDHISM** and **SCIENCE** in order to find the few documents dealing with both these concepts, but a good argument can be made that the combination is itself an independent single subject. Furthermore, to be referred in a vocabulary to a pre-coordinate term representing such a topic-combination, when it is based on a substantial body of existing documents, can help a searcher clarify what is really wanted. This does not mean that no further post-coordination need be done if the indexing vocabulary is a pre-coordinating one: two separate pre-coordinate access points may still need to be brought together, whether manually or interactively, to reach the desired result in a search. The use of index strings (see below) is the best of the methods discussed in this section for avoiding a need to post-coordinate.

The access points found in a vocabulary of this type were, and usually still are, called subject headings. Throughout this book, the term *access point* is preferred to the word *heading* but the latter is retained when this kind of pre-coordinate vocabulary is at issue; a subject heading is only one particular type of subject access point and must be distinguished from the other types discussed in this chapter. LCSH, the best-known example of this type of vocabulary, is functionally described as a pre-coordinating vocabulary. Its techniques were adopted early in this century by the emerging A&I services to index journal articles and eventually also influenced back-of-the-book indexing significantly.

Descriptors.   Post-coordinate searching caused a different type of vocabulary to come into existence in the 1950s as described on pages 91–92. This type does not, in general, permit a single access point to express more than one concept. If several concepts are involved in a particular query, their access points must be post-coordinated at the time of the search. A vocabulary of single-concept terms is called a thesaurus in order to distinguish it from a list of subject headings. Its individual access points are usually called descriptors or, more vaguely, just terms. The early experimenters with post-coordinate indexing called the access points *uniterms*, a word which has unfortunately disappeared from use. In that it implies one-term = one-concept, it is a more descriptive and memorable word for the purpose. The thesaurus is as influential in the late twentieth century as was the subject-headings list earlier; virtually all new vocabularies since 1960 are thesauri. In 1988, LCSH incorporated many external features of a thesaurus while not abandoning pre-coordination. In addition, for many years now LCSH has been gradually changing pre-coordinate terms into a term-plus-subdivision structure which can be post-coordinated more readily when loaded into a database management system; for example, **ELECTRICITY ON SHIPS** has become **SHIPS—ELECTRIC EQUIPMENT**. These changes are discussed further on pages 212–13.

Index Strings.   Although it comes into being because of the intellectual content of some actual document, either a descriptor or a pre-coordinate subject heading identifies a concept, not a document. It posits a subject and asks, "What documents concern themselves with this?" In contrast, permuted-word natural-language indexing focuses on a given document, saying "Here is what *this* document is about" and is in this sense more completely pre-coordinated than a subject heading can be. The rotated- or permuted-word system places each concept used as an access point in the precise context of the document which generated it. The advantage of providing a document-related context for any access point, natural-language or controlled, was never entirely forgotten, and as soon as electromechanical sorting machines made it economic, it returned as the KWIC/KWOC index but without vocabulary or structure control (see page 72).

In the mid-1960s, Derek Austin, responsible for the subject indexing of the *British National Bibliography* (BNB), proposed to add a measure of control to permuted-word indexing in order to achieve more intellectually coherent results in a context-based pre-coordinate subject index while still taking advantage of computer technology. In Austin's system, the cataloguer

1) composes a statement of the topic(s) of the document in its own context, paying some attention to choice of terms but not necessarily using a particular list of authorized ones and

2) codes the parts of that statement based on the syntactic and semantic functions of its words.

A computer program automatically produces access points for the document based on the words in the cataloguer's statement and on their functions and relationships as shown by the coding. Permuted-word indexing in this new controlled form is now generically called string indexing. The coded statement of the topic(s) of the document is the index string. Austin called his version of string indexing the PREserved-Context Indexing System (PRECIS). String indexing in general resembles permuted-word indexing and can be made to work using natural-language words. The control it adds lies in its imposition of a structure on a multi-term access point.[5] The advantages of string indexing are most obvious when it is used to index interdisciplinary writing, which is why there is heightened interest in the system today. PRECIS is more highly controlled than some other string-indexing systems because it incorporates a full cross-reference structure; that is, it controls both the structure and the basic vocabulary of the access point.

Comparisons.   One cannot tell just from the appearance of a word (**COLLECTIBLES; POLLUTION**) or a multi-word single-concept term (**BLACK HOLES; CREDIT CARDS**) whether it is a subject heading, a descriptor, a particularly short index string, or only some natural language waiting to be searched. Only the use of terms with respect to coordination and context differentiates the three types of vocabulary discussed here. The existence of supporting links in the retrieval system is what distinguishes any of these from natural language.

5. This does not preclude the possibility of a single word or term alone expressing the whole subject and context of a document. The one word **CHEMISTRY** must serve as the entire index string for a general textbook on that topic.

If a combination of concepts (for example, the credit card versus electronic account debiting as a method of payment), a special aspect (for example, credit card security), a relationship among two or more concepts (for example, the influence of credit cards on family budgeting), or parts of a concept (for example, the magnetic banding of the credit card) must be indexed, differences emerge among the three types of vocabulary and how they are searched. To exemplify them and emphasize their distinguishing characteristics, access points are shown below as each system might apply them to the same hypothetical book or article entitled *Language Study, Reading, and the Computer Lab in the American School.* They are given in alphabetic order in each case.

- *Subject headings* (following the LCSH model):

    1. LANGUAGE ARTS—UNITED STATES—COMPUTER-ASSISTED INSTRUCTION

    2. READING—UNITED STATES—COMPUTER-ASSISTED INSTRUCTION

- *Descriptors* (following the model of the Educational Resources Information Center's *Thesaurus of ERIC Descriptors*):

    1. COMPUTER ASSISTED INSTRUCTION

    2. LANGUAGE LABORATORIES

    3. READING INSTRUCTION

- *Index-string access points* (following the PRECIS model):

    1. COMPUTER SYSTEMS. Applications in teaching reading skills to students in schools in the United States[6]

    2. READING SKILLS. Students. Schools. United States. Teaching. Applications of computer systems

    3. SCHOOLS. UNITED STATES. Students. Reading skills. Teaching. Applications of computer systems

    4. STUDENTS. SCHOOLS. UNITED STATES. Reading skills. Teaching. Applications of computer systems

    5. TEACHING. READING SKILLS. STUDENTS. SCHOOLS. UNITED STATES. Applications of computer systems

The links or cross-references which are part of each of the three systems add many additional words from which the user might arrive at one or another of the access points in these examples. It is, however, typical that a string-indexing system makes more access points searchable directly (not via a cross-

6. The use of capitals and upper/lower case distinguishes what appears on the two lines of a BNB PRECIS access point. Not all string-indexing applications make this distinction. The capitalization of individual words in PRECIS is also computer-generated, based on the coding of the syntax of the string.

reference or other link) than is true in the other pre-coordinate system, that of subject headings.

The two pre-coordinate systems, subject headings and string indexing, are applied to general-knowledge indexing in two of the world's largest libraries. The Library of Congress' application of LCSH as seen in the subject index to the NUC serves as the model for how libraries everywhere use subject headings. Librarians' views of how string indexing works in practice are based on the British Library's application of PRECIS in the BNB. Nevertheless, not every subject heading is an LCSH-authorized one. There are other general lists of subject headings, the so-called Sears List being the most familiar in North America, and thousands of special-subject lists, many now quite old because thesauri are now in favour. Similarly, not every index string is displayed according to the PRECIS programs; there are over two dozen variants on the string-indexing theme, none as complex as PRECIS.[7] For example, some simply display all terms following the access element in alphabetic order, ignoring the niceties of a string's syntax. This would result, for example, in the following access points (among others) for the above hypothetical document:

> **READING SKILLS. Applications of computer systems. Schools. Students. Teaching. United States.**
> **STUDENTS. Applications of computer systems. Reading skills. Schools. Teaching. United States.**

Thesauri and their descriptors are more closely associated with a high degree of subject specialization in the databases of A&I services and special libraries. There is therefore no one pre-eminent thesaurus to serve as a model in the way LCSH serves as a model subject-headings list or PRECIS as a model string-indexing system. There are only the hundreds of different published thesauri, each covering a more or less limited subject field. The largest of them are the thesauri of major A&I services, many of which are now available in print form. It is typical for a database vendor to support a mixture of natural-language and controlled-vocabulary searching of the same database. This, and the number of vocabularies in operation among many databases a librarian works with, renders the present state of word-index searching very untidy. A professional searcher at least distinguishes when natural language must be relied on and when vocabulary control is in operation and learns the particular features of each controlled system encountered. Each system has strengths and weaknesses in answering particular types of query. Will there ever again be a time when most major indices and library catalogues are accessible using essentially the same searching methods, as was the case for a few decades earlier in this century? The computer, so good at enforcing standardization, has not brought stability in this respect.

---

7. Each variant is described briefly in Timothy C. Craven, *String Indexing*, Library and Information Science Series (Orlando: Academic Press, 1986).

The Topic and the User

Point of View

Anyone who spends years studying and writing about a subject field helps to construct and redefine both its language and its internal relationships and tries to lead readers to accept the same terms and viewpoints. Yet different writers present the same field in different ways and each searcher is influenced by the context of previous reading and thinking about the topic. It would simplify matters greatly if the question of what information a particular user wants and that of what information a particular document contains could be considered separately. They cannot. The librarian who uses a vocabulary either to index or to search an index (indeed, the cataloguer and the reference librarian are usually two different persons) must judge what choice of terms and which point of view might best help each inquirer. Figure 23 suggests the relationships among these, and between each of them and the bibliographic record which links them all.

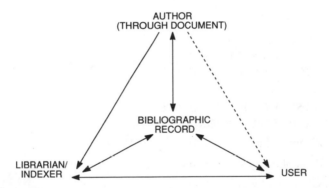

AUTHOR
(THROUGH DOCUMENT)

BIBLIOGRAPHIC
RECORD

LIBRARIAN/
INDEXER

USER

FIGURE 23. The interrelationships between author, user, and librarian showing the central importance of the biblographic record.

To the historian, Hugh Trevor-Roper's book *The European Witch-Craze of the 16th and 17th Centuries* is a social history of early modern Europe. To a psychologist, it is about mass psychology. To a theologian, it is a study of the perception of Satan. To a philosopher, it is about the misapplication of theories of good and evil. To a jurist, it is about the validity of evidence and confessions. To a sociologist, it is about the difference between the establishment and the outcast. What everyone agrees is *not* the subject of this book is witches or witchcraft. Which of the preceding is the viewpoint of the book's cataloguer, and is any particular cataloguer's view of its subject preferable to that of either the author or any given end-user? This illustrates the "mission: impossible" nature of the task of matching topics with actual documents. In the early 1980s, both the British Library and the Library of Congress applied to many of the same books subject access points authorized by the same verbal and classified vocabularies, namely, LCSH, DDC, and LCC. Two examples show how the same book can be viewed differently by equally competent professionals (to say nothing of their potential users).

- Title: *Worlds of Reference*[8]

    LCSH applied by LC:
    1. **ENCYCLOPEDIAS AND DICTIONARIES—HISTORY**
    2. **REFERENCE BOOKS—HISTORY**

    LCSH applied by BL:
    1. **INFORMATION STORAGE AND RETRIEVAL SYSTEMS**

    DDC applied by LC: **030.9**

    DDC applied by BL: **025.5209** (CIP, later revised to **001.5**)

    LCC applied by LC: **AE1**

    LCC applied by BL: **Z699**

- Title: *The Physical Environment at Work*

    LCSH applied by LC:
    1. **WORK ENVIRONMENT**
    2. **HUMAN ENGINEERING**

    LCSH applied by BL:
    1. **PSYCHOLOGY, INDUSTRIAL**
    2. **INDUSTRIAL PRODUCTIVITY**

    DDC applied by LC: **620.82**

    DDC applied by BL: **658.314**

    LCC applied by LC: **T59.77**

    LCC applied by BL: **HF5548.8**

In the case of differing LCSH applications, a user could in most cases get from an access point assigned by one cataloguer to that assigned by another through the cross-reference linkages because the terms in question fall within the same more general discipline. Sometimes, however, the points of view are so radically different that no cross-reference linkage exists at any level.

To accept a subject request at face value is therefore rarely wise. A request for *information* about abortion is reasonable, but a request for *an article or book* about abortion is almost meaningless. Is there a single document covering any subject (even one less controversial than this) in all its ramifications and from all points of view? To the degree a subject request is less comprehensive

8. I feel that this book, by Tom McArthur (Cambridge: University Press, 1986), has as its focus the very matter of this chapter, namely, subject analysis and its alphabetic and classified display. It is highly recommended as a nonlibrarian's view of this topic.

in scope and context (for example, physiological changes in hormone secretion following an abortion), the possibility is greater that something has been written with exactly the requested scope. Single points of view toward a topic are also common in documents, for example, describing techniques of, or giving the history of, abortion. In a pre-coordinate vocabulary, it is common to use a subdivision to express a point of view, for example, [topic]—**HISTORY**; [topic]—**PSYCHOLOGICAL ASPECTS**. Value judgements, however, are left to the end-user to make: that a book favours or condemns abortion, or what a psychological aspect of abortion signifies, is not normally revealed in its subject access points.

Relevance (Precision) versus Recall

To the child taking a first conscious look up on a clear night outside, the whole of astronomy is the topic *the sky*—a children's book on the topic is both general and short. To the post-doctoral fellow investigating black holes, astronomy is a thousand separate topics so diverse that the general term is almost irrelevant except as the name of the department that administers the fellowship. A general book on astronomy, however lengthy, is no longer of professional interest to this person. Between the two extremes, the lay adult of modest education may wish to find both a survey of the whole of astronomy and books with a detailed focus on an astronomical phenomenon (for example, eclipses), method (for example, spectrum analysis), or closely related topic (for example, life on other planets).

The most desirable documents to retrieve in response to any request are those whose *primary* focus is the topic in question and which deal with that primary focus from a point of view relevant to the user's need: in Ranganathan's apt maxim, the right book for the right person at the right time. Does the right document exist? Yes: often. If the match is obvious, the end-user finds it in the bibliographic file or stacks without professional help. The person who wants *any* document (and preferably *only* one) about a topic also normally finds it unaided: this person is unlikely to be very critical about which one best suits the purpose and is best served by using a natural-language index if one is available, not wasting the effort to deal with a vocabulary. At the other extreme, the user who wants *everything* bearing in any way on a topic is also rare. To answer that type of request, every available technique of subject retrieval must be used because each uncovers something the others do not. What results is an exhaustive subject bibliography compiled in a specific context and for a defined goal.

This is not what a library catalogue or A&I publication is intended to be: their purpose is to analyze subject content more impartially because they are expected to answer requests as yet undefined and even unpredictable. The person consulting a library catalogue or A&I publication usually wants something between the quick fix and comprehensiveness, that is, a high-quality selection of what is available within the scope of the collection or the bibliographic file consulted. It is precisely when nothing seems to meet this need exactly that professional help is called upon to locate, and to recognize as such, a number of peripherally relevant documents, each of which answers part of the need. Phrasing this in technical terms, the user wants to recall as few documents as is consistent with a high degree of relevance in each of them. To give someone investigating black holes a book on astronomy does not meet this criterion. It may represent low recall (one item) but it cannot be said to be highly relevant if only ten of its six hundred pages deal with black holes. Furthermore, a general book on astronomy is written at the level of a person wanting a survey of the field, not specialist information on any one part of it; thus its viewpoint also makes it less than highly relevant to the black-hole specialist. If no documents are available whose primary focus is the black hole, the more general book represents the highest-recall/highest-relevance material available and may have to serve until interlibrary loan can come up with something more suitable. There is presumably no such thing as no-recall/no-relevance as long as the collection has an encyclopaedia, but each user establishes a minimum threshold of acceptability of what is offered.

A synonym for relevance in this context is precision. The goal of every indexing/searching system is to be able to identify everything in the database which is precisely applicable to any given topic, that is, to maximize *both* recall *and* precision (relevance) and not to enlarge or diminish either at the expense of the other. If documents are available which precisely match the request, the goal is to retrieve them all. If no such document is available, the net must be cast more widely, but not so widely as to encompass much irrelevant information. In practice, higher recall (more documents retrieved) inevitably means lower precision (some of the retrieved documents are less than totally relevant). Conversely, higher precision (each retrieved document is central to the topic wanted) inevitably means lower recall. Concentrating on either is inevitably at the expense of the other, as acknowledged in the term *recall/precision balance*. Striking the best possible balance involves judgement, not measurement, and its constant adjustment in the course of a search.

What is closely relevant and what is only distantly relevant are usually difficult to determine from the subject index alone. It is the user's expression of satisfaction or dissatisfaction which results in terminating the search or making a further attempt to improve the recall/precision balance. A search often expands, and sometimes contracts, while in progress; not uncommonly it also shifts focus. A user often becomes more aware of what is relevant only while engaged in discovering what exists. The user cannot know, and even the librarian rarely finds out later, whether something better (or additional) exists but was completely missed in the search. When this happens, either the request-definition stage or the searching stage (or both) of the retrieval system somehow failed. It is much harder to determine and measure the failure rate than the satisfaction rate, but where this has been attempted, the failure rate is discouraging. Until it can be reduced, there is good reason to allow an inefficient redundancy in retrieval systems; for example by letting *both* classification and word-indexing, and *both* natural language and controlled vocabularies, do what each can do best even with the same request.

The Access Element: Specificity and Classification

Recall is primarily a function of the size of the file being consulted. The degree of precision possible is more closely affected by the choice of indexing terminology. Determining the form and wording of the access element is critical to both recall and precision. No user wants to be shunted among cross-references; direct access to the desired topic should be where the informed user first expects it.

Specificity

The index which can best maximize precision isolates subjects as specifically as the content of the documents listed permits. As Cutter put it, a book on the cat should be indexed under **CATS**, not under **MAMMALS** or **DOMESTIC ANIMALS**. Many more distinctions must, however, be made than the beginner in subject retrieval might wish. Every language expresses subtle differences of meaning: Inuktitut has many different words for the various kinds of snow. If it lacks a generic word for the cold white stuff, no indexer should impose one on material written for these people as if their own distinctions were meaningless. Because English vocabulary has been constructed from so many different cultural sources over so long a period, it may be the world's richest modern language in subtly different, but separately indexable, connotations. A significant difference between **DECEPTION** and **FRAUD** may be immediately evident to one trained in ethics or the law, but the layperson who happens upon one of these terms must be shown (by an associative link) that the other is also a valid access point for related material treated from another point of view.

The principle of specificity is the key to controlling the recall/precision balance regardless of whether the index is to support general or specialist searching. The problem is to know how specific is specific? Specificity is relative: to stretch the astronomy example on pages 197–98 to the breaking point, the sky is specific for the child, but general for the specialist in black holes. To serve beginners or those to whom a field is peripheral, one may authorize the use of, say, only a hundred broader terms (other than names). Provided they are well chosen, it should be possible to index any existing book, article, etc. in the field under one or another of the hundred. Thus music terms in a vocabulary designed for the retrieval of information about literature may be restricted to the level of **JAZZ** and **ROCK MUSIC**, allowing no more specific terms for the subgenres of either. Using this vocabulary, a book about the music of Jimi Hendrix shares the same access point as one about the music of John Lennon. The average number of items listed under each of a smaller number of terms is higher, but this is no disadvantage if the collection as a whole is small and the anticipated requests are fairly general. Precision may be desirable in the abstract but if there is nothing more precise in the collection to recall or no useful distinction made by searchers at a more specific level, what has this precision achieved? These are reasons why vocabularies containing many fewer terms than LCSH to cover all of knowledge, such as the Sears List, are valid in smaller libraries.

Adding a subdivision to a more general access element (for example, **ROCK MUSIC—ACID ROCK; MINERALS—COAL**) can improve the recall/precision balance but the user still finds the more precise topic in the file location of the more general one. Such an access point is not a pre-coordination: it does not show a relationship of two different topics. It expresses a single concept in terms of two of its hierarchical levels. It accomplishes the same thing in words as a classification scheme accomplishes using a notation. That is why it is called the alphabetico-classified approach. Using this approach, the number of access *elements* remains small even as the number of different access *points* grows larger and the individual access points become quite specific. The alphabetico-classified approach to constructing access points is now rare.

The other method of increasing precision is to authorize the addition of specific access points of the type **ACID ROCK, CLASSIC ROCK, FOLK ROCK, RHYTHM AND BLUES,** etc. as needed. Books about the music of Hendrix and Lennon are then no longer near each other in the subject file but are separated by the access points for many different topics, including **BACKGAMMON**. This was once known as the alphabetico-specific approach; Cutter called it a dictionary approach because specific terms are filed, as in a dictionary, without a primary concern for keeping classes of terms together.[9] Differences among the authorized terms of a highly specific vocabulary are necessarily more subtle. The greater the number of specific access points added, the more is related material scattered in the file or index, to be reassembled (if wanted together in a more comprehensive search) only by using links in the verbal catalogue and/or classification.

Levels of Indexing.   Into how many separate types should one divide the popular music of the 1960s for alphabetico-specific indexing? Can a group of different indexers or users agree both on the distinctions among its subtypes and on their naming? Unless the vocabulary is intended for a collection with a known clientele and type of use, it is better to have a more objective focus of specificity for indexing than an indexer's enthusiasm for the subject or users' supposed needs. Thus LCSH access points are based on the primary focuses of those documents-as-a-whole which get listed in the subject index to the NUC. A book's internal (back-of-the-book) index is expected to specify each concept, name, etc. treated significantly within its pages. The practical difference is clear:

9. The different connotation of the term *dictionary catalogue* used on page 71 came to be applied because Cutter's catalogue was also in a single alphabet of authors, titles, and subjects.

a three-hundred-page book whose internal index identifies five hundred separate subjects is very likely to appear under only one or two subject terms in the library catalogue. The principle of specificity is adhered to in each case at the level of the defined unit of indexing: at one extreme, the book as a whole; at the other, each paragraph or even sentence. This does not mean that a different vocabulary must be used at each different level of indexing; for example, LCSH can be used as a basis for back-of-the-book indexing. What it does mean is that the required level of specificity must be consciously determined and consistently applied.

The typical A&I publication falls between the extremes of the library catalogue and the back-of-the-book index. It generally attempts subject indexing in greater depth than the library catalogue, partly because journal articles and similar materials lack the equivalent of the book's internal index. The astrophysicist pursuing the topic of pressure broadening searches the A&I publication first because this topic is a likely focus of a journal article but a less likely focus of an entire book. The internal index of a general astronomy text is a last resort because it is unlikely to reveal anything new to this searcher. Some A&I publications, especially in the disciplines of science and technology, approach the depth of back-of-the-book indexing, providing perhaps a dozen index terms for a brief but specialized article. This is generally because the many processes, materials, etc. named in articles in those disciplines must be individually retrievable, not because the A&I service tries to divide the concepts themselves as minutely as a back-of-the-book index would.

Names.   Names of persons, corporate bodies, places, and works, established in the forms discussed in chapter 6, are the most highly specific of all index terms since each names only one individual. With such names, neither recall, relevance, nor specificity is a major problem. Information retrieved about John Lennon under his surname is totally relevant because *only* information about him as a person can appear there. This does not mean that his name should also be the index location for his musical style. Because name indexing is so relatively simple and sure, indexers sometimes get carried away with it and index every available name whether it has any bearing on the topic in hand or is merely mentioned in passing as an example. Similarly, many a searcher seizes on a name in a query even when it is not at all representative of the conceptual focus needed. While names can be traps, they are an implicit or explicit part of every vocabulary.

Classification in a Specific-Term Index

Is the concept more likely to be sought under the term **MUSIC, ELECTRONIC** or **ELECTRONIC MUSIC**? The answer to this difficult question depends on whether, in the particular case at issue, the typical user's attention is more likely to be concentrated on the nature of the distinction (in this case, electronic) or on the thing distinguished (in this case, music). This is not the issue of alphabetico-classed arrangement raised on page 200. Although the first of the two examples there, **ROCK MUSIC—ACID ROCK**, may seem relevant, it explicitly and separately names two different levels of a single hierarchy in the same access point, whereas **ELECTRONIC MUSIC** is merely a two-word access point expressing one concept. To invert it, making the second word the access element, looks rather like personal-name inversion to get the surname first. This is appealing when an adjective (the distinction) precedes a noun (the thing distinguished), as it usually does in English, because nouns are generally favoured as access points. Should the temptation to classify by bringing the various types of music together even in an alphabetico-specific listing extend to pulling jazz music away from the Js?

Because classification historically preceded specific-term indexing, indexers well into the twentieth century were wont to invert adjective-noun combinations. Cutter wrestled indeterminately with this issue but began the long process of weaning alphabetic indexing away from the grouping function and toward (1) the alphabetico-specific approach discussed previously and (2) what is called the direct approach: the naming of subjects in the word-order of their natural prose expression. This approach takes into account the assumption that any desired grouping of related material should be accomplished by classification and/or the linkages built into a vocabulary. However, the urge to group lingered, as expressed by the person responsible for the early application of LCSH:

> There is undeniably a strong tendency in the Library of Congress Cata-log to bring related subjects together by means of inversion of headings, by combinations of two or more subject-words, and even by subordina-tion of one subject to another. Yes, the tendency at times is so noticeable that it may seem as if an effort were being made to establish a compro-mise between the dictionary and the alphabetico-classed catalog . . . . the student and the investigator . . . are best served by having related topics brought together so far as that can be accomplished without a too serious violation of the dictionary principle.[10]

For decades, LCSH policy has been not to establish inverted access points. Many, however, like **LIBRARIES, SPECIAL** remain from the past alongside directly expressed counterparts in the same subject area, for example, **TECHNICAL LIBRARIES**. Presumably they will soon be revised.

Application of Descriptors and Thesauri

Although historically the most recent type of vocabulary, the thesaurus is the most uncomplicated one and its use is the easiest to describe. It is aptly named

10. J.C.M. Hanson, "The Subject Catalogs of the Library of Congress," in *Papers and Proceed-ings of the Thirty-first Annual Meeting of the American Library Association Held at Bretton Woods, New Hampshire; Bulletin of the American Library Association* 3 (September 1909): 389–90.

after Roget's eighteenth-century work whose primary purpose it imitates so closely.[11] This purpose is to display relationships among concepts more than to provide an indexing vocabulary tailored to a particular collection of documents. This may seem a subtle distinction, but it means that in practice, one consults a thesaurus as much to grasp the conceptual relationships of the subject field it covers as to find explicit terms to search in a given index. Both the subject-headings list and the string-indexing system are more explicitly linked to the indexing of the documents in a particular collection because they pre-coordinate concepts on the basis of what is in that collection. Since the thesaurus does not pre-coordinate, it views concepts more abstractly.

A descriptor in a thesaurus may be one word or more but it identifies only one concept. A qualifier may be necessary to specify a context for an inherently ambiguous term; for example, **DISTRACTORS (TESTS)**. This is not an attempt to impose or imply any context, point of view, or classificatory relationship. Nor does a descriptor imply any particular level or scope of treatment of that concept. The subject index at the back of a book is often composed of descriptors. If so, the access point **WOMEN—19, 74, 157** does not mean that the topic of women is treated generally, and reasonably completely, on each of the three cited pages. Far from it. The only implication is that there is some mention of the concept, in some depth or other, in some context or other, on each of those pages. It makes a difference to the user whether the reference is to the history of women's right to vote in the Netherlands, to women hippies in America in the 1960s, or to the incidence of throat cancer among Japanese women. Without a context, finding the isolated descriptor **WOMEN** can only result in frustratingly high recall and frustratingly low relevance, but in a back-of-the-book index, this context is normally provided by the very subject and point of view of the whole book, be it politics, sociology, or medicine. This is why descriptors are useful in back-of-the-book indexing in specialized areas but why their widespread use in the indexing of bibliographic files came only with the advent of the interactive file where they are easily post-coordinated with other terms to provide context and relevance. As many descriptors are applied to a document as are needed to encompass its principal focus. A document on the rehabilitation of patients with heart disease using massage therapy is indexed using separate descriptors for the concepts of rehabilitation, heart disease, and massage therapy. It is probably undesirable to index the concept of the patient separately in this context since the more specific term *rehabilitation* implies it.

Figure 24 illustrates characteristic features of a thesaurus. The linkages consist of any scope notes (abbreviated *SN*) as well as what are traditionally called cross-references. The latter are indicated in the thesaurus using conventional codes. A term authorized for use as an access point is linked with one or more instances of the following:

11. The reference is to Roget's original classified version, not the alphabetic arrangement produced by some modern editors.

1) a synonym; the code *Use for* (*UF*) is followed by non-authorized synonyms or other orthographic forms which also appear in the thesaurus; at its own location in the alphabet, each of the latter is followed by the instruction *Use* (*U*) and the authorized term(s)[12]

2) a term in the same hierarchy of meaning, but broader in extent and including the meaning of the starting-term, designated as a *Broader Term* (*BT*)

3) a term in the same hierarchy of meaning, but narrower in extent and included in the meaning of the starting-term, designated as a *Narrower Term* (*NT*) and

4) a term closely related to the starting-term, but in a way which cannot be expressed hierarchically, designated as a *Related Term* (*RT*).

Creating and displaying this syndetic structure (so described by Cutter in footnote 1 on page 177) requires close attention to logical rules. These have gradually been developed to the level of the ISO guidelines for thesauri cited in footnote 8 on page 77. Using the terminology introduced there, the first linkage expresses the equivalence relationship; the second and third, the hierarchical relationship; and the fourth, the associative relationship. A scope note is usually a more explicit way of expressing the associative relationship. The hierarchical relationship is normally indicated at only one higher (or lower) level than the starting term.

It has become common, although not universal, practice for a thesaurus to display its terms in at least two ways additional to the basic alphabetic display illustrated in figure 24.

1) Not every word of a multi-word term forms part of the syndetic structure. To avoid cluttering the basic alphabetic display of terms with such references as **RELATIONSHIP, PEER** *Use* **PEER RELATIONSHIP**, an index called something like Rotated Keyword Display is provided which lists every word in the thesaurus (perhaps excluding prepositions, etc.) in a single alphabet in a KWIC-index format.

2) Since the hierarchical relationships are shown minimally in the basic list (that is, at only one level higher and/or one level lower), a fuller display of all the logical links is useful. Cutter described this as a "synoptical table of subjects" and advised against it because of the "immense labor" involved.[13] The labour is no longer so immense be-

---

12. An older convention shows the code *x* instead of *Use for* and *See* instead of *Use*. The two terms need not have precisely the same meaning; for example, **PERCUSSION BANDS** *Use* **RHYTHM BANDS AND ORCHESTRAS** only means that for practical purposes, the indexer has decided to locate everything connoted by either of the two terms under one access point. This may be because the material being indexed does not make the distinction clear or because the index is for a group of users to whom the distinction, although real, is irrelevant (see pages 199-200).

13. *Rules for a Dictionary Catalog*, p. 80.

LANGUAGE PLANNING   *Aug. 1969*

SN   Planned language change directed to-
        ward improving the utility of a language
        or increasing its use in a given country
        or region.

NT   Language Standardization

BT   Planning
        Sociolinguistics

RT   Bilingual Education
        Bilingualism
        Educational Policy
        Immersion Programs
        Language
        Language Attitudes
        Language Maintenance
        Language of Instruction
        Language Usage
        Languages
        Multilingualism
        National Norms
        National Programs
        Official Languages
        Second Languages
        Sociolinguistics

FIGURE 24. A sample access point from the *Thesaurus of ERIC Descriptors*, 12th ed. (Phoenix: Oryx, 1990).

cause of the computer. These additional indices are not yet known by standard names but take the form of either or both of:

a)   a list called something like Descriptor Groups, in which each term in the thesaurus is listed as part of a broader class of concepts—the latter may be arranged alphabetically or in an explicitly classified order or

b)   a list called something like Hierarchical Term Display, in which the complete hierarchy of *BT*s and *NT*s associated with each term at *every* level is shown in association with that term.

Application of Subject Headings (LCSH)

The use of post-coordination in its proper context, the interactive file, is still new to many nonspecialist end-users. In contrast, most people are quite familiar with the pre-coordinate subject access point not only in library catalogues but also in telephone-directory yellow pages, back-of-the-book indices, etc. The very existence of LCSH is a factor in perpetuating pre-coordinate indexing. This largest of all vocabularies covers every subject area and represents some eighty years of thoughtful and continuous development and revision by subject specialists. However imperfect, illogical, or inconsistent it may be—and it is all of these—it is a practical tool for indexing and/or locating something relevant to almost any request. It has been adopted or adapted everywhere in the library world where English is the working language and is used in translation in other language areas. It is also used in many indexing functions outside libraries. At what expense would one redesign, much less reinvent, *this* wheel?

LCSH is the cumulation of currently authorized forms of all the subject terms and cross-references applied to bibliographic records by or under the authorization of the Library of Congress since 1898. The actual terms used, the amount of pre-coordination incorporated into any one access point, the choice of access element whenever two or more words are involved, the syndetic structure, and other aspects of LCSH have changed over time with socio-linguistic fashions, with changes in how concepts are treated in the books catalogued, and with periodic re-evaluations of the effectiveness of LCSH as an indexing vocabulary. A kind of superimposition as described on page 173 concerning changes in name access points has always applied in the Library of Congress' own use and maintenance of LCSH because although single terms are being constantly changed, at no time has the list as a whole ever been comprehensively revised. It contains terms in forms which would not be used if the concept were first encountered now but which continue to be applied to new books, for example, **LIBRARIES, SPECIAL**.[14] The importance of LCSH demands a rather lengthy description of its essential features.

Pre-Coordination

That a list of subject headings permits pre-coordination does not mean that every access point actually used combines several concepts; only some do. LCSH presents a pre-coordination in a number of ways, using, for example:

1) an adjective-noun combination in either word-order, for example, **PAPER CRAFTS; ADVERTISING, MAGAZINE**
2) a compound, for example, **LOCKS AND KEYS**; **CHRISTIANITY AND ECONOMICS**
3) a phrase, for example, **INCENTIVES IN INDUSTRY**; **EMPLOYEES, DISMISSAL OF**

14. As mentioned on page 202, that particular heading will eventually be replaced by **SPECIAL LIBRARIES**. In *The Subject in the Dictionary Catalog from Cutter to the Present* (Chicago: American Library Association, 1983), Francis Miksa analyzes four stages of LCSH development but with least attention to the current one. Each represents a significant overall policy change from the preceding one. Policy statements and interpretations of the application of current policy to individual categories of access points are part of the Subject Cataloging Division's *Subject Cataloging Manual: Subject Headings*, 3rd ed. (Washington: Cataloging Distribution Service, Library of Congress, 1988) [1 v., looseleaf]. Changes are published regularly in *Cataloging Service Bulletin*.

4) a dash-subdivision, for example, **WATER—FLUORIDATION**; **BIBLIOGRAPHY—DATA BASES**.

It cannot, however, be assumed that every access point which uses an adjective and a noun, a conjunction or preposition, etc. is a pre-coordination; for example, each of the following is a single indexable concept, not one that could be readily divided into separate concepts for post-coordination: **DELEGATED LEGISLATION; CEREALS, PREPARED; THOUGHT AND THINKING; DIVISION OF LABOR; OPERA—SOCIAL ASPECTS**. A parenthetical qualifier (for example, **SEX (PSYCHOLOGY)**) should not represent a second topic any more than it does in a thesaurus (see page 203), but in the manner in which LCSH is applied to particular documents, it sometimes seems to.

Using a dash (*never* a hyphen) is the most typical method of signalling a pre-coordination. In addition to indicating the pre-coordination of separate topics (for example, **LIBRARIES—AUTOMATION**), a dash may show that a topic is being pre-coordinated with:

1) a place, for example, **ARCHITECTURE—CANADA**; **CANADA—ENGLISH-FRENCH RELATIONS**
2) an intended audience, for example, **DOGS—JUVENILE LITERATURE** or
3) a form, for example, **LITERATURE—BIBLIOGRAPHY**; **CHEMISTRY—CONGRESSES**.

The use of place names in LCSH is discussed later in this section; form and audience are considerations in subject access which transcend types of vocabulary and are treated on page 217. The mingling of form/audience terms with concept terms gives rise to ambiguities; for example, does **CATALOGUING—PERIODICALS** apply to a book about how to catalogue a periodical or to a periodical about cataloguing? The same access point cannot serve for both.

Literary Warrant. LCSH is based on *selected* pre-coordination, not on the free pre-coordination of *any* two (or more) concepts. The latter is not pre-coordination at all. It might not even be post-coordination as much as merely chaos. Just as post-coordinating the surname **Cooper** with the given name **Richard** to locate a single person named Richard Cooper would be very inefficient (see pages 144–45), so, for example, post-coordinating the term **RELIGION** with the term **SCIENCE** (both of which are authorized terms in LCSH) is not an efficient way of approaching the concept "religion's interaction with science". This is not only because of the large number of documents to which each of those two particular terms is separately applicable but also because there is a cohesive body of existing writing whose precise focus is this combination of concepts. The existence of this body of writing gives what is called *literary warrant* to the establishment of the pre-coordination **RELIGION AND SCIENCE**, a warrant justified by the desirability of achieving high precision in the retrieval of the writings in question. This helps distinguish subject headings from descriptors, the latter being established for something closer to purely conceptual reasons, as described on page 203. If literary warrant appears more a pragmatic than a theoretical basis for action, it only emphasizes that LCSH is essentially a pragmatic vocabulary. Despite literary warrant, however, a particular subject heading is still to a degree independent of the intellectual content of any document, whether the document for which it came to be established or any other to which it is later applied. This is a major distinction between a subject heading and an index string applied to the same document.

One Book, One Access Point?   Neither pre-coordination nor literary warrant implies that one single subject heading must exist or be created precisely to fit the topical scope of each book catalogued. They only mean that if two concepts are treated in a document not as separate entities in relation to one another but as a self-contained and unified concept, a single access point should be available to express that unified concept. The origin of **MICROWAVE OPTICS** as a single access point is mentioned in this context on page 97; **RELIGION AND SCIENCE** is mentioned above. No recent document on either phenomenon could be said to deal with two separate topics. But the book *The Ethnic Origins of Nations* can still be said to deal with two separate concepts in relationship to one another—nationalism and ethnicity—and therefore properly receives two separate subject headings in the LCSH system. To engage in this hair-splitting is to make judgements which are often subjective but nonetheless essential to the nature of a pre-coordinate vocabulary. Thus a source of a new pre-coordinate subject heading is that book which finally convinces the subject cataloguer at the Library of Congress that topics once written about only in relationship to one another have merged into a unity. The wording of a title or subtitle may provide the final evidence needed. For example, the access point **FRAIL ELDERLY** was created on August 11, 1989, for the book *Aging in Place: Supporting the Frail Elderly in Residential Environments* because that single new topic was deemed to have emerged from its origins in what would previously have been expressed in the two separate access points **AGED** and **HANDICAPPED**.

The interdisciplinary nature of so much recent writing puts strain both on the process of creating new pre-coordinations and on the process of deciding how many separable topics a book treats. Some pre-coordinations authorized by LCSH may appear to go too far toward identifying a single document (or extremely few of them even in a highly specialized collection) and in so doing, bury some of the useful concepts involved in a welter of cross-references; perhaps **COAL MINES AND MINING—DUST CONTROL—WATER INFUSION** might be cited as an example of this.

Place.   Much writing deals with some aspect of a place as either (1) a topic whose focus is a geographic or a jurisdictional entity or (2) a qualifier of a non-geographic topic. These involve the coordination of a place name with a topic, with another place name, with a form, or even with several of these. It may take a moment just to realize what is meant by an access point such as **HERALDRY—SCOTLAND—ARCHIVAL RESOURCES—ENGLAND—OXFORD** (archival material located in Oxford but concerning Scottish heraldry). (This type of double-place subdivision was abandoned in 1990.) It may seem self-evident that some place/topic pre-coordinations are most likely to be sought under the place element (for example, **JAPAN—SOCIAL LIFE AND CUSTOMS**) while others are most likely to be sought under the topical element (for example, **BUDDHISM—JAPAN**), but Cutter found it so hard to decide which is which that he felt each such pre-coordination should be expressed in *both* ways.[15]

Like any other name, a geographic one must be expressed in the same way as an access element in a subject file as it is in a name file. However, the rules discussed on pages 161–63 do not adequately treat the naming of vaguer geographic units like metropolitan areas or multi-country coastal areas. Names for these are better defined by local usage; published vocabularies are often less than helpful. When it comes to using a geographic name as a subdivision of a topic, there is a further complication in whose resolution LCSH has not been consistent over the years. It is illustrated in two different access points: (1) **BULLFIGHTS—SPAIN—BURGOS** and (2) **BULLFIGHTS—BURGOS (SPAIN)**. The former pattern displays all material about local Spanish bullfights together (alphabetically subdivided by the city or local place) and separated from material about bullfights in France, Mexico, Portugal, etc. The debate between supporters of direct and specific identification and those who advocate a degree of classification in subject access points still rages in respect of place subdivisions. The Library of Congress has flip-flopped over the years, at one time routinely requiring direct geographic subdivision (the second example above); at another time, indirect subdivision (the first example above); and at yet another, dividing lead terms into some to be subdivided one way and some the other! As recently as 1987, the Library tentatively proposed changing from its then current policy of indirect subdivision to direct subdivision. The rule as of late 1990 is: always indirect. The indirect subdivision begins with the name of the country when a lower-level place is to be specified *except* in the case of provinces of Canada, states of the United States, and similar units of a few other specified countries where the highest named unit in the subdivision is not the country but the province, state, etc., for example, the purely hypothetical **BULLFIGHTS—CONNECTICUT—LONDON.**

Pre-Coordination and the End-User.   A common complaint of end-users about pre-coordinate subject access points is well illustrated by a very reason-

15. *Rules for a Dictionary Catalog,* p. 68, where he also acknowledges that for purely practical reasons, it is necessary to opt in each case for only one form. It is also in practice impossible to include in any pre-coordinate vocabulary or listing a cross-reference from each different place to each different topic or vice-versa; a few generalized references must serve to let the searcher know when it is better to search under the place name and when better to search under the topic.

able query: "Have you a list of the Canadian colleges where a wheelchair-bound student can be relatively mobile?" How does one arrive at the tortured but LCSH-authorized expression **UNIVERSITIES AND COLLEGES— CANADA—BUILDINGS—ACCESS FOR THE PHYSICALLY HANDICAPPED— DIRECTORIES** which precisely answers the query? This pre-coordination consists of three concept-segments, one place-segment, and one form-segment; two of the concept-segments are themselves pre-coordinations. The answer is that the end-user probably does *not* find the access point unaided but leaves it to the librarian to do so by following up more than one cross-reference in LCSH. Skilled use of the syndetic structure actually leads to this access point from at least a dozen different starting-points although the route is often less than clear. This type of combination calls out for an interactive post-coordinate search but, theoretically at least, pre- and post-coordination will arrive at the same result because of the syndetic structure associated with the former.

Pre-Coordination and the Cataloguer/Indexer.   The linkages in a thesaurus merely relate the meanings of single-concept terms to one another. In a pre-coordinate vocabulary, they bear the additional burden of helping to indicate how the terms are to be correctly assembled as building-blocks in a pre-coordinate access point such as the one in the previous paragraph. The five separate segments of that example can be assembled in no fewer than one hundred twenty different ways (see the **A B C D** example on page 92). The word *college*, the word *handicapped*, or the term *physically handicapped* will not be the access element in any of these permutations because none of them appears at the beginning of a segment; allowing any of those words to be an access element would vastly increase the number of possible permutations! Yet only *one* of the many possibilities, the one given above, is correct; any other is a misapplication of LCSH and would be of little or no use to a searcher because the whole syndetic structure of the list is designed to lead only to pre-coordinations which are correctly assembled.

LCSH cannot separately list every authorized pre-coordination; to do so would multiply the size of the print version, already ten thousand columns. If it authorizes the pre-coordination of one topic with the subheading —AC-COUNTING or of one place with the subheading —FOREIGN RELATIONS, corresponding pre-coordinations in the same form must obviously be permissible with many, if not all, other topics and places. A slightly more complex application of the building-block principle is shown in what are called multiples; for example, the pattern shown in LCSH as **ARTS, AMERICAN [FRENCH, etc.]—IRANIAN [etc.] INFLUENCES** authorizes the access point **ARTS, YUGOSLAV—JAPANESE INFLUENCES**. An instruction on the correct application of each different type of building block appears in the list but perhaps not always where a cataloguer or searcher would first think to look for it. A *see also* (*SA*) reference is the method most often used in LCSH to show

how to assemble building blocks correctly to form a pre-coordination. There is also a separate listing of the building blocks called free-floating subdivisions to supplement the instructions within LCSH and in the *Subject Cataloging Manual* mentioned in footnote 14 on page 206.[16] A new (that is, previously unused) access point may thus be created without an explicit change in LCSH if it involves nothing more than using available LCSH building-block instructions to form a new pre-coordination. Cataloguers elsewhere sometimes prefer to wait until the proposed new pre-coordination can be found on a Library of Congress bibliographic record—there are pitfalls in creating these solo.

Change and LCSH

LCSH may never have been thoroughly revised as a whole, but it is in a state of constant, even hourly, change. Every quarterly issue of *Cataloging Service Bulletin* throughout the 1980s lists some three dozen significant new subject access points (without any of their subdivisions) and a couple hundred major and minor changes of form and/or wording in existing ones. From time to time, a particular subject area undergoes a more systematic review and revision. In 1990, the Library of Congress began a far-reaching re-examination of the entire LCSH system which it expects will take a number of years and which may have radical results for its policies and practices of subject analysis. A conference on the troublesome technical issue discussed in the previous paragraph—the construction of access points involving subdivisions—will inaugurate this re-examination in May, 1991.

Ten editions of LCSH appeared between 1909 and 1986. Supplements and notification in *Cataloging Service Bulletin* were increasingly inefficient methods of publicizing its many changes. Beginning with the 1988 11th edition, a complete cumulation in printed form is promised annually to parallel the complete microfiche cumulation issued quarterly. Cumulations in machine-readable form are also issued regularly on tape and CD/ROM.

Changes in Terminology. Acting at one time in virtual isolation, the Library of Congress now shares the responsibility for formulating new subject access points with its partners in the National Coordinated Cataloging Program (see footnote 7 on page 118). It also considers the many suggestions of librarians who use LCSH and who are at times vociferous in their demands for terminology in keeping with current linguistic usage and viewpoints. Their concerns may appear more appropriate to public, school, and college libraries than to other academic and special libraries but since the early 1970s, Sanford Berman's ceaseless and sometimes intemperate prodding in favour of more socially acceptable terminology and the quicker inclusion of new popular terms has been instrumental

---

16. *Free-Floating Subdivisions: An Alphabetical Index*, 2nd ed., prepared by the Office of Subject Cataloging Policy (Washington: Cataloging Distribution Service, Library of Congress, 1990).

in effecting many changes. The Hennepin County (Minnesota) Library where he directs cataloguing operations maintains an independent subject authority file which has become a de facto supplier of new access points for LCSH. LCSH changes have been particularly numerous since the computer made it easier to implement them in existing automated catalogues. The Library of Congress now explicitly invites suggestions for additions and changes "in order to build a subject authority file that will be useful to other libraries receiving materials not acquired by LC or cataloging items at a depth not practiced by the Library of Congress."[17] This is a potentially major policy change, since incorporating new access points for this purpose will make LCSH increasingly like a thesaurus in being less closely linked to a particular collection.

Changes in Access-Point Structure. The MARC format provides for coding each dash-subdivision of an LCSH-authorized access point as a separate subfield. This makes it possible to search each subfield separately. It also distinguishes place and time subdivisions from each other and from other types of subdivision by using different subfield codes for these two factors, every other type of subdivision being coded identically.[18] Subfield delimiters are of little practical relevance when subject headings are loaded into a database management system which permits word-by-word post-coordinate searching, as is now common. In such a system, the pre-coordinate nature of any LCSH access point is compromised when a user searches it by its single words; the vocabulary becomes in effect a series of single-word descriptors devoid of the control exercised over access points as wholes. Thus the searcher can locate the word **SCIENCE** as a one-word access point, as the first word in **SCIENCE MUSEUMS**, as a word other than the first in **WOMEN IN SCIENCE**, or as a word in a subdivision, for example, **DEAF—EDUCATION—SCIENCE** or even **CLASSIFICATION—BOOKS—SCIENCE FICTION**. Adding the truncation feature, probably unwisely, one can even retrieve **SOCIAL SCIENCES**! This is a misuse of pre-coordinate access points which have been carefully (if not always logically) constructed in that context, as shown particularly in the last two examples above which do not even relate to the discipline of science. If such single-word searching is done with care after analyzing the topic(s) to be searched and identifying the relevant LCSH building blocks, it can be both effective and efficient, but in principle, it is not an appropriate technique for high-recall/high-precision results.

This is making LCSH perforce a *potentially* post-coordinate scheme, with profound implications for its maintenance and revision. Vocabulary control, once applied to a subject heading as a whole, is now more consciously applied to each of its separate conceptual parts because any one of them might be invoked

17. *Cataloging Service Bulletin* no. 41 (summer 1988): 83.

18. Each place and time subdivision can also be named in another MARC field (tags 043 and 045, respectively), not in words/figures but as a geographically or chronologically classified code for easier post-coordination. Not every library takes the trouble to code these.

separately in a post-coordinate search. One visible result is an increase in the use of free-floating subdivisions; for example, **BASEBALL MANAGERS** has become **BASEBALL—MANAGERS** and, with rather more changes of actual wording, **HISTORY, COMIC, SATIRICAL, ETC.** has become **WORLD HISTORY—HUMOR**. The basic problem remains, as always, to determine what must be left as an unbreakable unit of thought. For example, the pattern illustrated by **ITALIANS IN SWITZERLAND** was changed to the pattern **ITALIANS—SWITZERLAND** in keeping with the shift of practice noted above, but when those Italians are resident in the United States, the authorized access point is now not **ITALIANS—UNITED STATES** but **ITALIAN AMERICANS**, a single-concept access point. The concept of the single named ethnic group has been given precedence over that of the [people]-in-[place] coordination.

In the example on page 193, two LCSH-authorized subject headings are applied to the hypothetical book. Each happens to have three components separated by dashes. But among the six resulting separate components there are only four *different* ones: the other two appear in each of the two subject headings. The pre-coordinate nature of LCSH makes such a situation not only likely but even probable in the case of multiple headings applied to the same item. When subject headings are searched on a segment-by-segment or even word-by-word basis, it is annoying to have multiple hits for exactly the same item. Again, subject headings were not invented with their separation into component parts in mind.

Changes in Cross-Reference Structure. Through the 10th edition of LCSH, the hierarchical relationship in its cross-references had been shown only in one direction: from a more general to a more specific term. In addition, no distinction was made between a hierarchical and an associative relationship: both were accorded the status of *see also* references. When it was decided to make the linking apparatus accord more closely to that common in thesauri and described on page 204, this could not be effected piecemeal or over a long period. It therefore constitutes the most thorough one-time revision of LCSH yet undertaken. Linkages began to be established in accordance with the new practice in 1985. With the printed 11th edition of 1988, *USE, UF, BT, NT,* and *RT* completely replaced the former *see, x,* and *xx* links. Most *see also* links were also replaced but some of them had to be retained for the purpose mentioned on page 210. The conversion of links established prior to 1985 was accomplished by a computer program since it was impracticable to attempt it by human evaluation of each one; the years to come will see much clean-up of the snags resulting from the fact that the original links were not always logically developed. Figure 25 shows a single access point in LCSH as it appears in the earlier and the later styles, without any subdivisions.

Language planning (*Indirect*) (*P40.5.L35*)	Language planning (*May Subd Geog*)
sa Language policy	[*P40.5.L35*]
Languages—Political aspects	UF Languages—Planning
Languages—Revival	Planned language change
Languages, Artificial	BT Sociolinguistics
Standard language	RT Languages—Political aspects
x Languages—Planning	Languages—Revival
Planned language change	NT Language policy
xx Languages—Political aspects	Languages, Artificial
Languages—Revival	Standard language
Sociolinguistics	

FIGURE 25. LCSH in its printed 10th edition (1984, left) and 13th edition (1990, right) guises. The same subject access point is illustrated as from the ERIC thesaurus in figure 24 on page 205 in order to show differences of the content based on the special-subject orientation of the latter. Figure 37 on page 316 shows how the complete subject authority record can include more information than appears in the print version intended for the public.

Application of Index Strings

An index string is called that because it not only may be, but usually is, a pre-coordination of concepts, for example, **POLLINATION. CROPS. BEES.**[19] Like a subject heading, it is primarily intended for manual display and searching. Unlike a subject heading, it is intended:

1) to indicate a document's subject focus very precisely—the amount of pre-coordination is not determined or limited by an external list, such as LCSH—and

2) to be displayed in the index in its entirety under each of its significant elements—the user is therefore not at the mercy of cross-references to find at least one access element for the pre-coordination.

A string index can be used more effectively to help select documents useful to a search than indexing done via the other types of vocabulary because the entire context of the document being indexed is usually made fairly clear in the string. This may be seen in the example on page 193 which gives two LCSH access points and five access points derived from an index string for the same hypothetical document.

The larger number of access points is one reason why string indexing can concentrate less on the control of single vocabulary terms than do either thesauri or subject-headings lists; but it must concentrate more than even the latter on the *structure* of the resulting access points. As with LCSH, there is only one correct sequence of the remaining elements in the string following each access element. In PRECIS, the most complex of the string-indexing systems, only the sequence whose syntax is the most meaningful is generated by the program's interpretation

19. By convention, dashes are not used in the display of an index string because the succession of its parts does not necessarily represent subdivision of concepts, only their juxtaposition.

of the codes (called operators) input by the indexer. For example, the following access point is *not* produced for the hypothetical book in the previous example on page 193 because it does not make sense, a decision implicit in how the string was coded:

STUDENTS. TEACHING. APPLICATIONS OF COMPUTER SYSTEMS.
SCHOOLS. READING SKILLS. UNITED STATES[20]

Some publishers of monographic bibliographies use string indexing as did the BNB from 1969 through 1990 and a few A&I publications, for example, *Library and Information Science Abstracts*; *Historical Abstracts*. It is the least well known and understood of the three types of word-vocabulary-control discussed in this chapter. The real benefit of string indexing in general, and PRECIS in particular, lies in the intellectual discipline they introduced into the linguistic analysis of subject statements. PRECIS focuses attention strongly on syntactic and semantic functions, differentiating, for example, action, purpose, material, and agent in its coding. Such differentiation, sometimes called *semantic factoring*, is a part of every vocabulary; a restatement of its theory in a systematic yet practical way in the context of computerization has become part of the modernization of all subject indexing.

Which System?

Whether classification, subject headings, descriptors, or index strings provides the best indexing system to use in a given situation is rarely obvious. In North America, classification is often too readily dismissed from consideration. Each of the four methods should be able to deliver good recall with good relevance provided its implementation involves

1) complete concept-linking through the syndetic apparatus
2) competence in the subject field(s) in question among both those assigning the access points and those searching them and
3) technical skill on the part of the searchers in using the searching system, whether manual or interactive.

Few have dared to test the effectiveness of the four systems as such in controlled experiments because of the subjectivity of the variables.

String indexing typically provides more access points than either of the other two word-based systems directly, hence requires less two-step searching using cross-reference links. PRECIS has been proposed more than once as a replacement for LCSH in manual library catalogues. Both the cost (original

20. The full impact of this, perhaps more than of other examples in this chapter, can only be evident when it is seen in the context of the hundreds of other access points with the same lead term in an actual PRECIS index.

and continuing) and the disruption of so major a change prevented its serious consideration in the North American library community in the 1970s. The need for improved display of pre-coordinate access points, whether from LCSH or PRECIS, is now being bypassed by the interactive catalogue and post-coordinate searching. The rapid ascendancy of the latter is attested by the decision of the British Library to abandon PRECIS in its cataloguing operations as of November 1990, having already abandoned the application of subject headings on the LCSH model two years previously. It has, in their place, opted for the application of topical and geographic descriptors and is revising its existing PRECIS-based thesaurus accordingly. Any concept or place name requiring only one word is coded differently from a multiword expression of a concept or place name in order to deal with the concept-versus-word problem introduced on page 178. The system, named COMPASS (Computer Aided Subject System), is also designed to take account of the fact that data related to subject content may be searched among other data elements in a record as well as among these descriptors.

User-Friendliness

End-users tend to be less skilled in searching techniques, whether manual or automated, than librarians while the latter tend to be less familiar with the intellectual content of specialized subject areas than end-users. The pre-coordination built into subject headings, index strings, and classification schemes is extremely user-friendly to the searcher who finds it hard to define what is wanted in terms of isolated descriptors. It may be hard to locate a relevant pre-coordinate access point but once it is found, directly or through cross-references, the searcher has a sense of success unmatched in a post-coordinate system where doubt lingers about the utility of additional term-matching. Post-coordination may be a valuable tool in an interactive search but is no panacea. Other things being equal, it takes more knowledge of the topic being searched and more technical searching skills to get good results from a post-coordinate system than from a pre-coordinate one.

If pre-coordinate access points are the most *efficient* medium for searching a manual file, the process of post-coordination is almost essential for the most *effective* searching of an interactive file with its many indices. In many cases at present, and presumably for some time to come, the bibliographic data and access points compiled for an A&I publication, a national bibliography, or a library catalogue exist simultaneously both in a manual file *and* in an interactive one. The former can offer little choice as to how it is searched: once constructed, its indices are inflexible. How the latter can be searched is governed as much by the database management system into which it is loaded as by the file itself; it is not uncommon for the same interactive file to be available in the same library under two different database management systems (see page 116). In the case of A&I publications particularly, one library may buy (or have access to) only the manual version; another library, only the interactive version; a third, both versions. It is clearly economically impracticable to assign subject headings *and* descriptors *and* an index string to each document even if in many cases these would be almost identical. The skilled searcher knowledgeable in the subject field under investigation favours the interactive post-coordination of descriptors and this is the subject access method now being perfected the most systematically.

Subject, Form, Audience

Thus far in this chapter, it has generally been assumed that a controlled subject vocabulary is only used to identify what a document is *about*. Yet the user who wants a nineteenth-century children's fantasy does not care whether it is *about* magic mushrooms, life on the moon, or dwarves. All that is wanted is material written in a particular creative form (fantasy) at a particular time (the 19th century) for a particular audience (children). Yet each of these three aspects becomes a factor in a true subject search for a literary critique *about* nineteenth-century children's fantasy. This example illustrates why thesauri generally do not have form/audience components and why it takes further coding to make post-coordination work when form or audience is involved along with, or in place of, a topic. Form and/or audience is often combined with a subject in a search; for example, a dictionary of the French language or a collection of interviews on abortion directed at teen-agers. Whole library collections are divided on the basis of audience (for example, the children's, young people's, and popular reading collections) and on the basis of form (for example, the periodicals and government publications collections).

Because it is useful to control the vocabulary of these characteristics, subject-headings lists include form/audience terms as free-floating subdivisions, and classification schemes usually make provision for a separate component of the notation to express this characteristic. A form- or audience-identifier most often appears not as the access element but as a subdivision; however, it sometimes takes precedence. Both DDC and LCC, for example, prefer the classification of all bibliographies together, subdivided by the topics of the individual lists, rather than vice-versa. For a nonverbal creative work such as a musical composition, a form may be the only possible access point; for example, LCSH provides a form access point **SYMPHONIES** for scores and recordings of musical compositions of this genre as well as a subject access point **SYMPHONY** for works about this musical form.

Change

Even without the radical changes brought about by interactive and post-coordinate searching, no controlled vocabulary, whether of words or of logical classes, can remain static. The usage of natural language in titles, etc. does not remain stable either. Access via natural language is usually more effective in locating material in a new or rapidly changing field because the leading edge of novelty is expressed in titles, etc. In contrast, changes in any controlled vocabulary, including a classification scheme, must be made cautiously. It is not just a matter of inserting a new term or class; all the existing linkages must also be reviewed: not an easy task when the relationships of a new topic to the whole are just being developed by its investigators. Updated perceptions of existing topics must also be accommodated. This can involve much more than the simple renaming of, say, *moving pictures* as *motion pictures* or as *cinema*. A name change may imply a completely different connotation, such as both caused and accompanied the change from, for example, **NEGROES—UNITED STATES** to **AFRO-AMERICANS** in LCSH. Since they deal with the most current material, the compilers of A&I publications face both additions and meaning-shifts first; however, they are generally less concerned than the reference librarian about relating newer material to older.

When a topic such as cold fusion or the computer virus emerges in a field of the pure or applied sciences, a new name and relationship are quickly established even if they are not permanent. In the social sciences and humanities, the appearance of a new topic is more often gradual and undramatic, its relationships to existing topics indeterminate, and the moment of its baptism with its own name uncertain. In any discipline, the most significant investigators, writers, artists, etc. do not create new works about existing topics. They create new topics, even if these are at first perceived as merely extensions of existing ones. Marshall McLuhan's 1962 *Gutenberg Galaxy* reflected a decade of his thinking about the effects of mass communication. Most librarians at the time shelved it and listed it in their subject catalogues among works on the history of printing, a topic peripheral to both McLuhan's intent and the subsequent perception of the book by most of its readers. When domestic economy became family and nutritional science after pausing along the way under the guise of home economics, much more than a name change was involved.

There is a natural resistance to condoning rapid change in any subject indexing system for fear that a succession of changes will be necessary before a new topic and its name become stabilized. In a library catalogue, it is a major problem to decide how to deal with older material. Should what was written in the 1950s on information retrieval remain under the obsolescent access point **DOCUMENTATION** as a signal of the period and context in which it was written? Should older material on bibliographic automation remain classified with library administration? Is it reasonable to apply the current geographic name

Soviet Union to the description of a nineteenth-century political entity, or to continue to add to the existing grouping of material under **COMMUNISM** after the events of 1989/90? Locating information in LCC and DDC, but from newly emerging points of view, on such topics as political ideologies of the right and left, sexual mores, and environmental concerns is skewed by what many consider to be outdated juxtapositions embedded in the structure of those schemes. There is no simple answer to any of these concerns. The interests of users who want only a present-day perspective will always be in conflict with the interests of those interested in historical antecedents. Archivists do their subject indexing in the context of the period when the documents were generated, not in that of the period when they are presumably going to be used. There is much to be said for removing from a library's current subject catalogue the records for any material more than a generation old and letting footnotes and other such citations guide readers to the older material in a more appropriate subject context. As for shelf classification, the academic library's practice of placing older materials into storage solves more than just the space problem.

Every type of change identified above is more difficult to accommodate in a cooperatively maintained database. It is hard to find consensus among contributing institutions as to when and how to effect a change even when all agree that the change is desirable. Most libraries wait for a national agency like the Library of Congress to take the lead but its changes cannot yet be automatically and instantly incorporated everywhere. In particular, the North American view of classification more as a method of in-house physical location than of information retrieval tends to shunt classification changes to the bottom of almost everyone's priority list. Changing the relationships embedded in a classification scheme is more complex than merely providing new cross-references in a word vocabulary. The former is, however, probably more important because the word-links between old and new are generally more quickly and widely assimilated by users.

8

FORMATS

A typical bibliographic record forming part of a library's catalogue consists of

1) the data elements (see chapter 2) relevant to a given *document*, single words of some or all of which may be made accessible when the record is loaded into a database management system (see chapter 4)

2) controlled-vocabulary access points (see chapters 6 and 7) chosen to represent significant facts about the *work(s)* represented in that document and

3) housekeeping data relating to the *record* itself, for example, the name of the cataloguer, the date the record was last revised, a record-identifier number.

In terms of a manual system and its jargon, a format is the arrangement of all these pieces of information as a complete visible record on a physical medium (for example, card or printed page) as well as such clerical details of presentation as punctuation and capitalization. Traditional cataloguing rules prescribe both (1) the choice and structuring of data elements, access points, etc. and (2) the format.

Automation was one reason for rewriting cataloguing rules because computer programs are dependent on the explicit statement of facts, some of which are left implicit for human interpretation in the traditional manual record. One of the many confusions of automation is that the same machine-readable database may be searched interactively or output as a manual file. The manual format expressed in traditional cataloguing rules must therefore still be used even when machine-readable records are created, although some aspects of the manual format are irrelevant in the context of an interactive catalogue. In terms of an interactive system and its jargon, a format is what identifies to the database management software the type and/or function of each data element and each access point which might need to be separately sorted, searched, or output by that software for any predicted use. Traditional cataloguing rules, including AACR2, do not prescribe a format in this sense; it is left to a separate set of rules to prescribe the machine-readable format of a bibliographic record. In practice, the uses of manual and automated formats are merging, so a general definition of a bibliographic format must be quite abstract: it is a container for all the data comprising a bibliographic record, compartmentalized so that each unit of data, as defined by a particular system, can be separately identified and dealt with by whatever technology that system employs to handle the records.

Prose is a format for ideas expressed in words. Its phrases, clauses, sentences, paragraphs, sections, and chapters clarify their meaning in context. A bibliographic format does the same thing in roughly the same way. It is the grammatical structure, or syntax, of the bibliographic language referred to on page 27. In prose, what appears between parentheses is recognized as a qualifier or a brief digression. In a standard library-cataloguing format, it is recognized as a series title. In English, the basic syntactic order is subject/verb/object. In the language of bibliography, it is author-access-point/title/edition/place/publisher/date. The native speaker of English is not conscious of the basic order of the language because it is inbred from birth, but subtleties must be learned: the conditional subordinate clause may cause difficulty at first. Although the casual library user is rarely troubled by the basic bibliographic sequence of data elements, the novice can misinterpret bibliographic syntax when complex relationships are expressed in a compressed manner. The following statements imply quite different things; only by knowing how to use the bibliographic format in which they are expressed can one clearly convey in (or understand from) a citation what are the true facts of the particular document.

Terrorism, a bibliography. Supplement. Second edition. 1987.
Terrorism, a bibliography. Second edition. 1987. Supplement.
Terrorism, a bibliography. Second edition. Supplement. 1987.

Footnotes and short lists of references at the close of a chapter or book typically ignore those problems of bibliographic identification which cannot be conveyed in the simplest of formats. A huge file may nonetheless exhibit only a limited range of bibliographic situations and types of access points. If each of the tens of thousands of records in an A&I publication describes an article of personal authorship in one of a small number of journals, a quite simple format suffices because all the data elements are regular and predictable. On the other hand, a more complex format is required when

1) records for different ages and types of material appear in the same file
2) bibliographic relationships of many kinds exist among the documents listed and among their access points and/or

3) machine-readable records are to be shared among different catalogues and retrieval systems.

Situations of such variety, encountered regularly in library cataloguing, provide troublesome formatting problems.

Format Standardization

A variety of dialects still exist in the language of bibliography. A group of citations looks strange if half of them are composed according to the format imposed by one style manual and the rest according to that of another, but humans who can interpret the differences understand most of the details. The computer has been an effective prod toward a greater degree of standardization because unpredicted format variation is not tolerable to a computer program.

Style Manuals

A booklet of instructions on how to write a student term paper or thesis has long been known as a style manual (or style sheet, if it could be condensed onto one or two pieces of paper). It necessarily includes a format for making citations as footnotes or at the end of an article, book, thesis, etc. Most style manuals do not rule on bibliographic problems in any great detail; in particular, they devote little attention to the issue of access points since their purpose is largely restricted to the author-arranged listing of small numbers of documents (see page 68). There are many different style manuals prescribing a variety of citation practices. Some are in widespread and general use, others are used only in restricted circumstances. Inherent quality and general relevance is a major reason for the success of some manuals, but the ability of a producer to update one more often, advertise it more widely, or publish it more cheaply are also determinants. Probably all these factors have been operative in the ascendency of *The Chicago Manual of Style*, the style manual most favoured in the humanities and social science departments of academe on both sides of the Atlantic.[1]

Reference Manuals

The editors of academic and professional journals, often working with the A&I services which index them, are primarily responsible for a second category of bibliographic formatting standards called reference manuals, that is, guides for making bibliographic references (citations). Most of these began as the in-house rules of a journal issued to its contributing authors. Some are quite idiosyncratic but the fact that a single database vendor loads databases from many

---

1. *The Chicago Manual of Style for Authors, Editors, and Copywriters*, 13th ed. (Chicago, London: University of Chicago Press, 1982).

creators for searching and output using common software argues persuasively for more uniform practice. One result was the 1977 publication of the *American National Standard for Bibliographic References* (ANSBR), designed for manual records, as NISO standard ANSI Z39.29. In 1979, the editors of the leading English-language medical journals jointly agreed to its adoption in a slightly modified version. Another result was the publication by Unesco of a combination of a style manual and machine-readable format known as the UNISIST Reference Manual.[2]

Rules (Codes) for Library Cataloguing

When librarians first developed rules for formatting the records in their in-house manual catalogues, this was done as independently in each major library as it was in each A&I service. Early in this century, however, the development of union catalogues and the sale of Library of Congress cards were major incentives to librarians to reduce the number of variant cataloguing rules and formats. In the 1960s, librarians wishing to share machine-readable records quickly realized that they must use the same format or at least closely compatible ones. Cutter's 1876 *Rules for a Dictionary Catalog* (whose significance for controlled-vocabulary name and subject access points and for filing is described in chapters 6, 7, and 9) also prescribes a format for the description of documents which became the basis for Library of Congress practice and thereby spread throughout the English-speaking world. Radical revision of this format began in the 1940s but was only completed in 1969 and published as the International Standard Bibliographic Description (ISBD). AACR2 embodies ISBD in the context of the manual catalogue; the Machine-Readable Cataloging (MARC) family of formats encode it for application in a database management system. Both AACR2 and MARC also prescribe the formatting of access points; the latter extends even to prescribing much of what is called housekeeping data at the beginning of this chapter.

Within the library world of only twenty years ago, smaller libraries tended to apply very selectively the rules and formats devised by and for their larger counterparts; today it is possible to speak of a single library standard virtually worldwide. The increasing practice of merging selected A&I databases with the local interactive library catalogue makes the need to standardize formats between libraries and by A&I services more urgent. As they perceive a need for greater standardization in their descriptive finding aids, archivists are also beginning to adopt library formats as closely as their materials allow. Finally, as

---

2. Two hundred twenty-six English-language style and reference manuals, each at least five pages long and published between 1970 and 1983, are cited in John Bruce Howell, *Style Manuals of the English-Speaking World: a Guide* (Phoenix: Oryx Press, 1983). Howell's brief history of the style manual dates its first appearance to 1608.

the automation of information handling spreads, others are copying, adapting, or imitating the basic MARC format designed by librarians. Many aspects of it are applicable to non-bibliographic information.

Formats for Description in Manual Files

Formatting controlled-vocabulary access points is treated in the two previous chapters. This section, and the next one on the ISBD, are not concerned with formatting access points but only with formatting the data elements introduced in chapter 2: those which describe a document.

Monographs

The early printers unconsciously established the first bibliographic format in the late fifteenth century by implicitly agreeing on what data elements should appear on the title pages of their books and in what order these should be stated. They placed the titling and authorship of the work in this most prominent location. In the manuscript, information naming the scribe and/or dating the completion of writing appeared as a colophon at the end of the book. When the scribe became a printer, later a bookseller, then a publisher—each a business firm interested in what is now known as product identification—that firm began to display its name and corporate symbol prominently up front, along with the title and author's name on the title page. It took a little longer to get onto the title page a statement of change or updating of the content—that is, an edition statement, which, along with the dating, helps establish the currency of the information.

   The cover and half-title page may bear some of the same data, but these physical parts of the book are intended primarily for physical protection and the former is removed in rebinding; the twentieth-century dust wrapper serves as advertising and therefore cannot be relied upon to present bibliographic data in their most sober and stable form. How natural, then, for the standard biblio-graphic format still to be based on a transcription of the title page. This is very visibly the case in the traditional catalogue-card record where that transcription appears as a separate paragraph. Data expected on the title page but not ap-pearing there might be added if available elsewhere; they are then enclosed in brackets. All other data (for example, information on series, physical descrip-tion, and relationships) are visibly separated on the card from the title paragraph by typography and/or spacing. The close relationship between a title page and a Library of Congress record according to the rules followed there between 1898 and 1948 is shown in figure 26. It is interesting to note that since the series title is a relative latecomer to bibliographic data, it rarely appears on the title page and its location in the bibliographic record varies wildly from style manual to style manual and among different cataloguing rules.

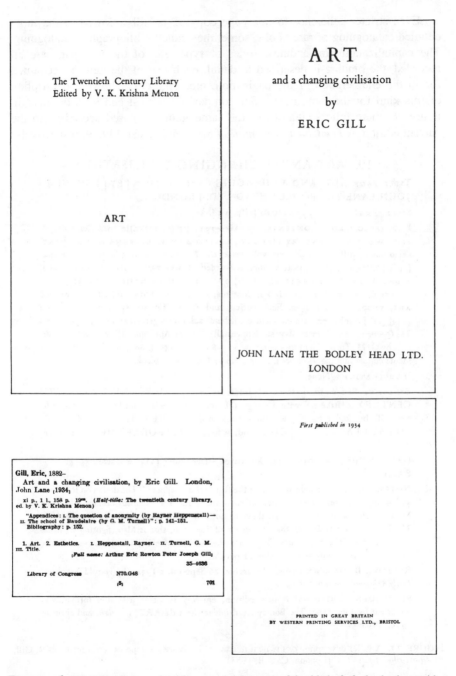

The Twentieth Century Library
Edited by V. K. Krishna Menon

ART

ART

and a changing civilisation

by

ERIC GILL

JOHN LANE THE BODLEY HEAD LTD.
LONDON

First published in 1934

Gill, Eric, 1882–
  Art and a changing civilisation, by Eric Gill. London,
John Lane [1934]
  xi p., 1 l., 158 p. 19ᵐ. (*Half-title:* The twentieth century library,
ed. by V. K. Krishna Menon)

  "Appendices: I. The question of anonymity (by Rayner Heppenstall)—
II. The school of Baudelaire (by G. M. Turnell)": p. 141–151.
  Bibliography: p. 152.

  1. Art. 2. Esthetics.   I. Heppenstall, Rayner.   II. Turnell, G. M.
III. Title.
              [*Full name:* Arthur Eric Rowton Peter Joseph Gill]
                                          35–4636
  Library of Congress   N70.G48
                              [5]   701

PRINTED IN GREAT BRITAIN
BY WESTERN PRINTING SERVICES LTD., BRISTOL

FIGURE 26. The half-title page, the title page, and the verso of the title leaf of a book, along with its Library of Congress catalogue card prepared according to pre-1949 rules for description.

Even stricter adherence to title-page copying is still followed in the more detailed cataloguing of rare books, sometimes called bibliographic cataloguing. The capitalization, line-endings, styles of type, etc. of the title page are all recorded, the binding is described in detail, each leaf of the item is accounted for in the enumeration of the pagination, etc. Figure 27 shows a description of this kind for the same item.[3] For comparison with it and with the card in figure 26, there follow citations of the same item composed according to the current edition of *The Chicago Manual of Style* and ANSI Z39.29, respectively:

29. ART AND A CHANGING CIVILISATION

TITLE-PAGE: ART | AND A CHANGING CIVILISATION | BY | ERIC GILL | JOHN LANE THE BODLEY HEAD LTD. | LONDON

SIZE: 7¼×4¾.   COLLATION: [A]⁸, B–L⁸.

PAGINATION AND CONTENTS: Pp. xiv + 162; [i] [ii] half-title to series worded: THE TWENTIETH CENTURY LIBRARY | EDITED BY V. K. KRISHNA MENON | ART, verso blank; [iii] [iv] list of other volumes in the *Twentieth Century Library*, verso blank; [v] [vi] title-page, verso printers' imprint worded: FIRST PUBLISHED IN 1934 | and, at foot: PRINTED IN GREAT BRITAIN | BY WESTERN PRINTING SERVICES LTD., BRISTOL; vii–x Preliminary; xi–[xii] Contents, verso blank; [xiii] [xiv] half-title worded ART, verso quotations from Ecclesiasticus and A. K. Coomaraswamy; 1–138 text; [139] [140] blank, verso author's and publishers' acknowledgements; 141–5 Appendix I *The Question of Anonymity* by Rayner Heppenstall; 146–51 Appendix II *The School of Baudelaire* by G. M. Turnell; 152 Bibliography; 153–8 Index; [159] [160] publishers' announcements concerning the *Twentieth Century Library*; [161] [162] blank.

ILLUSTRATIONS: None.

BINDING: Red cloth, lettered on front, at top, in black: THE TWENTIETH CENTURY LIBRARY with a design ('Laocoon'), specially made for the series by Eric Gill, blocked in black. Lettered in black on spine: TWENTIETH | CENTURY | LIBRARY | ART | ERIC | GILL | and, at foot: THE | BODLEY HEAD All edges cut.

DATE OF PUBLICATION: 1934. MS. dated 8 December 1933–6 January 1934. PRICE: 2s 6d.

NOTES: The following note appears on the flap of the wrapper: "The design on the cover and wrapper of this book has been specially made for *The Twentieth Century Library* by Mr Eric Gill, who writes: 'I can think of nothing more appropriate for a symbol for *The Twentieth Century Library* than a version of Laocoon, that is Man, fighting with the twin snakes of War and Usury. These are the powers of evil with which man in the twentieth century will have to settle, or perish.'"

REVIEWS: By Wyndham Lewis, *The Listener*, 26 September 1934. By Harold Nicolson, *Daily Telegraph*, September 1934.

SUBSEQUENT EDITIONS: A new edition, entirely re-set in a smaller format, was published by John Lane, The Bodley Head under the title ART, in 1946, and again in 1949. Price 5s.

FIGURE 27. A fuller description of the item illustrated in figure 26, reproduced from Evan R. Gill, *Bibliography of Eric Gill* (London: Cassell, 1953).

3. The classic analysis of this kind of description remains Fredson Bowers, *Principles of Bibliographical Description* (Princeton: Princeton University Press, 1949).

Gill, Eric. Art and a Changing Civilisation. The Twentieth Century Library. London: J. Lane, 1934.

Gill, Eric. Art and a Changing Civilisation. London: J. Lane, 1934. 158 p. The Twentieth Century Library.

Journal Articles

The systematic listing of journal articles in what we now know as A&I publications began in the early nineteenth century. A typical record copied from Poole's index (see page 110) serves as a model for analyzing the description of a journal article:

Cabinet System, English. (G. Bradford) No. Am. **118:** 1

The (inverted) title of the article, its author's surname and initial, and the abbreviated title, volume number, and page of the journal appear in a still familiar and totally intelligible fashion. However, we are now more likely to use a controlled-vocabulary access point than a title word to locate the article by its subject, and we tend to include the journal's dating and sometimes issue number along with its volume numbering. Poole was aware of the library cataloguing standards of his period but wished to save both space and time when listing so very many items. He therefore (1) presented the dating in an appended table of the indexed journals rather than as part of each citation, (2) abbreviated more than is now common, (3) used a dash to avoid repeating an access element, (4) omitted the final page number of the article, and (5) did not even necessarily transcribe an article's title exactly or that of the journal fully. This all bothered him enough that he apologized for his work as "crude and feeble on its bibliographical side."[4]

Poole's method of choosing and arranging data elements embodies three principles not in keeping with library-cataloguing practice of his time. Though he clearly had no intention of promulgating a new bibliographic style as such, his application of these principles became standard procedure for description in style and reference manuals by the early twentieth century:

1) desired data elements are given whether found in the source document or not (many authors' names in Poole's index are attributions)
2) data elements are arranged in an order based not on their appearance within the source document but on a fixed rule and
3) the larger unit (the journal of which the article being described is a part) is cited in an arbitrarily abbreviated form.

---

4. *Poole's Index to Periodical Literature*, rev. ed. (Boston: Houghton, Mifflin, 1882), v.1, pt.1:[iii]. On the other hand, Poole observes a difference between issue dating and imprint dating, which is rarely done any longer.

New Layouts, New Media: The Threat of Fragmentation

Conscious of the decorative aspects of their work, modern typographers no longer adhere so closely to the conventions of tradition concerning what should appear on a title page and how it should be stated. The informational value of the data and the needs of bibliographic control are often ignored in favour of a design statement or an advertising function thought to be served by a non-traditional presentation. The fashion for a simpler title page has chased some data elements to the verso of the title leaf and elsewhere. As desktop publishing flourishes, both the choice and the display of data elements are more and more often delegated to a clerk who is not paid to know and apply either graphic design or bibliographic traditions and who cannot be expected to know bibliographic purposes. In not fulfilling any expected title-page layout, the results are a challenge to bibliographic formatting.

A prominent and concise display of its bibliographic identity is possible in a document in one of the newer media, but its physical nature often makes the simulation of a quasi-title page impossible. From the label of a disc sound recording to the thin header at the top of a microfiche or the box containing the parts of a kit, each new type of document has its own way of revealing a title, authorship, publication details, etc. The publisher of nonprint material may provide an accompanying printed sheet to serve as identification but in doing so often introduces further inconsistency between that and the data given verbally, orally, or in some other way on the document itself. In the 1950s, as libraries began collecting more and more of the new media, the irrelevance of cataloguing rules designed only for printed books with traditional title pages was increasingly evident. For a time, bibliographic standardization was seriously threatened as ad hoc rules were devised with little reference to each other or to any book-based standard by many individual audio-visual departments often administered separately from libraries.

International Standard Bibliographic Description

The first departure from strict title-page transcription in library cataloguing was proposed in a 1945 Library of Congress study written chiefly by Seymour Lubetzky.[5] The resulting 1949 *Rules for Descriptive Cataloging in the Library of Congress* were widely adopted in North America from then until the Library of Congress implemented ISBD in September, 1974. In the 1960s, British cataloguers began modernizing their earlier (1908) format along similar

5. Library of Congress, Processing Department, *Studies of Descriptive Cataloging: a Report to the Librarian of Congress* (Washington: U.S. Government Printing Office, 1946). The landmark critique of the economics of library cataloguing which led the Library of Congress to commission this report is Andrew Osborn, "The Crisis in Cataloging," *Library Quarterly* 11 (October 1941): 393–411.

lines; their work led directly to ISBD. In 1966, in what was originally seen as only an economy measure, the Library of Congress was persuaded by one of its administrators, John Cronin, to copy, without further editing, into its own catalogues the bibliographic descriptions produced for current publications by some two dozen national bibliographies.[6] At the same time, the first machine-readable formats for bibliographic data were being developed, also at the Library of Congress. These two forces, international standardization and the computer, prompted a formal search for a modernized bibliographic format for the age of automation. They also provided a not-to-be-missed opportunity to stem the fragmentation of cataloguing rules by those dealing with nonprint materials, as noted earlier. Agreement was sought both internationally and among cataloguers of the various media on a single umbrella format so that the expensive work of writing file definitions for computer programming need not be repeated for each of a wide variety of essentially different formats.

Good will prevailed at the International Meeting of Cataloguing Experts (IMCE) held in 1969 under the aegis of IFLA. People from many countries agreed that differences in data-element formatting which resulted from differing national cataloguing rules were of little or no practical significance but merely stemmed from historical accident. Few compromises were needed to achieve an internationally agreed-upon format, which was named the International Standard Bibliographic Description (ISBD) and designed

1) to standardize the format of the descriptive portion of the bibliographic record for all types of materials
2) to make it easier to recognize data elements regardless of the language of their content and
3) to facilitate the computer-handling of bibliographic data.

Descriptive Elements versus Access Points

Controlled-vocabulary access points were excluded from consideration by the IMCE as they are excluded in the Library of Congress' Shared Cataloging Program mentioned earlier. International standardization of subject access points is inconceivable. As for name access points, the 1961 Paris Principles had already expressed a measure of international agreement and the 1969 delegates feared that their efforts to reach agreement on other formatting issues might not be successful if the remaining national differences over name access points were allowed to revive controversy. They restricted their discussions to the function of description. Separating the function of describing from that of access became

6. This policy, the one also referred to on page 118, was implemented under the name Shared Cataloging Program (later, National Program for Acquisitions and Cataloging (NPAC)). Accepting the records of the other agencies did not, and still does not, extend to the choice or form of access points.

a benefit, rather than a drawback, of ISBD in the context of computer formatting and interactive searching. The Library of Congress' 1949 *Rules for Descriptive Cataloging* had linked the two too closely. If a personal or corporate name chosen as the principal access point (main entry heading) also appears in the title proper, those rules remove that name from the transcription of the title. Thus the *Journal of the American Statistical Association* became, for cataloguing purposes, the author access point **American Statistical Association** followed by the title *Journal*: a single word and, being a common one, not used as an access point at all. Similarly, *The Complete Works of William Shakespeare* became, in those rules, the author access point **Shakespeare, William** followed by the title *Complete Works*. In the context of searching words in titles, now a common feature of the interactive catalogue, this is an intolerable distortion of a title. It also frustrates users who would recognize *JASA* or *Jl. Amer. Stat. Assoc.*, but never *ASA. J.*

Sources of Bibliographic Data

The title page of a book remains the most important source of the data required for its adequate description. ISBD calls the title page a chief source of information. A different chief source must be specified for each medium in which there is no formal title page or exact analogy. However, the arrangement of information on the chief source no longer governs either the choice of which data elements are to be included in the record or their arrangement in the record. These are governed by the format. Since data desirable in the record do not always occur on the chief source, ISBD specifies additional so-called prescribed sources of data. These include such locations as the verso of the title leaf, cover, and external reference sources, and they vary depending on the type of data element involved. Any data included in the record but not transcribed from either the chief source or from a prescribed source for the type of data in question are enclosed in brackets (see page 34).

Areas

ISBD specifies eight areas for bibliographic data, to be presented in a manual record in the sequence shown in the slightly abridged outline which follows. What appears in smaller type under the names of the areas is an enumeration of their elements as described in the next subsection.

    Area 1. Title and Statement of Responsibility Area

          1.1 Title proper

          1.2 General material designation

          1.3 Parallel title(s)

          1.4 Other title information

          1.5 Statement(s) of responsibility

Area 2. Edition Area

    2.1 Edition statement

    2.2 Parallel edition statement(s)

    2.3 Statement(s) of responsibility relating to the edition

    2.4 Additional edition statement

    2.5 Statement(s) of responsibility relating to the additional edition statement

Area 3. Material (or Type-of-Publication) Specific Data Area
[Used only for cartographic materials, printed music, computer files, and serials.]

Area 4. Publication, Distribution, etc. Area

    4.1 Place(s) of publication, distribution, etc.

    4.2 Name(s) of publisher, distributor, etc.

    4.3 Date of publication, distribution, etc.

    4.4 Place of manufacture

    4.5 Name of manufacturer

    4.6 Date of manufacture

Area 5. Physical Description Area

    5.1 Specific material designation and extent of item

    5.2 Other physical details

    5.3 Dimensions

    5.4 Identification of accompanying material

Area 6. Series Area

    6.1 Title proper of the series

    6.2 Parallel title(s) of the series

    6.3 Other title information of the series

    6.4 Statement(s) of responsibility relating to the series

    6.5 International Standard Serial Number (ISSN) of the series

    6.6 Numbering within the series

    6.7 Enumeration and/or title of subseries

    6.8–6.12 Parallel title of subseries, through Numbering within the subseries, the same as for 6.2 through 6.6
[The entire area 6 sequence is repeatable if the item is published in two (or more) different series, but the whole remains a single area.]

Area 7. Note(s) Area (repeatable, each note being a separate area)

Area 8. Standard Number, etc. Area (a repeatable area)

    8.1 Standard number: ISBN or ISSN (or other, yet to come)

    8.2 Key-title (associated only with an ISSN)

    8.3 Terms of availability and/or price

    8.4 Qualification(s) following 8.1 and/or 8.3

Every published item has at least a name (area 1), some facts concerning its origin (area 4), and a physical presence which can be quantified (area 5). Area 3 is used for data unique to a given medium, for example, the scale of a map, the numbering pattern of a serial. It is at present used only in the description of cartographic items, serials, music scores, and computer files. Whether any of the other areas exists in a given description is dependent on the availability of data for that area concerning the document being catalogued; for example, only a few books have an edition statement. An area for which there is no data relevant to the item is simply omitted.

Seven of the eight areas comprise a formal structure for the available data elements, which are usually derived from the document itself. The other, area 7, is the place for the cataloguer to state in a relatively unstructured way whatever cannot be put into the form or context of any of the other areas. The Note(s) Area should therefore logically be the final one. However, standard numbering was only devised in the 1960s and got tacked onto the end of the description as it then existed. In ISBD, it remained after the notes, illogically. Many of the relationships described on pages 45–46 must be stated in the Note(s) Area since other areas (2 and 6) carry information on only the two most frequently encountered types of relationship. Area 8 is sometimes used in practice, although not intended in theory, for recording standard numbers for related items, such as a paperback version or an edition distributed by a different publisher.

Elements

Each area is divided into a number of elements as tabulated above. Thus area 5, the Physical Description Area, makes provision for up to four elements as relevant to the item:

1) the extent; for example, number of physical pieces, number of pages, running time
2) other significant physical details; for example, presence of more than one colour, characteristics of fixing the information in the medium to indicate what playback equipment is needed
3) dimensions; for example, diameter of a disc, size of a container and
4) accompanying materials; for example, slides in a pocket attached to the back cover, the documentation of a computer file.

The elements in area 1, the Title and Statement of Responsibility Area, can be extremely difficult to separate cleanly from one another. It might have been more logical to locate titling in an area separate from the area which names authors but the grammatical linkage of a title with the name of an author is not uncommon in many languages, for example, *Five Scenes from Shakespeare* or *Bach's Greatest Hits*. This has important implications for interactive natural-language searching. Three examples may illustrate these; all are equally possible, given the vagaries of title-page wording particularly among conference proceedings.

> *Proceedings of the Third International Conference on Security*
> *Password control : proceedings of the Third International Conference*
>   *on Security*
> *Proceedings / Third International Conference on Security*

The name of the conference in question should be established as **International Conference on Security (3rd : ...**) in a name authority file (see page 161), where it may be made searchable word-by-word. However, the word **security** embedded in that name may well be sought as a natural-language title word by a user who does not understand the value of searching a name or subject authority file in such a case. In each of the above hypothetical cases, that word appears in area 1. In the first case, it is in the title proper; in the second, in the other title information; and in the third, in the statement of responsibility. The end-user has no reason to think of such a distinction while searching, yet few interactive systems make all of area 1 searchable on a word-by-word basis. It is not very efficient to do so for statements of responsibility when forenames (even initials) are their largest single component. Even making other title information searchable word-by-word significantly enlarges storage requirements, perhaps beyond the capacity of a smaller system. Each additional word indexed bears a continuing cost. This unpredictability regarding whether and how access is provided to an obviously useful word reinforces yet again the need to maintain, and to encourage searchers to use, controlled-vocabulary access points. It also demonstrates the need for clear documentation to searchers as to (1) which data elements other than controlled-vocabulary access points can be searched and which cannot, (2) where in the record word-by-word searching is available, and (3) what kind of truncation is supported, if any.

Punctuation

Formalized punctuation which indicates what kind of data is about to appear has always been a part of bibliographic formatting. Both long-standing British practice and that of *The Chicago Manual of Style* separate a place of publication from a publisher's name by a colon. Library cataloguing rules have long enclosed data elements relating to a series in parentheses. When ISBD was in draft in 1969, Michael Gorman suggested, and the Working Group concurred, that prescribed marks of punctuation should be used throughout the record more systematically than in previous practice and that punctuation should delimit areas and elements unambiguously.

The ISBD punctuation pattern is shown in the following skeletal record along with the capitalization pattern prescribed by AACR.

> Title proper [general material designation] = Parallel title : other title information / first statement of responsibility ; second statement of responsibility. — Edition statement / statement of responsibility relating to the edition, Additional edition statement / statement of responsibility for the additional edition statement. — Material specific details. — First place of publication ; Second place of publication : Publisher, date (Place of manufacture : Manufacturer, date of manufacture). — *extent of item : other physical details ; dimensions + accompanying material. — (Series title proper = Parallel series title / statement of responsibility for the series, ISSN ; numbering within the series. Title of subseries ; numbering within the subseries) (Second series with elements arranged within its separate parentheses as was the first). — *Note. — *Note. — *ISBN : terms of availability (qualification).

> (*An asterisk indicates where it is permissible to begin a new paragraph instead of using the period-space-dash-space to separate the areas.)

The use of what is now known as ISBD punctuation in the examples in figure 28 makes it at least possible to identify where a particular data element occurs in a record even if the script is unfamiliar. A colon preceding the words **ein Handbuch** clearly tells the clerk who does not know German that the word *Handbuch* is not the author's surname. Using ISBD, the book whose title page, etc. are illustrated in figure 26 on page 225 is described as follows:

> Art and a changing civilisation / by Eric Gill. — London : J. Lane, 1934. — xi, 158 p. ; 19 cm. — (The Twentieth century library)

In order to distinguish the prescribed ISBD punctuation from the natural punctuation which is still needed within names, titles, etc., the comma and period are only prescribed when the following element is unambiguous (a date, an ISSN, a new title). All other punctuation is stylized by placing a space before as well as after the mark, as shown in the skeletal record above and in figure 28. No mark of punctuation serves different purposes within the same area. The area-divider is a four-part mark: period-space-dash-space.[7] In addition to its utility for people who do not know the language involved, ISBD punctuation has direct counterparts in the content designators used in MARC (see page 293).

---

7. Since an em-dash is rare on a keyboard, this mark of punctuation is often shown as period-space-hyphen-hyphen-space.

ခေတ်ဟောင်း ခေတ်သစ် စာကြည့်တိုက်ခရီး, ၁၀၅၇–၁၉၇၃ / မောင်ကောင်းမြင့်. — ရန်ကုန် : စာပေဗိမာန်, 1978.

264 p., [4] leaves of plates : ill. ; 20 cm. — (ပြည်သူ့လက်စွဲစာစဉ်)

ਭਾਈ ਵੀਰ ਸਿੰਘ, ਸੰਦਰਭ-ਕੋਸ਼ / ਸੰਪਾਦਕ ਵਿਸ਼ਵਾਨਾਥ ਤਿਵਾੜੀ, ਹਰਿੰਦਰ ਪੰਨੂੰ, ਜਗਤਾਰ. — ਚੰਡੀਗੜ੍ਹ : ਪਬਲੀਕੇਸ਼ਨ ਬਿਓਰੋ, ਪੰਜਾਬ ਯੂਨੀਵਰਸਿਟੀ, 1974.

220 p. ; 23 cm.

Μιχαὴλ Περάνθης : εἰσαγωγή-βιβλιογραφίακρίσεις / 'I. M. Χατζηφώτη ; μὲ τὴ συνεργασία τῆς Νίκης Πολίτη. – 'Αθήνα : 'Εκδόσεις τῶν Κριτικῶν Φυλλῶν, 1976.

524 p. ; 21 cm.

FIGURE 28. ISBD descriptions in nonroman scripts from Library of Congress records. The access points are not reproduced.

Consequences of Data-Element Separation

For the nearly one hundred years of the domination of the Library of Congress unit card in North American library catalogues, it was natural to confuse the card itself with the bibliographic data it expresses. One could no more fragment or rearrange the latter than cut up the former with scissors and hope to have anything usable left. Merely by breaking the unit record apart, ISBD had several significant consequences. A minor one of these is the revival of an old practice of tagging, or labelling, record output; that is, stating in the visible catalogue record what *kind* of data element is being presented (for example, *DATE:*) as well as what data of that kind pertain to the particular item (for example, **1984**), as shown on page 296. It is possible to use the ISBD punctuation to generate the verbal tag or label but the development of the machine-readable coding described in the next section provided a far more efficient method of doing the same thing, so ISBD punctuation remains primarily for human, not computer, interpretation of the parts of a record.

Shorter and Longer Records. Of greater consequence, the definition of each data element separately provides a rationale and an almost clerical method for shortening a record when the fullest possible bibliographic information is not required. Each separate element can be defined as one to be included or excluded in a given record-output format. For a long time, the Library of Congress set a single standard of fullness for the many libraries using its cards both as derived records and as the model for their own original cataloguing. Yet rules allowing longer or shorter descriptions are nothing new. Cutter's full, medium, and short records are discussed on page 127. Of the commercial firms selling catalogue records (see page 111), some provide less, some more, detail than does the

Library of Congress. For example, the Wilson Company's cards produced from 1938 to 1975 contain no place of publication, no article at the beginning of a title, and no preliminary pagination, but normally include a summary or annotation. The issue did not arise whether these practices constitute acceptable departures from a cataloguing standard; they are simply an application of rules different from those taught in library schools as the national standard.

Rule 1.0D of AACR2, "Levels of detail in the description," returns some flexibility in this matter to a recognized standard.[8] The rule specifies which elements must be included (if relevant to the document being catalogued) for the result to be an acceptable AACR2 description at one of three different levels. If the user of the record knows which level of description was applied in that particular case, the record cannot be ambiguous even if certain information is absent. The effects on cooperation of some libraries producing records less full than others are discussed on pages 127–28.

The Family of ISBDs in Relation to Cataloguing Codes

In its first published (preliminary) version in 1971, ISBD applied explicitly only to printed monographs (books). Its immediate application in several national bibliographies demonstrated its practical value. It is possible to catalogue simple items with only the guidance provided in the table of elements and the skeletal record reproduced earlier in this section, but more explicit guidance is desirable in complex cases. This was particularly true when ISBD was relatively new and even experienced cataloguers were as yet unfamiliar with it. ISBD was incorporated in fuller detail and with more examples into cataloguing codes, such as AACR2, through the 1970s. In addition to remaining the original standard from which the catalogue-code versions derive, a separately published ISBD is useful in places where more detailed rules are not as likely to be used.

ISBD has expanded into a family of related formats because the original one designed for printed monographs and now known as ISBD(M) did not suffice to account for the peculiarities of documents in other media. Now, ISBD(A) exists for antiquarian, or pre-1820, books; ISBD(CM) for cartographic materials; ISBD(MRF) (formerly ISBD(CF)) for machine-readable (computer) files; ISBD(NBM) for nonbook materials; ISBD(PM) for printed music; and ISBD(S) for serials. *Guidelines for the Application of the ISBDs to the Description of Component Parts* constitutes the formerly announced ISBD(CP); it attempts to reconcile the conflicting interests of the library and the A&I communities in formatting the kinds of analytical records described on pages 258–60. Since 1977, the basic statement of ISBD principles and practice is to be found in

8. The choice of the word *level* in this rule is unfortunate, although perhaps unavoidable. In ISBD and on pages 249–62, the word is used in a very different sense related to the titling of different entities within the same publication, not levels of completeness in describing that publication in a bibliographic record.

ISBD(G), the *General* ISBD. This is the most succinct and abstract ISBD, the one which governs all the others so that they are kept consistent with one another. With different committees in charge of each specialized ISBD, this is essential but sometimes difficult. Both ISBD(G) and the specialized ISBDs are subject to regular review by IFLA committees; revisions of many of the original versions are now in force.[9]

Machine-Readable Formats

Any format, whether the grammatical format of a prose sentence or the ISBD format of a bibliographic record, breaks up information into manageable parts in order to help a user interpret it. A computer program depends totally on such help. If a manual record is not explicitly tagged or labelled, the human user normally finds an item's publication information by looking for a place name, not by counting past one or more instances of the period-space-dash-space punctuation to find the fourth ISBD area. How does a database management system recognize a place name? The human searcher knows where an individual record begins or ends by the blank line separating two records on a page or the fact that each is on a separate card. How does a database management system find the beginning and end of any information it must interpret? It can function only by finding codes, such as the single byte whose function is to say to it explicitly, "This is the end of the record." *Each* defined and separately manipulable data element in a record must be unambiguously identified in this way to the database management system. There are only two ways of doing this:

1) by storing each data element in certain known character positions, the same ones in every record, which the computer can locate by counting from a fixed point of reference (ultimately, from the beginning of the record) or

2) by associating with each data element a unique code which identifies the nature of the element while not being part of its content.

The two techniques are now used in combination with each other but they will first be described separately.

Fixed-Field (Fixed-Length) Formats

To be retrievable, a unit of information must be contained in what computer programmers call a field. Assigning to each field a fixed number of bytes and

9. All the ISBD publications identified in this paragraph are published by the agency now named the IFLA Universal Bibliographic Control and International MARC Programme; they are distributed by the British Library. See also Anthony G. Curwen, *ISBD Manual: A Guide to the Interpretation and Use of the International Standard Bibliographic Descriptions*, prepared at the request of the IFLA UBCIM Programme (Paris: Unesco General Information Programme and UNISIST, 1990). PGI-90/WS/16.

therefore an invariable location counting from the beginning of the record (the first alternative in the previous paragraph) makes both programming and running programs simple and cheap: what kind of data a field contains is defined only, but with certainty, by its location in the record. If what occupies character positions 36 through 39 of the record is always, and only, a year of publication, it is child's play to program for its identification, retrieval, output, etc.[10] Short-cuts are possible: provided every date in the database falls in the same century, only the two final digits of a date need be stored because a program can attach the same first two digits to these as a print constant at the time of output. Truncating a year to two digits is one of many techniques used in what is known as fixed-field formatting to save storage space and/or to ensure that each instance of a type of data can be expressed in a predetermined number of bytes.

However modern and capacious their computers, the majority of businesses still use this type of format because the data they process can generally be ex-pressed in fixed-length codes representing quantities, department names, stock items, etc. New codes are constantly being used to reduce complex naming sys-tems to fixed-length data elements, for example, the Universal Product Code (the ISBN is such a code) to identify a product, the social-security number to identify a person, and the library-circulation bar-code number to identify a transaction. Many bibliographically relevant facts can be expressed in code and assigned to fixed-length fields; for example, one byte suffices to show whether a document is a government publication or not: a predetermined code (for ex-ample, an x) shows that it is while another code (for example, a zero), or no code (a blank), shows that it is not.[11] Using the same single byte, one can even identify the type of agency responsible for the document (for example, local-level or intergovernmental) by replacing the x with an appropriate pre-determined code.

Any information which cannot be incorporated into a code or otherwise made to fit the assigned number of bytes in a fixed-length format must be omitted, either through internal abbreviation or end-truncation. Which bibliographic data elements can be abbreviated? How can a longer title be compressed into an inadequate number of characters without affecting its filing or the identification of the document whose name it is? If access points can be controlled in other ways, can their length be controlled? Of the more than thirty data elements

10. In this chapter and in the appendix, one machine-readable record is assumed to be a linear unit. In reality, a database management system is more likely to treat it as a number of linked parts, each stored and indexed in a separate file according to its type and the kind of processing demanded of it. The location (address) of a particular byte in the hypothetical linear sequence of the record is called its character position. The first byte in a sequence is always said to be in character position 0 (*not* 1). The byte in character position 1 is therefore the second byte, and so on. Perhaps confusing at first, this facilitates the mathematical calculation of addresses in a directory (see page 299) because the address, or starting character position, of any field is the address of the previous field plus the number of characters in that previous field.

11. A blank is not the same thing as a zero. It may be viewed as a code created by striking the space bar; it is a part of any character set.

defined in ISBD (many of them repeatable), one record contains most, another only a handful. A single controlled-vocabulary access point suffices for one document; another requires a dozen. How many fixed-length fields, and of how many bytes each, should be reserved for a single record, considering that every byte unused for significant data must remain in the record as a blank? Fixed-field formatting requires an unambiguous answer to every such question. No matter what the answer in each case, the results are undesirable: either truncation or a huge overhead of blank bytes in the database. Although fixed-length fields are applicable to many individual bibliographic data elements and library processes, they are, on the whole, inadequate for the information-retrieval purposes of bibliographic control. These purposes require a type of formatting in which a field occupies exactly as many bytes as the data comprising the field require and the record occupies exactly as many fields as are applicable to it.

Variable-Field (Variable-Length) Formats

Until librarians came along with their messy bibliographic data in the mid-1960s, hardly anyone thought it possible to operate computer programs except with fixed-length fields. Variable-field (or variable-length) formatting was initially developed largely with bibliographic demands in mind. This type of format permits the title in one record to begin in character position 25 and end in position 59, while in the next record it begins in position 46 and ends in position 187. All computer processing is based on locating the data to be processed via an address. Whereas in a fixed-field format the address of each defined data element is the same on each record in the database, an address in a variable-field format is meaningless until a record directory (see page 242) has indexed a field to it using data separators and content designators.[12]

Separators (Delimiters). The period-space-dash-space of the ISBD separates any two adjacent areas. It can appear several times in the same record because it does not bear the burden of specifying *which* area has ended or is beginning. A variable-field format requires two separators of this generic kind: one to mark the end of each complete field and a different one to mark the end of the complete record. However, it is useful to divide bibliographic fields into subfields as described in the next subsection. This means that a third unique separator must introduce each subfield. Each of these three separators must be a byte in the character set which is not used for any other purpose. There is no standard visual representation for these three delimiters and they cannot be alphanumeric characters which could be mistaken for the content of a field. The

12. The development of more powerful computers and expert-systems software offers promise for applying near-human intelligence to the recognition of fields of data by the nature of the data rather than only by embedded codes. This would significantly affect the nature of the format vis-à-vis input/output programs and facilitate data input.

written documentation of a system or format (including the appendix to this book) establishes some visible symbol for each.

Content Designators.   A machine-readable variable-field format must provide an explicit identifier, called a content designator, for every separate data element. Manual formats have always used marks of punctuation for this; for example, ISBD uniquely identifies a statement of responsibility by its preceding diagonal slash; LCSH always uses a dash to separate a subdivision from another one and from the access element; AACR2 encloses any qualifier to a corporate-name access point in parentheses. Older manual formats do not use punctuation as systematically but nevertheless capitalize and punctuate the beginning and end of a descriptive field as if it were a sentence. However, there are too few marks of punctuation to go around. If any other characters, especially letters, are to be used for the purpose (for example, *PL* to indicate that what follows is a place of publication), a way must be found to ensure that a content designator cannot be mistaken by a processing program for the content of the field itself. It helps if humans, who must do the coding, can easily remember all the content designators commonly used, but how is a program to know that *PL* is not the name of a city? The usual method is to use the same number of bytes for all content designators of the same type. By counting from a fixed reference point (the previous delimiter) through that number of bytes, the program first registers which particular content designator those bytes contain, then bypasses it to reach the first byte of the data element.

Fields and Subfields.   ISBD defines elements as they are grouped within areas; for example, a place, publisher, and date together constitute an imprint: three separate pieces of information which function as a unit. To preserve this dual nature of data in a machine-readable format, a field is defined as one complete ISBD area, one complete access point, one group of fixed-length codes, or one unit of housekeeping data. A field may be, and usually is, composed of more than one subfield; for example, the subject heading **BOOKS—CONSERVATION AND RESTORATION—TROPICAL CONDITIONS** is a three-part pre-coordination; the conference-name access point **Symposium on Symbolic Logic (3rd : 1987 : Waterloo, Ont.)** comprises a name, a serial number, a date, and a location. In each case, the parts are separately significant and to make them separately accessible for any purpose requires assigning a content designator to each.

The content designator of an entire field is called a tag. No two different types of field may be identified by the same tag but if a record contains repetitions of the same type of field (see next page), each repetition is identified by the same tag. A subfield is a single element, part of an access point, etc. identified by its own content designator called a subfield code. The first byte of this code must be the third type of delimiter described on page 239; since the number of possible types of subfield within the same field is limited, one additional byte suffices to identify the type of each possible subfield. The same actual subfield code can be used with a different meaning in each different field. There is nothing wrong with subfield *c* in a name-access-point field being a title of honour while in a physical description field, subfield *c* is the size of the item. This is the same as using a space-colon-space for several purposes in ISBD but only one purpose within any one field, or giving several telephone lines the same seven-digit calling code but never two within the same country/area code. The first subfield in a field is by convention almost always designated as *a*. Any others may be designated in alphabetic sequence (*b*, *c*, *d*, etc.) or mnemonically (for example, *v* for volume number; *l* for language). In ISBD area 4, the place is coded as subfield *a*, the name of the publisher as *b*, and the date as *c*; in the name-title access point **Mozart, Wolfgang Amadeus, 1756–1791. Concerto, piano, K.466, D minor**, the personal name is coded as subfield *a*, the birth/death dates as *d*, the title (*Concerto*) as *t*, the medium (piano) as *m*, and the Köchel number as *n*. The expected designation *k* for the key signature was pre-empted for a now-obsolete purpose which it must still serve in older records, so the key-signature subfield was rather arbitrarily assigned the unmemorable designation *r*.

It is common to incorporate some deliberate redundancy into formats for any kind of computer processing both to provide a double check against errors and to allow for flexibility in programming for a variety of applications. It would be feasible to make a content designator serve also as a delimiter, simultaneously ending one field and introducing the nature of the next, but the standard machine-readable bibliographic formats use both pure delimiters and content designators. Assigning content designators (tags, indicators, and subfield codes) to data elements, access points, etc. is called tagging the record because that corresponds with the process of manual-record tagging or labelling illustrated on page 296.

Repeatable Fields and Subfields.   There can be only one Title and Statement of Responsibility Area (ISBD area 1) in a record but that area may contain more than one unit of other title information. The Publication Area may contain two places of publication. Six subject headings for concepts may be assigned with two or more subdivisions in any of them. The same content designator must be used for each repetition of like data (each unit of other title information, each place of publication, etc.) because data of the same type must be treated the same in searching or output. The programmer implementing a database management system must know exactly which fields and which subfields may be repeated in order to write a workable file definition for the system. A format which permits a field or subfield to be repeated an unpredictable number of times within the same record causes significant problems for programmers. It is a major reason why microcomputers only recently attained the capacity to deal with the now-standard machine-readable bibliographic format in its entirety. It is also one of the reasons why a highly desirable kind of file organization in a database management system (the relational file structure) is at present still impracticable for the processing of bibliographic records.

Indicators.   Tags and subfield codes identify the parts of a record. Processing these parts may depend on defining to a program certain characteristics of the data; for example, which controlled vocabulary a subject access point comes from or, in a bilingually indexed database, whether the subject access point recorded in a field is in one language or the other. Without explicit identification, the computer cannot distinguish, for example, an LCSH from a MeSH access point or French from English. It is possible to do much identification of this kind using a single-byte code attached to a field. As another example, a person recognizes and ignores an initial article in any of several languages almost unconsciously when filing or searching a title. It is inefficient to program a computer to recognize every article in every language, but a one-byte numeral associated with a title field can constitute an explicit instruction to the filing program to skip that number of characters at the beginning of the title when placing that title in an alphanumeric sequence. A one-byte code used for such purposes as those described here is a content designator called an indicator. An indicator is only associated with an entire field, never with an individual subfield. Whether indicators are used at all, and how many there should be per field, varies among different formats. The processing program recognizes the indicator(s), if any, as the first byte(s) in every field, their number being defined for the format as a whole. The defined number of indicator-bytes must therefore be reserved in association with every variable field in every record even if in practice, significant indicators are used for only a small number of the fields in a given record and all the rest are coded as blanks.

Directory.   The delimiters and content designators described in the preceding paragraphs suffice to enable a program to locate the beginning and the end of any desired unit of data in a variable-field record provided it scans every character in each record. Searching is more efficient if at least the major content designators (the tags) can be scanned separately as a kind of table of contents to the record. This table of contents is called the record directory. An operating system or word-processing program creates a directory to a storage medium in which every file's name and size are associated with its location(s) on the storage medium. In the same way, the record directory indexes each field in the record by giving its (1) tag, (2) length, and (3) address relative to a fixed point of departure. Using a directory, the different fields in a record need not have addresses in any sequence which is meaningful to a person consulting the record visually, so an additional or revised field can be stuck in and addressed anywhere, making record revision technically simple. The directory consists of as many units as there are variable fields in the record. Each directory unit is of equal length so that a program can count past any number of them in equal increments. The input program which stores the completed records on tape or disk does all this counting and addressing; the human cataloguer is not bothered with it.

A database management system does not go through a process of directory-matching and address-searching every time someone consults the file. It does so only to create (or update) its own indices according to the requirements of the people who have designed the search parameters and user-interface for a particular application as described in chapters 4 and 10. These indices are the basis for all subsequent searching. Since the database management system uses the directory to create its indices, however, the most efficient indexing of the record is based on separate fields, a fact with major consequences for interactive searching. In practice, it requires the searcher to select the field(s) to be searched. The single-alphabet author/title/subject, or so-called dictionary, catalogue is therefore not the model on which the interactive catalogue can efficiently be based.

Label (Leader). A record in a manual file often contains some description of itself in addition to the description it contains of a document, for example, whether it is a new or a revised record, which cataloguer created it, whether its access points conform to a particular cataloguing code. A database management system needs quantitative information about the record, including how many bytes long the entire record is, the number of indicators common to every field, and the number of bytes in the standard unit of the record directory. Some of these facts (for example, the last two mentioned) are typically standard for an entire database and would therefore seem not to require stating in each separate record. However, if the format is intended for widespread adoption and considerable flexibility in operation, it must make provision for inter-system record compatibility and a little redundancy is a small price to pay. Finally, the processing programs must be told of any special format characteristics; for example, since formats for sound recordings, books, films, etc. must differ in the types of information they contain to describe the physical characteristics of the item, the processing programs must know which format variant to apply. The part of a record which contains such information as that described in this paragraph must be the first part to come to the attention of the processing programs, so the term *leader* was originally applied to it. It is now known as the label.

The First MARC Format

Punched-card equipment was well known in libraries for inventory and circulation purposes by the 1950s. Using this inherently fixed-field technology, librarians at first designed a unique format for almost every single application. By 1965, variable-field formatting was the subject of experimentation at the Library of Congress and other institutions, and the threat of format incompatibility which would inhibit record sharing was growing. The Library of Congress used its powers of persuasion and subsidized development gradually to convince the librarians of North America to adopt its variable-field format at least for the exchange of records even if they developed separate and simpler formats for in-house processing. In 1966 and 1967, tests of the first draft of the exchange format, by then named MARC, were undertaken to determine how it could support local cataloguing operations. These led to substantial revision of the draft and the MARC II format was issued in 1968. The II has long since been dropped. Until the late 1970s, only a large mainframe computer had the capacity to deal with all the features of the full MARC format, but selected data elements can be derived from this format and downloaded into whatever processing format a library's database management system can use. The reverse is less likely to be possible: any data element not separately identified in the in-house processing format cannot be used to recreate the exchange format. For example, many libraries used processing formats which could not accommodate subfields or field repetitions. Using the exchange format therefore usually meant receiving or downloading (sometimes called importing) records from a national agency but not sending them out to a cooperative database. This limitation was a major incentive to join a consortium or utility with adequate computer facilities to deal with MARC records and process them for member libraries as described on page 118. Now that programs are commercially available and microcomputer capacity is sufficient, more and more in-house systems use the MARC format in its entirety and can therefore also transmit a MARC record directly to another system. This is changing the nature of networking and making it more collaborative.

While there exist formats tied exclusively to the provisions of a particular cataloguing code, thesaurus, etc. and some which embody their own rules, neither of these conditions is necessary. MARC was intended neither to replace existing cataloguing rules nor to be valid for only one set of rules for either description or access. It is only the container for the data elements called for by whatever cataloguing rules, thesauri, etc. are employed to choose and state those elements. It was designed for sharing records even where the same rules are not in effect. In any case, it is desirable to be able to search, in a single interactive file, records created in accordance with various practices, older and current, as has always been the case in manual catalogues.

Although the data and their arrangement in a record may vary according to the rule applied, the catalogue card had become the standard record-exchange medium long before MARC arrived. It was therefore natural to make the MARC content designators reflect the appearance of the catalogue card so that MARC could serve the automation of catalogue-card production. For quite some time, this was virtually its only use. Alternative forms of catalogue display in libraries were then unknown. In this respect, MARC stabilized a little too early because the unit-record card, the bibliographic record format which became a part of its basic structure, was the final gasp of a dying tradition rather than the fresh beginning of a future one.

The intrusion of the ISBD and three AACRs have each required substantial changes and/or additions to the original MARC. As updating continues, all the provisions of the original MARC for now-obsolete pre-ISBD and pre-AACR practices remain; presumably there are libraries still converting into machine-readable form some records which embody these. There has been greater willingness to add to than to revise the format, making the full format cumbersome and in some respects mysterious to those who do not know its history well. It does not matter that the last note in ISBD area 7 bears a MARC tag numbered in the 500s and is followed by area 8, the ISBN, bearing the tag number 020. It is of much more consequence that the original MARC, based on the card format, preceded the rationalization of the uniform title as a general principle in AACR, Seymour Lubetzky's most significant contribution to bibliographic control. As a result, a uniform title, which is always an access point or part of one as described on pages 167–69, is often numbered in the tagging structure as if it were a descriptive data element, which it never is. This has perpetuated serious problems of understanding, displaying, and arranging uniform titles. Even reference librarians can be confused when this tagging anachronism is carried over into a misfiling of uniform titles in the output from a MARC database.

ISO2709

MARC works. Whether or not its design is perfect for its purpose is now immaterial: interlibrary bibliographic cooperation depends totally on it and it will never be replaced by anything significantly different. It was enormously costly to develop and to write processing programs for, so as soon as it proved useful in practice in the United States, it became a model to be followed elsewhere. In the interest of interlibrary cooperation, the Library of Congress was happy to support its worldwide spread and exercised little proprietary control. Almost everywhere else MARC was examined for adoption, the original was changed a bit to accommodate local needs. It was also improved, especially when examined by people not so strongly influenced by the old card format. Just as it took ISBD(G) as a more abstract guideline to keep the ISBD structure from fragmenting into incompatible parts (see page 237), so agreement had to be sought on a more abstract standard derived from the original MARC format, to which all the national variants would conform. In the meantime, A&I services around the world were also working toward machine-readable formats derived from their own practices rather than from those of library cataloguing. It was highly desirable for an international standard machine-readable format to take the A&I services into account if possible. In 1973,

ISO published its standard 2709, "Documentation—Format for Bibliographic Information Interchange on Magnetic Tape," which must be used in conjunction with other ISO standards relating to character sets and tape labelling. This is the same as the American ANSI Z39.2 and the British BS:4748. It regulates only the essential structural features of MARC as a variable-field format and is not even limited to bibliographic records. Librarians use this standard also to format records in name and subject authority files, including all links. Archivists use a format known as MARC(AMC) (MARC for Archival and Manuscript Control). ISO2709-based formats can be, and are being, used to process any kind of information requiring variable-length fields, bibliographic or other.

The delimiters, content designators, record directory, and label described above are all part of ISO2709 specifications. Only the following features are regulated in absolute terms:

1) the record and field delimiters are each described as a particular byte in the character set
2) every tag must be three bytes long and
3) the label must be twenty-four bytes long, with specified data in fixed locations therein (some bytes in the label are left undefined; a local use may be defined).

The label of each record specifies how many bytes are assigned to each unit of the record directory, how many one-byte indicators are used per field, and how many bytes are reserved for each subfield code. In practice, these three quantities are fixed for each MARC format and do not vary record by record.

The variable-length fields following the label and record directory are of three kinds. There are:

1) one record-identifier field
2) one or a very few fields called reserved fields in ISO2709 but known in North America (and in this book) as control fields and
3) any number of bibliographic-data fields.

The latter are the fields containing the descriptive areas and elements of ISBD, the controlled-vocabulary name and subject access points, and additional fields for retrieval codes: essentially the entire bibliographic record as described so far in this book and a bit more. ISO2709 is silent on how data elements, etc. are to be expressed in these fields since that depends on the type of document or object listed and the cataloguing or other rules applied to govern data selection and arrangement. This is the part of the record whose structure must be tied to a detailed individual format based on ISO2709, such as one of the many MARC formats. The permitted tag numbers for this part of the record run from 010 through 999.

Record-Identifier and Control Fields

The record-identifier field contains only one data element: a unique character string which programmers often call a control number, by which a database management system recognizes the record as a unit. All inter-record links to and from related records, access-point links to authority files, etc. must be made using this identifier. It does not matter what this identifying character string is: it can be all numeric, all alphabetic, or a combination, but no two records under the control of the same database management system can have the same record identifier. A Library of Congress card number is a record identifier in that Library's in-house systems because no two Library of Congress records can have the same number. But if Library of Congress records appear in another system along with, say, British Library and/or consortium members' records, then something additional, often a prefix, must make each identifier unique because the same number could come from each of several sources. If a local processing system generates a number at random as a record identifier, as is usually the case, the record identifiers of other systems (including those of the Library of Congress and of national bibliographies) are put into a bibliographic-data field, if kept in the local record at all. The record-identifier field is often treated as if it were of fixed length although in theory it need not be. ISO2709 prescribes that its tag be 001: the first variable-length tag in the record. It has no indicators or subfield codes.

The control fields are so called because they contain data useful for processing and searching. Confusingly, they are often called the fixed fields because they contain coded data which can be stated in a fixed-field structure. It was stated on page 237 that MARC includes features of both fixed-field and variable-field formatting. Information is given in the control fields both (1) in coded form for efficiency in storage and (2) in a fixed location relative to the beginning of their field for efficiency in searching. There is much potential for post-coordinate searching in the very large number of these codes which are defined in MARC. This potential has yet to be realized in most libraries. Some do not even bother coding all of them. The date of publication is stated in one of these fields as well as in the appropriate bibliographic-data field because it is more efficiently searched in a fixed field. Much of what is coded here is implicit, not explicit, in the rest of the record. The computer cannot determine which items listed are in the Farsi language by interpreting the meaning of title words as a human would, so if language is ever to be a search parameter, a program must locate an explicit language code. A fixed field is an efficient place to put such a code of a few bytes.

The following is a small representative sample of other coding provided, in one or a very few bytes, in these fields:

- places of publication (in three bytes, for example, *txu* for Texas, USA)

- physical characteristics (in one byte per characteristic, for example, *b* for super-8mm film)
- types of content (for example, *a* for autobiography)
- technical characteristics of content (for example, *j* for digitized stereophonic sound)
- types of publication (for example, *s* for a provincial-level government document, *l* for a conference proceedings)
- audience-level (for example, *v* for a secondary-school textbook)
- types of illustrative material contained (for example, *c* for portraits, *e* for architectural plans)
- housekeeping data (for example, the date of cataloguing, a code for the cataloguing agency, a code to show that ISBD punctuation is part of the record).

Each of these control fields is, as a whole, a variable field: more codes may be added provided they do not alter the character position of anything already defined in the field. Like the record-identifier field, a control field has no indicators associated with it. There are also no subfields because the character position of each code in the field reveals its identity. The appendix gives details of the coding of the control field for published monographs.

The MARC Family of Formats

The above subsections describe the structure of any ISO2709-based format, but the examples are all taken from what is actually done in the MARC format. The original MARC came to be called LCMARC and is now officially designated USMARC. MARC is no longer one format. It is a closely linked family of a score of siblings with no identical twins. Most were developed in the context of a country's national library and/or network; there are a few multi-country versions. All MARC formats are similar enough that they can be translated into one another using a fairly simple program. However, it would be inefficient if a national agency wishing to exchange records with many others had to write a separate translation program for each other agency's records received. IFLA therefore sponsored a universal MARC format (UNIMARC) for international record exchange. Unlike the older MARC formats, UNIMARC is consciously divorced from the appearance of the pre-computerized catalogue card. Its tags are therefore arranged more logically and their numbers often do not correspond to those for the same data elements in other MARC formats. Using it as an intermediate format, each national agency need only provide a translation program for its records into and out of UNIMARC. Record exchange within a country takes place in the national format. Countries with relationships as close as those between Canada and the United States continue to rely on bilateral format-translation. There is a particular compatibility problem within Canada because of the widespread use in Canadian libraries of commercial software packages written to process USMARC rather than CANMARC.

Non-MARC ISO2709 Formats

There are formats for bibliographic data outside the MARC family but still conforming to the ISO2709 structure. Two are important enough to note. One is the UNISIST Reference Manual referred to on page 223, designed for newer A&I services dependent on neither an established hardware/software package nor established cataloguing rules.[13] It embodies its own set of cataloguing rules which differ in some respects from the emerging international consensus developing around ISBD and AACR2. Its use is not widespread.

The newest and most sophisticated ISO2709-based format, the Common Communication Format (CCF), began as an attempt to bridge differences between the A&I community and the library community.[14] It is being used especially in parts of the world where the two groups have not become totally separated from one another by history or by economics. It is little known in the developed countries where MARC formats have become entrenched. Technically, the CCF represents a major advance in formatting because it provides for different levels of description within the same record as these are defined in the next section. It thus distances itself considerably from the origin of machine-readable bibliographic formats in the manual file where each record is an indivisible physical unit. It remains a significant failing of MARC formats that a record must remain a whole for all linking purposes so that a link can only be established between one complete record and another complete record. In the CCF, this is not the case.

Bibliographic Entities (Levels)

It has been stated more than once in previous chapters that many bibliographic files, and pre-eminently library catalogues of this century, are not merely collections of isolated records each of which provides information about only one item. They deliberately show relationships among different works and documents by means of

1) controlled-vocabulary name and subject access points (along with their cross-references): these link works related to the same person, subject, etc.

13. *Reference Manual for Machine-Readable Bibliographic Descriptions*, 2nd rev. ed., comp. and ed. H. Dierickx and A. Hopkinson (Paris: Unesco General Information Programme and UNISIST, 1981). PGI-81/WS/2.

14. *CCF: Common Communication Format*, prepared by Peter Simmons and Alan Hopkinson, 2nd ed. (Paris: Unesco General Information Programme and UNISIST, 1988). PGI-88/WS/2.

2) notes of several types in ISBD area 7: these mention the existence of other works or documents bibliographically related to the one being described and list separate works contained in it, even if these facts do not result in separate access points and

3) the principal access point and other name-title and uniform-title access points: these relate the various manifestations of the same work to each other.

This section examines an additional kind of linkage provided for in bibliographic formats: a linkage among the different records which either do exist or could exist for the *same* document when that document can have more than one bibliographic identity. Some formats accommodate this linkage better than others, as noted in the mention of the CCF, but all permit it to some degree.

What Does a Title Entitle?

Every bibliographic description must begin with a title, even if the cataloguer has to invent one ad hoc for a document lacking one. To look at this cliché from the opposite point of view, every title is entitled to appear at the beginning of area 1 of its own bibliographic description even if this does not always happen in practice. What different kinds of entities have titles? In this book, the important distinction between a work and a document is first made on page 5 and reoccurs *passim*. If a work is published in different editions, translations, etc., a uniform title collocates these in the file. If variant wordings of the title of a document appear on its title page, running heads, spine, etc., they are mentioned in an area 7 note and possibly warrant additional access points. The problem raised in this section is different: it is that of a document issued with more than one title, each representing a different bibliographic guise of the *same* work. Together, the several titles pose an identity crisis for both the document in hand and for the work(s) it embodies.

The title pages reproduced in figure 29 illustrate this problem. They are the first and last title pages of the six volumes of Churchill's war history as published in both its North American and its British editions. They raise a number of questions which may seem at first like pedantic hair-splitting but whose answers are significant in revealing how a user will search for any or all of the six as (1) physical document(s) or (2) intellectual work(s).

1) Did Sir Winston write one work in six volumes or six works which constitute a series?

2) Is the user more likely to search for Sir Winston's history of the war in an alphabetically arranged list under the title common to the six parts (that is, under **S**) or under each of the six separate titles (that is, under **G**, **T**, etc.)? The answer that the user would search under **C** for **Churchill** does not resolve the issue; the large number of records filed under his name must still be subarranged by their individual titles.

FIGURE 29. Two pairs of title pages for the same works, showing the effect of typography in emphasizing the titling of the different entities (levels).

3) Whether the user's information about Churchill's history of the war comes from references heard in conversation or from citations seen, how much are those references influenced by the wording, layout, and typography of the title pages of the documents in which they originate— that is, to what degree are a Briton and an American likely to search for, or cite, Churchill's history differently from one another because of the title which predominates typographically in the different editions?

4) In choosing which title to use as the basis of a catalogue record— that of the part (one particular volume) or that of the whole (all six volumes)—should the cataloguer be influenced by whether the library intends to acquire all six or only one or a few of them? (If the latter seems an unlikely decision in the Churchill case, it would certainly be taken in many other bibliographically identical situations.)

5) To describe all six volumes, should one prepare one bibliographic record (for the six volumes as a unit), six records (one for each volume), or seven? This last alternative is doubtless ideally preferable but
   a) it inevitably costs more money and
   b) it begs the question of how data elements will be presented for output or searching: each of the seven descriptions must begin with only one particular title in its area 1.

6) Would it have been easier or more difficult to arrive at a decision regarding questions 4 and 5 above in 1948 (when only the first part existed) or in 1954 (by which time all six existed)?

To complicate matters further, all these questions have somewhat different implications in the environment of the interactive catalogue than they do in that of the manual catalogue. Some of the problems implicit in the above questions may not be problems if the database management system used permits word-by-word searching, but only if one can search each word of *all* title elements of each record, not only of the title proper or even all of area 1. In whatever fashion the records for these volumes are created, one or another of the titles involved is going to end up in area 6 or area 7, either or both of which may be excluded from natural-language retrieval or may be retrievable only from an index different from that containing the title proper.[15] Another major problem of the interactive catalogue is that it is usual for only a few truncated data elements to be shown as the initial response to a search request under an author's name. Data in areas 6 and 7 of any record rarely appear on the terminal screen until a fuller display is specifically requested. How is the user to know for which

15. It is, for example, common for series titling to be incorporated in the name authority file. Series are subject to authority control because series titling can require links among variant forms found in different volumes of the series and between a series title and the name of an issuing corporate body. In the case of serials, however, the serial title does not generally enter the authority file, even though the same conditions can apply, because the variant titles, etc. are made additional access points rather than cross-references. This is another unfortunate anomaly caused by the preservation in an interactive file of features essential only to a unit-card system of cataloguing.

records to request this fuller display as the large number of Churchill's works are scrolling by and the initial display of their area 1 titles proper shows nothing which appears, *prima facie*, to be relevant?

Multiple Entities.   The Churchill example illustrates problems involved in dealing simultaneously with two different things: (1) a multivolume set or series and (2) a monograph in that series. Each of the two is a distinct bibliographic entity identified by its own title proper but both comprise the same physical item(s).[16] The title page reproduced in figure 30 is more complex: it explicitly identifies three entities, one of which is a serial. They are:

1) *Sublevel Caving in Relation to Flow in Bins and Bunkers*
2) *Analysis of Bulk Flow of Materials under Gravity Caving Process* and
3) *Colorado School of Mines Quarterly.*

The sixty pages in this single-piece item contain other titles, too: titles of chapters, sections, and subsections of the text. Those may be important to the person quoting or indexing a particular passage within the document, but are of no importance in listing it as a whole. Or are they? At the end of this late chapter in an already overlong treatise on the bibliographic record, we are less able than ever to clarify either the most significant definition skilfully avoided on page 11 in the first chapter (*What is a work?*) or the most significant policy decision sidestepped on pages 42 and 45 (*Should the work or the document be the basis of bibliographic description?*). That there are no rigid answers to either of these two fundamental questions is the thrust of this necessarily difficult section which the beginner may wish to skip.

However one chooses to cite, catalogue, or index this publication, none of the three titles appearing on the title page reproduced in figure 30 can simply be ignored. Ideally, all three should appear in any record for the item. The following discussion explores

1) how the AACR/ISBD/MARC format locates and relates the three titles in records of various kinds which should, or at least could, be created for the item
2) which kind of record is most appropriate under certain circumstances and

16. I use the unfamiliar term *bibliographic entity* reluctantly because either of two more familiar terms, *work* or *level*, might seem adequate. As noted on page 170, AACR2 uses the word *entity* in the sense intended here, but only once. Elsewhere, the word *level* is used with the meaning intended here—for example, (1) in ISBD's section on the Multilevel Description, (2) throughout the Common Communication Format mentioned on page 249, and (3) in AACR2 rule 13.6. However, among North American cataloguers, the word *level* is normally understood only in the quite different sense of a level of completeness in description (see page 127). *Work* is also a less than satisfactory term here because of its other meanings. The Churchill case is not that of a single work which as a whole bears many titles; rather, the six-volume history of the war is treated as a different work than the one-volume history of its final year. Neither the problem nor the bibliographic solution is the same as in case of the St. Matthew Gospel example on pages 141–42.

COLORADO SCHOOL OF MINES QUARTERLY

Volume 75   October 1980   Number 4

ANALYSIS OF BULK FLOW OF MATERIALS UNDER GRAVITY CAVING PROCESS

Part 1: Sublevel caving in relation to flow in bins and bunkers

Li I. Yenge

$12.00

Colorado School of Mines quarterly. -- Vol. 1 (1906/07) -
. -- Golden : The School, 1907-
v. : ill. ; 15-28 cm.

1. Mines and Minerals resources--Colorado--Periodicals.
2. Mineral industries--Colorado--Periodicals. I. Colorado
School of Mines.

Yenge, Li I.
    Analysis of bulk flow of materials under gravity caving process
/ Li I. Yenge. — Golden, CO : Colorado School of Mines,
1980-c1981-
        v. <1> : ill. ; 28 cm. — (Colorado School of Mines quarterly ; v. 75,
no. 4 ISSN 0163-9153-   )
        Bibliography: v. 1. p. 41-45.

        Contents: pt. 1. Sublevel caving in relation to flow in bins and bunkers.

        $12.00

        1. Carving mining.   2. Bulk solids flow.   I. Title.   II. Series: Colorado.
School of Mines, Golden.   Quarterly ; v. 75, no. 4, [etc.]
TN210.C68   vol. 75, no. 4, etc.   81-129
                                        622'.05 s—dc19
    [TN287]   [622'.2]   MARC
Library of Congress

Yenge, Li I.
    Sublevel caving in relation to flow in bins and
bunkers / Li I. Yenge. -- Golden, CO : Colorado School
of Mines, 1980.
        60 p. : ill. ; 28 cm. -- (Analysis of bulk flow of materials
under gravity caving process / Li I. Yenge ; pt. 1)(Colorado
School of Mines quarterly, ISSN 0163-9156 ; v. 75, no. 4)
        Bibliography: p. 41-45.
        $12.00

Guy T. McBride, Jr.
President

FIGURE 30. The title page of a single issue of a journal and a bibliographic record for each of the three entities it represents. The middle one, being a photoreproduction of a 1981 Library of Congress record, does not conform entirely to present descriptive cataloguing rules.

3) why in some cases one or more of these titles does *not* appear on a given record.

The relationship of each entity to the other two is explicit and unambiguous. It may be easiest to understand these relationships by analyzing the nature of the three entities, beginning with the physically smallest and therefore least comprehensive one.

1) The entity entitled *Sublevel Caving* . . . comprises sixty pages issued by its publisher as one physical piece. It is part 1 of *Analysis of Bulk Flow* . . . and is, at the same time, the whole of the October 1980 issue (volume 75, number 4) of *Colorado School of Mines Quarterly.*

2) The entity entitled *Analysis of Bulk Flow* . . . comprises (1) the entity described immediately above *plus* (2) either the whole or part of some later issue(s) of *Colorado School of Mines Quarterly*. The appearance of the words *Part 1* on the title page in figure 30 implies that the publisher intended to issue one or more additional parts later but neither its (their) eventual existence, titling, nor relationship to the *Quarterly* could be predicted with certainty. Bibliographic good intentions—even promises—are broken, if perhaps not as often as some other ones. *Analysis of Bulk Flow* . . . was in fact subsequently completed by the appearance of a second piece which also bears three titles: (1) *Analysis of Bulk Flow* . . . , (2) *Theoretical and Physical Modeling of Gravity Flow of Broken Rock*, and (3) *Colorado School of Mines Quarterly*, of which it is the whole of the July 1981 issue (volume 76, number 3). Two of these three titles are therefore common to both parts of this entity.

3) The entity entitled *Colorado School of Mines Quarterly* has been published as some three hundred separate physical items. Its publisher continues to issue more of them with the same title regularly because it is a serial publication. Libraries tend to preserve them in four-to-a-volume rebindings.

While it is not very common for a quarterly journal to devote each separate issue to a single, separately titled contribution by a single person, this example is far from unique. To compare it with the Churchill example is to see how little difference it makes to the *work* (in this case, what Mr. Yenge wrote) whether it be published

1) as a single independent publication—something simple to both list and search in a bibliographic file and for which the simplest format suffices

2) as a publication in a monographic series (a group of separate publications each of which also bears the same series title as all the others)[17]

17. A monographic series is also a serial publication when items are intended to be issued in the series indefinitely. Many, but far from all, monographic series are serials. One which is not is sometimes called a set (see page 53).

3)   as a single contribution gathered together into a monograph with other independently created contributions (one type of such publication is the anthology; another is the conference proceedings) or

4)   as an article in, or the whole of, an issue of a serial publication.

Which of these types of publication is actually achieved may seem to concern only the work's author and publisher. These people tend to forget that it also makes a great deal of difference to anyone who must list the work in an A&I publication, a bibliography, or a library catalogue and therefore also to anyone searching for it because each of these tools treats the entities it lists and indexes in a somewhat different context. It would simplify bibliographic control enormously if every work, however one defines that word, occupied the whole of, and only, one physical piece with only one title! There would then be no such thing as a serial, multivolume work, series, anthology, conference proceedings, etc. There would also be many unemployed indexers, cataloguers, and reference librarians because clerks could do much more of the bibliographic work and end-users could find much more of what they need without professional assistance.

Record Formats for Emphasizing Different Entities

The focus of each bibliographic record is the title proper chosen for its area 1. The formatting of every other data element in the record and the coherence and intelligibility of the record as a whole depend on how the other data elements are made to relate to that title proper. Each of the three records shown in figure 30 describes in some way the one physical piece whose title page is reproduced in that figure; two of them originated at the Library of Congress. Each record begins with the title proper of a different one of the item's three entities and therefore gives prominence to the entity primarily identified by that title proper. The records show how ISBD areas 1, 6, and 7 are used to clarify the trinitarian nature and relationships of the one physical document. These three records are now analyzed separately.

The record in figure 30 with the title proper *Colorado School of Mines Quarterly* is a serial record. It is also incomplete, or open, because the serial is still being published.[18] The word *open* refers to areas 3, 4, and 5, which contain blank spaces awaiting information not yet known. There is no area 6 because this is the most comprehensive entity involved in this case. One could conceivably list the titles of the individual issues of this serial, either totally or selectively, in area 7 as a contents note as in figure 32 on page 259 but this practice is rare in the case of a serial because the note would be of uncontrollable length. The librarian who anticipates problems of identifying separately titled single issues may choose, ad hoc, to analyze some or all sin-

18. This type of record is probably still better known as an open entry. For the reasons given in footnote 4 on page 17 and footnote 1 on page 65, the word *entry* is avoided here as elsewhere in this book.

gle issues in the local catalogue as described on pages 258–60. This, too, is rare because it is normally expected that any citation will inform a searcher when the cited work is a part of a serial, thus shunting the entire search-and-retrieval process away from the monographic route of the library catalogue and toward the serial route of the A&I publication. One might view the records in any A&I publication as contents notes linked to the records for whole serials which appear in library catalogues. The caution is that the two routes sometimes merge and that some bibliographic entities manage not to get onto either retrieval route.

The record in figure 30 with the title proper *Analysis of Bulk Flow . . .* describes a multivolume work not all of which existed at the time this record was made for its first part. The serial title *Colorado School of Mines Quarterly* appears in area 6 of this record because it is the title of a more comprehensive entity of which this is a part. The title of the least comprehensive entity, *Sublevel Caving . . .* , appears in area 7 in a contents note because it identifies part of the entity named in area 1. When this record was initially produced, only part of this entity existed, so, like the serial record described in the previous paragraph, this one is left open with blanks in areas 4 and 5. It is not, however, a serial record and therefore has no area 3. The Library of Congress eventually revised this record and closed (completed) it as shown in figure 31.

```
Yenge, Li I.
  Analysis of bulk flow of materials under gravity
caving process / Li I. Yenge. -- Golden, CO : Colorado
School of Mines, 1980-1981.
  2 v. : ill. ; 28 cm. -- (Colorado School of Mines
quarterly, ISSN 0163-9153 ; v. 75, no. 4, v. 76, no. 3)
    Bibliography: Vol. 1, p. 41-45; v. 2, p. 63-67.
    Contents: Pt. 1. Sublevel caving in relation to flow
in bins and bunkers -- pt. 2. Theoretical and physical
modeling of gravity flow of broken rock.
  $12.00 (per vol.)

  1. Caving mining. 2. Bulk solids flow. I. Title.
II. Series: Colorado School of Mines quarterly; v. 75,
no. 4, [etc.]

TN210.C68   vol. 75, no. 4, etc.    622´.05 s --dc19
[TN287]                             [622´.2]
                                          81-129
```

FIGURE 31. On the appearance of the second volume of the entity named in the title proper, the Library of Congress revised the middle record shown in figure 30 as transcribed here. Since this is a revision, not a new record, it retains the same record-identifier number, 81-129. See pages 129–30 for practical implications of updating existing incomplete (open) records in both manual and interactive catalogues.

The final record in figure 30, the one with the title proper *Sublevel Caving* . . . , is the only one to describe the single physical piece whose title page started this lengthy bibliographic journey. It is unlikely that any library would prepare this record because this entity is so self-evidently dependent on one or more other entities that citation to it in isolation would seem unlikely; in other words, a user is not likely to seek this title as such in a catalogue or A&I publication. Why this is self-evident, however, has more to do with the typography of the title page than with the wording of this title, which in itself is neither dependent nor unusual. There is probably a citation in some mining journal to this title, lacking adequate identification of its more comprehensive guises and therefore ready to trap some unwary searcher into looking for this entity, which lies buried without access in many a library. Despite the hypothetical nature of this record, it is worth noting with respect to the format that starting area 1 with this title makes it necessary to record not one but two more comprehensive entities in area 6. Since this is the least comprehensive entity of the three under discussion, any area 7 contents note on this record could only mention chapter or section titles from the text. This is rarely desirable unless any of those chapters, etc. represents something which could be defined and sought as a separate work.

Analytics; Multilevel Description. In the briefest description permitted by AACR2 rule 1.0D, no area 6 is required even if the title in area 1 is a part of a larger entity. A contents note is optional regardless of how brief or full a record is produced. For these reasons, any title identified above as belonging in area 6 or area 7 may never appear in the record produced by one or another agency. Even if a title is recorded in area 6 or 7, making it accessible is a separate issue. In a manual catalogue, it might or might not be made an access point depending on the library's policy and the cataloguer's ad-hoc judgement. In an interactive catalogue, it is more likely, but still not necessary, that access will be provided to such a title. If the assurance of access, or at least full description, is wanted for *each* entity involved, two ISBD/AACR-authorized formats are available, known as (1) the analytic and (2) the multilevel description. Analysis is the production of a bibliographic record for a component part of a host item when the latter—in this case, the *Colorado School of Mines Quarterly*—has its own record in the same file.[19] The Library of Congress records in figures 30 and 31 bearing the title *Analysis of Bulk Flow* . . . are therefore analytic records, or analytics. In this example, the component part has its own title page, so the analytic record is indistinguishable from a record for a separately published item which is part of a series. However, *any* part of, or work within, a document can be analyzed provided it has its own title, for example, a single hymn in a

19. The terms *component part* and *host item* are those used in the *Guidelines for the Application of the ISBDs to the Description of Component Parts*, a publication in the ISBD system (see page 236) which illustrates the details of using both the analytic and the multilevel-description techniques. These terms are used in this subsection to refer to any two entities having a part/whole relationship with each other.

hymnal or even (although probably not wisely) a chapter of a textbook. When the component part is not in any way a separate publication, a special analytic format is prescribed. The resulting record with the title of the component part in its area 1 is called an *In*-analytic because the word *In* states the part-to-whole relationship in a manner familiar from style-manual citation practice as shown in figure 32. Whether in area 6 or in an *In* note, the host item is described very briefly because its full record appears elsewhere in the file. Access points are provided for an analytic record on the same basis as for any other record except that none is provided for the host item because its access points are associated with its own separate record.

```
PR1272
.M57

Modern plays ...    London, J. M. Dent & sons ltd [1939]

    xii, 354 p., 1 l. 17.5 cm. (Half-title: Everyman's library, ed. by Ernest
Rhys.  Poetry and the drama.  [No. 942])

    "First published in this edition 1937 ; reprinted 1939."
    "Bibliographies" : p. viii-x.

    Contents.—Milestones, by Arnold Bennett and Edward Knoblock.—
The Dover road, by A. A. Milne.—Hay fever, by Noel Coward.—Journey's
end, by R. C. Sherriff.—For services rendered, by W. S. Maugham.


    1. English drama—20th cent.
```

```
        Coward, Noel.
          Hay fever / Noel Coward. -- p. 141-98 ; 18 cm.
          In Modern plays. -- London : Dent, 1939.

          I. Title.
```

FIGURE 32. Above, a record for the collection whose title page is reproduced in figure 2 on page 31. Below, an *In* analytic record for one of the plays in the collection. This analytic is displayed in the traditional card style.

The analytic record provides a full description only of the component part; the host item is treated more briefly. Conversely, the record for the host item describes only that entity fully and may or may not even mention the component part. The method of displaying full information about each of several entities within a single record is called multilevel description. Figure 33 shows an example. Access points for a multilevel record can be derived from elements presented at any of its levels. Although part of ISBD, multilevel description is unfamiliar in Anglo-American practice. An analytic record is a separate record from that for the host item. In the MARC format, analytic, monographic, and serial records are identified as such in the label and are linked by putting the record-identifier number of the other record in a linking field. Formats in the MARC family cannot deal adequately with the multilevel description because to do so requires links to *parts* of a record, something possible in the Common Communication Format (see page 249). The ability to link data in a Series Area of one record to that in a Contents Area of another and/or to a Title and Statement of Responsibility Area of a third is a major advantage of the CCF.

```
The Second World War / Winston S. Churchill. --
Boston : Houghton, Mifflin, 1948-1953.
  6 v. ; 23cm.

  1: The gathering storm. -- Boston : Houghton,
Mifflin ; Toronto : T. Allen, 1948. -- xvi,
784 p. : maps. -- Published in association with
the Cooperative Publishing Co.

  2:
    [etc.]

  6: Triumph and tragedy. -- 1953. -- xvi,
800 p. ; maps
```

FIGURE 33. A multilevel description for the American edition of the Churchill item two of whose title pages are reproduced in figure 29 on page 251. To such a multilevel description, access points may be added for any name and title involved and for the specific subject(s), as pertinent to the whole and/or to each of the individual parts.

Which, and How Many, Entities to Emphasize?

Neither a cataloguing code nor a record format can prescribe which of several possible entities is to be featured by recording its title proper in area 1 of a record. The deciding factor is sometimes the nature of the database being created; for example, *New Serial Titles* and *Ulrich's Periodicals Directory* contain records using only the title of a serial publication as a whole. The focus of almost every record in an A&I publication is the title of an individual journal article, conference paper, etc. The purpose of a trade or national bibliography is to list monographs as published; records in these bibliographic sources are based on the titles of books, sets, and series offered for sale or distribution. A bibliography of poetry or of plays is based in large measure on the titles of the component parts of anthologies.

Library Policies.   The catalogue of a general public or academic library offers almost intractable problems in this respect to both its creator and its user. It is traditionally expected to be all things to all users, yet economic circumstances rarely permit this. If each of many cataloguers determines on a piece-by-piece basis which of several entities present within the same document should be the basis for a catalogue record, consistency is highly unlikely. Policies are needed. The library's size and the publication history of the work in question arc often considered because they are more objective factors. The user wants Thornton Wilder's *Our Town* and neither knows nor cares if it comes in a separate book, a three-volume anthology, or a magazine of play scripts. Typically, a large library buys those literary works which have been separately published in that form. It also buys specialized A&I publications and many bibliographies which give access to the contents of anthologies, for example, *Granger's Index to Poetry*, or Monro's *Index to Reproductions of European Paintings: A Guide to Pictures in More than 300 Books*. For both reasons, it is not as dependent as the smaller library on local-catalogue access to the contents of anthologies. It is perhaps surprising that another objective factor is the medium of the work. There exist many commercial bibliographies which list short works of creative writing appearing in journals and anthologies. It is much harder to locate a sound recording of a performance of a short musical composition, so these are more often analyzed in the local library catalogue. In fact, until 1980 the Library of Congress bent the general rule of cataloguing the document rather than the work by preparing a separate record for each of the several works on a long-playing disc under certain conditions. Rule 1.1G in AACR2 still retains this provision as an option for certain types of material when a document has no collective title.

Whether the library acquires all of a serial or series is another factor in the decision as to which entity or entities should be represented in the catalogue. If the library subscribes to the *Colorado School of Mines Quarterly*, the two parts of *Analysis of Bulk Flow* . . . are separated from each other by the two intervening issues of the *Quarterly*; in fact, they are probably bound into separate physical volumes. Nevertheless, users are more likely to be directed by citations, etc. to the title of the whole journal. If, on the contrary, the library does *not* subscribe to the *Quarterly*, it has acquired *Analysis of Bulk Flow* . . . explicitly to serve an independent subject need and should undoubtedly bind its two thin parts together and treat them as a separate unit for cataloguing and shelving. If the same library acquires other parts of the *Colorado School of Mines Quarterly*, those are all dispersed to different locations on the shelves and one expects a series access point in the catalogue to make this larger entity retrievable. Thus it is reasonable for different cataloguing/shelving decisions to apply in different libraries.

Cooperative Databases.   Early in this century, analysis was generously provided in the catalogues of libraries of all sizes and types. In a special library, as much as half a catalogue might even today consist of records for journal articles, conference papers, etc. There are two reasons for a decline in analysis in general library catalogues:

1) the growing number and accessibility of A&I publications and monographic bibliographies which list and index the contents of the anthologies and journals acquired by libraries and

2) increasingly tight budgets of library cataloguing departments and the recent need to spend money and staff time more on automation itself than on expansion of services.

A&I publications and monographic bibliographies are properly viewed as additional instances of purchasing derived cataloguing. They provide bibliographic access to essential parts of a library's own collection. Yet their cost is almost always charged to a different part of the library's budget than its cataloguing function and they are rarely thought of as integral parts of that function. As a result, the gap between the bibliographic access they provide and what the cataloguing department provides is too often ignored when the administrator lays down a policy of no local analysis by the cataloguers. Analysis remains justifiable when the astute reference librarian can predict that a particular work physically produced as part of a larger entity will be hard to come across in a separately indexed listing when it is needed. It is the reference librarian, not the cataloguer, who should make such ad hoc decisions. Cataloguers and administrators should be willing to act on them.

The analytics which are produced in library cataloguing departments find their way into the databases of the bibliographic utilities to be shared by other libraries. Their value is well known to interlibrary-loan librarians, and it is no surprise that the library producing many analytics gets requests for items which other libraries actually own but have not adequately revealed to their own users in their catalogues. Sharing analytics has a major drawback, however: the variety of formatting options described in this discussion of bibliographic entities almost ensures inconsistency, even at times confusion, in identifying those entities. Deciding whether and by what technique to deal with them is probably the least standardized aspect of bibliographic control. This encourages librarians to foster projects of producing analytics in a uniform way for such things as microform sets and to share the cost of their production. Like the distinction between the work and the physical document, the distinction between different entities in a document remains both a theoretical and a practical challenge. Both distinctions represent different facets of the same basic problem: the perennial one of matching what the user can identify as a need with the document which best serves that need.

9

ALPHANUMERIC ARRANGEMENT (FILING)

Whether they come from a controlled vocabulary or natural language, whether they are put into an index by a human filer or a database management system, whether they are searched manually or interactively, whether they are in a single dictionary sequence of many types or divided into a set of sequences, one per type, and no matter in what order a database management system stores them internally in the computer, access points must ultimately be presented to the human searcher in alphanumeric order.[1] That *M* follows *L* and *5* follows *4* is neither rational nor logical but, because it is both arbitrary and conventional, it is universally acceptable. Unlike any other possible arrangement, it is almost independent of language and of subject knowledge.

Alphanumeric arrangement is not, unfortunately, totally independent of language. Semantic elements have crept into almost every filing rule ever devised although they are not essential to one. The inevitable linguistic problem in alphanumeric arrangement is the fact that there are hundreds of forms of the alphabet, among them the arabic, cyrillic, devanagari, hebrew, and roman forms. There are also several forms of numeric symbols, among them the arabic, chinese, and thai forms. Few people know the characters or numerals and their

---

1. Within computer storage, parts of any single record, whether bibliographic, authority, or other, are almost certain to be randomly distributed across one or more storage devices but, as managed by a database management system, the whole records are logically ordered by the record-identifier number (see page 247) assigned to each record in sequence by a program when it is created. From the perspective of the user, the indices created by the database management system according to the access points, etc. specified by the cataloguer and systems designer are in alphanumeric order. This makes the basic file essentially a register file, as described on page 70. This is why, when records are assembled from their several storage sources after a search of one or more indices, they are in the order of their record-identifier numbers and are presented in that way on the searcher's screen or printed output unless a sorting program is invoked to put them into some other order. Figures 13 (page 79) and 16 (page 94) illustrate this retrieval process.

conventional arrangement in every existing form. Nonphonetic writing systems may employ objective criteria for establishing the order of characters; for example, the number of strokes in a Sino-Japanese character may be one factor in determining its dictionary location. There is even on occasion more than one accepted arrangement for the elements of the same script, for example, the Japanese phonetic hiragana. A basic character can become a problem when modified (for example, a roman letter with a diacritic) because single-language conventions exist concerning the order of certain modified characters. The Danes, for example, traditionally file ø after z; the Germans traditionally file ü as if it were ue. Fortunately, in the few scripts in which a distinction exists between forms of the same character (for example, upper- and lower-case roman letters), the distinction is ignored in filing, which is why a controlled-vocabulary index is often displayed using only upper-case letters. The forms and traditional sequence of the twenty-six-character version of the roman alphabet are very widely known and commonly used even where this is not the vernacular script. The universality of this version of the alphabet also means that there are widely applied conventions of transforming characters from other writing systems into roman characters (see pages 275–79). A conventional order for the ten decimal digits (0–9, in their arabic forms) and for their numeric combinations is even more universally familiar.

Basic Filing Rules

Despite the common basis for alphanumeric arrangement implied above, there are many details to be settled by specific rule rather than by universal convention because different arrangements are equally feasible or useful in different circumstances. Cutter's influence lingers after a century of changes, including those wrought by the computer, in library filing rules as in so many other areas of library technical services.[2] The most basic matter which must be governed by a rule is whether a space constitutes a significant character or not. In what is called letter-by-letter filing, a space is ignored and **Newfoundland** precedes **New York** because f precedes y. In word-by-word filing, a space (nothing, a blank) is considered to be a twenty-seventh character of the alphabet and is assigned a filing location preceding the letter a (something). Also called nothing-before-something filing, this results in **New York** preceding **Newfoundland** because the space after the w precedes f. Letter-by-letter filing is not at all uncommon. Most telephone directories and many encyclopaedias adopt it, but it does not allow for the organizational features desirable particularly in multiple-access catalogues. Cutter therefore established word-by-word arrangement as the most basic principle of bibliographic filing, which it still is.

2. Cutter's filing rules appear as rules 298–344 of his *Rules for a Dictionary Catalog*.

The treatment of punctuation is another basic issue requiring regulation. Should any particular mark of punctuation act as a space, be ignored (which is not the same thing), or be treated as yet another (twenty-eighth, etc.) character with its own specified filing location? For example, how should the following access points be arranged? (They appear here in letter-by-letter arrangement with the title in italics; the initial article is ignored.)

> **Cooper and Lybrand, Inc.**
> **Cooper-Hewitt Museum**
> **COOPER RIVER (S.C.)**
> *The cooper's shoe and other stories*[3]
> **Cooper, Stephen**

Cutter prescribed what punctuation should appear in a controlled-vocabulary name or subject access point precisely so that his filing rules could take account of it to produce the arrangement he considered best for the searcher. He wanted to make all corporate subheadings (see pages 157–58) and subject subdivisions file as a group under their respective access elements. To effect this, he required, for example, a period to precede the subheading in **Vancouver. Fire Department** so that his filing rules would treat the name as if it were **Vancouver** [two spaces] **Fire Department**. Thus the last municipal department in this sequence, say, **Vancouver. Youth Assistance Agency**, still precedes the title *Vancouver Cityscape*.[4] However, Cutter's rules and all subsequent ones ignore punctuation within a title proper. Because a title is not a controlled-vocabulary access point, the control exercised by making punctuation significant cannot apply to it. Other than the ISBD punctuation which separates a title proper from other title information, etc., title punctuation is not predictable and in some respects is discretionary with the cataloguer.

Dictionary versus Divided Files

Different types of access points may have, or may begin with, the same wording. How should one arrange, for example, France (the country) and France, Anatole (the person)? This problem, those of punctuation illustrated in the previous paragraph, and many others are most troublesome in the dictionary catalogue in which personal and corporate names (the latter often with names of subunits), titles (including subtitles), and multi-word and pre-coordinate subject access points are all combined in a single alphabet. This is the arrangement typical of the North American library card catalogue during the century preceding computerization and of the older manual A&I publications. Most other bibliographic

---

3. Although *The Chicago Manual of Style*'s capitalization of title words is used throughout the text of this book, the capitalization used in the lists of filed access points in this chapter is that prescribed by AACR.

4. Current cataloguing rules require a qualifier to follow the name of a city, for example, **Vancouver (B.C.)** (see page 163). This creates the subfile of municipal departments in a different way but it does not affect the basic filing principle discussed here.

tools are divided at least in that they have separate indices of names, titles, subjects, etc. When access points of only one type appear in a single index, there are far fewer problems of alphanumeric arrangement. This is one reason why, even before automation, librarians were abandoning the dictionary catalogue in favour of the divided catalogue. Yet divided files are not entirely trouble-free. An access point of any type may contain more than one word and some of the words may have different functions, for example, to qualify or subdivide the first word or term. Even if every personal name had the simple and conventional structure of Surname-*comma*-Given Name(s), hyphens and spaced prefixes within a surname would still cause problems difficult of solution using only the basic rule of word-by-word filing.

From the user's point of view, any interactive catalogue is a divided catalogue because the database management system creates separate indices for different types of access point, for example, name, subject, ISBN, call number, title. The database management system searches one of these at a time although the results may then be combined. However, many older dictionary-style files are still to be found among useful reference tools, so every librarian must still be familiar with rules covering the greater complexities of their arrangement as well as with the more modern issues of computer filing discussed later in this chapter. The following example, arranged in three different ways, contains only name, title, and concept-subject access points without descriptive data elements. To avoid some additional complications, there are also no multipart access points such as name-title ones.

The first arrangement is a letter-by-letter sequence with all punctuation and spacing ignored. It is extremely easy to index and search using a computer. In creating the indices, the database management system simply takes out all spaces and punctuation. The person searching interactively keys in the words as words, including the interword spacing and any punctuation which comes naturally, but the searching software immediately removes the latter from the keyed input before presenting the result to be matched against the indices. This arrangement is not uncommonly found in monographic bibliographies where each of several indices contains only one type of access point; it is rare in other types of bibliographic files. The characters of the first two access points in the example are identical although one is a one-word subject heading and the other a one-word title. Only the third arrangement below distinguishes identical access points by type. The first two access points, therefore, would be ordered by whatever element appears next in the bibliographic record.

WOOD
Wood
WOOD—BIBLIOGRAPHY
WOOD CHIPS INDUSTRY—CANADA
Wooden shoes and windmills
Wood frame construction

WOOD, HENRY ANGUS [name used as subject]
Wood Lake (Neb.)
Woodlawn Cemetery
Wood (Pa.)
WOOD—PRICES
Wood-Rogers, Frank
Wood's function in interior design
Wood, Sir Daniel
Wood, stone, and glass as building materials
Wood-turning as an art
Woodward Stores and retailing in Western Canada
Woodward Stores, Ltd.
Wood, William

The next version is in strict word-by-word sequence. A mark of punctuation is normally converted into a space and no distinction is made between a single space and a combination of adjoining spaces. An apostrophe, however, is removed and not replaced with a space. The special problem of the hyphen is noted below. This arrangement is very common in monographic bibliographies and in A&I publications. Being relatively easy to program, it is the arrangement produced by the sorting subroutine of most library database management systems but, as noted before the first arrangement above, such a search is done on name, title, etc. indices separately. These search results would therefore normally be output showing the access points printed below in upper/lower case, in italics, and in full capitals as three separate sequences although in the same relative positions as given below. A separate instruction is necessary if the searcher wants the results combined for output in a single sequence such as that which follows.

WOOD
Wood
WOOD—BIBLIOGRAPHY
WOOD CHIPS INDUSTRY—CANADA
Wood frame construction
WOOD, HENRY ANGUS
Wood Lake (Neb.)
Wood (Pa.)
WOOD—PRICES
Wood-Rogers, Frank
Wood, Sir Daniel
Wood, stone, and glass as building materials
Wood-turning as an art
Wood, William
Wooden shoes and windmills
Woodlawn Cemetery
Wood's function in interior design
Woodward Stores and retailing in Western Canada
Woodward Stores, Ltd.

The hyphen, of which two occur in this sample, is more of a problem than other marks of punctuation. Here, it is converted into a space. This makes *woodturning* file in a very different place from *wood-turning* or *wood turning*, although all three are orthographically acceptable forms. When dealing with natural language, this situation arises frequently, for example, on-line and online, co-operation and cooperation/coöperation. Manual filing rules require the filer to make an ad hoc judgement based on the separability of the parts before and after the hyphen. For computer filing, it is only practicable to treat hyphens all one way (changing them into spaces) or another (removing them and not inserting a space). Because they are more troubled by hyphens in title words than in names, many database vendors choose the latter course, which causes **Wood-Rogers** to file as **woodrogers** almost at the end of the above sequence.

The final arrangement is essentially Cutter's. It is much more complex than either of the other two. It is the basis for the arrangement of virtually all manual dictionary catalogues in libraries and takes into account the function of each access point and each separable element thereof, usually using punctuation as a kind of content designator. Different rules may apply to different data elements and to different marks of punctuation because of their functions; for example, the word *Sir* is ignored when it is a title of honour in a name access point; it is not ignored when it appears in a title. Cutter prescribes the separate ordering of access points which are the same up to a significant mark of punctuation (no mark of punctuation is considered significant within a publication's title) by their different functions. His posits the following order for these: (1) person, (2) place, (3) subject, (4) title. In the example, the different access points beginning with the word *Wood*, followed immediately by a significant mark of punctuation, are first divided into the above four types. Only then is each subdivided by what follows. This still separates Wood (Pa.) from Wood Lake (Neb.) because the latter is not a place named Wood, to be subdivided by Lake: it is a place named Wood Lake, to be subdivided by (Neb.).

Wood, Sir Daniel
WOOD, HENRY ANGUS
Wood, William

The three above consist of the surname *Wood* followed by forenames arranged as a subfile.

Wood-Rogers, Frank
Wood (Pa.)
WOOD
WOOD—BIBLIOGRAPHY
WOOD—PRICES

The three above consist of a one-word subject access point with two subdivisions arranged as a subfile.

Wood

This is a one-word title. It completes the group in which the single word *Wood* is alone or is followed by a significant mark of punctuation. There follow the names, places, subjects, etc. consisting of two or more words of which the first happens to be *Wood*.

WOOD CHIPS INDUSTRY—CANADA
Wood frame construction
Wood Lake (Neb.)
Wood, stone, and glass as building materials
Wood-turning as an art

Finally, as in the previous version, there follow the access points where there is no space after the first four characters, the apostrophe being always ignored in filing. The comma in the corporate-name access point is, however, significant; it accounts for the relative position of the last two.

Wooden shoes and windmills
Woodlawn Cemetery
Wood's function in interior design
Woodward Stores, Ltd.
Woodward Stores and retailing in Western Canada

These examples show how every departure from letter-by-letter filing represents a further attempt to ensure that the user will find logical groups of material together in an alphabetically arranged file. Cutter was not the first person to think this would be desirable but he defined the groups most systematically. His conclusions were widely adopted in later rules. As more and more subtle interpretation of his method of grouping was needed in order to arrange or to search a large catalogue, library filing came to be called filing *as if* rather than *as is*; that is, the wording actually seen in an access point must often be translated into something a bit different. Further examples of *as if* filing which developed through the century are:

1) numbers appearing as arabic numerals and symbols such as the ampersand (&) are filed as if written in letters in the language of the element in which they occur

2) a name used as an additional access point (added entry heading) is placed in a separate group following the same name used as a principal access point (main entry heading)

3) an acronym is filed as a word if it is commonly spoken as a word but as a series of initial letters if not and

4) records for editions, translations, etc. of the same work are filed in a single group regardless of the sequence of the words in the record itself.[5]

---

5. AACR shifted the responsibility for deciding on and implementing this arrangement from the filer to the cataloguer who makes the decision to create an explicit uniform title for the purpose (see pages 167–70).

The complex filing rules developed by the Library of Congress represent the ultimate stage of such interpretive considerations, which were thought to be a benefit to trained searchers using a huge manual catalogue.[6] That these rules should have been imposed on freshman students in dozens of small colleges throughout North America was certainly never intended by their creators.

Coordination, Filing Rules, and the Interactive Catalogue

Once access points have been arranged, there remains the problem first addressed on page 96: rules for subarrangement are needed when more than one record has the same access point. This is essentially a question of coordination: bringing two or more access points and/or data elements into play simultaneously; for example, fifty books with the same author access point are subarranged by their titles. This coordination of author and title (uniform title when it makes a difference) is the most significant of all filing coordinations because it represents the practical functioning of the principal access point, the main entry heading, which makes possible the standardized identification of a work (see pages 169–71). On the unit record envisaged by every English-language cataloguing code for multiple-access catalogues since Cutter, this cohesive access unit consisting of (1) an author's name (if any), (2) a uniform title (if any), and (3) a title proper (which is always present) occurs either at the beginning of the record or immediately following any "added" access point, be that another name, a subject, a title, a form, or anything else. When it determines the filing arrangement of the record, this access unit, shown in figure 34, was intended to come into play as a whole. Thus the cataloguing rules, the filing rules, and the card format all conspired to give the main entry heading a major role in file organization in manual catalogues in order to keep the records for variant manifestations of a single work always physically together. The access points and data elements of a manual record are always permanently pre-coordinated with each other in a fixed sequence; if there could be only one such sequence, the one described above was considered to be of overriding importance and was therefore adopted as the rule.

The essence of the interactive catalogue as described in chapter 4 is that there need be no one fixed sequence. The *searcher*—not the cataloguer/filer—determines in what combination, if any, access points are to be retrieved from among the indices created by the database management system; for example, by using boolean operators. A computer-produced manual file such as one on COM may also depart from the record-sequencing prescribed for so long in card

6. Library of Congress, Processing Department, *Filing Rules for the Dictionary Catalogs of the Library of Congress* (Washington: Library of Congress, 1956).

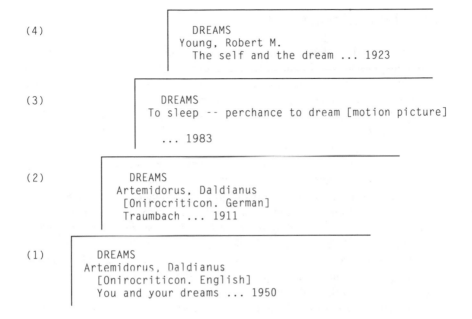

(4)

DREAMS
Young, Robert M.
   The self and the dream ... 1923

(3)

DREAMS
To sleep -- perchance to dream [motion picture]

   ... 1983

(2)

DREAMS
Artemidorus, Daldianus
[Onirocriticon. German]
Traumbach ... 1911

(1)

DREAMS
Artemidorus, Daldianus
[Onirocriticon. English]
You and your dreams ... 1950

FIGURE 34. The data elements following the subject access point **DREAMS** on these card-style records are fixed and are intended to determine the subarrangement of records under that subject access point unless a specific filing rule is invoked to contradict this subarrangement. It is becoming common for searching and output programs of an interactive catalogue to allow more flexibility (for example, to subarrange within a subject by publication dates or within any name directly by titles proper) or merely to subarrange any group of records retrieved by their serial record-identifier (or register) numbers. Any of these would result in a different arrangement of these four records.

catalogues. Again, the elements scattered throughout a stored machine-readable database are as easily assembled for print or COM output in one arrangement as in any other. This is not to say that a standard work-identifier (main-entry-heading-plus-title) is not useful, even for some purposes essential, as a factor in file arrangement. It is only to say that there are other purposes which the knowledgeable searcher can now pursue just as easily. Librarians are therefore exploring other possibilities in sorting the output from an interactive search. For example, records for works on the same subject are no longer universally subarranged by their authors' names but may well be displayed on a terminal screen or in a COM catalogue in the order of their dates of publication. The arrangement of records as they are retrieved and assembled by a database management system is not a generally useful one, as noted in footnote 1 on page 263. For formal output such as a COM catalogue, they are always resorted into whatever useful order the person responsible for ordering the output demands; for terminal-screen output, cost-cutting often dictates that no resorting is done and the searcher is both mystified and ill served by the resulting register order.

Filing by Computer

The *as if* filing which developed from Cutter's principles requires knowledge of the structure and purpose of each access point in order to arrange them correctly. Nevertheless, a high proportion of all the records to be filed into any manual catalogue are not problematic and can be correctly filed by an alert clerk with only a final professional check. No filer, professional or clerical, can file without frequent breaks from the boredom of the task: the mind wanders, observational powers diminish, and mistakes creep in. A one-percent clerical-error rate in almost any business is considered very acceptable but the misplacement of a thousand cards in a small hundred-thousand-card catalogue is not. Since the computer cannot make a clerical error, filing by computer would appear to be the ideal solution to both the high cost and the high error-rate of manual filing. Commercial publishers, including some A&I services, began using computers to sort the records in their manual bibliographic tools earlier than most libraries did because the latter were generally still maintaining card catalogues. For the sake of simple programming and cheaper computer runs, the commercial publishers were willing to sacrifice subtleties of arrangement.

Librarians at first scorned such a lax approach, seeing no reason to give up what they considered the superior file organization of the third (Cutter's) arrangement illustrated on pages 268–69. They pursued the writing of programs which would accomplish the latter but ultimately gave up: programming was too complex and execution time too lengthy.[7] The effort made librarians realize that their filing rules were perhaps unnecessarily complex, not only for computers but also for human searchers. The relative simplicity of the computer-based filing arrangements adopted by commercial publishers of telephone directories and other indices in the 1960s and 1970s came to appear more a virtue than a weakness, particularly in the divided files which were replacing the all-in-one dictionary arrangement. Logical groupings separated by the simpler filing rules could still be assembled by using additional cross-references or internal links in an interactive catalogue.

Filing by computer must be strictly *as is* to avoid major programming complications. The most noticeable differences between pre-computer and computer-based filing are therefore not related to the subtleties of the structure of controlled access points but to troublesome character strings, such as arabic numerals, initialisms, and abbreviations. These are a significant feature of natural-language access points, such as titles, search keys derived from abstracts, etc. Logical manual filing rules require that most of these be translated into complete words: the title *1812* becomes *Eighteen twelve*. It is totally impracticable to program for this, so a computer program will inevitably arrange the following access points,

---

7. See, for example, William R. Nugent, "The Mechanization of the Filing Rules for the Dictionary Catalogs of the Library of Congress," *Library Resources & Technical Services* 11 (spring 1967): 145–66.

all titles, in something close to the following order, although variants may be introduced by differing decisions as to which marks of punctuation to ignore:

> *The 2 x 2 game*
> *19th century prints and drawings*
> *35-cent thrills*
> *1940: the world in flames*
> *A.L.A. & you*
> *A.L.A.: a brief history*
> *Abbott and Costello go to the movies*
> *ALA and the continuing censorship battle*
> *Amadeus*
> *The American Library Association: a century of service*
> *Nineteenth-century European textiles*
> *Two by two into the ark*
> *The U.S. health system*
> *Uninvited and unwelcome*
> *The United States Army in the Second World War*
> *Universities of the future*
> *USA today*

The untrained searcher adapts easily to these computer-based rules because they are now used in virtually all directories, etc. Perhaps the librarian too familiar with the older style has more difficulty. Computer-based filing thrusts onto the searcher the burden of thinking, sometimes imaginatively, about what exact form an access point might take because the computer does not group logically similar but visually different forms.

Since a title is a natural-language access point, authority control is not available to provide individual cross-references or computer links from, for example, *19th* to *Nineteenth*. The searcher must simply come to know such basic rules as that a numeral files before *a*. The cataloguer may choose to add an additional access point under an alternative form for the single item being catalogued. Thus the record for Buchan's *The Thirty-nine Steps* may be made accessible by title under both **T** and **39**, but there is little point in adding a title access point under **N** for the title *1968, Year of Crisis*. In the case of any controlled-vocabulary name or subject access point (those discussed in chapter 6 and in most of chapter 7), the authority file provides the linkage mechanism and a searcher locates the preferred form either directly or through that link; for example,

> **A One Carpet Cleaning Ltd.**
> *search under* **A-1 Carpet Cleaning Ltd.**

Every time a revision of cataloguing rules alters the structure of access points, as was very much the case with the 1967 AACR, filing rules must also be revised to some degree. With the advent of the preceding issues raised by automation, the shoe was on the other foot and the cataloguing-code makers had to come to some accommodation with computer filing. In 1973, a Computer

Filing Committee was formed in the American Library Association; the word *Computer* was later dropped from the name in recognition that all filing would soon be done this way. It took the rest of the decade to overcome the prejudices of the past, to publicize the consequences widely, and to finalize rules which had some chance of acceptance.[8] These rules are designed for computer application in more than one way; for example, they identify how data elements are to be arranged both verbally and by specifying their MARC tags and subfield codes.

Standardization

Although many libraries have long adhered to a common cataloguing code in the hope that name access points might be exactly the same in different catalogues, an astonishingly large number of manual library filing rules exist. Their differences may be minor but their existence illustrates the feeling that a catalogue need only be internally consistent in its filing. Filing by computer has also not been entirely standardized. The 1980 rules of the American Library Association depart most significantly from the Cutter tradition in that they largely ignore distinctions among different punctuation marks and therefore among types of access point. In contrast, the rules published by the Library of Congress in the same year retain the traditional grouping of access points by type (surnames, jurisdictions with subdivisions, etc.).[9] Thus the American Library Association rules file **Canada Bank Note Co.** before **Canada. Census Division** while the Library of Congress rules file them the other way around in order to keep all corporate subdivisions of **Canada** together and before the access points for other corporate bodies whose names happen to begin with the same word. Both sets of rules recognize that there are advantages and disadvantages to either approach. The retention by the Library of Congress of some complexities sacrificed by the American Library Association committee reflects two assumptions:

1) more attention to logical groupings is needed in searching a very large catalogue where it is harder to see the forest for the trees and
2) the catalogue of a national institution is more likely to be searched by persons well versed in bibliographic practices than by casual, untrained users.

Some human interpretation and judgement is still required to implement either the American Library Association or the Library of Congress rules, resulting in programming complications.[10] A library may choose to ignore a particular difficulty rather than engage in complex programming or buy a more costly

---

8. *ALA Filing Rules* [by the] Filing Committee, Resources and Technical Services Division, American Library Association (Chicago: ALA, 1980).

9. *Library of Congress Filing Rules*, prepared by John C. Rather and Susan C. Biebel (Washington: Library of Congress, 1980).

10. John K. Knapp, [Review of both rules], *Journal of Library Automation* 14 (June 1981): 126–29.

system; for example, by permitting the title *Henry IV* to file as *Henry iv*; that is, between *Henry Is Coming* and *Henry Misses Out*. This means that filing systems in local libraries, in A&I publications, etc. actually differ from one another a bit more since computerization than they did just before. Any commercial software package for local processing has a built-in filing program over which the librarians have little or no control. How punctuation and nonalphabetic symbols are treated and how the results of searching more than one index are merged and displayed are likely areas of difference among these. Before purchasing software, it is essential to inquire closely into how it arranges output. It seems unlikely that a third major set of computer filing rules will ever be published for library use in North America. Those of either the American Library Association or the Library of Congress will be adopted or adapted for local systems. In the United Kingdom, the British Library published its own rules, which are very similar to those of the Library of Congress.[11] Filing principles, and a model result of using them, have also gone through the process of ratification by ISO. The former are expressed as standard ISO7154: "Documentation—Bibliographic Filing Principles." Since only limited agreement could be reached on the latter, it appears as an ISO technical report, TR8393: "Documentation—ISO Bibliographic Filing Rules." The two documents constitute an excellent study of the component parts of any type of access point inasmuch as they can influence filing at any level of complexity.

Nonroman Scripts

European academic and national libraries commonly keep records for material in nonroman scripts (for example, arabic, cyrillic, hangul) in separate catalogues, each arranged according to the filing conventions peculiar to itself. North American libraries have preferred to consolidate the records for material in different scripts in a combined file. This requires the romanization of anything which could affect filing, namely access points, even if the remainder of the record is left in the vernacular script.[12] Romanization is still sometimes, but more loosely, called transliteration: it is the conversion of nonroman characters into characters of the roman alphabet. It is not translation. Converting 日本放送協会 into Nihon Hōsō Kyōkai (or into NHK) is romanization; changing the Name into Japanese Broadcasting Corporation is translation. Romanization is not an issue only for large, academic, or automated libraries. A rapidly increasing number

11. *BLAISE Filing Rules*, by the British Library Filing Rules Committee (London: British Library, 1980).

12. Romanizing the data elements of a description has never been condoned by modern cataloguing rules, but until a character set (see pages 121–22) is available for a script and its use is affordable, a library is forced to romanize the entire record for computer manipulation.

of names of nonroman-script origin are encountered in everyday library work in English in even the smallest libraries, for example,

Peter Tchaikovsky: *originally* Пётр Ильич Чайковский

Anton Chekhov: *originally* А. П. Чехов

Sholem Asch: *originally* שלום אַש

Yukio Mishima: *originally* 三 島 由 紀 夫

Existing Romanization

The surname of the author of *The Cherry Orchard*, shown above in its original cyrillic form, appears in print on some title page in each of the romanizations shown below, the language of the title page being indicated in brackets.

Anton Čechov [English, German, Italian]
Anton Čechow [German]
Anton Čexov [English]
Anton Chehov [English]
Anton Chekhov [English]
Anton Czechow [Polish]
Anton Tchehov [English]
Anton Tchekhoff [English]
Anton Tchekhov [English, French]
Anton Tchékhov [French]
Anton Tchekoff [English]
Anton Tschechov [German]
Anton Tschechow [German]
Anton Tsjechov [Dutch]

As a modern current-events example from another script, the surname of the Libyan leader of the 1980s appears in various English-language news-media headlines with the initial letter *G*, *K*, or *Q*. Each of the above forms is called an existing romanization because it appears in some existing roman-alphabet publication. If a library collects materials in many languages, a few cases are sure to arise of differing existing romanizations of the same name, if not cases as extreme as those involving Mr. Chekhov and Colonel al-Qadhdhafi [sic: a romanization actually found in an English-language title].

Romanization is based on phonetics: it attempts to reproduce in the roman alphabet the sound of the character as it is pronounced by a native speaker of the language in question. It almost inevitably involves some distortion of the sound of both the original language and the language (or dialect) of the person who imposes the romanized form. A given roman character (or any combination of characters) is pronounced differently by speakers of different languages and often even by speakers of the same language. Romanization also involves orthography, a very imprecise art in most languages but particularly in

English, which is notoriously inconsistent in its rendering of roman characters in sound and vice-versa.

Multiple existing romanizations arise from the fact that cultural exchanges between, say, the Slavic and the Arab worlds (on the one hand) and speakers of various western European languages (on the other) began early, sometimes before the stabilization of orthography brought about by print. Speakers of each west-European language romanized the foreign words by sound and passed on their romanizations in diaries and published writings, often ignorant of different romanizations of the same words adopted by other writers. Thus a German hearing a particular sound made by a Russian visualizes an equivalent German word which begins *tsch* or *tch* while, at the same time, an American bystander hearing the same person visualizes an equivalent English word which begins *ch*. Throughout the nineteenth century, the English-speaking world got most of its nonindigenous musical tradition via Germany, the source of most printed scores, so English speakers accepted the Russian composer's surname as Tschaikowsky or (now more often) Tchaikovsky. For the most part, the literary and theatrical traditions came directly from Russia to Great Britain, so the surname of the Russian writer only begins with a *T* in an English-language source in the increasingly rare case of a publication directly influenced by Germans. In their original cyrillic script, the surnames of both the composer and the writer begin with the same character: Ч.

Systematic Romanization

Locating existing romanizations and using them as access points therefore inevitably leads to international incompatibility. This might not bother a librarian or user interested only in music, or only in literature, but when a library catalogue contains names from both fields as well as others, it is annoying. For a long time, therefore, librarians considered it more desirable to seek international agreement on what is called systematic romanization: the automatic equating of a given nonroman character with one or more specific roman characters. This requires agreement on a romanization table for the nonroman script in question—a kind of manual character set with exact equivalences like the one required for computer communication (see pages 121–22). Part of such a table is reproduced in figure 35. Applying a systematic romanization of the cyrillic script to the surnames of the composer and the writer named in the previous paragraph means that the same initial roman letter must begin both surnames, whether that be *C* or *T*.

Systematic romanization thus has undesirable results for the broadly educated library user familiar with both the composer and the writer. Once again, the cataloguer is accused of hiding things in the catalogue. Nor is there now, or soon to be, only one systematic romanization table for each script. ISO-authorized tables exist for a number of scripts but so do conflicting ones still

Vowels				Consonants		
					Initial and medial	Final
อะ, อั	a	อั๊วะ	ua	ก	k	k
อา	ā	อั๊ว, ว	ūa	ข, ฃ, ค, ฅ, ฆ	kh	k
อำ	am	ใอ, ไอ, อัย, ไอย	ai	ง	ng	ng
อิ	i	อาย	āi	จ	čh	t
อี	ī	เอา	ao	ฉ, ช, ฌ	ch	t
อึ	ư	อาว	āo	ญ	y	n
อื	ư̄	อุย	ui	ฎ, ฏ, ฑ¹	d	t
อุ	u	โอย	ōi	ฐ, ฒ	t	t

FIGURE 35. Part of the LC/ALA romanization table for Thai.

widely used in business, government, and libraries. In most North American libraries, and to a degree in the international English-language library community, the tables applied when systematic romanization is required are those proposed by the Library of Congress and sanctioned by the American Library Association.[13] Systematic romanization was required by the predecessor rules to AACR2, but this present code allows the adoption of either existing or systematic romanization depending on the circumstances. If systematic romanization is adopted, AACR2 does not prescribe the use of particular tables. In effect, it abdicates responsibility and leaves it to the individual library to decide how to romanize in each case. Most North American libraries naturally follow the practice shown on individual Library of Congress records. Since that library now leans in favour of existing romanization, the musical composer is finally taking his place under **T**.

Romanization is therefore recognized as an intractable problem unless everyone allows the *originator* of the nonroman-script message, and not the receiver, to determine the appropriate romanization. In the 1950s, the government of the People's Republic of China decreed the use of a particular system, called Pinyin, for romanizing Chinese writing in all roman-script publications issued in that country. This system differs substantially from the Wade-Giles system previously prevalent among English-language sinologists, journalists, etc. As the Chinese government came to be recognized by Western countries through the 1970s, it applied cultural and diplomatic pressure to have Pinyin adopted abroad and has been successful among all but the older English-speaking academics. In 1979, the *Time* magazine cover pictured Mr. Teng; ten years later, the same person

13. The basic tables and any revisions are published from time to time in *Cataloging Service Bulletin*. Index appears in no. 46 (fall 1989): 71–74

was so featured as Mr. Deng. The pronunciation by a native Mandarin speaker of the name of the country's capital city has not changed, but the romanization Peking has virtually disappeared from current Western publications to be replaced by Beijing—just as the form found in many earlier English-language books, Pei-ching, slipped from currency a long time ago. A new standard of romanization from the arabic script appears to be taking root on a more ad hoc basis as interest in Islamic topics grows. The English-language publishers of the Muslim sacred book are now clearly favouring, and thus imposing on common usage, the romanization *Qu'ran*.

10

THE RECORDS AND
THE SEARCHER

The bibliographic record in the singular, not the plural, features in the title of this book and is the focus of the previous chapters. Before the searcher finds the one record (or few records) most relevant to the query in hand, she or he must deal with a file, a book, a catalogue, or a database full of them. This problem is the focus of chapters 4, 5, and 9, but not from the end-user's point of view. The attention scattered throughout the previous chapters to searchers' needs demands a summary of the relationship between those needs and the current technologies of record display. This chapter might have been entitled "The User Interface," but the large and specialized existing body of writing going by that name suggests a more modest title for what is attempted here. Furthermore, much of what is in this chapter is more tentative than what appears in the rest of the book because user-reactions to the display of computer-processed information in large quantity is a very new interdisciplinary field of investigation involving logic and psychology as much as librarianship and computer science. Like the other chapters of part II, this one concentrates on the user of catalogues, A&I publications, and monographic bibliographies particularly in the context of bibliographic services offered by libraries.

A catalogue is always ideally located near the documents it lists. This is impossible when banks of card drawers will fit only in some Great Hall. If the file is a closed one, whether in book or CD/ROM form, copies can be provided for consultation on each floor or each division of a library and in the offices and homes of users, but must be regularly exchanged for the latest cumulation. An always-up-to-date interactive file is accessible online using compatible hardware and software anywhere. The additional cost of system capacity and multiple ports for multi-user simultaneous interactive searching is considerable for the library; the searcher required to pay the actual cost of the communication link to the online current file from a home or even a distant city finds that cost getting less all the time. Making the current catalogue available in the homes and offices of users and supporting it with adequate system capacity is among a library's best possible public-relations moves, but the administrator must be prepared to face constant pressure for costly extensions of the service.[1]

User Reactions to Manual and Interactive Searching

The microreproduction of large bibliographic files was begun before their computerization not only to produce low-cost copies but also, by reducing their physical size, to make large files quicker to consult and less intimidating. Computer searching is normally quick but still inherently intimidating to some users. By now, enough care has been devoted to the designing of user-friendly interface that the interactive catalogue appears to have become to most users a more welcome challenge than its manual predecessors. It is certainly less physically demanding than walking and stooping among drawers, taking books from shelves and flipping pages, or inserting fiches into a reader. Users are beginning to realize that the interactive catalogue can assemble more information in some more relevant ways than any manual file can. To the enthusiast, it has become an invitation to experiment. However, the less it costs to provide access to stored data elements, the more access points tend to be provided and the more complex becomes the task of finding what is relevant among them. Once the searcher realizes this, psychological hesitation may increase.

A user's persistence in pursuing a search, especially if it involves looking in several different parts of a catalogue, is a function of motivation. This varies not only with the person and the purpose but also with the file size. A look at an older card file tells much about motivation. In any larger group under a given access point, the first dozen or so cards are almost invariably more noticeably worn than the last ones. It must also be true of other types of file, even if it cannot be so dramatically proven, that the user is often exhausted before the relevant information in the file is. At least the size of an interactive file is not the initial discouragement it often is in the case of a larger manual file because its content is only visible a screenful at a time. This tends to provide more psychological incentive to continue browsing but it limits the searcher's ability to anticipate what might turn up around the next corner. Not seeing the forest for the trees and giving up as soon as a single tree of interest comes into view are extremely common failings of the inexperienced end-user in any system, manual or interactive; anything which encourages a user to stop without a positive reason to do so is not ideal.

---

1. As in chapter 5, the questions of whether a user fee should be charged and, if so, on what cost-recovery or profit factor it should be based are raised but not debated here.

The goal of lower-quantity recall but higher-precision retrieval is discussed on pages 197–99 in the context of subject searching, where it is the most difficult to achieve, but it applies to any search. The relative simplicity of post-coordination in an interactive catalogue makes that goal achievable more often than it is in a manual catalogue but it takes more prior strategy-planning on the part of the searcher. End-users are not well served by the librarian who implies that it is easy to find information in the catalogue. Librarians will continue to spend much time compiling short and highly relevant manual lists of citations from that catalogue in anticipation of predictable users' interests. The earliest advances automation offered to direct user-service included selective dissemination of information, or SDI: the regular automated matching of an individual user's statement of interests with all new additions to a database and the output and delivery to that user of the resulting citations.

The inexperienced searcher of an interactive file faced with either high recall but little precision, or no recall at all, is still usually stranded with less help about what to do next than is available in a manual file. When the innocent request *FIND SUBJECT* **BIBLIOGRAPHY** gets the response "There are 2,579 items. Do you want to see them?" most searchers will ask to see the first few on the screen, then flee to the comfort of human contact at the information desk in the hope of getting a more comprehensible answer. Those who design the user interface for an interactive file must show special sensitivity to the kind of guidance it must offer when users cannot readily see (and therefore mentally grasp) the scope of any component of a search. A large manual file may have just as many records accessible via that term, but as discussed in the next section, at least seeing the actual records makes it easier to grasp their organization and their relevance to the search.

More important, a search of a manual file retrieves the word **BIBLIOGRA-PHY** only if it is the first word of a controlled-vocabulary access point or a title. A searcher must know what an interactive file makes accessible in response to different commands in order to avoid reaching this word either as a single word within a controlled-vocabulary access point (in this case, possibly even as a form subdivision) or as a natural-language word anywhere in the Notes Area of a record. Which particular access-point index is to be searched for a particular need may not be self-evident; for example, series titles are often part of a name-index rather than of a natural-language-title index (see footnote 15 on page 252). If the particular index being searched is not explicitly stated on the screen throughout the use of that index, the user may, for example, forget that a subject search is under way if only names (as subjects) happen to appear in the block of access points visible at the moment. In the initial browsing stage of a search, it is typical for only access points to be shown on the screen with no item-descriptions attached to those access points. This leaves the searcher totally in the dark concerning what kind of actual documents or how many of them the search can retrieve until a further instruction is given to scan the associated records. That scanning is far more tedious on a screen than in any kind of manual file if any large number of records is involved.

Browsing versus Searching

There is a major difference in an interactive search between the operation of the *BROWSE* command and that of the *SEARCH* (or *FIND*) command. The former shows the searcher a segment of an index beginning at, or immediately before, the character string the searcher has keyed in and permits the browse to continue indefinitely as described on pages 103–4. Not all systems permit backwards-searching but it is desirable. The *FIND* command matches what the searcher has keyed in with what is in the index being searched and displays any result(s) of an *exact* match—nothing more. In this context, there is no such thing as a *search* of a manual file; every searcher *browses*, seeing as much of a sequence of access points and/or of complete records as there is the patience to assimilate. Starting at **WATER—POLLUTION**, one might go back in the subject access points as far as **WATER LEVELS** and ahead as far as **WATER RESOURCES**, especially if no different subject such as **WATER, RALPH** intrudes to break the train of thought.[2] The same is true of following up cross-references: a bit of success with the first one leads a motivated searcher to pursue others until the trail peters out conclusively.

Access Points versus Records.   With any manual file other than the rare pure register file, one browses bibliographic records directly under one or more types of access point: records and their access points are physically joined. In interactive searching, it is more usually necessary (1) to browse access points in isolation and (2) to select from the access point file(s) which ones to pursue; only then are the bibliographic records for actual documents displayed for browsing. In general, the more records—not merely access points to them—one can see at a glance, the greater is the motivation to proceed in the browse. Fifty or a hundred may be seen on a microfilm-reader screen or a pair of facing printed pages, but only one appears on any one card; the terminal screen is almost equally limited—one or two average-length records can fill it. What is worse, they disappear from the screen to make room for more and therefore dim in consciousness before the search is complete unless they are printed out immediately. To make more records visible at a time on a screen, many output programs display each item initially as a single line of a few truncated data elements, reminiscent of what once fit onto an eighty-column punched card. This gets perhaps fifteen or twenty onto the screen, each identified by a number in sequence (called an occurrence counter) so that it can be easily recalled later by that number.

2. One of the best features of Cutter's complex filing rule (see pages 268–69) is that, even when the access-point index consists solely of subject access points, a name-as-subject cannot intrude into the sequence of a concept and its subdivisions.

Knowing the *quantity* of records retrieved at each step of a search is a major factor in the user's decision as to how to modify the search if the immediate result is not satisfactory. Most user-interface systems display this quantity—but no actual records until another command is given—if there are more than, say, ten of them. This permits the user to modify the search in the hope of achieving less recall and higher precision when the quantity of records retrieved appears unmanageable or is the result of an obviously too broadly conceived search. One learns quickly from experience how and when to modify an initial search, but the casual user delving into a new topic has little basis for making such decisions before examining at least some of the retrieved records. Despite attempts to make searching software simulate the steps instinctively taken during a manual search, the file of machine-readable data remains ultimately as invisible as are the computer's procedures in sorting through it. The result is that the searcher has to have a kind of blind (which is not to say uninformed) confidence in the effectiveness of any given search strategy. Such confidence is good if it provides motivation to continue but is misplaced if the chosen strategy is not adequate to the task in hand. When the first relevant result appears, should the searcher persist in the hope of finding additional useful results or terminate the search thinking there is nothing more to be retrieved? This is the single most important decision in any search, yet how far to pursue particularly a subject search is rarely certain. It is even less certain when the result of an invisible process searching an invisible file is presented on a terminal screen than when a visible manual file can be further probed before the decision is made to end the search.

Response Time

Searching at a computer terminal is faster than manual searching provided the computer is busy doing its part of the job as rapidly as the searcher types. However, an inactive cursor causes frustration within surprisingly few seconds. The user cannot tell whether the system is down, is doing someone else's search, or is scurrying about assembling the requested records. A reassuring message on the terminal screen helps—it does when your telephone call is on hold—and perhaps the terminal should also play soothing music. If it is known at what times of day or week response time is likely to be slow, users may be notified to avoid these if possible. If priority should be given to certain users (for example, reference librarians on duty), the system can recognize and give priority in time-sharing to their passwords. Peaks in the use cycle and corresponding deterioration of response time may be expected when any new upgrading feature is added to the system.

Record Output

The visual presentation of data on the screen and the sequence in which the retrieved records are displayed within an access-point group are vital factors in determining whether a user will pursue a search further or terminate it. The latter issue is treated on pages 270–71 as a part of the discussion of filing. The unit-record format typical of the mid-twentieth-century card catalogue is historically the only one in which every data element is displayed under each access point. As noted above, the initial display resulting from an interactive search usually consists of very abbreviated or even truncated records so that more will fit onto the screen. The complete record, the one showing not only the data but all formatting codes and illustrated on page 295, is usually made available only to the library staff. End-users are normally given access to one or more versions differing in completeness; database vendors typically offer the searcher a choice of output formats.

The terminal screen at which an interactive search request is input is not necessarily the output device on which the response appears. Part or all of the result of the search may be

1) transferred directly as input to generate another search; in effect, this is what is done when a search is further modified interactively
2) stored on tape or disk for later processing or
3) printed in hard copy on a printer, whether that equipment is next to the searcher or at any remote location.

It may be useful to download into a separate file only selected records retrieved as the search proceeds, identifying those wanted by the occurrence numbers. These records can later be resorted or further edited for any use depending on the capabilities of the particular system.

Scanning and comparing records is greatly facilitated if access points and data elements can be noticed and distinguished from one another with little visual effort. In card and book listings, anything from paragraphing and spacing to different type styles and fonts and even colours have been employed to this end for centuries. It is now possible for computer output to be equally varied, whether in hard copy, microform, or on a screen, but whether from inertia or for economic reasons, computer output is still commonly displayed very monotonously in a single typewriter-letter style and sometimes even without extra intra-record spacing. Commercial considerations in home computing have dictated that multicolour display is the first type of variation to have much prominence. The so-called tagging of data elements illustrated on page 296 has returned to fashion for screen display. It is no longer considered *infra dignitatem* to tell the user that a particular name in the record is that of the publisher. The tagged or graphic display of a record, however, occupies more of the screen leaving even less space for additional records. Using windows to keep track of the progress and the process of a search is invaluable but not if they are so crowded that they drown out other necessary data. Although output programs would have to be specially written for larger and more capacious screens, the library market is surely large enough to warrant the cost of such a development. The possibilities of aural and graphic display are just beginning to be explored.

User Instruction

Users are not born knowing how to use files of bibliographic records. Instructing them is an old practice which has recently acquired a new image and name: bibliographic instruction. Students are taught early how to use a simple library catalogue; this is extended to the use of basic periodical indices before the end of primary school. College courses provide instruction in citation and in finding sources of subject information for term papers in A&I publications and in monographic bibliographies. Library tours given at every stage lay emphasis on the many signs and/or handouts available to explain the filing rules, the difference between sections of a divided catalogue, etc. Users are urged to consult a subject authority file in print or fiche form as described on page 177 to see the relationships among terms before starting a search; the access points in interactive files are increasingly linked directly to authority files so that the same kind of strategy planning can be done at one keyboard. Almost every monographic bibliography and printed A&I publication has a preface explaining its use and special features in detail; unfortunately, the same kind of documentation is rarely offered as conveniently to the user consulting an interactive file. Finally, a librarian is normally on duty to offer any additional help needed.

Using an interactive catalogue requires some technical knowledge not all of which can be taken for granted. Nobody needs instruction in how to turn pages or flip cards but what action to take, or what key to strike, at a computer terminal just to get started is not self-evident because it differs from system to system. So does the command needed to initiate a given type of search; for example, one system responds to *FIND*, while only *SEARCH* will get another going. A proposed international standard command language will take some time to be implemented.[3] When it is, it will no doubt be taught in schools along with other aspects of computer operation and information access. Even then, the casual user may still use an interactive system as if it were a manual one, searching in a unidimensional frame of reference. To date, more work has typically gone into improving interactive file structures and system search capability than in explaining a system to users in practical terms, whether through personal instruction sessions with a teacher, written documentation, or *Help* screens.

Menus versus Command Mode

When only a few records, or even none, are retrieved as a result of a computer search and the validity of the search strategy must be taken on faith, the less

3. See Margaret Morrison, "The NISO Common Command Language: No More 'German to the Horses'," *Online* 13 (July 1989): 46–52.

confident searcher wonders whether typing skill or command interpretation is at fault. A good system designer deals with psychological aspects of the person/computer interface as well as the technical aspects of access and display. The most supportive help available on a terminal screen is the menu. Menus are in effect a series of *Help* screens automatically offered at each step of a search. Each screen gives the searcher a limited number of options to choose from whenever a decision is needed in order to advance the search another step. This is like having a librarian watch every move and give instructions: comforting and helpful to the beginner but frustrating and unnecessary for the person who knows how to proceed. Experienced users do not like the typical simple menus which are the most common today. Programmers do, because they fix an invariable sequence of operations. Menu-based software is widely used regardless of the input/output device but is essential if the latter is a touch terminal lacking a keyboard, where the heat of the user's finger touching the screen over a displayed line or box activates the choice displayed there. Users who like the menu mode and/or do not type confidently appreciate the touch terminal but its vogue in library applications was brief except as a necessary help for the disabled user.

In command mode, the user simply instructs the program what to do. *Help* screens are available but must be called into play, usually with a function key. The instructions needed by most users to employ the basic commands can usually be given in a small number of instructions and/or a keyboard template. Some systems offer a choice of menu-mode or command-mode. Some offer both a simpler command mode and a more advanced one, the latter providing shortcuts in keying to accommodate searchers who have taken the trouble to familiarize themselves with command combinations, how to set global parameters, etc. without going through intermediate steps. Every advance in user-interface flexibility is of some aid to the experienced searcher but increases the potential complexity of the system for both users and programmers.

Searching by End-Users versus Intermediaries

Interactive searching directly by end-users is now commonplace in libraries. Neither wear and tear on hardware, potential damage to software through misuse, nor initial user unfamiliarity is any longer a major issue but other economic concerns remain as demands increase. Few libraries have readily met the budgetary demands of unexpectedly high usage. Databases and searching systems over which a library has direct control (principally its own catalogue) are permanently mounted, basic instructions are adjusted to the needs of the local clientele, and technical problems are forestalled by backup systems and repair facilities. As a library acquires the right to use other databases (for example, to connect with other libraries' catalogues interactively or by acquiring A&I databases on

CD/ROM), it becomes dependent also on the technical support of the originating system, any changes in which may have unwanted effects on the receiving system and/or users. Nevertheless, the local system can be programmed to act as a gateway to external databases for searching them alongside the local catalogue, almost transparently to its users. Where the library must pay a direct charge for connect time to use a remote searching system and/or database, it must control the cost. This makes it reasonable to maintain a policy requiring a librarian to conduct the search even if the end-user for whom it is done is accustomed to searching the same database in its print form directly and even if the librarian is no more adept or efficient at it than the end-user would be.

End-user searching of externally produced databases will inevitably spread beyond librarians' ability to control it even if that were desirable. Much of it is already being done outside libraries. Just as law firms and medical clinics have long bought bibliographic tools in their fields in print form for their lawyers and physicians to consult directly, they are now directly subscribing to the services of database vendors and acquiring their own CD/ROM workstations. What the librarian offers as professional help to an end-user will remain, as always: (1) generalized instruction in the use of bibliographic information and (2) detailed professional interpretation of particular requests and search strategies. The present period during which the librarian often serves also as a technician at the keyboard need not last long, which is good. Librarians cannot view the growth of end-user interactive searching as any more of a threat to their proper job than was making the library's own catalogue available for public consultation in the mid-nineteenth century. The only worrisome factor is that, as searching systems and databases become available directly in the home and office and there is less reason to go to, or telephone, the library simply to access them, fewer end-users may recognize when they need the intellectual help of the trained information professional.

A Perfect System?

No professional in any field can ever claim that the status quo is perfect. Yet few librarians in the first half of this century saw any way of improving upon the book and card file as methods of storing and searching bibliographic data. So long a period of stability in the use of these techniques led to unwarranted complacency concerning the details of their application and therefore the entrenchment of a limited number of particular filing rules, catalogue formats, access-point structures, etc. in a field which might have remained more flexible. Independently of, and prior to, the impact of the computer, there was significant challenge to this stability in the early 1950s, particularly in the area of access points. At the Library of Congress, while Seymour Lubetzky was challenging long-standing rules for formulating name access points, Judson Haykin in an adjoining department was overseeing a less visible but just as revolutionary revision of controlled-vocabulary subject heading practice, with the results discussed in chapters 6 and 7. Outside the Library of Congress (and, alas, therefore beyond the ken of many librarians who should have been paying closer attention), the new breed of information scientists were experimenting with access methods described in chapters 3 and 4: natural-language indexing and post-coordination.

By the 1970s, it was clear that the typical bibliographic file of any significant size would soon be the interactive file. The technology which brought this about was commercial and competitive: probably a blessing because it made the pace of change breathtakingly and mercifully rapid. Yet the transition to the fullest possible use of this technology is long and costly for libraries with their huge investment in existing databases, equipment, administrative organization, and staff expertise in obsolescent searching methods. The fact that there will forever be requests, particularly in the humanities, for data from older bibliographic sources means that any new system can never entirely supplant the old. In the early 1990s, what can be expected of bibliographic control is astounding to those who recall what was and was not possible in the early 1960s. However, to hold that the Perfect System now exists is either an ego trip or an advertising ploy; if not, why does every operational system still regularly announce or promise yet further enhancements? Both the technology and its intellectual foundations remain in the development stage. Another edition of this book may yet be necessary.

The system as a whole will not be perfect until it is composed of compatible components as judged by a single acceptable standard. How will the Perfect System be recognized when it does arrive? There is agreement on its features, if only in general terms. Hardware and software developers will long argue over how individual pieces of equipment, systems and applications programs, command languages and menus, and data formats can most efficiently achieve the following goals—and librarians will continue to debate how they can afford:

1) adherence to a standard format for all data of bibliographic significance, and standard protocols for file transfer, which transcend hardware and operating-system incompatibilities
2) the ability to maintain files containing both name and subject authority records and linked to multiple files of bibliographic records
3) the ability to search interactively for authority-controlled access points
4) the ability to search at least some additional data elements and/or fields for single words or terms, individually or in stated proximity to others
5) the ability to apply boolean operators at any stage of any search
6) the ability to accommodate the demands of simultaneous users, both for internal processing (updating, correcting, etc.) and for public searching, without serious deterioration of response time and

7) a user-friendly interface between the searcher and the database management system.

These characteristics of a Perfect System for automating bibliographic control may be more completely realizable than the basic functions of bibliographic control itemized on pages 7–8. Will the millennium arrive by the year 2000?

THE MARC FORMAT

The characteristics of variable-field formatting in general, and of both ISO2709-based formats and the subset of these known as MARC formats, are described on pages 239–48. To that description, this appendix adds sufficient detail

1) to show how any bibliographic format in the MARC family serves in the production and searching of manual and interactive library catalogues and

2) to permit the beginner to apply CANMARC or USMARC content designators to bibliographic records composed according to the current standards described in chapters 6, 7, and 8, for published monographs displaying no esoteric bibliographic peculiarities.[1]

As noted on page 245, there are many content designators in these formats which reflect earlier cataloguing practices no longer authorized by AACR2. These are ignored in this appendix. This appendix may therefore serve as a more user-friendly introduction than a complete coding manual, which for any MARC format is bulky, repetitive, and replete with detail required only infrequently.[2] Any difference between CANMARC and USMARC relevant to those content designators treated here is specified with an explanation enclosed in brackets.

---

1. The format described in detail herein is *Canadian MARC Communication Format: Bibliographic Data* (Ottawa: Canadian MARC Office, National Library of Canada, 1988) [1 v., looseleaf]. This format is virtually identical to *USMARC Format for Bibliographic Data: Including Guidelines for Content Designation*, prepared by Network Development and MARC Standards Office (Washington: Cataloging Distribution Service, Library of Congress, 1988) [2 v., looseleaf]. Lists of codes for languages, countries, etc. used in records are published as separate pamphlets in the USMARC documentation.

2. The entire USMARC group of formats is published in an abbreviated version, *USMARC Concise Formats for Bibliographic, Authority, and Holdings Data* (Washington: Cataloging Distribution Service, Library of Congress, 1988).

Four steps can be distinguished in a cataloguer's work in creating a machine-readable bibliographic record. First, the item is catalogued in accordance with accepted standards for descriptive cataloguing (for example, AACR2) and subject analysis (for example, LCSH and DDC), with the addition of some data elements and codes for local housekeeping information. For example, the following are determined to be the principal access point and area 1 in describing a hypothetical book:

> Roland, J.H. (John Harvey), 1943–
> The Kennedy days / John H. Roland and Ralph Beacock.

In the second step, each data element, etc. is assigned any appropriate content designator(s) (a tag, indicator, and/or subfield code) as specified by a machine-readable format (for example, CANMARC). Here, the cataloguer identifies the access point and ISBD area in the example as two separate MARC fields and assigns the following content designators:

- one tag: for the access point, *100*; for area 1, *245*
- two indicators: for the access point, a *1* (because the person has a single surname) and a *0*; for area 1, a *1* (because a title access point is desirable) and a *4* (because its first four bytes must be ignored when it is filed)
- a two-byte subfield identifier preceding each subfield.[3]

When the elements and content designators are input, something like the following should appear on the terminal screen:

> 100 10 ‡aRoland, J.H. ‡q(John Harvey), ‡d1943–
> 245 14 ‡aThe Kennedy days /‡cJohn H. Roland and Ralph Beacock.

In the third step, some codes are added to make explicit or more easily searchable certain pieces of information as described on page 247. Here, for example, the cataloguer realizes that the title proper *The Kennedy Days* implies that the book includes biographical information; verifies that this is true, and looks up the appropriate one-byte code to indicate this fact in field 008.

In the final step, a few characteristics of the record *itself*, not the item, are identified and coded for its label. Here, the cataloguer notes among other things that this example represents a revised record replacing a previously incomplete CIP record used for acquisitions purposes in the same system, and that it describes a monographic textual item; each of these facts gives rise to a code needed in the label. These four steps must be undertaken in accordance with the library's (or consortium's) policies concerning choice of standards, fullness of cataloguing, etc.

---

3. The first of these two bytes is the standard subfield delimiter (see pages 239–40) shown in this appendix as a ‡.

Input/Output Conventions

In practice, some professional cataloguers choose to write the data elements and access points on a paper workform pre-printed with the most-used content designators. The keyboard-input device is then operated by a clerk-typist trained to observe certain input conventions. Other cataloguers prefer to work directly at a computer terminal. An input program is designed or adapted for the local system to minimize repetitive routine keying. Some of these programs prompt for each expected data element in sequence by showing its content designator(s) automatically after the previous element has been input. Others display a complete screen of expected content designators; relevant data are inserted where applicable. In principle, any data or code which can be generated by a program should not have to be input individually by the keyboard operator. For example, the series description has been surrounded by parentheses in the Anglo-American cataloguing practice of this entire century and this ISBD area (area 6) has its own tags. A program can, on recognition of the appropriate tag, supply the parentheses as a print constant in any output product. As another example, the typewriter keyboard lacks the dash required in the ISBD area separator, but this difficulty is overcome by letting the program supply it and its surrounding spaces (or the optional paragraphing which may replace it) each time a tag denoting an ISBD field is encountered.

Writers of the first input/output programs in the 1960s and early 1970s considered how MARC-formatted data could most efficiently be keyed into a database and how they should appear in output seen by the user. The conventions they established were at first separate from the format itself and often not transferable from one system to another. They were also strongly influenced by the look of the standard card-form record then universally familiar. Inevitably, the appearance of consortia and cooperatively built databases required the standardization of differing local practices. Agreed input conventions now form an integral part of both USMARC and CANMARC. Some of them are not entirely logical or necessary (for example, with one exception which could easily be resolved with a little good will, all ISBD punctuation could be generated from MARC content designators) yet the introduction of MARC and the ISBD to local cataloguing operations was not simultaneous. Continuing retrospective conversion of non-ISBD records into machine-readable form also keeps the practical application of MARC and the ISBD separate to a degree, resulting in inefficient redundancies in their application.

The principal input conventions relevant to the descriptive portion of the record are:

1) ISBD-prescribed punctuation for the elements *within* an area is individually keyed
2) such punctuation is keyed along with any prescribed *preceding* space

but without its *following* space, immediately preceding the two-byte subfield code to which it is equivalent; the output program inserts one space wherever it removes the two-byte subfield-code[4] and

3) only the period is keyed at the end of an area; no punctuation is keyed at the end of area 6 since it ends in a print-constant parenthesis.

The principal input conventions relevant to access points are:

1) brackets enclosing a uniform title (see AACR2 rule **25.2A**) are not input[5]
2) dashes within pre-coordinate subject headings of the LCSH type are not input nor are any spaces inserted before or after subfield codes ‡x, ‡y, or ‡z
3) subject and/or other access points are not explicitly numbered in sequence
4) neither the word *Title* nor the word *Series* is input as a tracing to indicate the need for an access point consisting of the wording found in, respectively, the title proper or the first instance of an area 6 in the record—in the former case, the first indicator in field 245 generates the access point; in the latter, the existence of field 440 does so and
5) a period is input at the end of an access point unless the final character is a hyphen.

To illustrate these conventions, here is a traditional card-catalogue record for a hypothetical publication:

> **Smith, Jean, 1943–**
>   Collecting Canada's past / Jean & Elizabeth Smith ; photography by Ken Bell. — Scarborough, Ont. : Prentice-Hall of Canada, c1987.
>   220 p. : ill. (some col.) ; 27 cm. — (The Hobbyist's handbooks, ISSN 1523–5071 ; no. 5)
>   Includes bibliographical references.
>   ISBN 0–13–140467–9 : $29.95.
>   1. Collectors and collecting. 2. Material culture—Canada. 3. Canada—Social life and customs. I. Smith, Elizabeth, 1947– II. Bell, G. K. III. Title. IV. Series.
>   745.1′0971   NK1125   C87–10230–1

Here are the same data as they might appear on a cataloguer's terminal screen downloaded from the *Canadiana* database and with the French-language

---

4. On the typical input screen, where each subfield is displayed beginning on a new line as it is in the record on page 295, it is usual for the subfield code to appear at the beginning of the line. This leaves its equivalent ISBD punctuation lonely and illogically at the end of the previous element.

5. In the remainder of this appendix, AACR2 rule numbers relevant to the data under discussion are given in bold type in parentheses.

subject access point(s) in that database automatically identified by their indicator and removed:[6]

[Label]			nam0a*
001			870010231
008			870611
			s
			1987
			****
			onc
			a***
			[etc. for the 20 fixed-length elements of field 008; see below]
020	**	‡a	0131404679 :
		‡c	$29.95.
055	0*	‡a	NK1125
082	**	‡a	745.1'0971
		‡2	19
100	10	‡a	Smith, Jean,
		‡d	1943–
245	10	‡a	Collecting Canada's past /
		‡c	Jean & Elizabeth Smith ; photography by Ken Bell.
260	0*	‡a	Scarborough, Ont. :
		‡b	Prentice-Hall of Canada,
		‡c	c1987.
300	**	‡a	220 p. :
		‡b	ill. (some col.) ;
		‡c	27 cm.
440	*4	‡a	The Hobbyist's handbooks,
		‡x	15235071 ;
		‡v	no. 5
504	**	‡a	Includes bibliographical references.
650	*0	‡a	Collectors and collecting.
650	*0	‡a	Material culture
		‡z	Canada.
651	*0	‡a	Canada
		‡x	Social life and customs.
700	10	‡a	Smith, Elizabeth,
		‡d	1947–
700	10	‡a	Bell, G. K.

When the record with its content designators has been either downloaded from an external database or originally keyed in, the input program which stores it on tape or disk automatically completes it by

---

6. When necessary to avoid ambiguity, a blank (that is, the input equivalent of striking the space bar) is explicitly shown in this appendix as an asterisk (*).

1) placing a field terminator at the end of each field and a record terminator at the end of the record
2) composing the remainder of the label
3) composing a record directory which consists of each tag employed in the record along with the byte-count and address of its field and
4) assigning a record-identifier string for field 001 (the existing content of field 001 of a downloaded record is usually unacceptable for the local system, so is either eliminated or transferred to another field).

In an in-house processing package, the database management system also generates for its own indices whatever access points are called for by the designer of the system. This normally includes all those specified in the MARC record by access-point tags and/or indicators but may be expanded to include, for example, single words of specified fields.

Stored on a length of tape, the completed MARC record looks like the binary equivalent of the alphanumeric version shown in figure 36 on page 315. With local call number and holdings information added, the record can be transformed by appropriate programs into whatever selection and arrangement of data elements the library's policy calls for, from something as traditional as the unit card on page 294 to perhaps something like the following format, called tagged (or labelled) output:

TITLE:	Collecting Canada's past
AUTHOR:	Jean & Elizabeth Smith
DATE:	c1987
PUBLISHER:	Prentice-Hall of Canada
SERIES:	The Hobbyist's handbooks
LOCATION:	Holly Branch: 745.10971 SMI
	Oak Branch: 745.10971 SMI - Reference Use Only
FOR RELATED MATERIAL SEE SUBJECT FILE UNDER:	
	Collectors and collecting
	Material culture--Canada
	Canada--Social life and customs

A detailed description of MARC content designators completes this appendix. In order to relate the parts of the above record to this description, they are blocked out on page 315 and the addresses are shown explicitly in added subscript numbers. The address $229 = 0$ shows how the 230th character from the beginning (character position 229) is the so-called base address of data recorded in character positions 12 through 16 of the label as described next. All subsequent addresses within the record are calculated in relation to this "base-address" character position and each is recorded in its respective unit of the record directory.

The Label: The First Twenty-four Bytes

The required twenty-four bytes of the label contain the following data: the character positions occupied are given in the left margin:

0–4   The total number of characters in the record (including this label, the record directory, and all terminators and content designators), right-justified with leading zeros.

5   Record status code; one of the following:[7]

       n   new record
       a   previously partial record
       c   corrected or revised record
       p   previously a CIP record
       d   deleted record

6   Type of record code; one of the following (along with the next code, this indicates to the processing programs which version(s) of the control field(s) 007–009 are to be brought into play in interpreting the nature of the data elements in the record):

       a   language material (including microform)
       b   [for archival use]
       c   music, printed or microform
       d   music, manuscript (including microform)
       e   cartographic material, printed or microform
       f   cartographic material, manuscript (including microform)
       g   projected media (for example, slides; videorecordings)
       i   sound recordings (nonmusic)
       j   sound recordings (music)
       k   two-dimensional nonprojectable graphics (for example, paintings; computer graphics; transparencies)
       o   kits
       r   three-dimensional artifacts and naturally occurring objects

7   Bibliographic level code; one of the following:

       a   component part, monographic
       b   component part, serial
       c   collection
       d   subunit
       m   monograph
       s   serial

8–9   Two blanks: these bytes are not yet defined by ISO2709.

---

7. Throughout the following pages, the expression *one of the following* means that all the authorized possibilities are enumerated in this appendix. In contrast, *for example* means that the complete MARC manuals provide more possibilities, and only those most frequently encountered in practice are given here.

10	The numeral 2 which tells a program that the first two bytes of each bibliographic-data field (that is, of fields tagged 010 and up) are indicators, not part of a data element.
11	Another numeral 2 which tells a program that each subfield code comprises two bytes; thus whenever the program encounters the standard subfield separator (the ‡), two bytes (that separator and the next byte) must be skipped to reach the first character of the data element itself.
12–16	Base address of data, right-justified with leading zeros. This is the starting-character position (relative to the first byte of the *entire* record) of the record-identifier field, the required field bearing tag 001. In the record directory, the address of each variable-length field (that is, each field with a tag number) is given in relation to *this* character position. In other words, the starting-character position of field 001 becomes, for purposes of the directory and all further processing, position 00000 and the number recorded here in the label directs the programs instantly to that position. Hence, in the example appears the address *229 = 0* (actually, 00229 = 00000).
17	Encoding level code; one of the following:

0	full cataloguing done with the item in hand
1	full cataloguing done without the item in hand
3	an abbreviated record such as a subordinate record for a contents note
5	a record complete as to description and name access points but lacking controlled-vocabulary subject access points
6	a minimal-level record meeting a set standard (see page 127)
7	a preliminary record
8	a CIP record
z	the concept of a coding level is inapplicable to the record

18	A code noting whether and how ISBD is applied to the description: if AACR2 is followed, the only code applicable here is *a*.
19	Linked-record code: an *r* or a blank is used, depending on whether or not a related record must be accessed in order to process this record. The presence of a linking-record field (760 through 787) and sometimes a related-work note field (580) is associated with the use of an *r* in this byte.
20–23	Entry map: the numerals *4500*. The last two digits are at present undefined in ISO2709; the *4* and *5* refer to the number of bytes occupied by the second and third segments of each unit of the record directory.

The Record Directory

The record directory consists of a series of twelve-byte units, one such unit for each variable field in the entire record; that is, each field bearing a tag number.

The number of bytes in the entire directory is therefore twelve times the number of such fields, plus one byte for the record directory's field terminator. Each twelve-byte unit consists of

1) three bytes giving the field's tag
2) four bytes stating the total number of bytes in the field (including its indicators, field terminator, and all subfield codes) and
3) five bytes stating the address of the first byte of that field relative to the base address of data recorded in bytes 12–16 of the label.

The Record-Identifier Field: Tag 001

This field must occur in every record. It is imprecise to call it a *control field*, as is often done. Its sole function is to identify the record to the database management system whose programs manipulate the data in the record. The number of bytes in this field (including its field terminator), their internal arrangement, and whether any print constants are involved are up to the local system designer. It is usual, but not necessary, for the length of this field to be uniform for each record in the same database. The actual character string must be unique for each different record in the same database and is usually made up by a computer program as the new record is entered into the database. This field and the control fields described next contain neither indicators nor any subfields.

The Control Fields: Tags 005 through 009

Cataloguers commonly call these fields the *fixed fields* because the data they contain are in the form of codes, each containing a predefined number of bytes and occurring in predetermined character positions within the field. Any byte for which there is no significant data must therefore be input as a blank. Yet each of these control fields *as a whole* may be of any length, as is true of every tagged field in any MARC format.

The first control field, bearing tag 005, is often omitted in local applications. In it, the computer's internal clock records the date and time when the record was most recently changed. This can be expressed to a tenth of a second; for example, 19901215211847.5 means 9:18 and 47.5 seconds p.m., December 15, 1990.

The other control fields contain fixed-length codes of the type described on pages 247–48. CANMARC uses those tagged 007, 008, and 009; [USMARC does not use 009]. At least one of these fields must be present in each record. What is encoded here depends on

1) the physical medium of the document (for example, slides; kits)
2) the nature of its intellectual content (for example, music; maps) and
3) its bibliographic form (for example, manuscripts; serials).

The codes in character positions 6 and 7 of the label determine which of the possible meanings the database management system must attach to each code in these fields.

The following description of how to code field 008 for a monograph containing text (in popular terms, a book) serves as a model of how these control fields are organized for any type of material. CANMARC assigns meanings to 41 bytes in the 008 field for textual monographs; the 42nd and final byte of the field is the standard field terminator. [USMARC assigns the same meanings in the same positions except for the 41st byte, which it does not use, so its monograph-008 field is one byte shorter than that in CANMARC.] From one to six bytes are assigned to each of twenty different meanings [nineteen in US-MARC]. The cataloguer, unlikely to remember that the country-of-publication code occupies character positions 15–17 of field 008, is more likely to refer to that code as occupying *fixed field 5* by its position in this sequence of meanings. In the following description, therefore, both the sequential numeration of the meanings and the character positions are given, the latter in brackets.

1 [0–5]   Input the date the record is first entered into the file as YYMMDD; for example, *900220* for February 20, 1990.

2 [6]   Input one of the following codes to show what meaning is intended by the content of the eight following bytes:

    s   a single year of publication (**1.4F1**) occurs in area 4: that year appears as the next four characters and the following four bytes are blanks (this is by far the most common situation)

    b   the following eight bytes are all blanks because the year occurring in area 4 is before the Christian Era (B.C.) and must therefore be coded in field 046 rather than here (this cannot occur for a printed item)

    c   both a year of publication and a copyright year (**1.4F5**) occur in area 4: the former appears as the next four characters and the latter as the following four

    d   detailed dating used only for technical reports: a year appears as the next four characters; a month and day (MMDD) within that year as the following four (**1.4F** does not permit the addition of month and date in area 4, so in the descriptive part of the record they occur in area 7)

    m   initial and terminal years of the publication of a multi-part item occur in area 4 (**1.4F8**): the former appears as the next four characters and the latter as the following four; if the terminal year is unknown and appears as blanks in area 4, the figures *9999* are input here

n   the following eight bytes are all blanks because no date can be ascertained or estimated (a condition *not* permitted according to **1.4F7**)

q   a year containing a hyphen or question mark as specified in **1.4F7** is indicated by inputting this code here, then adding the earliest *possible* year as the next four characters and the latest *possible* year in the following four[8]

r   the work was previously published and this record is for a reissue or reprint of that publication (**cf. 1.11**): the year of the item in hand (the reissue, etc.) as recorded in area 4 appears as the next four characters; the date of the original appearance of the publication reissued or reprinted, as recorded in area 7, appears as the following four.

3 [7–10]   Input the four digits of the first year, or blanks, as specified in the code input in fixed field 2.

4 [11–14]   Input the second year, or blanks, or a month and day, as specified in the code input in fixed field 2.

5 [15–17]   Input the code for the first, or only, country (province, state) of publication named or implied in area 4 (**1.4B–C**). Each first-level component part of Canada, the Soviet Union, the United Kingdom, and the United States is represented by a three-character code whose final character designates the whole; for example, Ontario is *onc*. All other countries have a two-character code followed by a blank; for example, Chile is *cl**. If *[S.l.]* appears in area 4, input *xx** here.

6 [18–21]   Input up to four one-byte codes showing types of non-verbal material in the item; those enumerated in **2.5C** and a few others may be specified, for example:

         a   illustrations [that is, *ill.* appears in area 5]
         b   maps
         c   portraits
         g   music

If more than four such types are evident in the item, judge which are the four most significant ones to code. If there are fewer than four, input the final byte(s) in this group as blanks. If there is no such material in the item, input all four bytes as blanks.

7 [22]   Input one of the following intellectual-level codes or a blank if none applies:

8. The reason for this convention, as well as for coding **9999** for unknown terminal year, is to facilitate the use of inclusive dates and relational operators (see page 102) as an element in interactive searching.

j	juvenile
u	primary-grade material
v	secondary-grade material

8 [23]   Input one of the following codes for the form of the item or a blank if none applies:

a	microfilm
b	microfiche
c	micro-opaque
d	large-print
f	braille
r	regular print reproduction

9 [24–27]   Input up to four one-byte codes describing the nature of the item's contents selected from some two dozen which have been defined, for example:

a	the item is an abstracting tool
b	the item is a bibliography or contains bibliographic references
d	the item is a dictionary
i	the item is an indexing tool (but see also fixed field 13)
m	the item is a thesis
n	the item is a survey of the literature of a subject area
r	the item is a directory
x	the item is a technical report

(See fixed field 6 if more or fewer than four apply to the item.)

10 [28]   Input a blank if the item is not a government publication; if it is, input a one-byte code stating the governmental level of its publisher, for example:

f	a body at the federal/national level
i	an international intergovernmental body
l	a body representative of a local jurisdiction
s	a provincial or state body

11 [29]   Input the digit *1* if the item contains the proceedings, a report, or a summary of a conference or meeting; input the digit *0* if it does not.

12 [30]   Input the digit *1* if the item is a festschrift or the digit *0* if it is not.

13 [31]   Input the digit *1* if the item contains an index to its own contents or the digit *0* if it does not (but see fixed field 9 if the item is an index to other material).

14 [32]   Input a *0* or *1*; no other code formerly defined is relevant to cataloguing done according to current standards.

15 [33]   Input a blank if the work is non-fiction. If it is a literary text, input one of ten defined codes for types of literature, for example:

c	comic strip
d	drama (including television scripts, etc.)

> f   fiction
> h   humour, satire, etc.
> j   short stories
> p   poetry
>
> If more than one of these applies, judge which is the most significant.

16 [34]   Input a blank if the work does not contain biographical material or one of the following codes if it does:
> a   the item is an autobiography
> b   the item is an individual biography
> c   the item is a collective biography
> d   the item contains biographical material

17 [35–37]   Input the three-character mnemonic code assigned to the language, or major language, or first language, of the content of the publication; for example, English is *eng*; French is *fre*. Use field 041 to give additional information if there is more than one language or if the item contains translated material.

18 [38]   Input a blank if the machine-readable and the manual record for the same item are identical in their content (as is normally the case). Otherwise, input one of four one-byte codes to indicate the nature of the difference; for example, if the manual record contains words in a nonroman script but the machine-readable record is fully romanized, input an *r*.

19 [39]   Input a blank if this record contains purely original cataloguing (see page 112). If it is a partly or wholly derived record, input one of six one-byte codes to indicate its source (the most usual of these is the letter *l* for Library of Congress).

20 [40]   [This byte is not used in USMARC.] When a record is converted from one MARC format to another, the translation program (see page 248) sometimes cannot determine without human intervention what a particular byte in a control field or in a content designator should be, so it inserts a standard fill character. If no such character appears in the record, input the digit *0* here. Otherwise, input one of three codes to indicate where the fill character appears in the record. The use of fill characters should not be an issue in original cataloguing or among users of the same MARC format.

The Bibliographic-Data Fields: Tags 010 through 899

Some one hundred fifty fields with different tags ranging from 010 through 899 contain data including the ISBD description, name and subject access points including classification numbers, links with other records, and work- and document-identifying codes of many kinds additional to those represented in the control fields. This means that for every tag currently used in the format, there are almost five with no meaning assigned to them yet, or likely ever. However, a two-digit numeric tag would not have sufficed. A two-letter tag may have been preferable—some in-house systems translate the three-digit tags into mnemonic two-letter ones—but letter tags bring their own problems, not least those of application in various languages.

Tag-Number Order as a Reflection of the Unit-Entry Card

The tag-number sequence was established in the mid-1960s and therefore closely follows the order of the elements on a traditional Library of Congress unit-record card of that time. The sequence of descriptive data elements in ISBD largely conforms with it and some bibliographic tools (for example, the NUC register) still follow the tag-number order closely for all elements. However, those who design user-interfaces, whether for commercial OPAC software or for in-house adaptations, no longer feel constrained by the rigid application of this sequence and departures are increasingly common as descriptive data elements and access points are individually selected for display in various combinations for various purposes.

Approximately thirty different fields numbered from 010 through 099 include what appeared at the upper left corner of the traditional catalogue card: a call number, whether based on the Dewey or Library of Congress classifications, a government-publication numbering system, or a local shelf-location system of any kind. Since these are codes rather than words, codes of many other types also came to be assigned tags beginning with a zero; for example, codes concerning the record itself (its field-001 record-identifier number in other systems and/or bibliographies), codes concerning the physical identity of the document (the ISBN; a standard technical-report number), and codes other than classification symbols concerning the intellectual content (the form of a musical composition). Fields 090 through 099 are reserved for local call numbers and appended holdings information, for example, branch location.

In the unit-record system, the main entry heading (principal access point) occurs next, so four tags numbered in the 100s were assigned to a principal access point consisting of a personal name (tag 100), corporate name (tag 110), conference name (tag 111), or uniform title (tag 130). If the principal access point is the title proper, however, no field numbered in the 100s exists in the record and the 245 (title proper) field is also the principal access point. Other titles used as, or as part of, a principal access point (see page 168) are in fields tagged from 210 through 243. Thus when a uniform title is associated with a personal, corporate, etc. name as part of the *principal* access point identifying a work, that uniform title is not part of the same field as the name but is located in field 240. Conversely (and confusingly), whenever a name and its associated uniform title together identify a work in a *subject* or an *added* access point, they do occupy a single field; for example, in field 600. Access points other than the principal one (the main entry heading) are far removed from the latter in the sequence. Their tag numbers (from 600 through 830) follow those of the Note Area because they appear on the unit-record card after the notes, as the tracings.

Tags numbered from 245 through 599 convey the descriptive data elements in their ISBD sequence, but again the format of the pre-ISBD record determines the first digit. What are now areas 1 through 4 constitute a single paragraph on the unit-record card so its parts are all located in fields tagged in the 200s (beginning with 245). The very few tags used in the 300s are devoted to the physical description, now area 5, which in the card format begins a new paragraph. (It, and what follows of the description, were also set in smaller type on the Library of Congress printed card.) Data identifying series (now area 6) occupy tags numbereed in the 400s. Notes (area 7) are in fields numbered in the 500s, unfortunately defined and fixed in the tagging sequence before their skilful division into a score of distinct kinds in AACR2. The standard numbering schemes (ISBN and ISSN) were very new when the sequence of tags was established and had not yet been identified as the final ISBD area so they were consigned, not illogically, to the group of numeric codes whose tags begin with a zero. Tag numbers from 760 through 787 are used for links to other records and those from 850 through 886 for holdings and other miscellaneous information.

Table of Most Frequently Used Content Designators

In the following table, each tag number is followed by a brief definition and, when easily definable, the relevant AACR2 rule number(s) governing the content of that field. Two indicator-bytes must be associated with a tag each time it is used; their permissible values (numeric or blank) appear at the first two indentations. At the next indentation appear the most commonly applicable subfield codes (almost always alphabetic) used in that field, omitting the code's invariable first byte shown in this appendix as ‡. A verbal explanation of the use of an indicator follows a colon (:). A brief definition of the content of a subfield follows an equals sign (=). An appended table of uniform-title subfields describes the subfielding of any uniform title whether it occurs alone or as part of a name/title access point. It is referred to at each tag where it is applicable. An alphabetic index to the MARC content designators completes this appendix.

Content designation was chosen for mnemonic value where possible. For example, whether a personal name appears as a principal, an added, or a subject access point, its tag always ends in two zeros (100, 600, 700, 800). Furthermore, one of its indicators and many, if not all, of its subfield codes are identical in all these fields. Similarities of this kind are shown in the following detailed table as referrals to basic patterns. This may be an annoyance at first but it permits much compression in displaying the format and highlights its essentially simple structure. Many subfield codes were also chosen mnemonically for ease of coding, for example, *l* for *language* (see page 241). Their alphabetic sequence therefore does not necessarily express the sequence intended for output, which is governed by the cataloguing rules, the subject-headings list, etc. used.

When a field or subfield is repeatable (see page 241), its tag or subfield code is shown in the following table with an ® (this symbol is not part of the field or subfield designation). Repeating a field means repeating its tag, its two indicators, and all its subfields as many times as necessary. Repeating a subfield means repeating only that subfield, along with its two-byte subfield code, within the field.

010—Library of Congress Control Number for the record (formerly called the Library of Congress Card Number). In the internal database of the Library of Congress and in MARC records emanating from there, this number is the record identifier in field 001.

*	*	a	=	the number, including any prefix and/or suffix, but not the hyphen because that is output as a print constant after the second numeric character.

016—As for 010 but containing the control number for the record in *Canadiana* [not used in USMARC; see field 015].

015—As for 010 and 016 but containing the control or serial number of the item in any other national bibliography or bibliographies (subfield *a* is repeatable), each with a prefix denoting which bibliography it is from [USMARC uses this field also for the *Canadiana* control number].

020®—International Standard Book Number (**1.8**).

*	*	a	=	the number (omitting hyphens, which are output as print constants) and any parenthetical qualifier (**1.8B, 1.8E**)
		c	=	terms of availability (**1.8D, 1.8E**)

041—Language Coding.

0	*		:	no translation is involved
1	*		:	the item is or includes a translation
		a	=	language code(s) of the item's textual content
		h®	=	if item involves translation, the language code of the original and/or of any intermediate translation(s)

043—Code(s) for Geographic Area of Content.

*	*	a®	=	a seven-byte code designating an area associated with the item, usually an area mentioned in a subject access point (see also field 052)

045—The time period covered by the content of the item can be shown in this field using a complex time code.

050®—Library of Congress Classification Number(s) and any associated item number.

0		:	item is in the Library of Congress
1		:	item is not in the Library of Congress
	*	:	[USMARC uses this indicator to show whether or not the Library of Congress has assigned the number]
	a®	=	class number, including any cutter number which forms part of the subject class
	b	=	item number, for example, a cutter number for an author's name; a date; the numbering within a series

052®—Geographic-Classification Coding.

*	*	a,b	=	the Library of Congress Classification (omitting the prefix *G*) associated with a geographic area treated in the content (see also field 043); each cutter number goes into a repeatable subfield *b*

055—Similar to 050 for class numbers assigned by or on behalf of the National Library of Canada [not used in USMARC].

082®—Dewey Decimal Classification/Call Number, including prime mark(s) to show permissible segmentation.

0	*		:	taken from a full edition of DDC
1	*		:	taken from an abridged edition of DDC
2	*		:	taken from an abridged *New Serial Titles* edition
		a®	=	class number
		b	=	item number, as in field 050
		2	=	number of the DDC edition used

100—Principal access point (main entry heading): a personal name **(21.1A; chapter 22 as to form)**.

0			:	name contains no surname **(22.8, 22.10, 22.11, 22.16)**
1			:	name contains a single surname
2			:	name contains a multiple surname **(cf. 22.5C)**
3			:	name is that of a family or dynasty (possible as a subject access point)
	0		:	(the only possibility under current input conventions)
		a	=	the name, including given names, initials, and other elements not specified below for other subfields
		b	=	numeration of a person identified by a given name **(22.1A)**
		c®	=	term of rank of a noble person **(22.6A1)**, title of honour or address **(22.12, 22.15)**, or a qualifier other than a fuller form of name(s) **(22.13–.16, 22.19)**
		d	=	dates **(22.17)**
		e	=	optional relator **(21.0D, 21.36C)**
		q	=	fuller name forms in parentheses **(22.18)**

110—Principal access point (main entry heading): a corporate name **(21.1B; chapter 24 as to form)**.

1		:	the name is or begins with the name of a jurisdiction **(24.3E, 24.6, 24.18–.26 and chapter 23 as to form)**
2		:	any other corporate name (except that of a conference, for which see field 111) given in direct order, including any parenthetical qualifier **(24.1–.4, 24.6, 24.9–.11)**
	0	:	(the only possibility under current input conventions)
	a	=	the main heading: the part of the access point preceding a period
	b®	=	a subheading **(24.13–.14, 24.18–.19)**
	n,d,c	=	number, date, and/or location of a meeting or conference appearing as a subheading, as in field 111 **(cf. 24.13 type 6, 4th example)**
	e	=	optional relator **(21.36C)**

111—Principal access point (main entry heading): the name of a conference (but not as a title proper or as a subheading of another corporate body) **(21.1B2d; 24.3F, 24.7 as to form)**.

2		:	the name is in direct order
	0	:	(the only possibility under current input conventions)
	a	=	the conference name including any parenthesized qualifier (except the following, which are in separate subfields:)
	n	=	the sequential number of the conference **(24.7B2)**
	d	=	the date of the conference **(24.7B3)**
	c	=	the location of the conference **(24.7B4)**
	e®	=	a subordinate unit of the conference

130—Principal access point (main entry heading): a uniform title without a preceding 100, 110, or 111 field being applicable **(21.1C; chapter 25 as to form)**.

0–9		:	number of characters to ignore in filing
	0	:	(the only possibility under current input conventions)
	a	=	the uniform title; also uniform-title subfields as on pages 313–14

240—A uniform title following a 100, 110, or 111 field (see page 313) **(cf. 25.1–.2)**.

[the first indicator is differently used in CANMARC and USMARC to show whether this title appears on certain output products and whether it is wanted as an access point]

0–9		:	number of characters to ignore in filing
	a	=	the uniform title; also uniform-title subfields as on pages 313–14

243—A field used like field 240 for a collective uniform title **(25.8–.11, 25.34)**.

245—Title and Statement of Responsibility Area **(1.1)**. If there is no 100, 110, 111, or 130 field, subfield *a* of this field is the principal access point (main entry heading) and the first indicator must therefore be *0*.

0	:		no additional access point (added entry heading) is provided under the wording in subfields *a*, *n*, and *p* (see also field 740)
1	:		additional access point (added entry heading) is provided under the exact wording of those subfields
	0–9	:	number of characters to ignore in filing
		a =	the title proper **(1.1B)**
		b =	parallel title(s) and other title information **(1.1D–E)**
		c =	the remainder of the area **(1.1F; cf. 1.1G)**
		h =	general material designation (GMD) **(1.1C)**
		n® =	the number of a part/section of a work **(1.1B9, second example)**
		p® =	the name of a part/section of a work **(1.1B9, first example)**

250—Edition Area **(1.2).**

*	*	a =	edition statement **(1.2B)**
		b =	statement(s) of responsibility and subsequent edition statement(s), etc. **(1.2C–E)**

260—Publication, Distribution, etc. Area **(1.4).**

0	*	:	(the only possibility under current rules)
		a® =	place of publication, etc. **(1.4C)**
		b® =	name of publisher, etc. **(1.4D–E)**
		c® =	date(s) of publication, copyright, etc. (see character positions 6–14 in field 008, and **1.4F**)
		d,e,f =	place, name, date of manufacture **(1.4G)**

300®—Physical Description Area **(1.5).**

*	*	a® =	extent **(1.5B)**
		b =	other physical details **(1.5C)**
		c =	dimensions **(1.5D)**
		d =	accompanying material, including its physical description in parentheses **(1.5E)** [in USMARC, this is subfield *e*]

440®—Series Area **(1.6)**, provided the wording in this field is also used as an added access point (added entry heading).

*	0–9	:	number of characters to ignore in filing
		a =	the series title **(1.6B)**
		n® =	number of a subseries **(1.6H)**
		p® =	title of a subseries **(1.6H)**
		x =	ISSN **(1.6F)**
		v =	volume numbering or other sequential designation **(1.6G)**

490®—Series Area (**1.6**), provided the wording in this field is *not* to be used as an added access point.

0	*	:	no access point for the series is provided
1	*	:	an access point for the series is provided but it takes a *different* form from that provided by rule 1.6, usually because (a) chapter 21 requires something other than its title to be the series' principal access point, (b) the series title varies from item to item in the series, and the variant chosen for the series access point differs from what is found in the item described in this record and therefore transcribed here, or (c) multiple titles (for example, of both series and subseries) appear within one set of parentheses in the Series Area but only one is wanted in a single access point. A *1* as a first indicator switches the program to any field(s) with a tag beginning with *8* (800, 810, 811, 830) for the form of a desired access point to identify the series.
	a®,v,x =		subfields as for field 440; *n* and *p* are not used; *a* is repeatable for the resumption of any title information following a subfield *x* or *v*

5XX—The format provides for some fifty different fields, most of them repeatable, whose tags begin with a *5*. These contain data in the Note Area (**1.7**). Most have blanks for both indicators and allow only subfield *a*. In some, however, indicators are used to generate print constants. The most frequently used of these fields are:

        500®—General note

        503®—Bibliographic history note (**1.7B7**)

        504®—"Includes bibliographic references" and similar notes (**2.7B18**)

        505 —Formatted contents note (uses indicators) (**2.7B18**)

        520 —Abstract, annotation, or summary note (**2.7B17**)

        534 —Original version note (**1.11F**): this field permits many subfields (**cf. 1.7A4**)

600®—Subject access point consisting of, or beginning with, a personal name.

0–3		:	type-of-personal-name indicator as for field 100
	0	:	source: Library of Congress (name and LCSH authorities)
	1	:	source: Library of Congress (for children's literature)
	2	:	source: National Library if Medicine (MeSH)
	3	:	source: National Agricultural Library
	5	:	source: National Library of Canada
	6	:	source: *Repertoire des vedettes-matière* (French)
	personal-name subfields as for field 100		
	t	=	title; also uniform-title subfields as on pages 313–14
	x®	=	any "dash" subdivision except those of the following two types:

y®   =   a period (time) subdivision
z®   =   a place subdivision

610®—Subject access point consisting of, or beginning with, a corporate name (including that of a political jurisdiction as such).

    1–2   :   type-of-corporate-name indicator as for field 110

        0–6   :   source-of-access-point indicator as for field 600

                 corporate-name subfields as for field 110; other subfields as for field 600

611®—Subject access point consisting of, or beginning with, a conference name.

    2   :   type-of-conference-name indicator as for field 111

        0–6   :   source-of-access-point indicator as for field 600

                 conference-name subfields as for field 111; other subfields as for field 600

630®—Subject access point consisting of, or beginning with, a uniform title.

    0–9   :   number of characters to ignore in filing

        0–6   :   source-of-access-point indicator as for field 600

        a   =   the uniform title; also uniform-title subfields as on pages 313–14

        x,y,z =   as for field 600

650®—Topical subject access point.

    *   :   first indicator blank [USMARC uses it to designate the level of the subject]

        0–6   :   source-of-access-point indicator as for field 600

        a   =   the topical subject access point

        x,y,z =   as for field 600

651®—Subject access point consisting of, or beginning with, a geographic name (a political jurisdiction as such, with or without a corporate subdivision, is considered a corporate body and therefore located in field 610).

    *   0–6   :   source-of-access-point second indicator as for field 600

        a   =   the geographic name or place element

        x,y,z =   as for field 600

6XX—Additional tags beginning with a 6 are provided for subject access points assigned according to different principles from those of traditional Library-of-Congress-style cataloguing, for example, PRECIS; descriptors from a thesaurus.

700®—Additional (not principal, not subject, not series) access point consisting of, or beginning with, a personal name (see **21.29–21.30** for all 7XX fields).

    0–3   :   type-of-personal-name indicator as for field 100

      0–2   :   second indicator designates differences in the type of access point (*0* = alternative, *1* = secondary, *2* = analytical); these are significant for some filing arrangements
personal-name subfields as for field 100

      t   =   title (**see 21.30G**); also uniform-title subfields as on pages 313-14

710®—Additional (not principal, not subject, not series) access point consisting of, or beginning with, a corporate name.

   1–2   :   type-of-corporate-name indicator as for field 110

   0–2   :   second indicator as for field 700
corporate-name subfields as for field 110; other subfields as for field 700

711®—Additional (not principal, not subject, not series) access point consisting of, or beginning with, a conference name.

   2   :   type-of-conference-name indicator as for field 111

   0–2   :   second indicator as for field 700
conference-name subfields as for field 111; other subfields as for field 700

730®—Additional (not principal, not subject, not series) access point consisting of a uniform title.

   0–9   :   number of characters to ignore in filing

   0–2   :   second indicator as for field 700

   t   =   the uniform title; also uniform-title subfields as on pages 313–14

740®—Additional access point consisting of a title for the publication being catalogued *other than* (a) the uniform title for the work (see field 730) or (b) the title transcribed in subfields *a*, *n*, and *p* of field 245 (see last paragraph of **21.30J1**).

   0–9   :   number of characters to ignore in filing

   0–2   :   second indicator as for field 700

   a,h,n,p=   subfields as for field 245

75X—Additional tags beginning with *75* are provided for added access points assigned according to different principles from those of traditional cataloguing.

760–799—The format provides for some dozen different repeatable fields in this range of tag numbers in which the relationship between documents described in different bibliographic records can be shown, and in which the control numbers of the records can be linked. Their most frequent use is to link records for earlier and later serial titles.

800®—Access point for a series, *not* in the form recorded in the Series Area but established as a personal name followed by a title (see **21.30L**

for all fields from 800 through 830). An series-access-point field tagged 800, 810, 811, or 830 may be required either because of the presence of the digit *1* as the first indicator in field 490 or because a series is mentioned in a 5XX-field note such as field 534.

0–3   *   :   type-of-personal-name first indicator as for field 100; second indicator blank

personal-name subfields as for field 100

t   =   title; also uniform-title subfields as below

n,p,v =   subfields as for field 440

810®—Access point for a series, *not* in the form recorded in the Series Area but established as a corporate name followed by a title.

1–2   *   :   type-of-corporate-name indicator as for field 110; second indicator blank

corporate-name subfields as for field 110; other subfields as for field 800

811®—Access point for a series, *not* in the form recorded in the Series Area but established as a conference name followed by a title.

2   *   :   type-of-conference-name indicator as for field 111; second indicator blank

conference-name subfields as for field 111; other subfields as for field 800

830®—Title access point for a series, but *not* exactly the title recorded in the Series Area.

*   0–9   :   first indicator blank; second is number of characters to ignore in filing

t   =   title; also uniform-title subfields as below

n,p,v =   subfields as for field 440

850®—Symbol(s) to designate the institution(s) holding the document described in this bibliographic record. More detailed information can be given in field 851. These fields are important, for example, in the databases of consortia and bibliographic utilities used for interlibrary-loan searching.

886®—Foreign MARC information field. Used to contain data formatted according to a different version of MARC which cannot be automatically translated into the local version.

Uniform-Title Subfields. In fields 130, 240, 243, 630, 730, and 830, a uniform title is the initial element and is located in subfield *a*. An access point in any of fields 600, 610, 611, 700, 710, 711, 800, 810, or 811 may be a name-title access point (see **21.30G** and **21.30M** for those in fields 700, 710, and 711). In these cases, subfield *a* is occupied by a personal, corporate, or conference name, so the title is located in subfield *t*; the title portion of such an access point is nevertheless considered a uniform title for coding purposes. In all the above cases, content designation is provided as follows for the additions to the basic uniform title which are either permitted or prescribed in AACR2, **chapter 25**. Of these, subfields *h*, *k*, *l*, *n*, and *p* are widely applicable; the others pertain chiefly to legal, musical, and scriptural works.

d®	date of treaty signing **(25.16)**
f®	date of work **(25.5B, 25.18A13, 25.30E)**
g	miscellaneous; for example, name of second party to a treaty **(25.16)**
h	general material designation (GMD) **(1.1C, 25.5D)**
k®	form subheading; for example, *Selections* **(25.9, 25.18A9, 25.34C3)**
l	language **(25.5C, 25.18A10, 25.35F)**
m®	medium of music performance **(25.30B)**
n®	number of the part or section of the work **(25.6A2)**, numeric identifier of a musical work **(25.30C)**
o	statement of arrangement of a musical work **(25.35C)**
p®	name of part or section of the work **(25.18A1–9, 25.32A)**
r	key signature of a musical work **(25.30D)**
s	version **(25.18A11–12)**

For example, the name-title subject access point for a book *about* Beethoven's Rasumovsky Quartets is coded as follows:

600   10   ‡aBEETHOVEN, LUDWIG VAN, ‡d1770–1827. ‡tQUARTETS, ‡mSTRINGS, ‡nNO. 7–9, OP. 59.

The Authority-Link Fields: Tags 900 through 999

CANMARC provides fifteen repeatable tags in this group, one for each type of non-subject controlled-vocabulary access point possible in the record and one for linking the fields involved. They are used to record cross-references involving these access points and to link the English and French equivalent forms of access points. [USMARC does not use any tag beginning with a *9*. It relies solely on the authorities format to keep track of cross-references.] Separately published CANMARC and USMARC formats exist for authority data; that is, to record in authority files the forms of access points and their cross-references separately from the bibliographic records in which they are used (see page 81). USMARC also includes a separately published format for holdings data. All these formats are structurally the same as the bibliographic format described in this appendix since all are a part of the MARC family of formats. A MARC format for the symbols and text of a classification scheme is at present being devised. The MARC-formatted subject authority record shown as part of figure 37 illustrates how the same general structure, and even some of the same tag numbering, applies to this as to a bibliographic record.


```
0 0 7 8 8 n a m * * 2 2 0 0 2 2 9 0 a * 4 5 0 0│0 0 1 0 0 0 9 0 0 0 0 0

0 0 8 0 0 4 2 0 0 0 0 9│0 1 6 0 0 1 4 0 0 0 5 1│0 2 0 0 0 2 6 0 0 0 6 5

0 5 5 0 0 1 1 0 0 0 9 1│0 8 2 0 0 1 9 0 0 1 0 2│1 0 0 0 0 2 4 0 0 1 2 1

2 4 5 0 0 8 2 0 0 1 4 5│2 6 0 0 0 5 8 0 0 2 2 7│3 0 0 0 0 4 1 0 0 2 8 5

4 4 0 0 0 4 9 0 0 3 2 6│5 0 4 0 0 4 1 0 0 3 7 5│6 5 0 0 0 3 1 0 0 4 1 6

6 5 0 0 0 3 0 0 0 4 4 7│6 5 1 0 0 3 7 0 0 4 7 7│7 0 0 0 0 2 9 0 0 5 1 4

7 0 0 0 0 1 6 0 0 5 4 3 F│3 8 6 5 7 4 1 0 F│8 7 0 6 1 1 s 1 9 8 7 * * *
                        229=0                 9

* o n c a * * * * * * * * * * 0 0 1 1 * * e n g * * 0 F│* * ‡ a 8 7 0 0
                                                       51

1 0 2 3 1 F│* * ‡ a 0 1 3 1 4 0 4 6 7 9 * : ‡ c $ 2 9 . 9 5 . F│0 * ‡ a
           65                                                    91

N K 1 1 2 5 F│* * ‡ a 7 4 5 . 1 ' 0 9 7 1 ‡ 2 1 9 F│1 0 ‡ a S m i t h ,
             102                                     121

* J e a n , ‡ d 1 9 4 3 - F│1 0 ‡ a C o l l e c t i n g * C a n a d a '
                           145

s * p a s t * / ‡ c J e a n * & * E l i z a b e t h * S m i t h * ; * p

h o t o g r a p h y * b y * K e n * B e l l . F│0 * ‡ a S c a r b o r o
                                               227

u g h , * O n t . * : ‡ b P r e n t i c e - H a l l * o f * C a n a d a

, ‡ c c 1 9 8 7 . F│* * ‡ a 2 2 0 * p . * : ‡ b i l l . * ( s o m e * c
                  285

o l . ) * ; ‡ c 2 7 * c m . F│* 4 ‡ a T h e * H o b b y i s t ' s * h a
                            326

n d b o o k s , ‡ x 1 5 2 3 5 0 7 1 * ; ‡ v n o . * 5 F│* * ‡ a I n c l
                                                      375

u d e s * b i b l i o g r a p h i c a l * r e f e r e n c e s . F│* 0 ‡
                                                                 416

a C o l l e c t o r s * a n d * c o l l e c t i n g . F│* 0 ‡ a M a t e
                                                       447

r i a l * c u l t u r e ‡ x C a n a d a . F│* 0 ‡ a C a n a d a ‡ x S o
                                           477

c i a l * l i f e * a n d * c u s t o m s . F│1 0 ‡ a S m i t h , * E l
                                             514

i z a b e t h , ‡ d 1 9 4 7 - F│1 1 ‡ a B e l l , * G . * K . R
                               543
```

FIGURE 36. A MARC record as the computer "sees" it. *F* is a field terminator; *R* is the record terminator. A vertical line marks the end of the label, of each directory unit, and of each variable field.

```
ACCESS UNDER: Night people (May Subdivide Geographically)
USED FOR:     Night owls (Persons)
              Nighttime people
              Nocturnal people
BROADER TERM: Persons
- - - - - - - - - - - - - -

000  00532nz***2200181n**450b
001  sh*86006451*
005  19861211161704*8
008  860930i**anannbab************a*ana******
040  **  ‡a DLC ‡c DLC
150  *0  ‡a Night people
450  *0  ‡a Night owls (Persons)
450  *0  ‡a Nighttime people
450  *0  ‡a Nocturnal people
550  *0  ‡wg ‡a Persons
670  **  ‡a Work cat.: Melbin, M. Night as frontier.
670  **  ‡a Web. 3  ‡b (Nocturnal; Nocturnalism; Night owl)
670  **  ‡a Hennepin ‡b (Night--Social aspects)
675  **  ‡a NYT Index; ‡a Thes. Psych. Index
```

FIGURE 37.   MARC-formatted subject authority record.

Index to MARC Coding

This is an index to the content designators tabulated in this appendix. A number in parentheses designates a character position within the designated field. The term *common subfield* refers to the table on pages 313–14. The double dagger (‡) is the subfield delimiter.

INDEX

Please refer to the Table of Contents for a systematic survey of the topics treated in this book.

A separate index of CANMARC/USMARC content designators immediately precedes this index.

The filing is word-by-word; an acronym or initialism is unpunctuated and treated as a single word.

An acronym which has assumed independent status in the library literature is so indexed; a cross-reference or duplicate indexing appears under the spelled-out form.

The letter *n* following a page number indicates that a footnote is the only mention of the topic on the page. Similarly, *fig.* refers to the figure on the page.

Examples and figures per se are not indexed, but a significant concept, definition, or primary source illustrated only by an example or figure is indexed.

Page numbers on which the term is merely defined are printed in italics. Definitions of obsolescent terms are so indexed, but are then cross-referred elsewhere for substantive discussion of the concept. The following concepts, treated integrally throughout the book, appear in this index only if a definition as such can be noted: A&I publications; access; bibliographic records; catalogues; databases; files; indices; information storage and retrieval systems; libraries; monographic bibliographies.

Ronald Hagler, professor at the School of Library, Archival and Information Studies at the University of British Columbia, holds master's degrees in library science and Latin and a Ph.D. in library science. He has published articles in several journals including *Library Trends, Singapore Libraries, LRTS,* and the *Canadian Library Journal* and was honored with the Margaret Mann Citation in 1990 from the Cataloging and Classification Section of the Association for Library Collections and Technical Services for his work with AACR2. He was also the co-author of *The Bibliographic Record and Information Technology* (ALA, 1982).